WHAT YOU MADE OF IT

WHAT
A MEMOIR
YOU
1987–2020
MADE
C. K. Stead
OF IT

AUCKLAND
UNIVERSITY
PRESS

To Kay
Oliver, Charlotte and Margaret
and to whānau (including my sister Frances)
and friends everywhere

AROHANUI

The world as you found it
Catullus

was neither
benign nor malign
but what you made of it.

Also by C. K. Stead

Poetry

Whether the Will is Free
Crossing the Bar
Quesada
Walking Westward
Geographies
Poems of a Decade
Paris
Between
Voices
Straw into Gold
The Right Thing
Dog
The Red Tram
The Black River
Collected Poems, 1951–2006
The Yellow Buoy: Poems 2007–2012
In the Mirror, and Dancing
That Derrida Whom I Derided Died

Fiction

Smith's Dream
Five for the Symbol (stories)
All Visitors Ashore
The Death of the Body
Sister Hollywood
The End of the Century at the End of the World
The Singing Whakapapa
Villa Vittoria
The Blind Blonde with Candles in her Hair (stories)
Talking about O'Dwyer
The Secret History of Modernism
Mansfield
My Name Was Judas
Risk
The Name on the Door is Not Mine (stories)
The Necessary Angel

Memoir

South-West of Eden: A Memoir 1932–1956
You Have a Lot to Lose: A Memoir 1956–1986

Criticism

The New Poetic
In the Glass Case
Pound, Yeats, Eliot and the Modernist Movement
Answering to the Language
The Writer at Work
Kin of Place: Essays on 20 New Zealand Writers
Book Self: The Reader as Writer and the Writer as Critic
Shelf Life: Reviews, Replies and Reminiscences

Edited

Oxford New Zealand Short Stories (second series)
Measure for Measure, a Casebook
Letters and Journals of Katherine Mansfield
Collected Stories of Maurice Duggan
Faber Book of Contemporary South Pacific Stories
Werner Forman's New Zealand

First published 2021
Auckland University Press
University of Auckland
Private Bag 92019
Auckland 1142
New Zealand
www.aucklanduniversitypress.co.nz

ISBN 978 1 86940 946 3

Published with the assistance of Creative New Zealand

creative nz
ARTS COUNCIL OF NEW ZEALAND TOI AOTEAROA

A catalogue record for this book is available from the National Library of New Zealand

Book design by Carolyn Lewis
Cover design by Spencer Levine

Cover images: Front – Courtesy of the Gerrard and Marti Friedlander Charitable Trust
Back – Copyright *NZ Herald*/Brett Phibbs

This book was printed on FSC® certified paper and other controlled material

Printed by 1010 Printing International Ltd

Contents

By Way of Introduction

Rounding off *You Have a Lot to Lose*, and believing I would not live to write an account of the years that followed my departure from the university in 1986, I wrote that, despite my endless perambulations between New Zealand and the 'out there' world, I still thought of myself as 'a loyal Pākehā New Zealander with deep and abiding attachments to Tāmaki Makaurau'. In today's very generous Radio NZ review of that book Harry Ricketts described it as 'memoir rather than an autobiography' – autobiography, he suggested, being about oneself, memoir about oneself and other people. Somewhere in *Le Rouge et le Noir* Stendhal says a novel is like a mirror walking along a road. These which now become three memoirs are that kind of writing – not fiction, but the report of one who consistently reflects, looking out rather than in and reporting what he sees. These are my encounters and engagements with the world of books and writers, and of teaching and writing about them. I am not interesting except insofar as I meet, engage with, and report upon, interesting people, places and events. The world reflected in my ambulant mirror is primarily literary, but behind it constantly is the broader image of politics and society.

What You Made of It completes the more than thirty years of my literary life after I left the shelter of the university to be a full-time writer; but the narrative this time is only roughly chronological, broken into chapters each of which centres on a scene or theme, and on related places and persons. As with the previous two I claim that this is as truthful to memory and to the written or printed record as I can make it; but it is not (and could not be) comprehensive. Some people who have been important in my life are absent, sometimes for reasons of privacy, discretion, accident, or simply for the convenience or the imperatives of narrative. Three of these 'oversights' are given an Appendix – but there could be many more. Even my family are mostly background to a literary life – but to treat them otherwise always threatened to expand the memoir beyond reasonable limits.

Every book creates its own rules as it goes, and the writer, while acknowledging his part, indeed his responsibility for every word, is aware of a kind of helplessness, and will say, if only to himself, this is the best I could do, being the person I am and given the chances life and the gene pool threw my way. In these scary midwinter/Matariki nights, when coronary symptoms remind me of my dire prognosis, I think of the benign words of the bronze statue of the writer in Dubravkin Put at the end of my story 'Last Season's Man': 'Old friend, you must know there's no Justice. That I am here and Tomislav is not is neither right nor wrong. The Universe is indifferent and does not love us. Everything is Chance.'

C. K. S.
Tāmaki Makaurau
23 June 2020

1. Oxford and Consequences

Dan Davin and etc.

I begin with Dan Davin and Oxford, not because the man or the location is more important than other persons or places that will figure in this book, but because they are a focal point for stories: there are lines out from the man and the place, interconnections with what is to follow. Dan was a writer, and Oxford a notable academic hub. My ambition had been to be a writer, full-time; and the academic world was the one I hoped to escape from, though without entirely turning my back on it. So to begin with Dan's death will serve as a symbolic stepping-off point for the story of Stead, recently retired from his professorship at the University of Auckland and now well launched on his new freelance literary life.

In my copy of Dan's book of memories of literary friends, *Closing Times*, there is a clipping of his death notice in *The Times* saying the funeral will be at 11.30 at the Oxford Crematorium, Headington, 1 October (1990). I have scribbled on it the train I would take, 'Paddington 9.50 – 10.40'. I was in London and had just a day or so before farewelled Kay at Gatwick on a plane back to New Zealand, so would go to the funeral alone.

I remember Bruce Purchase as Master of Ceremonies. Bruce was a New Zealand actor we had got to know in London during my 1965 sabbatical leave, because his wife at that time, Elspeth Sandys (later to be Maurice Shadbolt's penultimate), had been a student of mine. Bruce had been attached to my old friend of student years, Susan Davis; and we had seen him on the stage at the Old Vic. His contribution to the occasion was notable not just because he brought an actor's voice and skill to his delivery but because his friendship with the Davins, both Dan and Winnie, in Dan's last days and weeks, had been close. Bruce was the son of a soldier who had served in the NZ Div. in World War II, like Dan had been wounded and decorated, and had survived the war but not for as many years as Dan. These were facts which were of enormous importance to Dan and gave Bruce a special place.

Fleur Adcock, another friend, delivered two poems, Dan's 'The gorse blooms pale', and Donne's 'Death be not proud', in her usual reading style which always sounded to me faintly admonitory. The New Zealand High Commissioner Bryce Harland spoke well – movingly – of Davin as the decorated soldier and author of the official New Zealand war history of the Battle of Crete. I had been involved with Bryce in the purchase of a flat in London for use by New Zealand writers – the Labour government's, and more specifically minister Michael Bassett's, gift to our literary community to celebrate New Zealand's sesquicentenary, 150 years since the signing of the Treaty of Waitangi. Last details of the flat were to be discussed with Bryce over lunch at New Zealand House a few days later.

Davin's purely Oxford and academic/publishing connections also figured in the obsequies, probably more importantly; but I mention these Kiwi connections to emphasise how inescapable New Zealand had been in Davin's life, and how few the 'degrees of separation'. He and Winnie had become expatriates, but the bonds with home had not been severed. In his last years he had seemed to leave his homeland behind as an intellectual preoccupation; but he must have known by then that if he had a place in anyone's history it was New Zealand's, not Great Britain's where he might once have hoped to leave an enduring mark.

To me the funeral seemed adequate, but no more than that. I felt that if it had been a purely New Zealand event it would have been more expansive, with even the possibility that it might go wrong, that someone would behave badly, or speak out of turn, but more fitting for the man Dan had been. It may be they were constrained and allowed only a fixed time; but it was an Oxford funeral, proper, itself wearing a dark suit.

My inevitable pilgrimages to Oxford had begun at the HQ of what James McNeish had called the Kiwi-Oxford Mafia, 103 Southmoor Road, Davin's address. This had been when I was a postgraduate student in Bristol on a scholarship from New Zealand in 1957–59. It was the height of the anti-nuclear movement in the UK, and our presence, Kay's and mine, as visitors, had been added to by the sudden eruption of the three Davin daughters, Anna, Bridget and Delia, with Anna's boyfriend Luke Hodgkin, the four just back from a CND rally. So a connection had been established with Dan, I very much the insignificant junior and subordinate; but I admired him and liked Winnie. Dan had the kudos, the mystique, of the returned soldier, meaningful especially to one who had been, as I had, a child during World War II, who had grown to consciousness with it, and yet had been too young to take part. That war experience gave Dan authority and confidence; but also with it came the nostalgia of knowing that for him nothing like it, nothing quite so intense or significant or memorable, could happen again. That certainty, and the fact that he had left New Zealand and was in a position which did not make a return seem practicable, put him twice removed, from 'his best years' which is how he characterised the war, and from his roots. It was a dilemma he could not escape except by writing about that place, or that time, or both, so memorably that a new and more splendid identity would be forged. But, whether because of the demands of his work as assistant to the Secretary to the Delegates at

Oxford University Press, or because he lacked the necessary talent, or more simply because too many hours were wasted in the pubs of Oxford where he held nightly court, he had fallen short and seemed to know he had, and to be saddened by it. At the time of that first visit I had written to Frank Sargeson that I'd just read Dan's novel *The Sullen Bell*, 'essential reading for New Zealanders in Britain', I said, but its prose was 'lifeless'; and Frank had written back that Davin's talent was 'marginal'.

There were a number of things Dan had told me, or told the company when I was present, during those 1950s encounters, that I remembered and reminded him of when he came on a visit to New Zealand in the early '60s, and Kay and I drove him and Winnie about during the Auckland part of their stay. One was that his eyes had learned to detect instantly the presence of an N and a Z in close proximity anywhere on a page of newsprint and would home in on it at once to confirm that it was or was not New Zealand; and almost equally, caps R and C would catch his wandering eye to check whether they signified Roman Catholic: Dan the Roman Catholic from New Zealand, though he had lapsed from one and departed from the other, was so, inescapably and ever.

Another was his memory of undergoing his *viva* examination at Oxford and being asked how one part of his examination answer connected with the one that followed. Across the desk he could just make out his script and with a faintly pencilled squiggle and 'n.s.' in the margin. He considered the question and then said, 'I'm afraid they don't really connect, Sir. Bit of a *non sequitur* I'm afraid' – which earned a nod of approval. And then there was a story about being invited after the war to visit Windsor Castle where General Sir Bernard Freyberg, on whose staff Dan had served in the Western Desert, had been appointed the Lieutenant-Governor. After dinner and drinks and so on, all retired to bed. Dan got up to find himself one more drink, achieved this, and then, uncertain of directions returning to his room, opened a wrong door to find himself looking at an enormous double bed in which Sir Bernard and Lady Freyberg were sitting up side by side, each reading a copy of the *Slough and Windsor Daily Times*.

As we drove the Davins about and I reminded Dan of these anecdotes he seemed surprised, impressed by them as feats of memory, but also pleased (I suppose) because he was the one remembered. He must already have taken note of my respect-bordering-on-fondness for him (he reminded me of my father, also Irish Catholic by upbringing and leftist by temperament) and I felt I had received from him, not approval exactly, but a sort of provisional accreditation which must in the immediately following years have been ratified by my publications, literary and critical. So I had been given the job of editing Oxford University Press's second World's Classics *New Zealand Short Stories* (1966 – Dan had edited the first in 1953). Davin's biographer, Keith Ovenden, writes that 'Stead was a controversial choice in some New Zealand quarters at the time but Davin was steadfast in his support for him at OUP'.

The work was well under way in 1965 when I was on my first sabbatical leave and I visited the Davins again, with the usual round of a meal at 103 Southmoor Road and then an hour or two at Dan and Winnie's local, at that time the Gardener's Arms where Dan had a chair recognised as his and reserved for him. On another visit that year Dan took me to the cottage in Dorchester which he used as an escape from the pressures of work to get on with his own writing. He showed me his desk scattered with papers and books of reference and – on that occasion – detailed maps of North and South Islands. I was struck by this and referred to it a number of times in letters to friends because I saw it – and welcomed the warning – as an example of the expatriate New Zealand writer losing his grip on his subject. When I wrote to Frank Sargeson I said I didn't want 'to become a Davin'. This was absurd – we were quite unlike – but I was always looking for, and finding comfort and reassurance in, examples that could be made to mean I had done the right thing in putting myself where I was, at home and becoming 'a New Zealand writer'.

I never discussed with Dan the choices I was making in 1965 for the second Oxford New Zealand stories; but I remember very clearly how difficult some of them were, and that one I wrestled with was Davin himself. The stories chosen had to be subsequent to those available for the 1953 selection. I would have liked to find among his more recent stories (there had been a few in *Landfall* and elsewhere) one that seemed good enough, but none of them did. He had been persuaded by his friend Julian Maclaren-Ross that some of his pub anecdotes were too good to be thrown away over drinks and would make respectable short stories. It was advice he'd acted on, not always to good effect. It was critically exacting of me to turn thumbs down on them; and my thought now is that surely I could have stretched a point for our Oxford icon. His stories can't have been disastrously bad; and it would have been a courtesy, even a kindness.

I never got any hint from Dan that he cared; but he probably did – and it seems to me it was an oversight which might have added to the degree of his displeasure when he believed, later on, that he had good reason to be displeased with me. This came when I wrote my long critical article about John Mulgan. There was a convenient myth about Mulgan that he had been denied a Rhodes scholarship because he had revealed leftist leanings, which had been unwelcome to a conservative university hierarchy at the time of the Auckland riots in 1932. My own political inclinations being what they were, this was a myth I would have been happy to promote. The problem was that when I looked into it I found there was no basis for it in fact. John Mulgan's editorial in the student paper, *Craccum*, which was supposed to have revealed these 'leftist' leanings, was not only anonymous – it was ambiguous as well, siding clearly with no one; and his academic record had declined over the three years of his Bachelor's degree. He and his two rivals for the scholarship had been rated equal in social and sporting achievement; so the decision had to come down to academic merit, and Mulgan came in third. That is what my quite lengthy article (which dealt with other matters, including his novel *Man Alone*) reported. It was true that the Governor-General of the time had liked Mulgan and asked the University of Auckland to reconsider; but the university was right to ignore this request. What basis for paranoid theory would it not have promoted if the university had allowed viceregal preference to override academic attainment?

A myth, especially one with political or religious implications, even one completely baseless, is something only to be challenged or disturbed by someone prepared to receive buffets and brickbats. I'm not sure I was prepared, but the buffets and brickbats came. The subsequent issue of *Islands*, in which the article first appeared, had ten pages of letters about it, only two endorsing what I had suggested. Mulgan's angry sister, Lady Dorothea Turner, urged Keith Sinclair, at that time writing a history of the University of Auckland, to look into it and prove Stead wrong. Keith looked, and reported back that he could not, because I was not. Lady Turner, and James Bertram, another promoter of the Mulgan myth, complained that I had used my professorial position to check and report on Mulgan's academic record which should have remained private; but I was unrepentant. Mulgan was long dead, and continued concealment of the record was perpetuating in effect a defamation against E. P. Haslam, who was supposed to have won the scholarship in 1934 unfairly and at Mulgan's expense.

The Mulgan controversy (as it became) was a cudgel Davin was happy to take up. In a letter to Keith Sinclair he referred to my 'damn silly article' and asked whether I was 'off my chump'; and reviewing in *The Review of English Studies* my collection of essays *In the Glass Case* where the Mulgan essay was reprinted, he fixed his sights on it, speaking for 'older scholars of at least equal distinction' whose opinion I had ignored. Looking at this review again I can only see it as evidence of Davin's decline – so long-winded and laboured, so elaborately and unenlighteningly metaphored, so unfocused except on the Mulgan essay, and even there confused, failing ever to come to grips with what the essay actually asserts. I find it hard to imagine that even Davin's most stalwart supporters would want to defend it.

Janet Wilson,* in *Kite* (no. 20, July 2001), an unbound supplement to the *Journal of New Zealand Literature*, reviewing my novel *Talking about O'Dwyer*, decided not only that the character of Donovan O'Dwyer was 'a portrait of Dan Davin', but that it was unfair to the original and a 'revenge' for Dan's review of *In the Glass Case*. 'Why', she asked, should my character 'lack Davin's impressive achievements as writer, publisher, editor, historian and critic?' Because, I replied, O'Dwyer was neither writer, publisher, editor nor critic, but a don in ancient history, a man who half-believed he was living under a Māori mākutu. The character of O'Dwyer was indeed partly drawn from, or not wholly unrelated to, the character of Davin. He was an Oxford University man, ambiguous about his relationship with his homeland New Zealand, spending a good deal of his waking life in local pubs, and with some sense of having failed to quite make his mark. But he was not Davin.

In replying to Janet Wilson I said it was strange she should chide me for representing Davin's life as less than a success story when she had herself edited a book about him in which there was a persistent subtext of failure, frustration and disappointment. Dan, his biographer Keith Ovenden records, had wanted to be Secretary to the Delegates of Oxford University Press, but had to settle for assistant to the Secretary. He had wanted to make his mark as a fiction writer, and had not really done that. So insofar as O'Dwyer could be seen as in any way related to Davin, it was hardly a misrepresentation.

As for the novel as 'revenge': I had completely forgotten our (Dan's and my) sharp exchange about his review when I came to write *Talking about O'Dwyer*. Insofar as Dan was there in the novel at

* Another old friend, daughter of the writer Phillip Wilson, long-ago colleague in the University of Auckland English Department, and now the wife of friend and fellow-poet Kevin Ireland. The book of reminiscences of Davin she edited was called *Intimate Stranger*, Steele Roberts, 2000.

all (modified, qualified, by the fact that O'Dwyer was also and more importantly Major Humphrey Dyer, commander of D Company, 28 Māori Battalion during the Battle of Crete) he is represented affectionately. It's true the opening chapter of the novel has a group of O'Dwyer's colleagues sitting around a table at dessert and wine after dinner at high table, acknowledging his merits but at once undermining each positive with a corresponding negative. This conversation is observed by the novel's central character, Mike Newall who, however, does not himself contribute to it; and I think the effect is more a criticism of Oxford than of O'Dwyer. But it is true that I heard some of these comments, the positive and corresponding negative, about Davin around just such a table at St John's College when I was Senior Visiting Fellow there in 1996.

TO REVERT NOW TO A VISIT to 103 Southmoor Road, the Davins' house, in 1965: I remember family and friends standing around talking prior to the usual pub-visit. The meal was over and we were briefly divided into ones and twos, waiting for a decision to be made. In the midst of this I found myself in conversation with the Davins' young friend and protégée, Nuala O'Faolain, a student at Oxford on a scholarship from Dublin. The memory is clear and vivid because the rapport between us was so instant and so electric. I remember her as beautiful, but possibly because I am more an ear than an eye person, and the voice and Irish accent were so soft and irresistible. I don't remember what we talked about, but at some point she took me by the wrist and said I should come out with her on to the back garden and look at the moon. There were clouds out there, no visible moon, but I saw stars. One of us quoted Keats: 'haply' (perhaps) 'the Queen-Moon is on her throne, / Cluster'd around by all her starry Fays;'

> But here there is no light,
> Save what from heaven is with the breezes blown
> Through verdurous glooms and winding mossy ways.

She said we should 'kiss in honour of Keats', and she gave me the name of a pub close to the British Museum where she always went in the late afternoon on days when her research took her to the Senate House Library. I was to look for her there. I said I would, and thought I would, but later decided if we were to meet again it should be by chance, not by an act of will. It didn't happen.

Keith Ovenden, the Davin biographer, makes it clear that Nuala and Dan were lovers for a number of years, and that he had represented her in his novel *Brides of Price*. Ovenden says of this:

> Dan's way of life owed much to Winnie's tolerance. Her sense of his needs in their relationship, and her willingness to adjust to them, coupled with his unshaken need for her companionship and intellectual strength, made their marriage imperishable. Dan's mistresses were always defeated by it in the end.

I assume Nuala was one of the 'defeated' – though Ruth in *Brides of Price*, said to be her portrait, is represented as being secretive and having other lovers at the same time that she is willing to share the bed of the novel's first-person narrator, Adam Mahon, the Davin figure.

When, after Dan's death, Janet Wilson edited her book of reminiscences about him, she invited me to contribute. I declined, afraid it might be like one of those photo-ops where one sees a group of political hopefuls straining to be as close as possible to the PM. There was some of that, inevitably, when the book appeared; but what seemed to me by far the truest and frankest contribution came from Nuala. She was quick, almost brutal, in dismissing Dan as fiction writer, and describing him as a man deluded about himself. But having said that she paid him the most dazzling tribute:

> He taught me things and introduced me to people and dined me in places like his London club. But it wasn't for any of that that I cared for him. And it wasn't for him as a man: I didn't

> find his Churchillian looks or his measured self-presentation particularly attractive. But he never did or said one thing in our relationship which wasn't supportive and companionable and decent. He was a difficult man, and I was young and erratic. And the times were heady. Yet we knew each other for ten years or so without a single unaffectionate moment.

She also wrote:

> Winnie didn't like me. But she was scrupulously fair to me [. . .] She put up with the likes of me with many a sardonic glance. But she was such a giving woman that she often forgot she didn't like me, and made me an omelette.

In 1987 I had forgotten Nuala when I attended, with John and Christine Kelly, a Yeats conference in Monaco. Shortly after it began we were informed that recent reports suggesting the bones removed from the first grave of Yeats in Roquebrune and now reinterred at Sligo in Ireland had been the bones of the wrong man. Since it was planned that one excursion for the conference was a visit to that first grave and memorial stone in Roquebrune cemetery, the mayoral authorities wished to assure us that no such error had been made, that the bones sent to Ireland for reburial after World War II had been those of the poet. One of the journalists who had written up this story in Dublin was Nuala O'Faolain; and far from reassuring everybody, this formal announcement led to a revival of doubt, which has continued ever since. Yeats had died in Menton in 1939 just before the outbreak of war. During the war the body had been mistakenly removed from its tomb and reinterred in a common fosse; and when the post-war request came from Dublin for removal and reinterment in Ireland, the scramble to find the right set of bones had not, despite these embarrassed assurances, resulted in anything but renewed uncertainty. This was a subject I would revert to in my novel *The Secret History of Modernism*.

It was almost ten years later again that Nuala published *Are You Somebody?* She had become a much-respected Irish journalist and feminist; but this book made her famous. In 2002, when Kay had gone to London to be with daughter Margaret for the birth of a grandchild, I found that each day I spent time and care preparing myself a meal, and then it seemed to be gone in a flash. I was not used to eating alone, so decided I would play myself a talking book, which I found did slow the process down and make the meal seem more civilised and sociable. Among the books I got through in this way was Nuala's *Are You Somebody?* which she had recorded in the lovely Irish voice and accent that had seemed so electric and dangerous in 1965.

In 2008 when I was flying to a poetry festival in Venezuela I read the news of her death. She had died aged 68 of cancer, and I wrote her a sort of In Memoriam poem, 'Talking Book' (i.m. Nuala O'Faolain):

> Last night on the long haul
> Auckland to Santiago
> I read in the *Guardian Weekly*
> that you were dead
> whom I met at midnight once
> in an Oxford garden.
>
> Your voice was smoky Irish
> it quoted Keats
> and there breathed between us
> the promise to meet again.
>
> Long after and alone
> I listened to you reading
> the book that had made you famous.
> Each night, over the meal I'd cooked
> and wine

you gave me your story,
your sensibility, your solipsism,
your many regrets.

Our promises were empty of course –
only an effect
of youth and the night.
Here in Santiago
snow has touched the farthest mountains
with the white silence
of a perfect disregard.

I'm uncertain how perfect that disregard was, but it made a good last line and put a distance between us which was not what I had felt in the moment of reading the news.

Talking about O'Dwyer

Talking about O'Dwyer is my Oxford novel. But it is also my Croatia novel and my Crete novel. And of course the roots of its story are in New Zealand and New Zealanders – possibly too much of a good thing, too many exciting narrative threads for one novel; but it was published by Penguin *here* and Harvill (slightly revised and improved) *there*, and got good notices at both ends, including one by Paul Binding in the *Times Literary Supplement*'s Books of the Year (2000) saying 'I don't know why everyone isn't talking about *Talking about O'Dwyer*, C. K. Stead's intricately worked and compelling novel.' And there was another, equally luminous, by John de Falbe in the *Spectator* (27 May 2000) who concluded 'It seems incontestable to me that C. K. Stead is among the very best contemporary novelists'.

I lament the fact that Dan didn't live to read it, and especially to read the review in the (wait for it) *Wairarapa Times* that said 'Stead is proving to be a master of finding ways to talk about what it means to be a New Zealander'. Wasn't that what Dan would have wanted said of himself as fiction writer? It's perhaps naïve of me to believe he would have thought it had done justice to New Zealanders at war, but perhaps he would; and he would surely have thought that element – showing New Zealanders to ourselves – more important than the decline of the character of O'Dwyer in Oxford.

Talking about O'Dwyer is also my Māori Battalion novel, and there are not many of those, just one by a Pākehā. But the Māori Battalion in World War II had to begin with a Pākehā commander, which is my excuse – if fiction writers ever need an excuse for where their imaginations take them. I have, after all, also written an account of the childhood of Jesus of Nazareth and his school friend Judas Iscariot.

The story of the story began for me when I was a student and found a friend in young fellow-poet and Latin scholar Rob Dyer, whose father had been, indeed, the Pākehā commanding officer of D Company, 28 Māori Battalion early in World War II and during the Battle of Crete in May 1941. Rob, when we had got to know one another well, told me the story his father had told him – that during the Crete battle and the retreat from Maleme airport, one of his men had stepped on a mine. His legs were shredded, he was in acute pain, bleeding profusely and certain to die, could not be carried with them in their retreat, and did not want to be left to the mercies of the German paratroopers who might take a frightful revenge for the fact that the New Zealanders had shot and killed so many of them while they were coming down from the skies. The wounded soldier's Māori mates and Major Dyer made sure that the wounded man was clear about what he wanted, and then Dyer, taking responsibility as commander, said in Māori 'Thy will be done', put a gun to the soldier's head and shot him.

When Dyer returned home at the end of the war he went to the Māori soldier's marae and told elders what he had done. He was received with courtesy and understanding, but a mākutu was put on him, not because he had shot the soldier, but because he had shot him in the head and the head to Māori is sacred. The tribal area was just north of Whangārei where the Dyers always took their family holidays, and now it was felt (to young Rob's great disappointment) they could not go there again. It was partly to explain this that Humphrey Dyer told his son what had happened.

Rob was still a child, perhaps nine or ten, and it had made such an impression, had so burned itself into his consciousness, that he retained it throughout his life as a revealed and terrible truth, one which made his father, not a killer, but a man of enormous courage and principle. I saw no reason to doubt it; and though it lay dormant for many years, it was probably always waiting to be seized upon and used in a work of fiction.

There was a brief period when my normally affable relations with my always marvellous and sometimes maddening publisher at Harvill, Christopher MacLehose, were less than harmonious, and as a consequence my only historical/family novel, *The Singing Whakapapa*, was published by Penguin NZ. I should perhaps have persisted for UK publication but I was glad to have it done, that part of 'my material' (as Maurice Duggan would have called it) made use of and left behind.

With *Talking about O'Dwyer*, however, Christopher and I began to get back together again. Penguin did a New Zealand edition and Harvill and Harvill Panther, the rest of the world; so once again there was a wide range of reviews, and translations – in this case into Spanish (*Recordando a O'Dwyer*), German, Croatian, Slovenian (all three of these as *Makutu*). To one trying to live by his writing, these larger print runs, foreign translations, and film options of which there were always, as the number of my novels grew, one or two and sometimes three alive at any one time, were important. The film options always seemed to lapse, usually for lack of necessary finance, before a movie was made, but they brought an income. *Talking about O'Dwyer* was to engage the interest of a young hopeful movie-maker who would renew her option on it for a number of years before giving up for want of sufficiently well-heeled backers.

By this time my life as a full-time writer had fallen into a pattern – a new novel followed by a new collection of poems, and then another . . . The novel might take eighteen months or two years to complete, and the poems perhaps a year. There would be many other things written in this period, including reviews and literary articles, occasional lectures, attendances at book festivals and my own book launches. And there was travel for research, including usually a summer period in France and England. It was the life I had spent all those years as a university teacher working towards. Now I had it and was pleased with it, though it was never easy, and sometimes challenging, with (because I am the person I am) a sense of being constantly involved in a wrestle with Fate. One grew more adroit in what Eliot called 'the intolerable wrestle with words', because, though 'practice' does not 'make perfect', it does 'make better than before'; and though there might be a slight, slow dying down of youthful fires, there were qualities like ease, confidence, cunning, and something like wisdom, to make up for them.

I was appointed Senior Visiting Fellow at St John's College, Oxford for the 1996–97 academic year and Kay and I were given a two-storeyed house on the corner of Woodstock and Plantation roads. Two of our children, Charlotte (with two children of her own) and Margaret (no children at this time) and their husbands were living in London, so we saw a lot of them and had Christmas 1996 together. It was an exceptionally cold winter – the fountain outside the Radcliffe Infirmary froze and so did parts of the river, and there were reports of swans caught in the ice. I was finishing *Villa Vittoria*, or had finished it, and seemed to be writing mostly poems – the Oxford poems in *The Right Thing* date from that year. Our house had a walled garden at the back, and was only a walk away from the college, or, in a different direction, from the suburb of Jericho. The University Parks were close and I ran there to keep fit. We dined from time to time in the college, and I sometimes had lunch there. We went up and down to London by the Oxford Tube (bus) which was cheap and took less than two hours. It was in many ways an idyllic life, and yet I didn't stay the full academic year and would be quite glad to get back to quiet Tohunga Crescent and summer.

Some months before I'd had news that two young Croatian editors, Jadranka Pintarić and Ljiljana Šćurić, had discovered my 1984 novel *All Visitors Ashore* and proposed to bring out a translation in Croatian; and now, while we were still in Oxford, Kay I were invited to the launch in Zagreb. It was still winter, late January, and though the war caused by the break-up of the former Yugoslav federation appeared to be over, it was in everyone's mind and conversation. Feelings were still tender. There were refugees and accusations of 'ethnic cleansing', new revelations of horrors and atrocities, and a court was set up by the United Nations in The Hague to try perpetrators of alleged 'crimes against humanity'.* All of this was in the air; and there was also in Zagreb still a sense of the old communist dispensation, with the government of Franjo Tuđman distributing favours undemocratically to its supporters, of whom my publisher, Hrvoje Božičević, was clearly one. He and his architect wife wore the finest clothes (her fur coat went to her ankles), met us at the airport in a chauffeur-driven Mercedes, installed us in a flash hotel (the Esplanade) and took us to the finest restaurants. We had press conferences, appearances on TV, a meeting with a senior government minister, and generous gifts. New Zealand's ambassador for the region, Judith Trotter, was summoned from Rome to attend, and the launch, held in a jazz club, was lavish. It must have been on this visit that the idea of a novel, or part of a novel, that would exploit New Zealand's long-standing connection with the Dalmatian region came to me – and I would return to Croatia very soon to explore it further. So there were two fictional ideas, which could have been two novels, or might merge into one. If it was to be just one, at its centre would be the Māori Battalion and the shooting of one of its soldiers by

* It was for this court that my old friend, and translator of *The Death of the Body* into French, Tony Axelrad, worked for a number of years.

his own commanding officer. What part the Croatian (Dalmatian) connection had to play in it would not become clear until later.

THE NOVEL ABOUT DYER was already in my head, and Dan Davin, who had been wounded in Crete and had written the official New Zealand war history of the battle there, made the connection with Oxford. Aspects of Davin and aspects of Humphrey Dyer would combine to make the character of O'Dwyer; and it was the curse put on him for shooting his wounded soldier in the head that, in the novel, would condemn O'Dwyer to an unhappy life in Oxford. It was fiction: but like every fiction it had some basis in reality.

Oxford had made a strong impression on me – not so much its academic identity (though that could not be absent), but more its physical location, its scene, its ambience. I was happy to locate O'Dwyer there. At the beginning of the novel his funeral has just taken place, and dons of his college, which I called Bardolph's but based on St John's, retire after dinner at high table to a room where dessert and port or Sauternes are taken (with snuff if anyone chooses) and where the talk includes a good deal about the man whose obsequies some of them have just that day attended. Each good thing remembered about O'Dwyer is qualified by something less than good, and sometimes bad. O'Dwyer's colleagues are in two minds about him; and among them only Mike Newall, also a New Zealander, knows the secret of his having killed one of his own soldiers, and the consequent mākutu. After the dinner Newall talks to an old don, Bertie Winterstoke, and begins to tell the great deal he knows about O'Dwyer, including the shooting and the consequent curse; and this provides the framework for a novel which has to move about in time and place, but will keep coming back to Oxford and these two, Mike and Bertie, 'talking about O'Dwyer', continuing the conversation until the story is completed. I think this structural aspect, and the licence it gave me to roam about those Oxford scenes I had enjoyed so much, was what preserved my feeling of being in control of the narrative. Newall is the character most like myself, and I made him a lecturer in philosophy. Bertie Winterstoke is something of an old buffer, good for jokes and good at them, conventional, a 'type', the name hinting at 'Bertie Wooster', but as a character I think believable. It seemed to me Oxford was full of such men.

I had always said I would never write about a place I hadn't visited (a rule I broke when I wrote *My Name Was Judas*) so the writing took me to Crete. I went in May 1998, the time of year when the battle took place and so the time of the annual commemoration. And my investigations at home took me to New Zealand Defence Force Archives, and National Archives. In the latter I found an item which was a special gift to the fiction writer, because it cast the story I was telling in a new and more dramatic light. What Humphrey Dyer had told his son about the shooting had been the kind of thing a soldier father would tell his nine- or ten-year-old son. The truth was much harsher, and Dyer, burdened by it, had set it out in a notebook and deposited it in the National Archives. One has to suppose he thought the true story would come out after he was dead, and preferred to tell it himself – because the circumstances had seemed at the time, and must still have seemed in retrospect, to justify what he had done.

What he recorded was that, once it was decided the island could not be held, the Māori Battalion, which had fought so fiercely and well, was given the role of rearguard in the retreat – the hard part, holding the line while the rest made their escape. So the Battalion fought, retreated, fought again, always being last to leave. They were fighting over a landscape of alternating olives and reeds, rising gradually towards the mountains they would have to cross to meet with a British ship or ships that would wait for them on the other side of the island. In a late stage of this action one of Dyer's men stepped on a landmine and his feet and lower legs were shattered. His two best mates refused to abandon him but picked him up, one holding each arm, and dragged him on with them. Dyer could see Germans appearing and disappearing among the olive trees getting rapidly closer. He ordered them to put down the wounded man but they ignored him. He was sure if they persisted with this rescue attempt, which couldn't succeed, they would all die. He could have run on ahead of them, leaving them to the oncoming Germans. Instead, he took out his revolver and ordered them again to drop the wounded man and save themselves, and when they refused again, he shot the wounded man in the back of the head.

It was a moment of high drama in which everyone acted bravely; but Dyer's action was also, as my characters conclude when Mike Newall gets to tell it late in the novel, unlawful. The irony is that Dyer/O'Dwyer (at this point fiction and fact are indistinguishable) could have shot one or both of the men carrying the wounded one, for disobeying a lawful command in circumstances of battle; but he had no legal right to shoot the wounded man. So he saved a situation by himself disobeying army law. This is something that would have fascinated Davin and I wondered whether he'd heard about it when preparing his official war history. It is very likely that he had, and that all such incidents (of which there were probably many) were omitted from the official record.

I was keeping Rob Dyer informed about what I was writing, not wanting the novel to take him by surprise when it appeared. He seemed to accept he could not prevent my using his father's story, but I could see that it did not please him; and now his response, when told of my new discovery, was total rejection. At once, and as often afterwards as we reverted to the subject, Rob flatly refused to accept my version – which, as I was to point out many times, was not mine but his father's. All this was going on by letter between me in Auckland and Rob in Paris where he was living with his fourth wife, with whom he had by now had three sons – Professor Nathalie Mauriac Dyer as she called herself (or as Rob called her), combining her own distinguished family name (she was the granddaughter of the Nobel Prize-winning author François Mauriac) with Rob's.

To Rob the advent of three sons quite late in his life was immensely relevant to the story I was telling. He had always believed, without any authoritative Māori confirmation so far as I could tell, that the mākutu on his father had extended to himself, and had been the reason for his failure at Oxford and why none of his previous marriages had produced a son. In Australia he had been married to a woman connected to, or descended from, the composer Rimsky-Korsakov, and either to her or to a subsequent (possibly Iranian – I am unclear of details) wife he had had two daughters. Then there was an American wife he brought to New Zealand to live, some time in the late 1970s or early '80s, and who I think had a daughter to him. That marriage also foundered, but it must have been during this sojourn in New Zealand that he made moves to have the mākutu lifted. He wrote me a number of subsequent letters about this, and what he described sounded so inauthentic, so un-Māori, I wondered whether his leg had been pulled by a Māori joker; or he had been seen as a naïve and easily duped source of ready cash. The lifting had involved chants, prayers and the cutting of chickens' throats, which to be effective had to be repeated by the 'tohunga' every month I think at the full moon for a year, after which the mākutu was gone.

Rob believed all this, and repeated it to me in several lengthy handwritten letters. For him, its efficacy was proved by the advent of his three sons to Nathalie. The mākutu had been lifted! I have no idea what happened to the previous wives and their three apparently unimportant daughters; but the sons were adored, and as the years went by they proved to be, Rob assured me, 'brilliant'. Considering that their mother was a Mauriac, a professor at the Sorbonne and a significant editor of the letters of Marcel Proust (to whom she was also related), and that Rob himself, before his self-immolation in Oxford, had been a scholarship boy and a distinguished Latinist, this was not in the least unlikely. But because it fitted so tightly into what Rob believed about his father and the mākutu, my discovery of the little notebook in New Zealand National Archives and the confession it contained could not be accepted. Rob closed his mind to it, and in all his letters to me thereafter simply went stubbornly over the old ground: that after consultations with the wounded man and other Māori soldiers, his father had shot a man who was begging to die.

Once in the year 2006 Kay and I were in Paris and Rob invited us to dinner. Nathalie was very charming, very distinguished, and the sons were impressive young teenagers. Nothing was said about Rob's father or the curse. All that, it seemed, was between the two of us, and by letter. Rob, whose work after that brief stint back in New Zealand, had been as a teacher of Latin, Greek and classical studies at the Hotchkiss School in Lakeville, Connecticut, was now retired to Paris with his family. His French didn't appear fluent enough for him to be in very close and easy communication with the sons in what was clearly their first language, but this impression may have been incorrect, and in any case relations between them in English seemed warm. With Nathalie less so – and though Rob was there for the dinner, it appeared he had been consigned (with the dog) to living downstairs in a smaller apartment also owned by Nathalie, or the Mauriac family. Anyone who has read my novel *The Necessary Angel*, in which a New Zealand lecturer at the Sorbonne is married to a distinguished French professor and editor of Flaubert, will recognise that I took this broad outline from Rob's situation. Otherwise there is no resemblance. Rob's personality was not in the least like that of my character, Max Jackson. All he had done for me in this novel (and only by example – we did not discuss it) was to give me the 'case' of such a marriage. I learned a lot about the internal workings of the Sorbonne in writing it, but not from Rob nor from his wife. My best informant was my friend Professor Claire Davison to whom (along with daughter Margaret) the novel is dedicated.

I don't know whether Rob ever read *The Necessary Angel*, and in 2017 I heard that he had died. I googled his name hoping for details and found, together with a good image of him, looking very nice and quite sane, some of his poems in what I've called 'Rob's grand manner', including one addressed to Karl Stead that begins

How can we desert the day
who storm through the mists of morning?
Shall not some untold age proclaim us
the gods who did bestride the untamed hills
and crown a common place in verse?

and ends sinisterly

But my voice shall return in the roll of thunder
with the notes of the ages strummed on a tuning fork
and the sound of water beneath the dark Minoan prows.

You say I live betraying, Karl;
mark only what my dead voice brings you from the past.

A message from beyond the grave! I think he meant I had accused him of betraying New Zealand by choosing to live abroad, which was probably an implication of a verse letter I had addressed to him when we were both very young.

Some years after *Talking about O'Dwyer* was published I had a call from Harawira Pearless, recently appointed by the government an official historian to D Company, 28 Māori Battalion, in which Dyer and his victim had served. Kay and I invited Harawira for coffee. He seemed to know everything about Major Dyer's shooting of the wounded soldier, and also about Rob Dyer's version of 'what happened' and what followed, most of which he shrugged off as a side issue, untrue, unimportant but sad.

With his full facial moko and his easy-going, smiling way with questions of fact and inference, Harawira seemed not so much an academic historian, more an emanation of a spirit, the wairua of the Māori Battalion, able to absorb equally fact and fiction, as if the difference was to be noted, but no cause for alarm.

More recently again (15 January 2020) Rob's French son Michel visited Kay and me. When I mentioned that Rob had written several contradictory accounts of the curse and its lifting Michel just smiled (a smile that recalled his father vividly) and said, 'Dad would do that.'

Crete, Croatia, and credibility

What part of all this would make its way from life into fiction was for me as much a matter of chance, or inner compulsions, as of will. Oxford had been so vivid it had to be there – which is perhaps why I left before my term there was up, while it was still vivid, before it became 'ordinary' as it had for Dan Davin. And then there was the dramatic Humphrey Dyer story: this had been waiting around so long, pressing for attention. So Oxford, Crete, and the Māori Battalion, improbably, began to merge. But then it was while we were in Oxford that Croatia had summoned me, and that was another unavoidable vividness asking to be included. Fictions began to form of their own accord in the hours around 3 and 4 a.m. when I was often awake for an hour or so, and open to invasion. That these different elements would come together seemed inevitable, because they had arrived together in my life, in my imagination. To make the narrative coherent and plausible – that was my job. It was what 'going to work' now meant for me. The result could not be an easy read, conventional fiction, a convenient going-to-sleep sort of novel, where writer and reader snooze off together. If I had to work at it, so would the reader.

When my Uncle Don went off to the war he came to say goodbye to us. I was seven years old. He took me on his knee while he talked to Mum and Dad and I was conscious of the almost sandpaper texture of his battledress – a texture I would remember when I encountered it again in my own battledress as an eighteen-year old CMT soldier, 328175 Signalman Stead. At the last minute Uncle Don gave me a clasp-knife for a going-away present. It seemed an important moment and I could think of nothing to say but a shy thank you. One of the blades of this knife ended in a fine point, and I soon learned to flick-throw it at a tree so that it stuck there. One day my throw missed the tree and the knife disappeared into an ivy-covered rock wall behind it. I hunted for it for days, fearing that if I didn't find it Uncle Don might be killed. Then news came that he was 'missing in action'. I hunted more frantically, and further news came that he was alive but a 'prisoner of war'.

Uncle Don had a Māori wife, Auntie Trixie, my favourite aunt, and their son, 'Little Donnie', came to live with us 'for the Duration', so my sister and I had a part-Māori (as you were allowed to say then) first cousin at school with us. The 'part-Māori' cousin was part source of the character of Joe Panapa's son, Frano, in *Talking about O'Dwyer*. Frano is killed on his motorbike, so the other element in the making of his fictional character was my friend Ian Lamont who died in the same way at the age of eighteen. The knife is also there in the novel. So are the aunt and uncle, one Māori, one Pākehā, but their genders are reversed because it is the Māori uncle who must go off to war with the Māori Battalion.

I mention these connections, not because it's important the reader should know them – not at all – but because it illustrates the way so much in fiction comes from random 'realities' in the writer's life. It's like running something up in the kitchen: a bit of this, a bit of that, thrown into the big pan with the arbitrary chopped onions which just happened to be there in the pantry . . .

I already knew the Oxford scene well; and the New Zealand location out of which much of the story would spring was Henderson, West Auckland, which Maurice Gee had made his own (calling it Loomis), and where Kay had grown up. I had been to Croatia, now to be an important element in the story; and I planned to return there very soon. But first I had to have my feet on the ground, and eyes, ears and nose alert, in Crete – and at the right time of year, May, when the battle had been fought. I flew from London via Athens and checked in to a small hotel on the seafront at Hania. I took no notes at the time and had lost my appointments diary in France, but I have a vivid recollection of that small harbour enclosed by a sea-wall, and of waking to flickering light striking up from the glassy water on to the ceiling of my room; and of going out on the balcony and seeing a fisherman standing in his small boat and sculling towards and through the harbour entrance. There was such a vivid sense of the exotic, as it would similarly have struck the New Zealand soldiers – and that same sense persisting as I had breakfast, and then discovered the market, and travelled by battered commuter bus in the direction of what had been the crucial Maleme airfield, the one that had to be defended at all costs if the enemy were not to fly further military supplies in. The cost in lives was high and still the battle for the airfield was lost, and Hitler's extraordinary march through Europe continued. I sat on the shingly sands remembering what I had known even as a child, and getting my bearings of the battlefield.

The landscape had not changed; there was the same hill (107) that had to be held against the assault of the paratroopers because it commanded the airfield, and in the end was lost by the New Zealanders. There were the same olive groves through which much of the battle and the 'fighting withdrawal'* occurred – the inlets from or to the sea where a kind of tall reed (which Ezra Pound, encountering it in another part of the Mediterranean region, described as 'bambooiform') grew in profusion. In the days that followed I became accustomed to this ambience without it for a moment ceasing to seem rich, exciting, and foreign. I found Suda Bay and the vast, sad Allied cemetery where our soldiers are buried alongside Aussies and Brits; and the separate German cemetery, on hill 107, the hill we lost, where German losses are recorded and their more than 3000 dead are buried. I attended some of the commemorations, including one attended by Judith Trotter, called from her post as our ambassador in Rome to represent New Zealand diplomatically as she'd done less than a year before in Zagreb for the launch of my book.

---

* Davin's biography by Keith Ovenden is called *A Fighting Withdrawal*, Oxford University Press, 1996.

So much of this was destined for the novel that would be *Talking about O'Dwyer*; but there was a feeling of surplus, of more than a novel alone could 'use', and the result, when I returned to the UK (I was staying once again in Oxford) was the sequence of poems, 'Crete', which concludes

Last Post, Suda Bay

Should we disturb you
my dead compatriots
so well-placed here?

Should we disturb ourselves?

Your silence is absolute
unless we pretend
it's you who speak in the wind.

Not forgotten
but unfathomable.

More vivid than yesterday
and like yesterday
gone beyond call.

Would it all come together coherently? That's something I worried about constantly, never sure (and still not) of the answer. My first source, Rob Dyer, had drifted so far from fact, and so close to or over the border of sanity, his approval could no longer be expected or sought; but for Paul Binding in the *TLS* and for John de Falbe in the *Spectator*, clearly it worked as a novel. Mark Williams, who seemed to approach it expecting trouble when he reviewed it for the *Listener*, found it 'lucid' and a 'narrative elegantly constructed'. 'A strength of the book' he wrote 'is the dramatisation of a cultural experience neither Maori nor Pakeha, although it touches both.'

I was relieved by that and other warm responses; but when I look at it now I can't read it, except here and there. I'm too aware of how much the effort of holding together and managing all those far-flung elements cost me. But at the same time I relish some of the moments of wit, some of the jokes between old Bertie Winterstoke and Mike Newall, and the way the story comes back to them, and thus to itself, as they ramble from one to another of those hallowed Oxford locations I had loved, encountering them as I did in middle age rather than in youth when they had seemed to friends like Don Smith intimidating and overbearing. I relish too the end-of-a-marriage exchanges, at once brisk and clever, fond and grim, between Mike and Gillian; and not least Mike's assault on her serious Anglicanism in Chapter 9, with his parable of the Bowser of the Holy Spirit on the back side of the moon.

Postscript 1:

In October 2019 while he was working on the second volume of his biography of Maurice Shadbolt, Philip Temple sent me a copy of a postcard I had sent Maurice dated 4/10/90 after the Davin funeral. It was of a Joan Miró 'Aidez l'Espagne' poster which I explained I'd chosen because Maurice would remember hearing, as I did, that Dan was said to have felt guilty because he'd gone to Oxford rather than to Spain to fight for the Republic. In the same card I told him I'd had 'an amiable dream about you. We were trying to walk along together so we could have a good talk – but we were going in different directions.'

It was an appropriate comment on Dan and a perfect image of my relations with Maurice. See Chapter 14, p. 340 for Maurice's positive response to *Talking about O'Dwyer*.

Postscript 2:
As late as January 2001 Rob and I were still arguing about the shooting of the wounded soldier. And in an email of that date I wrote:

> I gave a talk about the novel to a U3As group on the North Shore last week. A man of about 80 came up afterwards. He said he'd been in the Battle of Crete and it had been such an event in his life he'd read everything that had been written about it since. He said, 'I've only previously read two accounts that gave me the feeling of the battle as it really was. Yours was the third.'

Postscript 3:
Davin's second collection of short stories, *Breathing Spaces*, was not published until 1975, which perhaps explains my failure to find anything of his suitable for the Oxford *New Zealand Short Stories* (second series) 1966.

2. France and French and the French

Smith's Dream, Tony Axelrad, and Uzès

My first novel, a New Zealand political fantasy springing from my obsession with (and opposition to our participation in) the Vietnam War was written in the late 1960s. Hutchinson in London had published my novella, 'A Race Apart', in their *New Authors Short Story One*, 1961, and my first book of literary criticism, *The New Poetic*, in their University Library series in 1964, so *Smith's Dream* went to them first and in due course was accepted. There followed a delay which to the still inexperienced writer seemed unduly long; and then, after a contract had been drawn up but before it was signed, came news of some kind of upheaval in the firm, accountants overruling editors, and the offer to publish was withdrawn. Impatient, I gave up on the idea of publication in London and settled for Longman Paul in Auckland who had published my first book of poems, *Whether the Will is Free*, in 1964.

The New Zealand Literary Fund chaired by Professor Ian Gordon declined to recommend a grant, a decision said to be on the ground that the novel, though 'well written', was 'political'. This was usually a fatal blow to the publication of New Zealand fiction in those days, but my editor, Phoebe Meikle, was determined, Blackwood Paul was willing to take the risk, and *Smith's Dream* came out as a hardcover in 1971, followed within a year by a paperback reprint in which I made one radical change to the ending – Smith who had survived at the end of the first version, simply by 'walking away' from the conflict, was now killed, and the honour of 'political commitment' in an 'age of anxiety' was upheld.* The novel did well – it was found to be one that otherwise reading-resistant boys especially took to; and its success was assisted by the idea which got about on talkback radio, that the fascist-tending PM Volkner, who calls in American troops against left-wing rebels in the hills, was really based on Prime Minister Rob Muldoon.

When a version of the story appeared as the Roger Donaldson movie *Sleeping Dogs* in 1977, with Sam Neill as Smith, Ian Mune as Bullen and Warren Oates as US Colonel Willoughby, *Smith's Dream* was reprinted with a 'still' from the movie on the cover, and the commercial success of the novel was assured. There was a period when almost every New Zealand secondary school child had 'done' the novel (often together with the movie) in English; and I'm still approached by people (including my motorised Parnell postman just last week) who tell me they read it at school.

At some time in 1990 I had a phone call or letter from someone unknown to me, Anthony Axelrad, to tell me he was doing a translation of *Smith's Dream* into French. My view of French literature and culture tended, not untypically among Anglophones, to be respectful and even somewhat exalted, so I very much liked the idea of a translation into that language. But was *Smith's Dream* the right novel? I had moved on to other fiction, both before leaving the university in August 1986, and more rapidly after that date. *All Visitors Ashore* was published in 1984, *The Death of the Body* in 1986, *Sister Hollywood* in 1989; and by 1990 I seem to have been well on the way with *The End of the Century at the End of the World.* I responded gratefully to Tony (as I would soon know him) but

* An account of these matters will be found in *You Have a Lot to Lose*, pp. 167–69.

suggested *The Death of the Body*, which had just been translated into Swedish, and with versions soon to follow in German and Portuguese, was more likely to be received with interest in France.

Tony and his partner of that time, a Frenchwoman, Gisèle, drove up from Wellington at the end of 1990 or the beginning of 1991, stayed in the Takapuna motor camp, and Kay and I took them to dinner in Parnell. This was our first meeting, and since Tony was to figure a good deal in this part of my life I will sketch his background.

Anthony Axelrad was technically English (he held a British passport, and by this time a New Zealand one) but had grown up in France, first in Paris, then in Nice – so although both his parents were British and spoke English at home, they sent Tony to French schools. He told me, with a linguist's precision in such matters, that his English vocabulary when in his teens would have been about 1500 words. As a consequence he regarded French as his first language. But self-identification can't have been simple. In Nice, his schoolfellows, a mix of local Niçois and recently arrived 'Pied-Noirs' from Algeria, identified him by his accent as Parisian and therefore alien and disliked, or at least not favoured.

At the end of his years of schooling Tony had signed on as a deck-hand to a Liberian-registered ship whose crew were mainly Serbo-Croat-speaking Dalmatians. He had studied Russian at school (his mother, who had lived through the Blitz in London during the war, had forbidden him to study German) and with the help of that language, was soon getting by, gaining confidence in his ability to see a new foreign language as a problem but not an obstacle.

His life before we met had a fascinating international irregularity. He had been a sailor, a student, a translator, an insurance salesman; he had hitch-hiked thousands of kilometres through Europe, worked in South Africa on a crayfish trawler and then as crew on a yacht; had been a taxi driver in Sydney, done two thirds of a degree in Russian in Nice, and a whole degree in geography in Wellington.

No need to unscramble all of this. In South Africa Tony met his first wife, Sheelagh, and they were married in 1974. After various employments, travels and adventures they enrolled themselves as full-time students at Victoria University in Wellington. Their son Eric was born in their first year and Sven in their third. The stresses of their life told on the marriage however, and Sheelagh left Tony for another man. When she found herself badly treated she asked Tony to assist her escape with the two boys (by now aged nine and seven) – which he did, helping her arrange a return home to South Africa. Relations between them have remained civil over the years, and he has been in regular contact with Eric and Sven, now adults.

So was Tony English or French? He always seemed perfectly fluent in either language, educated, or sufficiently well-read, in the literatures of both, and a fascinating mix of characteristics, some that one would call 'French', and others equally 'English'. There was even, picked up along the way, a hint of South African-Dutch in his accent, and he was comfortable to be considered, after years in New Zealand, 'a good Kiwi'. I sometimes thought he would have made a good character in a novel by Simenon, slightly mysterious, difficult to identify, international. At the time of first getting in touch with me about *Smith's Dream* he was employed by the Department of Internal Affairs in Wellington as a translator.

When we met, Tony was living with Gisèle whom he had got to know during a brief return to France. But Gisèle's experience of New Zealand, he later told me, was like that of my Frenchwoman Louise in *The Secret History of Modernism*: she had brought to New Zealand a French romantic, perhaps Gauguin-inspired, idea of 'the South Seas', and found herself disappointed and unhappy in chilly and windy Wellington, with little English and only Tony's English-speaking associates for friends. By the time I met them (though I was not told) she was already thinking of returning to France.

Tony had wasted no time taking my advice by letter that *The Death of the Body* might be a better prospect for French publication than *Smith's Dream* and had already begun his translation before our meeting. I suggested that when it was complete he should send it to Christopher MacLehose whose French wife, Koukla, acted from London as an agent for French publishers. By February 1991 he was writing to say his translation was on its way to London. In due course it was accepted by the Paris publisher POL (upmarket, they also published Marguerite Duras) and was produced in the classic French plain off-white paperback format which gave it, to one familiar with such things, a feeling of French seriousness, weight, purpose.

Meanwhile Gisèle had gone and Tony had met Pat in Wellington in 1992. Pat was English-born and had come to New Zealand with her family when her father was recruited to install radar at Dunedin's new airport, and then radio-telecommunications west of Auckland. When that and other contract work was completed he was ready to return home with his family; but by this time Pat, a young adult, had decided to stay. When Tony met her she had been married for twenty-four years. There were no children and the marriage had unravelled. She and Tony fell in love, decided they should marry and that they would live in England. They came through Auckland in October 1993 on their way to London and Kay and I gave them a farewell dinner at a Turkish restaurant in Newmarket.

My subsequent dealings with the Axelrads always had a strong literary aspect. Tony was continuing as a literary translator and did French versions of novels by Australian writers Robert Drewe, Fiona Capp and Julia Leigh. But he was himself a writer of fiction, both in English and in French, never entirely certain which language his stories would be most at home in – an ideal uncertainty for a translator but perhaps not so good for a writer. His subjects for fiction ranged widely, as his life had – France, South Africa, New Zealand, Australia – and I was confident I would see them one day in English or in French.

When I was setting out to write this part of my story I asked Tony (with whom I'm in fairly regular email contact) what had first brought him to New Zealand. His reply is worth quoting in full, because it shows aspects of his character, and particularly his quality as a writer, which even in English seems to me French:

I never liked or felt at home in Nice. A character in Fiona Capp's novel *Last of the Sane Days* sums up its sinister flashiness in one sentence: 'The brighter the sunshine, the darker the shadows' (p. 104). As a teenager I escaped into books and maps. The concept of *les antipodes* fascinated me: the farthest you could get from Nice was a place called New Zealand – two big islands in my atlas, lots of blue, green and brown. The following extract from my memoir describes my first sight of the South Island:

> Eight weeks later, while the *Serafin Topić* was loading grain in Mount Maunganui, the crew organised a football game: the Engine Room vs. the Deck. It was wonderful to run after a ball on lush New Zealand turf after a long sea voyage that took us through the Panama Canal to Long Beach, California, and then across the vast expanses of the Pacific to the antipodes. My first sight of Aotearoa, the land of the long white cloud, is still etched in my mind's eye half a century later. I was working on deck in the wake of a force-10 storm that had battered us for thirty hours when Nostromo, the bosun, told me to report to the bridge. Captain Sunj greeted me with a smile and pointed to the horizon: '*Novi Zeland*.' Between the heaving dark blue of the ocean and the paler blue of the southern sky rose the snowy barrier of the Southern Alps. Later that morning, the pilot took us through the Otago Heads, where hundreds of sheep were grazing peacefully on the hillsides, so close we could hear their plaintive bleating. It felt as if I'd landed on a different planet: '*là tout n'est qu'ordre et beauté, luxe, calme et volupté*'.*

* A line from Baudelaire: 'There, there's only good order and beauty, luxury, peace and pleasure.'

When we left New Plymouth in February 1969 I knew I'd found the place where I wanted to live. In the notebook where I recorded quotes, song lyrics and poems I wrote the following in French: 'Nouvelle-Zélande, terre de rêve. Je reviendrai, mais pas seul.'* The promise was fulfilled on 20 March 1978. In answer to your question, and however unlikely it may sound, what took me to NZ was a dream.

THERE WAS ALWAYS, IN ADDITION to all the literary connections, a feline element to the Stead–Axelrad engagements. Pat has a rare talent for taming feral cats; and my first task when I met up with them after their return to London was to look after and feed the current stray, Zoe, while Pat and Tony went on holiday. To me Zoe was the most unsociable and affection-resistant animal (and Kay calls me a cat whisperer) I have ever encountered. This was in 1995 and it was a convenient arrangement – I would have rent-free occupancy of their flat in Tufnell Park in return for taking care of Zoe while they were absent. Later, in Saint-Maximin in France, I would again be in charge of this Impractical Cat (who would have presented Old Possum with an exceptional challenge), and learned to get even close enough to stroke her fur, but only by lying near her on my stomach in the grass and, slowly enough for the movements to be almost imperceptible, to wriggle and edge towards her. Any sudden movement and she would fly in terror into the undergrowth and be missing for the rest of the day.

In London Pat worked as an accountant and Tony (the Simenon character again) as station assistant at Goodge Street and other stations on the Northern line of the London Underground. But France and *la langue française* called, especially to Tony. He was a natural linguist, and although he was enjoying his work on the Underground, it was, I think, always in the nature of an escape from

---

* New Zealand, land of dream. I will return but not alone.

serious commitment. The internet brought about new possibilities. You could set up as a translator and have work come to you, and return it completed, entirely online. That meant in turn that you could choose your work location – somewhere close to your ideal – and Pat and Tony began to hunt for such a place. They were systematic, with a kind of orderliness that seemed to me very French, taking into account aesthetics, climate (Tony's time at sea had made him unusually weather-conscious), house prices, cost of living, and general ambience. They settled finally on the village of Saint-Maximin just outside the town of Uzès in the south-west of France, 20 kilometres north of Nîmes and perhaps 30 west of Avignon. This was a region often referred to by the English as Provence but, being west of the Rhône, is strictly Languedoc-Roussillon.

Tony and Pat bought a house there, just outside the village on the *chemin de la Coste*, with perhaps a half-acre of garden and a small swimming pool. There was an upstairs bedroom and a sunroom both looking over a valley of vineyards, cornfields and sunflowers, towards the main road between Uzès and Remoulins, beyond which the land dropped again, gently towards the river Alzon, with dark green hills beyond again. It was like a landscape by van Gogh, and I remember it all so exactly because for the next perhaps twenty years I was to spend usually a month, sometimes two, of every European summer there – for a few years alone (with Zoe while she survived) and then with Kay after she retired from the University Library in 1998. With us there as guardians, the Axelrads took their summer holiday. Tony would never let us pay rent. He said it was because he did not wish to be involved in the nightmare of French tax bureaucracy this would entail, but I think it was because he was by nature generous, and because as the years went by we became good friends.

Tony's experiment as freelance translator was not unsuccessful but I think it was more stressful than he had expected. There was the uncertainty of whether work would come in and so the feeling that every request must be satisfied; and then gaps causing anxiety, followed by rushes of more work than was convenient. So when he was offered a position as translator with the court set up in The Hague by the United Nations to deal with war crimes during the recent war in the former Yugoslavia, Tony was ready to take it – first on trial, leaving Pat in Saint-Maximin, and then permanently, renting a flat there for themselves as a couple. At some time after this transition the Saint-Maximin house was sold; but not wanting to sever their connection with that lovely region, indeed wanting to return to it from time to time and perhaps retire there, they bought a smaller house in the village itself. It was mostly unoccupied, and they invited us to continue as before, taking holidays there.

This was a region first known to Kay and me and to our children for two misfortunes: while I was holding the Mansfield Menton fellowship in 1972 we had camped a night under the famous Roman *Pont du Gard* on the river Gardon, and next morning our van, with faulty steering I had not known about, had run off the road putting Kay overnight in hospital and sending us all back to Menton rather than on to our intended destination, Spain; and roughly a decade later, on a tour around France with then teenage daughters Charlotte and Margaret, our car, parked overnight in Arles, had been broken into and our luggage stolen.

But the region was also known to me from my studies of French literature: it contained the town of Tarascon which had given its name to Daudet's fictional character Tartarin, the gullible game-hunter whose lies and self-deceptions made him a hero; and it was the location of the famous mill from which Daudet had written his *Lettres de mon Moulin*, stories, written in a classically limpid French, which included the beautifully sad 'La Chèvre de Monsieur Seguin'. I knew too that Racine, whose play *Andromaque* I had tried, as a student, to turn into a modern poetic drama, had spent a year or two of his youth in and around Uzès. It was in Tony and Pat's library I found and re-read Victor Hugo's novel *Les Travailleurs de la Mer*, and recognised for the first time that the end of my novel *All Visitors Ashore*, in which Curl Skidmore runs along the beach and over the rocks waving the red towel to the ship in which his lover is departing, had been – not modelled on, because it was unconscious, but powerfully influenced by, memories of the end of the Hugo novel which I had studied and been moved by as a student.

We usually flew from London to Nice where we picked up a hire car and then, after a few days' return to Menton for fond memories and, often, meetings with the current Katherine Mansfield Fellow, it was off west towards Saint-Maximin. Once settled, there would be visits to Avignon and Nîmes, and north to the region around Barjac where some of our New Zealand friends had retired (Ted and Joan Sturmer), or spent the European summers (Mike and Linda Gill, Mary Gee); or we might drive east to Maussane-les-Alpilles where Stephen and Natasha Spender had their *gîte*, *Mas Saint-Jérôme*, and where Natasha had made the remarkable English garden she wrote a book about which Christopher MacLehose published.* Occasionally there was a visit further afield, westward to Avèze where the novelist A. S. Byatt – Antonia – a friend of many years, spent much of every summer away from London, writing and swimming in the pool she said her Booker Prize had paid for, eating her evening meal (together, of course, with her visiting friend or friends) in the local *auberge*, always with a glass, or at most two, of champagne from a bottle that was put aside for her so she could return to it the following evening.

But the hire car was mainly for our drive, every afternoon, to the village of Collias for swimming in the Gardon. This was the same river that flows under the *Pont du Gard*, and Collias is five or so kilometres upstream from that most remarkable of Roman remains. The Gardon is not as big a river as the Rhône, but wide and deep enough for the swim across and back to be a good workout. There were steep rocky bluffs on one side from which children jumped, climbing higher as courage or recklessness increased. It was a healthy river, with large fish always to be seen; and sections

---

* *An English Garden in Provence*, Harvill Secker, 1999.

of fast-flow you could ride with downstream, and others slower and deeper for simple swimming and exploring the depths. There were canoes for hire and arrangement for canoe and canoeist to be picked up further downstream and returned where they began.

And then there was the routine that gripped and enchanted me quite as much as the swimming, and which I still recall with nostalgia, often retracing its paths in half-waking hours in the night. This was the morning walk that took us from Saint-Maximin by a rough unsealed road past vineyards and crop fields (and one quite remarkable wheatfield that blazed scarlet with poppies in spring and early summer), past olives and cherry trees, and now and then a stone *capitelle* in which shepherds or cowherds had sheltered overnight in ancient times – and then down into woods on a rough walking track past a chateau and a mill-house, along the track beside a small stream, the Alzon; and then climbing up into the centre of the compact town of Uzès by paths which either brought us out at the cathedral, or (a slightly shorter route) at the hospital – and so into the centre for coffee, sometimes in the *périphérique*, more often in the central town square, *la Place aux herbes*. After that there would be minor shopping matters, mainly bread and perhaps cakes from the *boulangerie*, and then the walk home in the often quite extreme heat, stealing a few grapes along the way, if it was late enough in the summer, to quench thirst and provide a minimal sugar-shot. These small thefts were quite unacceptable by French notions of propriety, breaches of the *contrat social*, but the vastness of the fields of vines, and a sort of British informality in such matters, rendered them not only morally insignificant, but practical and almost virtuous. We were never apprehended.

Saint-Maximin, the Roman aqueduct, Amanda, the storm . . .
I was fascinated by the aqueduct system that ran from Uzès to the *Pont du Gard*, and on down to Nîmes. In the first century CE the

Romans had had a significant garrison at Nîmes (site of France's highest recorded modern-day temperatures) and more water was needed than could be found close at hand. A copious and constant source, known in modern times as *la Fontaine d'Eure,* welled up from an underground aquifer under the walls of Uzès; but how could that water be sent to Nîmes? For Uzès itself it must have been carried up in buckets or loaded on to donkeys, which even into the twentieth century were among the region's most significant labourers. But Nîmes was 20 kilometres distant, and between came the valley through which flowed the Gardon. Without mechanical pumps the river was useless to a town divided from it by the intervening landscape – those high bluffs the children jumped from. But suppose the water from the *Eure* could flow by means of an aqueduct across the intervening valley, it could then run on by gravity all the way to Nîmes. To get the passage across the valley of the Gardon would require an immense structure. So a stone bridge was built across the river, then another on top of the first, and a third on top of the second: thus the immense and extraordinary triple aqueduct that is the *Pont du Gard.* From there a steady downward path was found or created, a system of channels and tunnels through which the water flowed to Nîmes for the next five hundred years, until new and sufficient sources were found in or near the town itself.

The path of the aqueduct from the *Fontaine d'Eure* to the *Pont du Gard* passes just below Saint-Maximin, and I enjoyed hunting for surviving parts of it, no longer still functioning, but remarkable as relics of Roman ingenuity.

When we first visited the *Pont du Gard* in 1972, heading for Spain from Menton, it was not, as it is now, a World Heritage site, and much less closely guarded and controlled. It was still possible then to climb to the top tier, the one through which the water flowed in Roman times, and I got up there with our two older children, Oliver and Charlotte, aged eight and five. I don't think we went all the way across; but at least we can say we have walked more than a few scary steps, in that ancient elevated watercourse, towards the point on the opposite side where the descent towards Nîmes begins.

Even in summer the weather in that region of France can spring surprises. In 2002 daughter Margaret came from London to visit us with husband Guy and their new baby, Joseph. I was writing my novel *Mansfield* and wanted a quick second look at the coastal town of Bandol and the hotel Beau Rivage where Katherine Mansfield had her first serious tubercular haemorrhage. Kay and I made it a day-visit and, heading back in the late afternoon, stopped in Maussane to look at menus (a regular pastime for travellers in France) when an enormous flash and a crack of thunder unleashed sudden rain – so extraordinarily hard and heavy that we retreated to the car, both drenched in less than a minute. It seemed best just to press on slowly through the almost blinding downpour, reflecting idly that when Louis XV said 'Après moi le déluge' he must have had something like this in mind, and that it was a better image of the French Revolution than what we inhabitants of islands mean by 'rain'.

When we got back to Saint-Maximin we found Margaret and Guy alarmed but excited, wanting to go out and look at it, and at its effects. So they went, leaving us with baby Joe. They reported that the Alzon was already over the road, cutting off the direct main road from Saint-Maximin into Uzès. That evening we went for a meal to a restaurant in the nearby village of Saint-Siffret and were turned away because it had become a shelter for refugees from flooding. Next day we found a way into the town by a back route. Bread was being rationed (bread is like life itself in France, which is why Marie-Antoinette's possibly apocryphal 'Why don't they eat cake?' is such a symbol of aristocratic incomprehension). There were queues for bread, and people with pails lining up at a water truck delivering safe drinking water. The Gardon was in serious flood and, as we were to see in the next day or so, had washed away houses and a restaurant along its banks near Collias. There was one beautiful stylish house built on a shelf of rock overlooking the river at Collias, and Margaret and Guy had thought perhaps if it was ever for sale they might buy it. It had been swept away entirely – there was nothing left but the shelf, and nothing since has replaced it.

The road over the *Pont Saint-Nicolas* between Uzès and Nîmes was also washed away and would not be open again for almost a year. The supporting bridge was intact but the river, almost unbelievably considering the depth of the valley below, had risen right over it, and left a large tree behind in case anyone should be in doubt. We saw cars lying in the middle of cornfields, where they had been carried and dropped by the floodwaters. Around thirty people in the region had died, drowned or struck by lightning. There was chaos everywhere; and our visitors were happily trapped with us, unable to find their way home to London until the waters began to recede.

IT SEEMS A TRUISM THAT WHEREVER you travel in the world if you are a New Zealander you will meet a compatriot, and very likely one with whom you have fewer than six degrees of separation – more like one or two. The one we met in Saint-Maximin was the surprising Amanda Taylor-Ace, proprietor of *La Maison de Maitresse* which, together with another New Zealander, Hester Bullen, she ran during the European summers as a guest house and cooking school. Amanda had had two marriages and two divorces, a child from each, and now described herself as a free woman. She had sold her child-care business in Takapuna, and some Auckland property (including the Takapuna North post office) to buy and restore two adjoining houses in the village for her guest house. Our few degrees of separation were that at the time of our getting to know her, Amanda's current partner, or best male friend, was Alex Witten-Hannah whose family and rather grand residence on a lifestyle block at Karekare on Auckland's west coast were well known to us because we'd had a bach at Karekare since 1975. Alex recognised us at Suzie's café in Saint-Maximin and took us at once to Amanda's house for a meal and wine and what became an impromptu party.

Alex was a lawyer in Auckland and seemed to have an informal coming-and-going relationship with Amanda who herself came and went following the summers between France and New Zealand. Alex had broken up with a wife, there had been a divorce and a bitter and protracted custody battle over their children (I think there were twins), and it appeared the wife had talked, in a wine-fuelled moment, of wanting to put a contract on Alex to have him killed. Word of this got back to Alex, and he decided to use it against her, involving the police and having an undercover detective pose as a killer ready to remove Alex for a sufficient sum. The ex-wife seemed to acquiesce and was duly charged with conspiracy to murder. The matter came to trial, and she was found guilty but because the defence had shown that Alex himself was involved in this plan for his own death, she received a suspended sentence. There were reports that on each day of the trial Alex had been accompanied by a colourfully dressed current partner, who chanted magic spells over him. I'm not sure whether this benign sorceress was or was not Amanda. Daughter Charlotte made a short story of it, 'Pity', in her brilliant collection *Opportunity*,* by focusing on the parents' love of the disputed child, so that both the mother's thought of having the father killed, and the father's turning knowledge of her careless talk back as a weapon against her, are seen with pity. The real subject is the father's and the mother's equally powerful parental instinct.

The *Maison de Maitresse* was two eighteenth-century houses, at right angles one to the other, with a connecting terrace, a walled garden and generous swimming pool. At the front was Saint-Maximin's small village square and an ancient well, and from the back a view over a landscape of cornfields and vines. Amanda's temperament was lively, affirmative, devoted to good food, good wine, and good fun. She has written a book about her life,

* Charlotte Grimshaw, *Opportunity*, Vintage, 2007.

My French Affair, with a subtitle *How a Kiwi Woman Found Her* Joie De Vivre *in the South of France*.* The book is interspersed with many excellent French recipes. One of its chapters begins:

> I love men and I love sex. I particularly love younger men and I love sex with them. In France I have had many lovers most of them more than 20 years younger than me. I doubt this would have been the case if I'd stayed in New Zealand.

Amanda was born and brought up in New Zealand, and though her French mother taught her Kiwi kids nothing at all of the French language she taught Amanda a great deal about French cooking. So Amanda was into her middle years before the idea of starting a new life in France came to her, and she began only then to learn something of the language. There's a French expression when people are being modest about their linguistic skills, *Je parle français comme une vache espagnole* – I speak French like a Spanish cow. I have the impression that Amanda's French – or more precisely her pronunciation, her accent – is of the *vache espagnole* variety, except that no Spanish cow could be so fluent. It just rolls out in a steady stream, always warm, friendly, enthusiastic, and is always understood.

Saint-Maximin was once a typical French rural village with its own *boulangerie*, its café and post office. Now it has none of these. There is a Carrefour supermarket half way between the village and the town, but you need a car to stock up with food for several days. When Kay and I first visited there was still the traditional French café, run by a Swiss woman, Suzie, which also offered basic meals. But when Suzie sold, it was to a couple who planned to make it into an upmarket restaurant. The terms of the purchase, which had to be approved by the mayoralty (*M. le Maire* in France has considerable power in local affairs), required that the café continue

---

* *My French Affair*, Random House NZ, 2012.

providing drinks during regular hours, whereas the new owners were really only interested in a restaurant offering a proper lunch menu on certain days, and dinner in the evenings. So the young proprietor's mother-in-law was put in charge during the daylight hours, it seemed with the intention of giving surly service, or none, and driving customers away. (We went there just once during this difficult time of transition, with a friend and, asking for glasses of wine, were told there was none!) Gradually the 'regulars' dwindled and vanished, and soon we had only a restaurant for tourists and summer visitors – very attractive, fine dining, but another feature of Old France gone forever.

For winters the town would be a better place to live than the village; but even Uzès, after the good weather and the tourists are gone, is probably not, as it can seem in summer, an ideal location for retirement living; so it did not surprise me that, after Tony retired from his job in The Hague, he and Pat sold the Saint-Maximin house and retired to a compact English city, Norwich, where he continues his writing, and the recreation of cycling he had taken up seriously in Holland, while Pat's recreation is swimming in the local pool. Both are serious readers, Tony in French and English, but also in Dutch as a consequence of his years at The Hague. They have a small black and white cat, acquired in Holland and called Kitty, not as neurotic as Zoe, but at once timid and demanding, the temperament of a Janet Frame, but whether with her genius or not only other cats (and perhaps birds and rodents) could say. From time to time on visits I have seen Kitty flash by on her way upstairs to her own little room, but she never stops to exchange pleasantries.

England, or was it the English language, or perhaps two British passports, had won. When the Axelrads stayed with us in New Zealand I thought Tony liked the idea of a return here, especially if they could live in Auckland, and particularly Devonport; but house prices were rising steeply, Pat's choice was firmly for England, and Tony, less decided in his preferences, accepted that. I suppose where a true linguist lives may be in two or four or more places at once, without moving at all; but in our recent exchange about what it was had taken him to New Zealand in the first place, he ended surprisingly, 'With the precipice of Brexit looming, I still hope Pat will see the light and accept to up-anchor and enjoy our sunset years in the South Seas!'

For me France has always been something of a marvellous elusive unreality, touched so often and over so many years, both as location and as language-and-culture, and once in youth in the form of a young woman, I feel I know it very well – well enough to know there's a sense in which I don't know it at all. It has been for me an aspiration, what Henry James might have called 'the Unachieved Thing', its attraction continuing for precisely that reason. It has given me a feeling, not so much of failure as of always falling short on the brink of success. Success has been just around the corner, and will still be there when I die. This is not to suggest I don't know a lot of French literature and French music, or that I can't, when pushed to the wall, understand spoken French or make myself understood in it. But people like Tony Axelrad are my measure of my own inadequacy.

I have written often about my certainty that a good deal of this un-success began in the third form at the crucial age of thirteen, when I learned French for the first time, and off the page rather than by ear. Along with this goes my (I believe unanswerable) point, that those born blind learn to speak fluently whatever language they are exposed to, while those born deaf do not (and were once designated 'deaf-and-dumb'). Language is a matter of ear not eye, and should never be taught by sight until the ear has done its learning. I am still and forever burdened with the habit of trying to 'see' the words as I hear them spoken, rather than going instantly from sound to comprehension.*

* See e.g. 'The Sweetshop Window: One New Zealand Writer's Engagement with French Language, Literature and Society', *Book Self*, Auckland University Press, 2008, pp. 49–69.

Kay and I returned to Uzès for one or two summers after the Axelrads sold their house in the village, renting in the town itself, and loving it quite as much. My France is not only Uzès and the Languedoc. It is also Menton and the Mediterranean, and (of course) Paris. I have poems about both, including a long one called *Paris*, published as a small book with illustrations by one of my students, Greg O'Brien; and my last novel, *The Necessary Angel*, is set entirely there, in the milieu, physical and social/intellectual, of the Sorbonne. But walking in those Uzès woods past mill-house and chateau; or swimming in that river with its still green depths under sun and shadow; or eating French food and drinking French wine in that classic *Place aux herbes* with its ancient arcades and its starlings squabbling raucously at evening; or sitting out of doors in the village while its summer swallows conduct their Battle of Britain with invisible enemies before sundown and the moment when the bats and Hegel's 'owl of Minerva' take over: these are locations and states of being that make one reflect on the human spirit, and what it is enriched by, and how places have grown in value by human occupation – how history and culture and nature have developed in unison there, and how we New Zealanders are inextricably linked to, and enriched by, our European past, and foolish if we try to sever inherited connections.

3.
The Home Front

Getting off-side

Although after leaving the University of Auckland in 1986 I spent some part of every year overseas (usually but not always in the Northern Hemisphere summer), I still spent much more time at home than away; and while away I was always 'a New Zealand writer'. At home I was not infrequently involved in some kind of public argument or literary scrap, often with a political edge. I had some 'cred' as a dependable leftist. I had joined the Labour Party at age seven, and though I was not now an active member, no one would have suspected me of voting for anything but the left. I had been very active in the protests about our participation in the Vietnam War, about the Springbok tour, about Bastion Point – one of those people Rob Muldoon would have dismissed as belonging with the 'Rent-a-Demo crowd'. There had been a slight wobble which the lefter-than-left might have detected when David Lange and Roger Douglas came to power as PM and Finance Minister. I saw that they had inherited from Muldoon a serious financial crisis and that radical measures were necessary – and (like Lange) I thought Douglas was the man for the job. I remembered sitting a few years earlier alongside him at Bob Chapman's dinner table and agreeing that politicians had to do what they saw was necessary, not what they thought would make them loved – and for a time I thought that was what Roger was about. In other words I was loyal to Labour, and took longer than Jim Anderton, and Lange himself, to recognise that we were being taken, not down a traditional Labour (Keynesian) path, but off to the right into the dark night of the School of Chicago – Friedmanite theory, Reaganism, Thatcherism, the shadows of which still linger.

That wobble was soon left behind and I was back with Labour, as Labour was with itself, and with my old badminton partner Helen Clark.* But I remember that interim as rocky, a period of bitter argument and recriminations. My academic studies, if anyone had thought to inspect my political credentials there, might have caused doubt and difficulty; but only because the question I pursued so often, of how if at all poetry and politics can work together, was itself difficult. My conclusion was always the same (the same that W. B. Yeats had come to), that on the whole they can't; that politics was by its nature (and necessarily) crude, operating on the basis of general truths and broad brushstrokes, while poetry had to be subtle, refined, complex and sometimes opaque. My three prime, twentieth-century Modernist literary figures, Yeats, T. S. Eliot and Ezra Pound, had all been, by my notion of political respectability, deplorable – two of them anti-Semites, all terrified of 'the Mob' and what it might do if it got loose in their precious bailiwick. But I had never suggested otherwise, or defended their politics. I was sure I knew all three as well as I knew my best friends: that I would have had little common ground with Yeats whose romantic-mysticism I found quite alien; that I could have had civil conversations with Eliot but would have deplored his subtle theological evasions and High Anglican dishonesties; and that I might have been entertained by Ezra while

* Helen and I formed a foursome with Keith Sinclair and Joan Anderton (now Caulfield – she was Jim Anderton's wife at the time) to play at the University of Auckland's new gym.

finding his ranting egotism exhausting and his opinions distasteful. Sometimes my close study of Pound, and my ability to make sense of him where others saw only confusion and madness, caused raised eyebrows and suspicions (Keri Hulme once suggested I might be a fellow-fascist); but usually these were murmurs and grumbles from people not sure enough of their ground to make anything of their suspicions. My Pound studies belonged with arcane academic pursuits that could be ignored. What was always surprising to me, and why it was a question worth pursuing, was how these three, among the finest, subtlest and most conscientious craftsmen in poetry, could seem to embrace one or another (as it seemed to me) kind of irrationality. Auden, another major poet, had been, as a young man, reasonable in his commitment to the left as Hitler rose to power and we all lurched towards World War II; but as he aged, Auden had drifted back into Toryism, Anglicanism and English public school-Oxford snobbery, his face wrinkling with the decline as if a bad fairy had put a spell on his cradle from which, despite the wonderful technical command and clear-sightedness of his youth, there could be for him no escape in his declining years.

So much for my academic identity, not left behind when I left the university, but of less public interest. But as a writer about social and political matters, and about New Zealand in particular, it was my intolerance of what I saw as varying shades of bullshit that got me into trouble. I was not good at what as a family we called 'humming and swaying'. Humming and swaying was what our friends and allies of the left did when a general affirmation was called for which involved cutting corners with the truth, a little insincerity, a smackerel of hypocrisy. Questions about 'race, gender, class' often produced this – everyone pretending that an issue which was complex and called for subtlety, could be covered by an agreement that X was good and Y was evil, and that all who cast doubt or thought otherwise were fools, racists, or tools of capitalism. When I reviewed the Wedde/McQueen *Penguin Book of New Zealand Verse*, which promoted itself as, and was praised for being, the first to include poems in Māori, I pointed out that the versions in English offered as footnotes to the Māori texts were either bad poems or bad translations, and I couldn't say which because I did not know Māori – but neither did the editors! This was unacceptable – doubly so because it was true.

I received numbers of letters from writers congratulating me privately for this frankness and honesty; but in public it was deplored and I was accused by Michael King of advocating 'the ethnic cleansing of New Zealand literature'. This was in the time of the war in the former Yugoslavia, when 'ethnic cleansing' was a term, and a horror, constantly in the news.

'The New Victorians', the piece with which I concluded *Answering to the Language*, my second book of critical essays, is full of such statements, accurate, clear, ringing, but unacceptable. I read them now with surprise, so much sounds fresh in style – 'hard, bright, clean, particular' – and truthful. Here's an example about the Mervyn Thompson case:

> Watching [a TV interview] I felt that a dominant moralism (as distinct from morality) was beginning to dictate the behaviour of everyone in public life. Nothing was allowed to be a true and simple expression of human sexuality and the male psyche. The intellectual community was being corrupted by a childish desire to be 'good', and could only be made healthy if enough people forgot about 'goodness' (pleasing Mummy and Daddy) and thought instead about authenticity.

For such social commentaries I got many public rebukes and many private congratulations. I often felt bruised by the former and irritated by the latter, wanting to reply 'Don't tell me you agree with me, tell your disapproving friends; have some courage – tell the world!' Those essays seem for the most part as true now as they did then. I'm glad to have published them; but I know I wouldn't want to say those things now. Have I too become inauthentic? Is the mind, like the eyes and ears, blurred by old age?

To some extent I was at odds with myself because I was politically and socially liberal – even by inclination radical – but academically conservative. On the one hand I deeply deplored our typical English-speaking punitive habits in dealing with crime, which punished the poor and deprived for behaving as the poor and deprived always do – lawlessly. This meant Māori, who predominated among the poor and deprived, predominated in our prisons. I wanted change, and saw only fear and revenge where there should have been pity and reform. I looked to Scandinavian models, and saw Garth McVicar's Sensible Sentencing Trust, and Bob McCoskrie's Family First movement, as benighted enemies of enlightenment and progress; and I deplored both National and New Zealand First for their populist pandering to the Kiwi (and Anglophone) punitive norm when all the evidence against its efficacy was publicly available. I favoured trade unions, graduated taxation that would hit wealth hard, a wages policy that would go some way to level affluence in New Zealand, and a completion of the welfare state to include teeth, eyes and hearing, which was part of Labour's plan in the 1930s but had been overtaken as the capitalist model reasserted itself in the 1950s and '60s. I was in other words (and am) both temperamentally and intellectually a fairly hard-line Keynesian man of the left.

On the other hand I cared deeply about the English language and about literature in that language (including New Zealand's). I was resistant to ideas strongly prevalent at the time that it was wrong to correct the written language of the schoolyard because that undermined the confidence of vulnerable youngsters who needed self-belief. I favoured an education system that exposed young people to the best in literature; and the streaming of classes according to ability, so that those with real talent would not be held back by those who lacked it. This led me into arguments with secondary school teachers, and on a wider front with those among them who wanted to revise our history and our literary history in favour of moral worth, desert rather than distinction. I was for the traditional 'white male' canon rather than the creation of new ones in which women, the brown and the poor were discovered to have produced writers of genius, neglected only because they were women or brown or poor.

Obviously the canon would include the Brontës, and Jane Austen, and George Eliot – but it always had; and even by the early twentieth century women like Wolfe and Mansfield were changing the picture. It was not that the canon would go on being predominantly dead, white and male – and I had never been anything but eager to recognise, with total indifference to sex or race, new talents. That was what I considered was needed – indifference to everything but quality. The great and always undervalued advantage of the accepted canon was that it gave educated people a common ground for discourse. That common ground was worth more even than (if it could be said to be unjust) justice.

There was a kind of rightness about all this; but was it too inflexible, too hard-line, unrelaxed, combative? Didn't my bullshit detector home in too ruthlessly on the half-truths and sincere insincerities by which what was supposed to be 'my side' argued its case? Maybe so – but how refreshing those essays look now, how clear-eyed and sharp and truthful. I was one voice, and a good one; I didn't have to turn myself into a choir and try to sing all the parts.

After I left the university I began to write an occasional column in the somewhat 'glossy' magazine *Metro*, and this offered me an outlet for what I might have thought of as 'straightening' the record, but was soon giving me a reputation as a spokesman not only for the right, but for the Right. A good example is that, arguing for greater assistance for the poor and the dispossessed, I said (and I am probably responsible for the fact that this became one of Don Brash's slogans) one should 'target, not race but need'. If this were done, the majority in need being Māori, Māori would benefit most, but without leaving out those in need who were not Māori. In principle this was true; but once Brash and those who supported him took it up it got gathered into the anti-welfare anti-tax arguments of the affluent and greedy, and became surreptitiously an argument against assisting Māori at all. There is a *mea culpa* here, for sure. When I look at the thirty or forty years since I was involved in these culture wars, I have to concede that New Zealand society is better for having had the policies I sometimes criticised and sniped at; that colonialism had done so much harm to Māori collectively that it was Māori most of all who were in need of massive direct assistance, and a chance to do things in their own way. I should have told myself what I had been telling anyone listening to my work as an academic, that politics was not poetry and had to work in broad brushstrokes, boldly, even crudely, if there was to be an outcome.

The Death of the Body

I also got off-side with the feminist movement. Again my 'cred' should have been good, or at least acceptable. I had grown up in a household with an atheist grandmother ('Religion is the opiate of the people' she told me, attributing it to Karl Marx) who loved to sing hymns but only for the singing not for the song; with a music teacher mother, a Fabian socialist who kept her professional sign and qualification up on the front of the house, using her unmarried name, Olive Karlson; and with a sister who, nicely but firmly, insisted on her priority as the older one. My father figured in his role as senior Labour Party person and trade union secretary, but mainly as the working father, the provider, and veggie gardener, who handed his fortnightly pay packet over to his wife, the 'good manager' who gave him a small allowance out of it for pocket money. He was given to rage at intervals but always seemed on the back foot, which was why I had sympathy for the traditional male, the wage-slave, who could be expected, if able-bodied, to be called upon to go to war; and I found it difficult to see women as if victimhood was their normal or natural role.

Kay was a working wife, a librarian, who had gone to some trouble after the children were born, travelling to Library School in Wellington for periods to acquire a professional qualification; and our two daughters were encouraged quite as much as our son to get university degrees. They both graduated in law and arts, both practised law for a time, and then gravitated back to literature, Charlotte the writer, Margaret the publisher. When I was in trouble with the feminists I felt my whole family backed me – including Oliver, who wrote a letter to the paper saying the idea that I was an old-fashioned male sexist was nonsense. 'In the Stead family the women go out to work and the men mind the kids' – an exaggeration of course but making his point with comic overemphasis.*

As critic I had corrected John Middleton Murry's misrepresentations of his relationship with Katherine Mansfield and how it was reflected in her work; and I had promoted the neglected work of Sylvia Ashton-Warner. As writer my first two fictions, 'A Race Apart' and 'A Fitting Tribute', had first-person female narrators; and the same would be true later of significant parts of the novels *The End of the Century at the End of the World* and *Mansfield*. No one could plausibly suggest that I was blind or indifferent to, or uncomprehending of, the female psyche.

The university situation described in my novel *The Death of the Body* (which might struggle to find a publisher if it were offered now) is one of sexual liberation, a continuation of the mood of the '60s, and before the late-1980s dark cloud of the AIDS scare (combined perhaps with economic uncertainties) closed over and a new puritanism set in. The professor of philosophy, Harry Butler, is having an affair with one of his students, while his wife, Claire, exhibits another aspect of the time by following the teachings

* At the time he was full-time at home minding his son while writing a thesis, I used to relieve him one day a week. Oliver has a PhD in Art History and a Master's in Library Science and is currently Curator, Drawings, Paintings and Prints at the Turnbull Library.

of a Sufi-style guru. Harry's professional interest in a famous philosophical crux, 'the mind/body problem' of René Descartes, is parodied or paralleled by his wife's chanted mantra, 'I am not this body, I am not this body', in the room where he was supposed to be writing his 'definitive study' of that crux, but now taken over by her Sufi shrine; and the practice as distinct from the theory (philosophical or spiritual) is acted out in Harry's sex with his student on the floor of his university office. The simultaneously light-hearted and yet intellectually serious pursuit of these questions is what would make the novel (I suspect) unacceptable in the age of the 'Me Too' movement; and yet it is precisely that quality of profoundly serious comedy which makes me still want to claim *The Death of the Body* as one of my best pieces of fiction.

While I have been thinking back, recalling the sexual libertarianism of the university in the 1970s and '80s, a memory has come to me of an event which illustrates the atmosphere of that time, its peculiar flavour. It was in the early '80s and I was sitting at my desk reading work done by my creative writing class. Outside the rain was bucketing down, when my door flew open and a young woman hurtled in. She stopped, looking bewildered, as if expecting to be somewhere else. My room was at the end of a short corridor so there was no possibility that this door led anywhere else than where she found herself, in the office of Professor Stead whose name was on the door.

She looked finally at me (the door had somehow closed behind her) and said, 'I'm soaked.'

I could see that. She had no overcoat, her clothes clung to her and her long wet hair hung heavy, partly over her face.

She asked did I have a towel she could mop herself with and when I said sorry but no I didn't, she asked didn't I have whisky in my filing cabinet? Or gin?

I told her no, sorry, no whisky, no gin.

She said she thought professors always had spirits in their filing cabinets.

None in mine, I said. I was on the brink of becoming brisk and forbidding, sending her on her way, but she was so strange, and so wet – and perhaps needy. There was such an odd air about her, I was curious and delayed.

Professor X, she told me, had whisky in his filing cabinet.

This didn't surprise me. X* had been drinking a lot in recent years and I'd noticed his hands sometimes shook in the mornings.

You must know him well, I said.

I thought her reply was 'I do. I had his baby.' I begged her pardon and she repeated it with an ironic smile.

Responding to the smile, which seemed to excuse a moment of levity, I said that was careless.

She shrugged, suddenly serious and said she wasn't sorry. She loved it – loved *her*. She loved her baby – *X*'s baby – now a toddler.

I asked did X know and she said he did but denied he was the father. I had a sharp feeling, an intuition, that all this was true, including the baby, and that it probably was X's. It would not be out of character for him to get himself into such a scrape (to use the word the Shelley/Byron set would have used for such crises) and to deny paternity. This was not something to be explored further. I stood up, and said 'Well then . . .' hoping this would make it clear she should go.

In a rush she told me that she taught English at an Auckland secondary school, that her classes studied my poetry – and *Smith's Dream* too – and that if I came on the 'Writers in Schools' programme I would be welcome. *She* would welcome me.

So she had hurtled through my door knowingly. I thought of Professor X's baby and told her I was too busy these days for the Writers in Schools programme. I got up and saw her out as nicely as possible. I directed her to the women's loo where she might be able to find a towel and dry herself. I wished her well and was apologetic. She might be precarious, might need help, but I didn't want to have to be the one to deliver it.

---

* Not a member of the English Department.

THAT WAS PART OF THE ATMOSPHERE that produced *The Death of the Body*. The novel was also written partly in the light and shadow of the physical assault by radical feminists on the English Department's lecturer in drama, Mervyn Thompson, said by his attackers to be a 'rapist'. Mark Williams, who was a junior lecturer in the department at that time and so had some feeling both for the facts and the atmosphere, sees my novel in that context, but too narrowly, as if the Thompson affair is the novel's real subject.* Harry Butler in the novel has to deal with the activities of the Women's Collective in his department, who wish to expose and end his affair with a student, and have him punished for it. The student herself will not cooperate with them and neither will his wife; and between them wife and lover frustrate the attempts by the Collective to have him held to account, though he seems to emerge from the drama comically diminished. This novel was seen by some as 'anti-women', whereas the point of view of the novel (if it can be said to have one) is that the radical feminists of the time were less liberators of oppressed women and more accurately seen as manifestations of sexual puritanism. Interactions between male and female, which if they are to be analysed, discussed and represented in works of art call for subtlety, delicacy, dexterity, had become politicised, and acts of heterosexual love, almost by definition, rape. Mark Williams describes the central subject of the novel, correctly I think, as 'the conflict between feminist activists and academic liberals'. It is a battle which, with the assistance of the AIDS scare, the feminist activists were to win – and this is perhaps represented by the last glimpse the novel offers of Harry:

> What is that look in Harry's eye as he stands staring down at his desk? It's certainly not triumph. But not despair either.

---

* The attack on Thompson is discussed in my previous autobiography, *You Have a Lot to Lose*, pp. 378–79. Mark Williams' discussion of the novel is in his book *Leaving the Highway: Six Contemporary New Zealand Novelists*, Auckland University Press, 1990.

It's something so neutral it's hard to be sure what it is. Probably just acceptance, as a well-trained dog accepts when you chain it to its kennel for the night. It is, after all, quite a long chain, and an unusually well-appointed kennel. [. . .]

From now on that door between Harry and Edith will remain more or less permanently ajar. His Thursday seminars will take on a more structured character. He will become a more disciplined academic, a more compliant husband, a more dutiful father, a more dependable person. He will even patch up his differences with the Dean. [. . .]

Yes it's acceptance, and yes it's wry. Is it also the death of the body? Who can say?

The Treaty, the London flat, and the Tonya Harding of NZ Lit.

The left often embraces a package and expects its supporters to accept and affirm it whole, not in bits. If you make exceptions to your affirmation, you are frowned upon. If you reject too many items, and especially if you are seen to do this publicly, you will be reproached, deplored, ultimately you will be banished from the favoured fold. You will become an apostate. That is where I found myself in the 1980s and '90s; that is where my bullshit detector consigned me – I had become an apostate of the left. As certain pieties about women and Māori became established and accepted as right and proper I began to dissent. If it was respectable to be a dissenter, a dissident in Eastern Europe, as was the case in those days, why should it not be respectable here and now?

The fact of general disapproval came through to me sometimes like a quiet breeze but with a faintly offensive odour, other times a loud wind – and with it at the same time came approval, often from those I did not approve of myself. Eliot has a line 'then fools' approval stings, and honour stains' – rather snobbish of him it seems in context, and I did not think those who liked my opinions fools. In fact I did not write thinking who might like or dislike what I wrote; I wanted to like it myself, to feel that it met difficult questions with subtlety and accuracy.

In his 1990 book *Leaving the Highway*, Mark Williams has a chapter, 'C. K. Stead's Adversary Stance', in which he discusses these areas – the old class race gender nexus, but most particularly race and gender – in which I was seen to be stirring the pot, harassing my own tribe, making trouble. What I thought I was doing was challenging pieties, linguistic sloppiness, that 'humming and swaying' which *l'équipe* Stead found insufferable. Those who disapproved of this sniping and carping would have asked 'Why bother if the cause on the whole is good?' 'Mainly,' I would have replied, 'out of a sense of scrupulousness.' I was, to use the title of one of my books of essays, *Answering to the Language*.

Recently I replayed a 1990 *Frontline* TV discussion of the Treaty of Waitangi in which half a dozen 'experts' (Paul Temm, Mason Durie, Claudia Orange, Mira Szászy, with Hekia Parata and Shane Jones as backup), all of one opinion, were lined up to confront an audience in which a few people like myself of another or other opinion were scattered to give an impression of fairness, of debate, of catering for a variety of points of view. Watching it now, having shifted my ground on these matters, I was expecting to be embarrassed. But what struck me with real surprise as the programme ran on, was how reasonable I seemed, how firm and clear – and relaxed. There was no sign of my 'abrasive personality' (Williams' description). I appeared amused by the situation I found myself in, and said so: it had been promoted as a debate but set up to produce one view at the expense of any other. One who was not pleased with this arrangement was Ian Wards, who had been Chief Government Historian for close on twenty years and must have known as much about the Treaty as anyone present, but who had been assigned a place in the crowd rather than at the front where he belonged, because his view did not accord perfectly with what was by now the correct, the official, one.

The Treaty itself, I said when I got a chance to speak, was conceived as if between two nation states, Māori representing Aotearoa, and the Crown, Great Britain. The Brits understood that sovereignty was being ceded; the Māori probably thought they were retaining it. But now the two entities making the agreement had become, over time, so different, it was hard to see how the Treaty could any longer mean whatever it had been understood to mean in 1840: 'the Crown' now meant, not Great Britain but New Zealand, and 'the Māori' were those of New Zealand's citizens who were of the Māori race. So if Māori, you were now of both parties to the Treaty; if Pākehā, of only one. All of us could claim whatever rights being a New Zealander conferred; only Māori could claim the rights conferred by being Māori. That was the basis for the complaint that making every law conform to the Treaty gave Māori more than equal rights under it – as our parliamentary system did also.

All this still seems to me true; and it was a truth which the Mason Duries and Claudia Oranges, the Paul Temms and Mira Szászys, slid evasively over. But what the CKS watching the programme in 2020 would ask the CKS sounding so at ease and at home in the public eye of 1990, is this: does it matter that the basis for action may be (as the Treaty was once called) 'a legal nullity', if it is being used as a means to correct the unacceptable imbalances in our present-day society – those injustices which put Māori constantly at the wrong end of statistics in wealth, employment, education, crime? By all means describe the Treaty, its circumstances and implications then and now, clearly and accurately; cut out the 'humming and swaying', the insincerities and false pieties about it; but if it's working, embrace it! In other words, the clear-eyed and cheerful purist of 1990 has become the old man of 2020. He has become a pragmatist, though still less than quite certain which is 'better'.

Mark Williams tried to understand what I was doing during this period after leaving the university, and concluded that it was a strategy to gain readers. Now that I was emerging from a previous identity as poet and academic and becoming novelist and social critic, I was creating a public for my new work. He ascribed to me a deliberateness, a degree of calculation, that I can say was not how it seemed from the inside. Did I gain readers by writing these articles and appearing on these programmes? Perhaps I did, but that was not why I wrote them and followed them up in public appearances; and I think it likely I might have lost as many readers as I gained – or perhaps more. But there was no calculation – that was the point really: I was constantly asked what I thought, and I answered. It was what Allen Curnow characterised, with a mixture of respect and anxiety, as 'Karl's candour'.

WELLINGTON WRITERS FIONA KIDMAN and Lauris Edmond were in the forefront of a movement which was forcing New Zealand (and it was happening worldwide) to take women writers seriously. I got on well with them, did useful things in the name of the writers' organisation, PEN, with Fiona, had good literary conversations with Lauris, and good public readings with both.* But we fell out over 'the London flat'. I put it in inverted commas because it is still remembered as the occasion when New Zealand writers collectively shot themselves in the foot. Fiona has given her own uneasy account in her autobiography *Beside the Dark Pool* (pp. 159–73).

I was in Wellington as chairman of the Literary Fund Advisory Committee when I heard that Fiona had suggested the government might buy a house on an island owned by her and Lauris's friend Dudley Kelly who would sell it for $235,000 if it could be used as some kind of retreat for artists and writers. Although Fiona insisted this was a lot less than the house was worth, it was steep for the time, and especially for a house accessible only by row- or

* I have written in *You Have a Lot to Lose* (pp. 252–53) about both women writing me complimentary poems, Fiona publishing hers in the collection *Flying to Palmerston* and feeling later, in her autobiography *Beside the Dark Pool* (Vintage, 2009, p. 81), that she had to explain it as a mistake.

motor-boat. Though I didn't doubt it was a romantic spot, I didn't think one could entirely rule out the possibility that the idea of a getaway for arts people might be Mr Kelly's ploy to get off his hands a difficult-to-sell property which he acknowledged he and his wife were getting too old to make their home.

However, the suggestion had been put to Michael Bassett, then Minister of the Arts, and he asked a group of writers to canvas the idea and report back. Some found it an attractive idea, though the island was remote and access by boat inconvenient; but more attractive, if the Minister was of a mind to spend money on a writers' retreat, would be somewhere less remote and inconvenient – in or close to a major city; or better still (the truly bold idea) why not overseas?

By the time I next heard from him Bassett was indeed of such a mind. I don't think there had ever been, since the time of Joseph Heenan who contrived to get a special state pension for Frank Sargeson, a Minister so well disposed towards New Zealand writers – a goodwill that was not destined to last. Bassett had even thought of buying the Villa Isola Bella, the Mansfield house in Menton, but had had a report suggesting it might be unstable and need expensive repair work. He thought seriously about Sydney, and since Kay had a brother-in-law there, a mathematician and head of East Sydney Tech, but also a man who knew the property market, Bassett suggested I go there and look for something that might be suitable as a writers' retreat. I did that, but by the time I got back with a lengthy report and proposals, Michael had moved on, becoming more ambitious on behalf of writers. He had been in touch with Bryce Harland, our High Commissioner in the UK, thinking London might be the way to go.

That seemed improbable, but I supported it wholeheartedly. Bassett had access (via Cabinet approval) to a fund of Lotteries money that was to be used for commemoration of New Zealand's sesquicentenary (150 years since the signing of the Treaty of Waitangi) and this might be tapped for the purchase. It was a rare opportunity. I'd usually had academic access to accommodation in the UK, and I knew it was the roof over one's head rather than the cost of getting there that had prevented writers who would have liked to make the visit from going. The Menton fellowship had worked to the benefit of most of the writers awarded it; in some ways London and everything it offered (including the English language) could be even better. The two, London and Menton, might in the end even be combined. What a writers' fellowship that would have made!

It was later complained that Bassett favoured me unduly when he sent me to look for a suitable flat; but I was, at that time, the New Zealand-based writer who knew London best. I went willingly, of course, and worked in conjunction with Bryce Harland, to whom I reported every move. So Bryce and I recommended, and the government bought, a flat in Ridgmount Gardens in Bloomsbury. It was in easy walking distance of the Russell Square (Piccadilly line), Goodge Street (Northern line) and Holborn (Central line) Underground stations; walking distance also from the British Museum, University College London, the Senate House Library, Charing Cross Road with its bookshops, and Oxford Street for shopping. The major West End theatres were all in easy reach; and it was not far at all to the river and the South Bank, with the Royal Festival Hall, the National Theatre (three theatres in one), the British Film Institute, and Shakespeare's Globe. Just to reel all these off revives my sense of how well we did, what a great gift to our writers it was, and what a loss when National won the election of 1990 and Doug Graham as Minister of the Arts, persuaded that our writers did not much favour the idea, sold it. Then, of course, our writers put up a collective howl of outrage that this benighted Bolger government had taken from them, had deprived them of . . . etc. etc.

But the writers had themselves created the negative impression which, though it didn't excuse Graham's action, at least made it publicly plausible and even politically astute. Fiona, backed always by Lauris, had made no end of a fuss about the fact that her friend Dudley's retreat-by-rowboat had been overlooked in favour of London; that there had not been sufficient 'consultation'; that the self-serving C. K. Stead had been listened to rather than the writing community at large; that the choice had been a harking back to colonial times. Twenty-three writers signed a public letter of complaint along these lines – the usual suspects, plus Maurice Gee who later wrote to say it was a mistake and he regretted it – another case of the public assault and private 'sorry – I didn't mean it'.

A *Frontline* television programme along these lines was made, presented by Ross Stevens and focusing especially on the fact of 'Bloomsbury', as if the word signalled, not a present-day thriving and multicultural location and community constantly in flux, but only a mode of writing now outdated and best forgotten, a faded icon of former times. We were shown the disaffected writers gathering at the open door of Vince O'Sullivan's office, convened there for a protest meeting to which the cameras were not given access, but were scarcely needed. Their letter with its twenty-three signatures would soon appear in the press.

I was interviewed and said my piece, believing naively that since I'd had the chance to explain, all would be clear and all would be well. I was inexperienced and had no notion how television cuts and splices to suit itself, how it could prove to the satisfaction of the world that the world is flat if it wanted to. Fiona's flat world was sold to New Zealand, and the London gift to our writers was duly lost.

Seen from a journalist's point of view the TV programme scored two direct hits. They had asked for copies of correspondence between Bassett and Stead on the subject, had been refused, had invoked the OIA, and received copies but with deletions by the Minister. They then got hold of uncensored copies from (I suppose) a leaker in Bassett's office and so were able to expose what he had deleted. It was the end of a letter from me in which I said if he wanted someone to occupy the flat and buy the necessary household equipment it would need, I was going to be in London soon and would do that. This was offered as evidence of my self-interest in the project. I was going to be in London anyway and was trying to hurry the project along. After this revelation I never went near it and the High Commission had to pay for someone to do what I would have done for nothing. But the programme had scored.

Its second direct hit was that Bassett, nervous about dealing with press and public on the one hand and his Cabinet colleagues on the other, anticipated certain questions and suggested how I should answer them. The programme then interviewed us separately, noticed we gave the same answers to the same questions, and was able to alternate images of us saying the same things. It was cleverly done and we looked like a couple of bad conspirators, the sort of guys you wouldn't buy a used car from. Each asked, for example, were we friends, we both said 'I've never been to his house'. It was true, but it looked like a lie. 'Cronyism!' – that was the cry, and the programme described me as 'the Godfather of New Zealand literature'.

Both of these hits could be seen as the kind of mistake a nervous Minister makes when hounded by the media. There had been no need to delete any part of my letter – my suggestions were reasonable, but we looked bad when they were undeleted and exposed. And he should not have primed me to give answers he was going to give himself. They were truthful but were made to look otherwise.

Bassett and Labour were under pressure. Lange and Douglas had finally fallen apart. Lange had announced his 'time for a cup of tea' on progress towards Douglas's flat tax policy. (On that score, if the programme had probed, it might have discovered that the cronies did not see eye to eye: Bassett would go with Douglas in the direction of what became the ACT party; I remained loyal to Lange and Labour.) Douglas was out of the Cabinet, Labour was plunging in the polls, and Bassett was struggling to get his gift through without it becoming public and consequently ensnared and dragged down as the Labour ship floundered towards the defeat of 1990. Fiona blew all that by making her complaints very public, and a press, looking for anything that could be turned against the government, made the most of them.

So the gift was made, and lost. Bassett got no thanks. Maurice Shadbolt and I resigned from PEN, and Maurice, with a candour all his own, blamed 'the garrulous and graceless prima donnas'* Lauris and Fiona, for the loss. 'New Zealand writers' he said, 'deserved all they did not get'. Fiona's account in *Beside the Dark Pool* returns to the 'we don't need Europe' provincialism of the time, but inhibited now because in the interim she has had the Menton fellowship and fallen in love with France. You can read her voice into every sentence she writes on this subject, and I wouldn't buy even a new car from it – certainly not a piece of real estate.

But it was a sequence of events that gave me part of the material for my novel *The End of the Century at the End of the World* in which Cabinet Minister Dan Cooper (not in the least like Bassett, indeed more like me) struggles with a similar political bind, trying to preserve at government expense the cottage in which a woman writer (unfortunately for the project, his aunt) lived and wrote her brilliant fiction. He is subjected to harassment by television, and the unique and beautiful cottage, a literary landmark, finishes under the bulldozers.

THERE WAS ANOTHER *FRONTLINE* programme, also presented by Ross Stevens, this one in 1994, on the question of my transgressions against the conventional wisdom of the time, following me around the country as I promoted my novel *The Singing Whakapapa*. Cathie Dunsford, Keri Hulme, Kevin Ireland, Dick Scott and Roger Robinson were asked, one by one, what they thought of my recent utterances on the page and off the cuff. Cathie, an ample lesbian writer who had been a tutor in the Auckland English Department

---

* Fiona's account wrongly attributes this insult to Bassett, and cites it as an excuse for her own rudeness.

during my final years there, was jolly and affirmative: she and I disagreed, of course, but 'Karl and I would sit down and have a good argument' about whatever the issue might be. Keri, on the other hand, adopted one and then another pained pose, and grumbled, half-voice, that the sharp literary critic Stead was in danger of killing the sensitive young plant of our literature. Kevin was affirmative – Stead was 'questioning the catch-cries and sloppy thinking of the time – and that's great!' Dick Scott thought Stead had a great brain and made people think; but Dick believed he had found himself in the character of Maurice Scobie, the old hard-line Marxist in my novel *The End of the Century at the End of the World*, and he seemed to feel that my having put Scobie to death by cancer was some kind of punishment or revenge for something he, Dick, had done. This was bizarre, because if there is a hero in the novel I would say it was Scobie. His final lunch with Laura is I think one of the best fictional scenes I have written, and everything in it redounds to Scobie's credit. It even occurred to me that Scott had liked finding himself as Scobie (it does rather flatter him) and could only, in all modesty, refer to it at all by pretending to be aggrieved. Scobie is irreverent, playful, full of jokes, but unwavering in his political commitment even though it is to 'the God that failed' (as Stephen Spender called the Marxist cause). Dick's interview finished with the concession that Stead was providing 'useful grit' to our literary scene. Finally there was Roger Robinson, who needs a new paragraph – a sort of quarantine ward all to himself.

Roger was chair of a committee set up to implement a new syllabus of English in secondary schools, and I had opposed vigorously its proposed 'Eight modes of language'. Whether or not that had anything to do with his evident ire in this interview Robinson, looking strangely mad-eyed, wanted to argue that I was a ruthless and destructive critic. 'People are afraid of Stead,' he said fearlessly. 'He goes for the jugular.' His example was that I had said Patricia Grace was 'a female icon in New Zealand's centennial year of Women's Suffrage'. This had seemed to me positive, an affirmative statement, but Roger smelled a rat in it. 'Stead is vicious,' he insisted; 'he's the Tonya Harding of New Zealand literature' (Harding being the American champion skater who had employed someone to break the kneecap of a rival). 'Stead is not as good a novelist as Grace, so *down* comes the crowbar on the kneecap.'

I was invited to respond to this. I couldn't – it was so extreme, so remote from civilised discourse, so wide of any perceivable mark. I said the interviewer could hunt through every word I had ever written and would never find anything even remotely approaching it for malice.

I return to this now after a quarter of a century because it's an illustration of how the dark clouds gathering around my public image in the 1990s made it possible for quite extravagant and baseless things to be said about me in public places, and the accuser not be held to account. My response subsequently was to shrug Robinson off as inconsequential, 'a journeyman of literature'. That still seems to place him accurately. But seeing the replays of these TV appearances and interviews now, what strikes me is how relaxed and cheerful I seemed – and how lucid.

In the uncut version of the programme sent to me by its producer Peta Carey, there is a charming moment filmed in the Christchurch Square. Ross Stevens asks had I ever written a fictional character meant to be a revenge on a real person. I thought he had the Dick Scott/Maurice Scobie idea in mind and said, 'No never.'

'What about Michael Friend?'

I twigged at once and said, 'Ah that one.'

'I thought,' Stevens says, giving the camera the full benefit of his good looks, 'that that was *me*.'

He was referring to an exchange in *The End of the Century at the End of the World* in which Laura asks, about the television programme that has gone disastrously wrong, 'Who did the questioning?'

Dan replies, 'Michael Friend. God he's such an insect. He wears leather slip-ons with no socks.'

'They're very fashionable Dan.'

'Maybe, but there's something so . . .'

'Unctuous?'

'It's that handsome smile. I'd rather have Perigo. He might slug you but at least you know it's happening.'

Stevens and I were grinning at one another. 'You're the exception,' I told him. It was an entirely good-natured exchange; and although he did wear leather slip-ons without socks, and did have the journalist's tendency to win you over with a smile when he intended to stab you in the back, I liked him and enjoyed my tour around the country with him and his team, and a charming young woman from Penguin whose name eludes me. He was excellent at his job and impressed me by something else – that he was fluent in French. It was Ross who taught me that if you wanted to use the super-polite subjunctive form of 'Voulez-vous?' you did not, as I had done with him (meaning to be ironic), say 'Veuillez-vous?' (followed by the infinitive) but just 'Veuillez?'

I recall with pain the grim irony that Ross was diagnosed with an incurable cancer at this time. I have a clear recollection of his telling me about it. He was standing on our back lawn by the plum tree while his team set up camera and lights in the Lockwood 'office' we'd had built in place of a grape and passion fruit covered fibro shed there when I left the university. His face as he told me was suddenly full of rage and refusal, as if it was saying it was healthy and handsome and would reject this diagnosis and would not die. What flashed into my mind was Thomas Nashe's 'A Litany in Time of Plague':

> Beauty is but a flower
> Which wrinkles will devour;
> Brightness falls from the air;
> Queens have died young and fair;
> Dust hath closed Helen's eye
> I am sick, I must die.
>   Lord, have mercy on us.

Vince and the dark corners

I mentioned in *You Have a Lot to Lose* (p. 254) that as I observed the way Vincent O'Sullivan operated in New Zealand's literary undergrowth I thought of him as Duke Vincentio in Shakespeare's *Measure for Measure* who manages the state in secret and in disguise, and is referred to as 'the old fantastical Duke of dark corners'. I've described there how Vince wrote a reader's report for Auckland University Press on Curnow's collection *An Incorrigible Music* which very nearly scuppered its chances of publication, and how a group of us in Auckland rescued it; and above I've noted that the meeting to work up opposition to the London flat purchase was convened in his office, and that he was one of the twenty-three signatories to the public letter of complaint about it.

Around 1991 or '92 Faber in London invited me to edit a collection of contemporary South Pacific stories. I gave some thought to whether I was the right person for the job. Albert Wendt knew the Pasifika part of the field much better than I did, but he still tended to anger and resentment in dealing with Pākehā New Zealand, and that would have to be a significant part of the content; and in any case I was now a freelance writer outside the protection of the university; if I was offered a job and it was one I could do, I should take it, so I agreed. In my introduction when the selection had been made (1994) I made a (not very successful) effort to claim a right to be doing this task:

> My childhood was charged with the aura of Oceania.
> My mother had spent much of her childhood on remote
> Pacific atolls – Nauru, Ocean Island, Malden Island, Makatea
> – where her father, a Swedish sea-captain, had worked
> laying deep-sea moorings and serving as harbour-master.
> Her reminiscences were rich in nostalgia and romance and
> our house full of Pacific island photographs . . .
>
> But the people who are seen from the homeland as colonials, and through perhaps two generations see themselves thus,

> are to the indigenous the colonizers. And colonization is both sought and resisted, desired and resented. The new culture, superior in its technology and the affluence it can create, is eagerly encouraged by the same indigenous people who deplore its destruction of their own, and who are at times driven by it to loss of confidence and despair.
>
> In small island states like Niue, the Cooks, and Western Samoa, the indigenous population remains predominant, and much of their culture survives; but economic pressures and modern appetites lead to dilution at home as well as emigration, usually to New Zealand.

The blurb explained that this collection was 'the fifth in a highly successful series of short fiction from around the world . . . [showing] the tremendous range of South Pacific writing in all its richness and variety' – a statement which might have been near enough to true but for the behind-the-scenes exertions of our own Duke Vincentio. I had chosen writers from the Cook Islands, Papua New Guinea, Fiji, Samoa, Tonga and Niue, together with a dozen New Zealanders. All seemed keen to be included and signed up for it. There had only been one refusal, O'Sullivan, himself an anthologist who perhaps thought he should have been given the job I was doing. He was a capable writer of short fiction and it would be hard to explain his absence, but I didn't think the damage was irreparable. He gave no reason for declining to allow his story to be included, but I should have seen it as a warning.

And then, almost on the brink of printing, I had word that three Māori writers, Keri Hulme, Patricia Grace and Witi Ihimaera, and one Samoan, Albert Wendt, had changed their minds and did not want their stories included. I was at first inclined to say they should be held to their legal contract; but Faber could hardly be expected to publish stories against the will of the writers. It seemed to leave me no option than to give up the whole project and hand it over to someone else. But Faber's Robert McCrum, who was in charge, said if I did that there would be no South Pacific stories in the series. Faber could not afford the time and expense it would take to start again from the beginning, so the region would not be represented. I knew a lot of the Pacific writers were excited at this opportunity to have their work seen on a wider stage, so I agreed to let the book go ahead with the holes that had been shot in its fabric – but only on the condition that I could add a 'Note on absences' to explain why those essential names were missing.

What I could not say was what I knew of how the exodus had come about. Like the makers of the TV programme about the London flat, who I supposed had a spy in Bassett's office, I had spies in the English Department. I was shown a copy of a fax that had gone from Albert Wendt to Witi Ihimaera, who was in Menton on the Mansfield fellowship, telling of a lunch during which Vince O'Sullivan, on a visit to Auckland, had persuaded Albert that I was an unsuitable person to do this anthology and that he and Witi should withdraw their stories. Vince, the message went on, was already in touch with other Māori writers and had hopes that Keri Hulme and Patricia Grace would also withdraw, and so encourage others to follow suit. A day or two later a fax from Witi to Wendt came in through the department office (beginning 'Ça va, Albert?' to show he was learning French) saying if others were withdrawing he would join them.

My strongest moral support in this mess came from Allen Curnow. A group of writers, led by Jim Baxter, Alistair Campbell and Louis Johnson, had got wind in advance of the proposed contents of Allen's 1961 *Penguin Book of New Zealand Verse*, and had written to Penguin in London with complaints that the anthology was inadequate in its representation of younger writers. This had caused no end of anxiety, trouble and expense to Curnow. It was comforting to have now his warm and unequivocal support; but just as there had been some grounds for the complaints against his anthology, so there were for complaints against mine. I had done my work conscientiously; but it should have been edited by a Māori or Polynesian, or even someone representing the strange mix the South Pacific had become – a Fijian Indian writing in English for example. That way it would have avoided the criticism that it was another example of appropriation, and the corrupting temptations the colonial power could hold out to the indigenous. Faber could offer world attention in a way no local publisher could match. There was no mass exodus: Vince's big four were the only absconders; but the ship was holed at the waterline.

I thought it was bad form, bad behaviour, to agree to one's work being included and then withdraw at the last moment, intending at least to rock the boat, and hoping to sink it. And I resented O'Sullivan's 'dark corners' way of sabotage, its lack of frankness and courage; but I deeply regretted taking the project on in the first place, and even more, not pulling out when the four withdrew.

I remember the launch of that book in Wellington as an extremely embarrassing occasion. McCrum had told me I was, or had seemed from London, 'the Big Cheese' in this part of the world, so I had been an obvious choice; and then he made a launch speech in which he said, less crudely, but pretty much the same thing, seeming to apologise for his mistake. I've forgotten what I found to say in response, but it wouldn't have been Big Cheesy. There was a dark brooding atmosphere which at this time I encountered often in what I liked to call our village capital. I was no longer welcome there, and glad to get out.

4.
Identities

What is a Kiwi?

If you ask that question now anywhere outside New Zealand the answer as like as not will be a fruit. That comes from our own folly in renaming what were in my childhood known as Chinese gooseberries 'kiwifruit', which *of course* got shortened to one word. I have a dim recollection that the publisher Chris Cole Catley told me proudly she had been on the advertising agency or publicity panel which made the recommendation.

I suppose I am a Kiwi but I prefer New Zealander; and I'm not one of those who object to being designated Pākeha – a term, however it came about, defining me as a New Zealander of European descent. (It may well in time extend to a New Zealander of any ethnicity other than Māori – but I don't think that has happened yet.) The kiwi is a flightless bird, and when I was a professional academic concerned with such questions I suggested that T. S. Eliot had sometimes signed his letters, or his light-hearted contributions to literary journals, 'Apteryx' (the Latin word for the kiwi) to signify his flightlessness. It was part of his un-Romantic or anti-Romantic pose.

When I wrote my autobiographical *South-West of Eden* I described my forebears on my mother's side, because they went back further into our history than the Steads who were Catholic Irish, late nineteenth-century arrivals; and I used family material again from my mother's side in my novel *The Singing Whakapapa*. From my grandmother Caroline Karlson (married to the Swedish mariner Christian Karlson after whom I was named) I learned that her two grandfathers were John Flatt, an English-born Church Missionary Society catechist, and Martin McDermott, 'a Scottish settler'. Those are the 'facts' as I recorded them. But Kay had a call while I was away overseas from a Mrs McDermott who explained that her husband was also descended from Martin McDermott, and that her family had recently explored the records and discovered that their/my forebear, the 'Scottish settler', had in fact been an Irish convict, transported to Australia at the age of nineteen, sentenced to seven years, extended to nine when he had escaped from the chain gang at Parramatta.

Kay and I have checked on this and the dates, and the data on his release, confirm that it is so. We have even visited the barracks in Sydney where the convicts slept in rows of hammocks, the building now preserved as a memorial, in which the names of those housed there in the year of the 1828 census are sand-blasted on a glass panel, each with his crime. Great-great-grandfather Martin's was 'bleach-green theft', described in other documentation as 'theft of calico'. Calico was put out on the village green to bleach in the sun and young Martin had stolen some – I hope for use by his poor mother. For that he was sent so far from home he could never hope to return; so having married in Sydney after his release, he removed himself to the Bay of Islands, presenting himself as a Scottish Presbyterian, setting up in business there, and later in Auckland, as a trader in plumbing supplies. He must have prospered, because my grandmother remembered the long line of funeral carriages stretching down the hill from Ponsonby and heading for the Symonds Street cemetery where his large marble gravestone was still identifiable in the 1960s but seems now to have fallen on its face so the inscription is no longer visible.

Did John Flatt, missionary catechist, know that his son was marrying the daughter of a convict? It's possible he did. He was a redoubtable character who, as I've recorded elsewhere, gave evidence in 1838 to a House of Lords inquiry into 'the State of the Islands of New Zealand', and exposed the extent to which his employer, the Church Missionary Society, was acquiring Māori land without approval from London – a revelation that led ultimately, through a number of years and many twists and turns, to the dismissal of Henry Williams when he refused (or was unable) to give up the land he had acquired and made over to his family.

On the other hand John Flatt may not have known, and Martin McDermott may have managed to keep the convict's usual marks from chains on the ankles, and any back scars from the lash, hidden from all but his wife. Certainly my grandmother knew nothing of this or I'm sure she would have told me with a certain relish. His release papers also mention a 'Britannia Woman and anchor' tattoo on his upper arm.

So that is the genetic mix on the female side in the making of this Pākehā – English, Irish and Swedish – missionary, convict and sailor – together with the mysterious but crucial contribution of the women who defined themselves only as mothers and home-keepers. Kay and I were never in any doubt about our national identity; and even in Australia, whose inhabitants are nearest to us in history and collective behaviour, the differences were plain. But we sometimes asked ourselves when we were first travelling outside New Zealand whether we were more akin to British or to Americans. When we were with American friends Lee and Jack Bartley we felt closer to British; with British friends, Robin and Elisabeth Marleyn, more like Americans. So much of our education, our political structures and social habits, were British it seems an idle speculation; and yet the popular culture we'd learned in childhood and youth – music and movies – had been American. There was an unspoken snobbish-British understanding that they were 'inferior'; but they were part of what had shaped our consciousness. In the household of my childhood everyone loved American movies; and I remember the puzzlement I felt hearing my parents trying to decide whether or not they would go to a movie tonight, and deciding not to. How could you make that choice if you were free to make the other? – which they could always do because my grandmother (Caroline Karlson) lived in the house with us, a permanent baby-sitter.

And she was our movie fanatic. She had a regular order at a bookseller in Balmoral for what she called 'my books' and they were all magazines which included news and gossip from Hollywood. She went alone to the 'pictures' (as we called them then), usually the five o'clock session (her 'tea' would be kept hot for her), mostly walking, with holes cut in her shoes to make room for the bunions. If there was a movie she liked, especially a musical, she might go five nights in succession. I think she was a fantasist, a novelist *manqué*, who lived out fictions based on movies and on the 'facts' about the stars learned from her 'books'. She was a simple, redoubtable woman, and if she had lived to read my novel *Sister Hollywood* she would have been sure I was a worldly success beyond her wildest dreams. I should have dedicated the book to her memory, or to my sister Norma, or both, but I had incurred such debts of gratitude to Cal Bedient and other friends in LA who had helped me with it, I felt they had precedence.

I was never exempt from this family passion for 'the pictures' and could sometimes succumb to it extremely. I remember holding the attention of my fellow 6A class at Mt Albert Grammar in what was called a 'study period' while I recounted in great and sequential detail the story of a movie called *Golden Salamander*; and in my late teens I was so impressed by a Kirk Douglas movie with the unintentionally comic title *Young Man with a Horn*, about the jazz trumpeter Bix Beiderbecke, I seriously wondered whether I could take up the instrument myself. It must have been the music that had so grabbed me, because I always considered Kirk Douglas's acting melodramatic and more than slightly absurd. Doris Day's singing would have been an added attraction – she had such a soft lyric quality and the notes were always dead true.

So 'America' featured in our lives mostly as movies and popular songs. There were two singers in the house – 'Nana', the hymn-singing atheist who also sang the popular songs of the late nineteenth/early twentieth century, and Karlson, who sang the popular songs of the day – Bing Crosby, Nat King Cole, Doris Day, Dean Martin,* Frank Sinatra, the Mills Brothers, the Andrews Sisters . . .

And then when 'our boys' had gone away to fight in the European war it was the American boys who had swept in to defend us against the Japanese in the Pacific. Kay and I both remember that invasion, its excitements, its chewing gum and milk shakes, its dancing, silk stockings and chocolates for big sisters. And then as suddenly as they came they were gone, the war was over and 'our boys' came home.

Soon we were young adults, politically conscious and disapproving of 1950s America, with its Korean War, and its Cold War that asked us to see Russia, in our childhood the heroic ally, as the present danger, and Germany, the old enemy, as the new friend. One of my earliest published poems was the militant (after the later style of R. A. K. Mason) 'Sonnet for a New Zealand soldier killed in Korea' which ended

> Fed on the manufactured truth you stilled
>   An older boredom in the gamble of guns and shells
> And paid the debt calmly when your loss was billed.
>   Your epitaph is the age-old cry that tells
> How you died 'fighting for peace' – words fogged in sighs.
> In the arms of our hate you were strangled by a knot of lies.

---

* I fitted a line from Martin's 'Everybody Loves Somebody' into my poem 'Lullaby' (*Collected Poems, 1951–2006*, p. 268) so I could put a little Dean-style croon into my reading of it.

Crude political stuff, but no worse than President Kennedy's *'Ich bin ein Berliner'* at the Berlin Wall, which was too much for those of us who still clung to the socialist ideal. We hated America's McCarthyism, but still learned its popular songs and loved what Hollywood offered – Humphrey Bogart and Marilyn Monroe, *Casablanca* and *Some Like It Hot*, and catch-phrases like 'Round up the usual suspects' and 'Nobody's perfect'.

So being anti-American went together with being one of America's client cultures – and that confusion or contradiction continued through the Cuban Missile Crisis, the Vietnam War and beyond. I'd had my first taste of grown-up America, its power and enchantment, when I was invited to New York for an academic conference in 1963.

Then Kay and I and three small children, heading for the Mansfield Menton fellowship by sea in 1972 had called in at New York, and returning by air had stopped off at San Francisco to visit old friends Lee and Jack. Sabbaticals in 1977 and 1984 had taken us outward and homeward through Los Angeles; and during my time still employed by the university but freed by my research fellowship to accept invitations abroad, I had extended my 'North American experience'. I loved especially the return route from London that took you north-west over Ireland, up over southern Greenland and the polar region and then down through northern Canada and the United States – ten hours of mostly daylight if you chose your flight-time right, flying with the sun, much of it over white frozen seascapes, lakes, and snow covered mountains where the firs or whatever conifers they were could be discerned down there in the vastness as trees, but minute, mysterious. In those days with a window seat you could keep the blind open and sit imagining animal life going on down there, marvelling at the spectacle and what human technology had brought us to. (Now there would be complaints of too much light spoiling others' enjoyment of their TV screens.) And then there were a few days in Los Angeles, Santa Monica usually, with thoughts and explorations for what was brewing towards a new novel.

1. Karl at home, 1986, the year he left the university, photo by Robert Cross. McCahon's *Rocks in the sky, series 1, no. 1* behind. *Copyright Robert Cross*

2. *(Above)* With friends above the *Pont du Gard* (Roman triple aqueduct) near Uzès, which figures in Karl's novel *Risk*.

3. *(Below)* The Steads' ample house in Oxford, corner of Woodstock and Plantation roads, courtesy St John's College where Karl was Senior Visiting Fellow, 1996–97.

4. (Left) Supper with Antonia Byatt at the *auberge*, Avès, France, where she drank only champagne.

5. (Below) Punting near the Mill House, Low Tharston, with Anthony Thwaite (poet and editor) and Ann Thwaite (biographer). (See Appendix.)

6. *(Above left)* Photo by Karl of Maurice Shadbolt in Menton, with his wife Barbara Magner and their daughter Brigid. Maurice was already deciding the apartment the fellowship provided was unsatisfactory and would soon leave.

7. *(Centre left)* Karl with Roger Morton (see Appendix) on the back deck at 37 Tohunga Crescent, with 'the Lockwood' (Karl's office) behind.

8. *(Below left)* Kay and Karl at the Axelrads' house in Saint-Maximin near Uzès, France.

9. *(Right)* Tony Axelrad, translator of *The Death of the Body*, staying with the Steads in Auckland.

10. Karl at the Katherine Mansfield memorial room, Menton: one of many revisits.

11. *(Above)* Karl 'on location' while writing *Sister Hollywood*.

12. *(Below)* Roger Donaldson at home in Santa Monica.

13. Covers of *Sister Hollywood*, clockwise from top left: German translation, Fischer, 1998; Harvill paperback, 1994; US hardcover edition, 1990; 1st UK edition, Harvill hardcover, with jacket photograph of the Civic Theatre, Auckland, by Werner Forman.

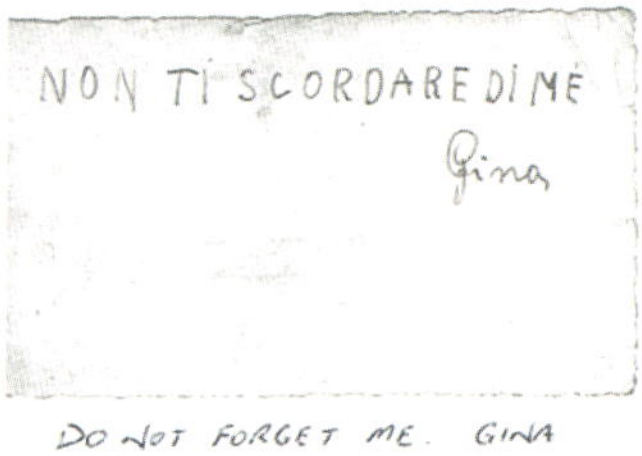

14. *(Above left and right)* The secret in the soldier's wallet – Gina's photograph, and her hand-written message on the reverse.

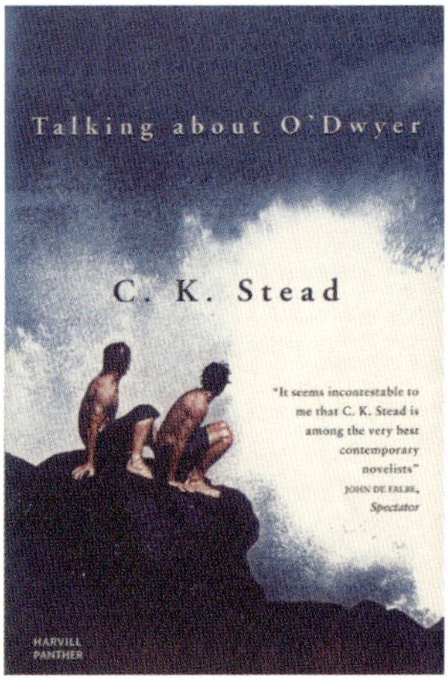

15. Covers of *Talking about O'Dwyer*, clockwise from top left: Harvill Panther trade paperback, 2002; Harvill UK hardcover, 2000; Penguin NZ paperback, 1999; Slovenian translation, 2006; German translation, 2001; Spanish translation, 2004.

I called the last chapter of *You Have a Lot to Lose* 'Sligo, Gateway to the World'. That was because when I flew off to lecture at the Yeats Summer School in Sligo, leaving my last class behind, I was beginning a new life as a full-time writer. In Sligo I met two Americans who would be, in quite different ways, significant in this part of my story – Helen Vendler and Cal Bedient. Helen, a Harvard professor, was widely acknowledged as one of the most important critics of modern poetry, and she was there, as I was, to give one of the plenary session lectures with which each day began. Hers was on the collection Yeats called *The Winding Stair*, mine on *The Tower*. I was astonished to find a very accurate news report of my lecture on what appeared to be an ordinary page of the *Irish Times* (19 August 1986) and on the same page a column by Nuala O'Faolain complaining that lawyers made a mystery of their profession and kept numbers qualifying to practise down so their earnings would be correspondingly high. On the same page were reports of bail refused in a kidnap case, a helicopter rescue for an injured Italian footballer, three Poles charged with burglary in Cork, a new Irish stamp promised to mark Peace Year, and a heroin seizure and consequent drugs charges. Books and ideas, in other words, were just part of Irish life, and did not need to be sequestered in the back of the paper. This was literate and bookish Ireland, where I could have lived as a writer tax-free. The report of my lecture mentioned that I was on my way to London for the launch of my third novel, *The Death of the Body*.

Helen Vendler was what I think of as the prototype high-powered Eng. Lit. academic, discovering meanings in poems that were certainly there, but some of them probably having arrived by instinct or accident, ratified in retrospect rather than achieved by deliberation. She was suited especially to late Yeats, because he had indeed become in his later years a planner of everything, working his poems up from prose drafts, labouring them into their tight-fitting suits of myth and form. They were great feats of structural engineering, as far as can be imagined from the Keatsian ideal that poetry should come 'as naturally as the leaves to a tree'; but I think even Yeats might have been surprised at what Helen discovered in them.

So I respected her brilliance with a practitioner's reservations. But there was no need to say any of this, and we got on well, liked one another, respected each the other's intelligence, and formed then and later a joke 'Atheists' Alliance'. Helen and I, and Ann Saddlemyer who gave the Sligo lecture on Yeats's wife Georgie Hyde-Lees, were the same age, fifty-three-year-old senior academics, and we would meet again the following year when the Princess Grace Irish Library in Monte Carlo called together a group of a dozen or so 'world experts' for a conference on the subject of 'Yeats the European'.* The following year Helen invited me to Harvard where I recorded poetry in their library's Poetry Room, attended a Harvard Fellows dinner in my honour, heard a lecture by John Cage which he had designed (successfully) to be meaningless, and gave one myself intended (also I think successfully) to be meaningful.

Cal Bedient, also met at the Yeats Summer School, a professor of English at UCLA, was not a specialist on Yeats and was in Sligo to learn, not to teach. He invited me to let him know next time I was passing through Los Angeles; and his charming little house in Santa Monica, with its slightly bizarre but gracefully post-modern décor, was to figure in my next novel. He himself, or a simulacrum, would figure as the Canadian poet Alban Ashtree in the story I called, in its final form, 'The Name on the Door is Not Mine'.

Cal Bedient and Santa Monica, Blake Nevius and Sherman Oaks

After Sligo *The Death of the Body* was launched in London and I did the usual launch things, including an interview with Edward Blishen

---

* The papers we three gave at the Monte Carlo conference are included in *Yeats the European* edited by A. Norman Jeffares, Rowman & Littlefield, 1989.

on the BBC *World of Books* programme and a reading at New Zealand House, and then headed home with a stop in Los Angeles to call on Cal. I would be back the following April, this time for a significant period, and with a purpose.

It was on one of these flights home I'd had the idea for what would be my next novel. I remembered my older sister Norma had met a young man and woman, Australians, actors on their way, they told her, to Hollywood. Norma was still a senior schoolgirl but had gone down to the Auckland waterfront (something Kay tells me the Auckland Girls' Grammar headmistress warned them never to do) with a friend, also from the school, the two hoping to meet interesting travellers and tourists off the passenger ships that tied up there. On this occasion they had struck up a conversation with the Australian couple and Norma had thought them very glamorous, especially the young man who had asked for her address promising he would send her a postcard from Hollywood. She'd given it, not expecting to hear from him again, but she must have made an impression because after some months the promised card came. He and his friend were loving Hollywood, had secured an agent and were hoping to have work there soon; and meanwhile had made friends with Humphrey Bogart and Lauren Bacall (he called them Bogey and Betty) and was acting as an occasional crewman on their yacht *Santana*. He said of this famous couple that they were 'both swell guys'. My sister was impressed, and so was I; but (not wanting to be a spoilsport) I did not tell her how that 'swell guys' struck me as a false note, a bad sign. Already this young Australian was taking on the slick talk of the place, assuming a role in a Hollywood story of success and fame to come.

This single (as I saw it) false note had stuck in my memory all these years and was the beginning of my notion of the character of Rocky Tamworth, the failed actor and alcoholic of the novel *Sister Hollywood*. And my notion of how my sister might cope with him, and with the situation she might find herself in there, was to form the character of Arlene, the narrator's sister, really the novel's hero. My idea was to imagine a family like our own, but larger and rather more (or perhaps I should say even more) turbulent, from which the older sister disappears suddenly, without explanation or any evidence of force or reluctance – rather the reverse. She seems simply to have gathered up her things, emptied her bank account, and absconded. So this movie-loving family, the Harpers, distressed (the mother tending to bouts of hysteria, the father to rage), try to continue life as normal, including their ritual Saturday night at the local cinema, the Capitol in Dominion Road where front-row seats 'upstairs' are reserved for them.* So they are watching the latest Hollywood movie, all together, when the missing older daughter, or someone remarkably like her, appears in the role of a secretary, taking something out of a filing cabinet for a businessman. But that's all – she has no importance as a character in the story and is not seen again. Was it really the missing daughter or just a lookalike? They hope to see her again in another movie. Perhaps she is on the way to stardom – but that one shot is all they have to go on.

This was the idea on which the novel would be founded – that Norma, not a schoolgirl but a young working woman, shorthand typist aged about nineteen or twenty, had met a young Australian (unaccompanied) stopping off in Auckland on his way to Hollywood; she'd spent some time with him, fallen in love, and had either run away with him or followed him – not telling her family, whose turbulence she'd had enough of and wanted to escape from, cutting all ties; and the story would be largely of how she fared with the young Australian in Hollywood, while at the same time it would keep the narrative of her family alive, and of a younger brother, a version of myself, who would continue to wonder what became of her, and in the end, after several decades and the deaths of their parents, would track her down still in Los Angeles.

* The Capitol still exists as a movie theatre but only what was the upper floor remains in use. I must have been taken to my first movie there in 1938 or '39.

I wanted to set her defection slightly back in time to the great period of pre-television Hollywood, and to keep the larger picture of political America, including McCarthyism as it affected Hollywood, alive in the story; so it was going to involve research – both reading and library records, and on-the-spot 'location' work. That was where Cal Bedient came in. He had invited me to call on him any time I was passing through LA. I did that – and when it was clear we got on well together he invited me to stay and later arranged for me to have the use of the house of a friend who was going to be away in Europe. Cal's house was in Santa Monica, less than a mile from the ocean and the pier. The friend was another UCLA professor, Blake Nevius, now retired, and his house I was to occupy was over the Hollywood Hills in Sherman Oaks. These, Cal's and Blake's, were models for the two houses my two principal characters were to occupy. His name, the young Australian's, was Bruce Burns but he had decided to go by the acting name Rocky Tamworth in preparation for the movies he would star in. Her name was Edie Harper, but she changed Edie to Arlene to remove herself further from home and family, and when she married Rocky became Arlene Tamworth.

The outlines of the story were clear in my head but the detail was going to be crucial – place especially and its ambience, weather, cityscape, plant and bird life, manners, and especially the whole terminology by which Hollywood operated and communicated. Having a clear purpose always made me learn quickly and retain as long as needed; and just as, later, in preparing for and writing *My Name Was Judas*, I would become for the period of the writing and for a short time afterwards quite expert and confident in theological and biblical matters, so for the writing of *Sister Hollywood* I became fluent in the language of the film studios and movie-making.

Around this same time I had upgraded my technology, acquiring my first word processor – a rather large box-like machine which sat on my desk in the Lockwood 'office', with a screen like a small TV, and a separate keyboard with mouse. It was not portable, so on the move I was still confined to handwriting in notebooks; but it was an advance. And Roger Donaldson had become interested in the idea of a movie of *The Death of the Body*, and had supplied me with a computer program for movie scripts, which I had begun to use in doing a treatment, and then a screenplay, of that novel.

But now, April–May 1987, I was first sharing Cal's house, and then occupying Blake's in his absence, absorbing place – locations that figured in the mythology of Hollywood, streets, boulevards, cafés and restaurants, cemeteries where the famous were buried under famously elaborate and bad-taste headstones; and at the same time doing serious research in the library of UCLA, and especially, on Wilshire Boulevard, the library of the Academy of Motion Picture Arts and Sciences (the one that awards the Oscars) where almost anything you needed to know on the history of 'the Industry' could be found. For me there was the same kind of excitement in this that there had been when I was a postgraduate student in London doing research into the literary history of the early twentieth century. Doing my hunting in the Academy library, to come upon stencilled copies of the original cast-lists for movies of my childhood –

> M-G-M STUDIO September 6 1946
> THE LADY IN THE LAKE
> CALL BUREAU CAST SERVICE

and then all the actors and actresses from major players down to what were called 'Bits' – this was genuine research, necessary for the novel I was planning, but exciting just for itself. I felt like the hunter when the quarry at last comes in sight. I was not worrying about whether the novel to result from all this would be good or bad, applauded or derided – this work was its own reward.

I tracked down the houses where important immigrant figures, Bertolt Brecht and Salka Viertel who would figure in my story, had lived. I visited studios – Burbank and Universal, Paramount with its iconic gate and water tower. And there was an occasion when Hollywood came to me rather than I to it. I was driving Blake's car around Hollywood and came into a street that seemed to be blocked by a police car, so I backed up and turned, and found that way now also blocked. Then I saw a cop with her gun out, crouching and looking up to a sharpshooter on a shop veranda or roof. I got out of the car, crouching to avoid any random gunfire, and looked up at the man with a rifle who did not appear to be hiding nor preparing to do bad things. For a moment I could see him clearly and he pulled a face at me that signalled 'Bugger off!' It took a few seconds then to pick out where the cameras were placed and recognise that I was in the middle of a bit of movie-making, and unwelcome.

On the same day I saw a shop-window display with statuettes of Beethoven, Elvis Presley and the Virgin Mary, together with some quite large Disney animals, and a sign HAVE A HAPPY EASTER – but nothing suggesting a crucifixion. Cal Bedient in my mind belonged in that world of inventiveness and display, eccentric and at moments bizarre – though he was also slightly apart from it in the sense of being intellectual, highbrow, and a poet. But only in California could the two cultures, 'high' and 'low', be so interconnected and so interacting that quotation marks were needed around the distinguishers. Cal's 'school' was UCLA (University of California at Los Angeles) and there was no clear British-style snobbery to mark the distinction; one would have to go east and north, to Harvard and Yale, and perhaps Columbia, to find it.

Cal had two cars, a beat-up Range Rover for ordinary use, a 1959 Thunderbird (he called it his T-bird), hectic blue with spectacular chrome fins, for important occasions. Cal crooned over its 'sculptured' metal, and then said 'but I'm an aesthete' – as he was indeed.

The first time he took me out to see a show we went in the Range Rover. It took an hour to get there, first on the freeway, then up into the Santa Monica mountains and Mulholland Drive, with fog down in the valleys. It was at the Palomino Club, a single-storey building in North Hollywood which, like so much of LA, is a sort of super New Lynn or South Auckland. We paid $17 for two, bought drinks and tacos and guacamole, and found seats. First came the Rhythm Pigs, who were pretty good, then the star of the night, Gail Warning, who was better – with volume, intensity and true notes, and wearing a mini-skirt and felt hat of the kind my father used to wear, but with a feather. Finally, late into the evening came Screamin' Jay Hawkins, a star of the 1960s, forgotten for a time but recently risen from the dead, whose voice was still pretty good but whose feature – the one that had once made him famous and so had to be included – was that at intervals his singing turned into a protracted and very loud scream.

On the long drive back we talked about literary criticism. Cal had annotated what I had published on Eliot's great poem, 'The Waste Land', and, not wanting me to read it, had hidden it under a pile of other books; but since he was gone every morning before I got out of bed and I was alone in the house some part of every day, I'd naturally rummaged (as one does – as *I* do) and had come upon it. Cal had also published a little book on the same great poem. He was the kind of critic Eliot himself had called 'the lemon squeezer school', critics who found so much in a poem, and spelled it out so laboriously, it made readers weary and bewildered, often unconvinced and sometime rebellious, and left the poet himself (Eliot reported) astonished to discover what he was said to have done. This was like Helen Vendler on Yeats. They were both lemon squeezers, but Cal was not as brilliant or famous at it as Helen. My own literary criticism was much less exhaustive than either, content to touch here and there on what was best, and how it worked, and move on leaving the poem to do its magic uncluttered by too much commentary. It was a kind of criticism which from Cal's point of view left too much unsaid, as his, from mine, was that it said too much. But I knew what he thought of mine, and he did not know I knew.

So we drove through the Los Angeles night, not with Gail Warning, nor the Rhythm Pigs, nor even Screamin' Jay Hawkins still sounding in our heads, but skirting around one another, not quite saying what we meant, but hinting at it; until in a moment of frankness I allowed myself, 'Well, Cal, the proof of the critical pudding is in *who wants to eat it*.'

That silenced him; it silenced us both, and we drove on, he perhaps crushed, perhaps angry, and I feeling guilty. It's the kind of exchange, like a wrestling match, which can sometimes bring boys closer together.

Cal seemed a prototype American in being will-driven, believing that he should be able to set himself stern goals, and that if he didn't achieve them it was some failure of character. When working at home he sat at his noisy manual typewriter set up on a desk in his bedroom, typing at a prodigious rate, sighing and groaning, with his formidable stereo system playing favourite discs or tuned to a local radio programme that broadcast continuous classical music, the sound as loud as the typing was fast. Also in that quite small room there was a baby grand piano (not a small item) with the lid down and ten framed portraits – his son and daughter twice each, three of Jean Harlow, one of Clark Gable, one of Marilyn Monroe, and another Hollywood star, possibly Montgomery Clift. Each was in a quite elaborate silver art deco frame. It was the frames he valued especially, but the stars added Hollywood lustre. There were injunctions to himself headed GOALS on a pinboard above the desk – to fast every other day; to stop once a week to talk to someone not usually spoken to; to run three days a week, and 'work out' three other days (there were weights on the back porch and a rowing machine in the sitting room); to absorb one new musical piece, or movement, each day and one new poem; to set aside, every second week, one night for telephone calls; to go to one cultural event each week; to cook a new dish each week . . .

It was the programme of a middle-class superman, and I assumed it was why he appeared constantly stressed – because he was (surely) constantly failing – though he did keep up fasting every second day. Stuck around the typewriter were smaller typed injunctions in thin strips: 'Push the edges out a bit: fire struck between stone.' 'You have not dared enough.' 'Every sentence a new ring, a particular rhythm and measure.'

His idea of relaxing was to do the ironing while watching replays of *Star Wars*. On the few occasions when we were both at home working during the day he might emerge from his room to get himself (if it was an eating day) another bowl of granola and milk and find me making myself a cup of morning coffee. The stereo was too loud for conversation, but I might signal towards its source and shout, 'That's something familiar.'

It was a piano work. 'Liszt,' he shouts.

I listen and then, 'No. Wagner.'

He repeats, 'Liszt.'

Another pause to listen and then, 'No, Cal – that's Wagner. *Tristan*.'

He goes in and returns with the sleeve. 'Liszt's transcription of Wagner' – so we're both right (sort of). I try to embark on a conversation about Liszt as Wagner's father-in-law, but we can't talk above the racket and go back to work.

At night he turned off the stereo and turned on a machine which created 'white noise' – a sound like rain on the roof or rushing air, which he found necessary (together sometimes with sleeping pills) for a good night.

Cal was kind and helpful, and though he made me anxious, we got on well together because I was, or felt I was, alert to every lurch and swerve of the inner man, and responded in advance of any possible outburst. It was like sailing a yacht in variable and occasionally stormy weather. I was occupying his seventeen-year-old son's bedroom and the plan was that I would move into the Amfac Hotel nearby when the son returned from camp; but as the day approached Cal said I should stay on with them – that there was a pull-out bed in the sitting room I could use for another week until Blake Nevius's house was available. He would put the rowing machine out on the back deck with the weights.

I had told Cal about the novel I was planning and he got into the spirit of my research, taking me to famous locations and coming home from his day at UCLA with one or two videos of vintage movies which we watched together. The second time we went out in the evening it was to see an old movie at a cinema in Brentwood, and Cal asked would I mind if we went in the T-bird which had no seatbelts. He dressed for this in white balloon pants, a colourful shirt and white flat hat. I dressed as well as I could, but had nothing that could match my driver. I avoided the shoes I'd bought at Dress for Less. They were cheap and comfortable and I was walking many miles every day; but I'd noticed Cal notice them and that they made him wince. They were not just Dress for Less shoes: they *looked* Dress for Less. Then, as if apologising for the wince, which he'd noticed I noticed, he told me he envied my ability to stay thin without fasting. I told him I envied his copious head of hair, and all was well again.

People in the streets applauded the T-bird as we drove by, Cal slowing so its beauty could be seen and appreciated. When we parked people crowded around and asked questions about it. On another T-bird excursion he took me to Musso & Frank's, the restaurant both Hemingway and Scott Fitzgerald had frequented. It still had the original panels and cubicles, the leather seats and murals, and we ate a meal of kidneys and bacon, drank red wine and talked – seriously, like the two middle-aged professors we were – about Fitzgerald's novel about Hollywood, *The Last Tycoon*, which he'd left unfinished; and about *The Great Gatsby*, and how the 1974 movie with Robert Redford and Mia Farrow was good to look at but missed entirely the elusive magic of the novel – not a perfect novel, we agreed, but mysteriously successful in a way nothing else Fitzgerald had done could match.

I used the UCLA Library a lot, and had help in my research from two men, Joe Beaton and Jim Generoso, who were knowledgeable about Los Angeles or Hollywood, or both, and took me on tours of important sites. I went with Cal to a reading by the poet Louise Glück. Cal had written about her and had the academic's loyalty to the subject he has made his own. She read a sequence which was to be her next book, about having been 'wounded in her heart' in childhood by the arrival of her two sisters. One died, but the other tormented her and caused her to become anorexic. Was this, I wondered, the A. S. Byatt/Margaret Drabble syndrome? But Antonia had not made it a theme of her writing (nor stopped eating); and these poems were read in a dreary solemn monotone. The effect, I told Kay in a letter, was oppressive, like being shut up in a box with a ravening ego that didn't even want to get out. 'She never looks *out* – never sees the world out there, so there's a lack of texture.' But I didn't doubt her competence as a poet; and the reading was followed by a pleasant party put on by one of Glück's admirers, with light food and wine in a garden. The admirer and husband had trained local scrub jays, so if either of them held an unshelled nut high in the air, a jay would swoop down out of the trees and take it; or if a nut was thrown into the air it would be taken in flight.

I gave a lecture on Yeats to one of Cal's senior classes. Next day he put on a farewell dinner for me (the cooking was sensational, the people clever and colourful) and the day after I moved to Sherman Oaks.

The circuit

Cal and the mother of his children were separated or divorced. At first after the break-up they had taken turns occupying the joint home in Santa Barbara up the coast, Cal sleeping alternate days in his office at UCLA; but the son had persuaded him to buy the little house in Santa Monica so he could go to a school that would allow him to advance his interest in heavy metal (the music, not the substance) and the former wife remained, I think with a new partner and the daughter, in what had been the family home.

So I assumed that though Cal had a professorial salary and a reasonable level of affluence, this division of assets had imposed financial constraints. His piece of Santa Monica real estate would not have been inexpensive (there were many front lawns with the warning sign ARMED RESPONSE, meaning 'Try burgling us and we'll shoot you dead'); his interior was a monument to good taste, good living, occasional fine dining, and affluence; but it did not match the house I moved to next. Blake Nevius had never been married, and the house he so generously and trustingly left me in charge of represented the accumulations of a lifetime, not of wealth as Los Angeles can mean it and loves to display it, but of real affluence, and of good taste quite the equal of Cal's. Blake's closets, I told Kay, contained about one hundred shirts, twenty-one jackets, thirty-five pairs of trousers, and seventy-eight ties, none looking old or frequently worn. I didn't count the shoes but there were many pairs, none of them Dress for Less. His housekeeper, an Ecuadorian grandmother of possibly forty-five, did not live on the premises but came and went, discreetly doing my dishes, checking on my need for supplies, washing my clothes and ironing them so I found even my newly pressed pyjamas on a hanger like a suit. A team of Mexican gardeners swept in at regular intervals, cutting lawns, trimming hedges, raking leaves, weeding and tidying garden beds. It was all done very quickly and unobtrusively, and they were gone again. But the garden itself was dependent, as everything growing in Los Angeles was, on water from Northern California (hence the great Roman Polanski movie *Chinatown* about water as power in Los Angeles), and being in residence I was in charge of the sprinklers. It reminded me of Brecht saying that if you scratch the surface here you discover the desert just beneath it. It was all lovely; but it needed money to maintain it, and it needed water if it was not to revert to chaparral.

My move suited the novel perfectly. Rocky fails as an actor, and Arlene finds herself not acting but screenwriting; and as their affluence increases thanks to her successes, they are able to move from the little house rented in Santa Monica to the house in Sherman Oaks, with its verdant hillside, its jays and mocking birds, squirrels and coyotes, pepper trees and bougainvillea, and hummingbirds hovering around the flowers in hanging baskets.

> She missed the breeze that came up Pico from the sea and cooled the little house on Pacifica Street. But here there was a sense of openness. She could climb the hill behind the house and look out across a still largely wooded, or at least scrub-covered, gully. There were houses among the trees. The suburb was growing all the time, but she had a feeling of escape as she drove down from Mulholland to her own space where to some degree plants and birds and animals still obeyed their own rules. Gophers ruined the lawn. Deer wandered down the slope in the early morning and chewed flowering shrubs. There were coyotes in the hills. Mocking birds cackled and shouted down the chimney when she was trying to concentrate on a script. Sun wrecked the roses someone had planted at the front of the house, and the hot dry wind from the mountains started small fires when the oily chaparral ignited spontaneously in the summer heat of the gullies.

Place has always been an essential part of my writing, both poetry and prose, and Los Angeles I received as an ample gift of location, as it was also in terms of events and characters and history. The political background of the time was drawn in too, as HUAC (the House Un-American Activities Committee) carried out its McCarthyite investigations into Hollywood 'communists', and the more liberal-tending members of the acting community, led by Bogart and Bacall, pushed back against the black list and took a delegation to Washington which Arlene joins. There was also the execution of the Rosenbergs (which I remembered myself from student days) making it a time of political agitation, anger and grief.*

---

* It was said that Ethel Rosenberg had been told that President Eisenhower would commute their sentence to life imprisonment if she would confess that they were spies. She refused, insisting they were not. The day of their deaths is mentioned in the first sentence of Sylvia Plath's novel *The Bell Jar*.

There were the famous gossip writers, Hedda Hopper, Sheila Graham and Louella Parsons, and the trade papers, the back lots and sound stages, the rushes and reshoots, the studio boss with his clichés and boasting – such good material for stories, for a story, and I felt (hoped – but believed while writing it, which meant the sentences spun along with confidence) I was making one that would draw readers in and hold them, wanting to know 'What next?' and 'How does it end?' The dialogue was sharp and clever, because Arlene had to be sharp and clever. Antonia was to tell me she saw Arlene as a model for young women, and an inspiration. Would anyone after this novel suggest I was unsuited to writing female characters, or uncomprehending of the female psyche?

Having Blake's car to drive made me freer to explore far and wide. It was a Chev and I sang as I drove the Donald McLean song about Miss American Pie and someone driving the Chevy to the levee . . . remembering, as I drove and hit the high notes, 1972 and the family's progress up the coast of America listening to that hit of the year on our radio with its aerial through the cabin porthole.

There were Los Angeles things I saw and couldn't use – Forest Lawn cemetery for example, with its Wee Kirk o' the Heather where Ronald Reagan's first marriage (to Jane Wyman) had been 'solemnised'. Its vulgarity was too extreme for anything but the kind of satire Evelyn Waugh had made of it; but it was part of the big picture, the ambience my characters functioned in. But on the other hand to drive down Sunset Boulevard to the Pacific and to eat at Gladstones restaurant; or to visit a house on Pacific Palisades where Charles Laughton had lived in fear that his mansion might crumble under him and take him down the cliff to the Pacific Highway; to find Grauman's Chinese Theatre, or stand on the dingy corner of Hollywood and Vine where young men and women had hung about in the great days of movie-making hoping their ravishing good looks would be noticed by a talent scout – these were places that were already becoming part of the story.

Men in middle age, and their marriages

I was back with Cal less than a year later, travelling on a Fulbright scholarship that took me around California, Arizona (with a helicopter flight over the Grand Canyon), Nevada, then north to visit my friends, John Edwards, now professor of zoology in Seattle, and Mike Doyle professor of English in Victoria BC. I had sought this travel grant to advance the writing of *Sister Hollywood*, but as so often happened in my life, the writing outran my plans for it, and I think by the time I was doing that tour a draft of the novel was already written. So this circuit took my mind for a time off *Sister Hollywood* and my anxieties about it (there were anxieties about every book until I moved on to the next, and the anxiety moved to the new one) and made me think about men of my age and their marriages. Cal I think was younger by a few years; John was perhaps two years older and Mike maybe three or four. Cal's household I've described, and the fact that his marriage seemed to be over which had left him seeming less than happy. John, my friend from NZ Army days (CMT)* was living with two of his four sons in a nice suburban house in Seattle. This was the family home abandoned by the wife, Ola, who was somewhere nearby in an apartment. What struck me about the household was its orderliness, its ambience of good reading, good music and good cooking, the civility of the sons and the brilliance of the one who was a linguist and who spoke Chinese fluently on the phone when someone called. John was, Kay said, of my friends the one most like me in temperament, and he and I talked, as we had always done, completely at ease with one another. He took me to his cabin in the Cascade Mountains and we climbed a couple of thousand feet through woods, and cooked salmon over a fire beside a rushing stream. He told me he and Ola had taken counselling and he had tried to adjust to her needs, but

* John, as well as a scientist, was a notable mountain climber who had been part of the team that achieved the first (and probably still the only) winter ascent of Mount McKinley. One of the team died, and John survived a fall into a crevasse. He died in 2015.

that as he made each change to suit her she demanded more, or other, and in the end she left in any case, not wanting to be with him any more. There had been no violence, no infidelity (or none acknowledged), but I could see his toughness and meticulousness, and that he might be difficult to live with. It was just the end of a marriage, and he was learning to do without her.

And when I got to Victoria, across the water from Seattle on Vancouver Island, I found Doran and Mike Doyle's marriage seeming on the brink of ending, not turbulently but, to Mike at least, sadly and inexplicably. Doran was just drifting away from him. She had become quite a radical feminist, but with none of the anger and asperity that sometimes went with that commitment. The dissolution was happening in slow motion, with a sort of wry sad smile – Doran's, not Mike's.

Theirs was a big rambling untidy house with a slight but not excessive flavour of hippiedom. They'd had three sons and then adopted a daughter from the Indian reservation; and when it came time to buy a new car Doran had said she would take that in hand. Mike didn't argue but was surprised to find she had sold the previous regular four-door family car and bought in its place a utility vehicle with a tray – for transporting vegetables, she explained, from or to the reservation. Like John and Ola, Mike and Doran had produced impressive and successful male progeny. It was as if, with the addition of the Indian daughter, 'the project' had been completed and now she had other things to do, other places to go, which included into the arms of another woman. It hadn't been quite declared yet, but one could see the signs that it was coming.

Mike was the opposite of John, sluggish where John was energetic, tentative where John was emphatic. He would not have made the effort John had made to rescue the marriage; but if he had tried, I'm sure it would have made no difference. He and I talked books and poetry, and I gave a semi-public lecture while I was there. It was a warm-up for one I was to give in Liège and in

London, marking exactly the centenary of the birth of Katherine Mansfield and T. S. Eliot who had been born only two weeks apart in September–October 1888, and who had known one another as young writers in London.*

On one of our walks along the shoreline Mike stopped off at a dingy house with many ill-fed, ill-dressed (or undressed) infants and two struggling parents, to drop off some St Vincent de Paul vouchers that would help them out in their poverty. As we came away Mike said, 'That's like the house I grew up in.' He had been born into London Irish poverty, and his mother had died of TB when he was only four. His father, an uneducated Irishman but a reader of Balzac and Dickens, had clearly passed on a considerable intellectual potential to Mike, now notable as critic, biographer, poet and professor, affluent and socially successful. He had had to travel so much further than John and I had, from our beginnings in suburban Mt Eden; and perhaps he still bore a few deep scars as a consequence. Long ago, before Mike and I became colleagues and then friends, I had written a less than kind review of his first book of poems, and had used a line by T. S. Eliot, 'the pleasant whining of a mandolin', to characterise it. There was still, just faintly like an echo of a distant past, a tone like that about Mike, in his poems and in his life, and though he sometimes made me impatient, I admired and respected him all the more for what it represented. His talent and his achievements were real, and though I was not to see him again after this visit, we kept up regular email exchanges until his death in 2016.†

So of my three fellow-professors, Cal was the will-driven mad American, John the meticulous mountaineer, and Mike still the Irishman with his faint mandolin-like inclination to whine: how did I measure myself against them? I flew on to give my Eliot/

* 'Katherine Mansfield and T. S. Eliot: A Double Centenary', *Answering to the Language*, Auckland University Press, 1989, pp. 149–61.

† I wrote an obituary for Mike in *New Zealand Books*, March 2017.

Mansfield lecture, first at the University of Liège, and then New Zealand House in London; and it was while I was in the course of this somewhat frenzied circuit that I became aware of being in an overdrive of energy, confidence and impatience with the world that moved so slowly and was so often '*wrong*'. I was in this state of mind when I went with Antonia Byatt to a lecture at *l'Institut Français* on the subject of a short story which Balzac had called '*Le chef d'oeuvre inconnu*' – 'The unknown masterpiece'. It had been translated by Anthony Rudolf who at that time I didn't know, but whose accompanying essay interpreting the story as Balzac's foresight and prediction of what modern painting would become, I found completely unconvincing.* After the lecture the floor was open for discussion and I pitched in – not rudely, but emphatically. As Antonia and I walked away afterwards I said I'd sensed her displeasure at my expressing my disagreement so unambiguously.

She said she didn't like male competitiveness.

But it was nothing to do with competition, I told her. It was about some things being unconvincing, utterly implausible, *wrong*.

She was silent for a while, and said finally, 'You see very clearly, Karl, but sometimes there are things you *don't* see'.

'What I don't see,' I said, 'is usually the Emperor's clothes.'

A day or two later I flew off to visit Helen Vendler at Harvard.

Lissom in Xanadu

I returned back from Boston, staying a few days in a friend's apartment in New York, and then on to Los Angeles again. The 1988 presidential election was coming to its climax, and the Democrat candidate, Michael Dukakis, decided to give his eve-of-election-day (November 7th) address at UCLA – the same night Cal had booked

---

* See 'Only Connect . . .', *Shelf Life: Reviews, Replies and Reminiscences*, Auckland University Press, 2016, pp. 370–78. At the time I wrote that essay I did not know, and neither did Anthony Rudolf remember at the time I discussed it with him, that he had been present on the London occasion.

me to do a poetry reading there. I expected no audience at all, but Dukakis was by now looking like a boring loser, and though he did draw the expected large crowd of never-say-die Democrats, mine in another part of the campus was small but quite respectable.

Sister Hollywood came out in London from Collins in 1989, with a jacket photograph by Werner Forman of Auckland's Civic Theatre, and in New York from St. Martin's Press, also hardcover, with a face on the jacket that might have been Jean Harlow's. A German translation came from Fischer Verlag; and a couple of years later Christopher MacLehose did it as a handsome trade paperback from Harvill.

Reviews were good and in good places – *Times, TLS, LRB, The London Magazine* – ample for the publisher to put together one of those 'stellar' promotional presentations for reprints and translations. At home Michael King described me as 'the most stylish writer of New Zealand fiction', and Iain Sharp wrote: 'Stead writes the way Torvill and Dean skate – very few people can put together such luminous sentences.'

All of that sounds like success; and from the point of view of a full-time writer, the novel paid its way, gave me what might be called 'a living wage'. But it should also be said that there was a certain reluctance in New Zealand to notice *Sister Hollywood* or to approach it in a friendly fashion. There were writers whose work was always warmly received. I was not one of them. This was the time when *Metro* published an article by Stephen Stratford called 'Why the literati hate C. K. Stead'. No one attacked *Sister Hollywood* front on, deplored it, or suggested it wasn't a pretty good read; but there was an unmistakably grudging, unfriendly tone.

An unnamed reviewer in *Salient* confronted the problem frankly. Stead was 'no stranger to controversy'; he had been 'making waves in the small pond that is New Zealand's literary scene'; 'had been scorned by some as provocative and insensitive'; and though 'his efforts to encourage intelligent debate' had been 'seemingly sincere', they had created barriers. But this reviewer got past all that and even liked the novel: 'Dominion Road to Hollywood and Vine – it's the stuff dreams are made of.'

Meanwhile my other American on the opposite coast, Helen Vendler, was writing to tell me of troubles similar to my own at home – that she was being 'trashed' by various reviewers because, 'though I see the point of the feminists and the Marxists, I can't subdue aesthetics to morals'; and that with the retirement of one of her colleagues she was the one left in the Harvard English Department wanting to lecture on lyric poetry, which in the mood of the moment was being decried as 'a hermetic, court-devised white male hegemonic non-populist genre, unavailable to enquiries about race, class and gender'. She wrote, 'I too loved having you around. It was a bracing experience to have an atheist by my atheist's side – it hardly ever happens, everyone is so mealy-mouthed and pious. I'm very happy that our names were linked by your reviewer.'

I had sent her my latest collection of poems, *Between*, and she told me 'I keep coming back to the Clodian Songbook, if only because they seem to hold the erotic life and the literary life in one sour but true embrace. I xeroxed them for Dabney Stuart who let me borrow *All Visitors Ashore*. I know you better for having read the latter, *mutatis mutandis*, and enjoyed it as a letter rather than as a novel.'

I wrote a poem for Helen in thirteen-syllable triplets which ended

How make a locked
box for the lady
famous for keys?

How cook for one
whose sure taste will
locate the secret

ingredient?
Rationalists, yet for whom
poems bespeak

a First World, what's
common between
us is open to

public view. No
secrets – only perhaps
a hint that

once, in a parallel
life, lissom
in Xanadu,

we may have danced
away our innocence
and the night.

5.
The Datson Story

Norma

I had two sisters, Norma, my senior by two and a half years, who was an important presence but not really a powerful one in my childhood, and Frances, seventeen years younger, so it sometimes seemed to me she was my first experience of what it was like to be a parent. Norma is now dead, and Frances a recently retired deputy principal of a school in West Auckland, an expert in what is called Reading Recovery. I have never written directly about either, but it's true that there were elements of Norma's character and personality went into the making of Arlene in *Sister Hollywood*. Norma and I were very different, and she seemed to me often inscrutable. I was strong on opinion and said what I thought; she was talented at silence, and the question was always what was being hidden – a great deal, or not much, or something in between – indifference? As a young woman she was pretty and cheerful and laughed a lot, and blushed when she laughed.

After Auckland Girls' Grammar and I think a year at Auckland Business College, Norma worked as a shorthand typist in the Lands and Deeds Department in Auckland, and acquired there the nickname Rusty because of the laughter and the blush. A Mt Albert Grammar school friend told me she was sexy and I supposed she was, though I saw her just as my big sister and therefore a category that was unique to me, quite distinct from girls I might think of in that way.

The sometimes inscrutable shorthand typist Norma with the ready laugh could be made believably into the shorthand typist Arlene who becomes a talented Hollywood screenwriter; but it has to be said that by the time I was writing *Sister Hollywood* I had known a number of highly intelligent and verbally adroit women, not least (and not only) Kay to whom I dedicated the novel.

I think I was seventeen when Norma married John Datson, a returned soldier ten years her senior. I was groomsman at their wedding. John's best man was Graham Perkins, his closest male friend, who had served with him overseas. My wedding present was a tea-trolley, an absurd domestic vehicle very fashionable at the time, on which you loaded cakes and scones, teapot, hot-water jug, milk jug and sugar bowl, and whatever spoons, forks and knives were necessary to the ritual, and wheeled it all into the 'front room' where you were serving 'afternoon tea' to visitors. It must have cost me quite a lot, earned in one of my school vacation jobs – freezing works or wool stores or post office. I had also to buy my first suit for the occasion.

John had been at Seddon Memorial Technical College in Auckland with Graham Perkins and Kendrick Smithyman,* and had left after only three years. The war came, and as soon as he was old enough he'd been 'called up' for service. Now he qualified for a 'rehab loan' and 3 per cent mortgage, and John bought a section in Rockfield Road, Penrose, not too far from MacEwans Machinery where he worked as the buyer. He built a small tidy three-bedroom brick house on it – all absolutely 'suburban' and proper, the prototype of the time, with space for a veggie garden at the back

* Smithyman dedicated a poem to Graham in his first book, *The Blind Mountain*, hence the opening three lines of my poem dedicated to Ken, 'Kin of Place', *Collected Poems, 1951–2006*, pp. 231–33.

and rich volcanic soil. John had a 'good steady job' – and he and Norma were launched; they were on their way! They would have four children, two boys and two girls. Ahead lay the 1960s–70s and its hazards, from which their children would not entirely escape harm, but would survive. The hazards and the harm, and the survival, only made them a typical working man's family of their time. The war receded but was still remembered by those of us who had lived through it – vividly by those who'd been part of it as John had, right through NZEF's participation, first in the Middle East and then in Italy.

He had a lot of stories about the war, most of them funny and well told. He made us all laugh. 'Rusty' laughed too, and blushed. When he talked about Italy it was most often about a town, Senigallia on the Adriatic coast, where his 'outfit', an intelligence unit of the New Zealand Scottish Regiment, were housed for some considerable time. Now and then (not often) John would mention the 'little friend' he'd had there, Gina. Was I being over-inventive, or the accurate sibling observer, when I thought these rare references to Gina produced, not Norma's laugh and blush, but her inscrutable face?

But the most significant fact in the Datson family's life as it went on and as the children grew up was that Norma in her thirties developed multiple sclerosis. Its onset was not rapid, but there was a succession of attacks, each leaving her just that fraction more disabled, less steady on her feet. By the time she was in her forties she was walking with the help of two sticks; and at some time I think in her fifties it was a wheelchair. Alterations were made to the house so she could continue to be the housewife, though it involved difficulties, adjustments and continual struggle. John was a hero, having often, as the years passed, to lift her in and out of her chair and in and out of their car. As much as the war ever did I'm sure this tested him and he rose to it unfailingly. She was courageous too, uncomplaining, coping. If any in our whānau deserved medals, they did.

John died at the age of seventy-three when Norma was sixty-four, and from then on she was on her own. The children were all married, coming and going, mostly living out of Auckland. They helped when and how they could; I think there were some meals-on-wheels provided; and after a time a home help or nurse came three times a day to help her in and out of bed and to shower. Kay and I (but Kay more than I) visited to talk and take her to the pictures, calling a disability taxi to get her to and from the cinema.

Soon it wasn't possible for Norma to continue alone in the house and it was understood she would need to be moved into a care-home. She never complained about this; but unknown to us she had decided she'd had enough of life, and wanted to leave what she and John had accumulated – the house in Rockfield Road and a bach at Stanmore Bay – to be shared among their children. The cost of keeping her in the care-home would not, as the rules stood at that time, be borne by the state, so it would eat into the children's inheritance. That was part of the reason for her decision that the time had come to die. Also, she was approaching her biblical 'three score years and ten', and ahead lay only an accelerating succession of MS setbacks – loss of sight, loss of speech, inability to feed herself: it was all well known and documented, and at the time there was no cure, no remediation. So she kept some of the drugs she received aside, and when she had enough to kill herself, left notes for her children and took them.

She had timed it carefully so she would be dead before the daily visitor was due; but as it happened her older son, Jim, who had a key to the house, called unscheduled and found her, alive but unconscious. He read the notes and was faced with a dilemma: clearly she intended and wanted to die, but could he take responsibility for letting it happen? He rang Frances. She was his aunt but there was only a year in age between them and they had known one another well since childhood. Frances told him what he too thought was the case, that he had no choice and must call the emergency services. He did that and Norma was saved.

When we next saw her she told us what had happened, but not about Jim's involvement. She pretended she had made a mistake about the timing and the home help had found her. She said her drugs were now being closely monitored and she was being subjected to 'counselling', which seemed like an invasion – but she could laugh at it. It was another human contact and it passed the time. She showed for the moment no wish to repeat the attempt, and we had happy meetings. I think she felt she'd tried and failed and would wait on her fate. In any case she was now to go into the care-home for the aged and infirm and there would be no possibility of killing herself there.

Again she was brave, but she didn't like the place – how could she? Her brain was clear and sharp but all around her were variously infirm or helpless people, most of them much older than she was. We saw more of her then, visited her on Sunday mornings to have coffee and talk, or during the week to go to a movie. She and I talked a lot about our childhood, some of which had been presented in rather heightened colour in *Sister Hollywood*, a novel I think she liked because she saw herself in Arlene. The three of us laughed a lot. Her death came slowly, but she never reached the degree of helplessness she had anticipated and feared.

She was transferred to Auckland Hospital and died there surrounded by whanau, including daughter Kathy's Māori husband Barry who insisted death should not be hidden from the children – so they all came and went from the bedside, playing or talking outside and returning. Norma's breathing seemed to signal there would be no return to consciousness. After her death she was laid out at her son Graham's house in South Auckland. Graham's partner was also Māori, and Māori protocol prevailed. Again the mokopuna came and went. Their eyes were fixed at first on Norma's face, but soon strayed to the television, and the scene, though not without a sense of loss and grief, managed to be also relaxed and almost normal – as if 'Granma' was still, though no longer alive, a soothing presence. The funeral when it came was more traditionally Pākehā – but there was no doubt the death had taken on a different, warmer and somehow less stark ambience because of that Māori influence.

The only poem I wrote about Norma (an exercise in the syllabics I was using a lot at the time) was written in 2006 in Menton on 6 June, our father's birthday which may have been what set me thinking about her. At that time her son Jim had not told us of his part in her 'rescue' from the attempted suicide – so the poem repeats her own less than complete account of that episode.

My Sister and M.S.

A catheter was the last straw. My sister
made 'a rational decision' – it was time
to die, but she misjudged

the dose – or was it the hours those drugs would take?
'Saved', she was told her medication would be
watched – no more hoarding her pills

and to help her beat her Black Dog there would be
counselling. She was marking time now, hanging
fire, but it wasn't all waste.

Sometimes we visited her in that Home for
the Helpless – sat in the sun looking over
the lake, our backs to Bedlam;

sometimes wheeled her to see a James Bond, or
something romantic. Talking about the past
she laughed so much I worried

she might fall out of her chair. Death came in its
own slow time. She was laid out in her son's house
all the grandchildren Maori

and Pakeha goggle-eyed until someone
turned on the TV which stole their attention.
At her funeral I thought

I couldn't speak, then spoke, remembering a
photo of her in school uniform with three
friends, and another up north

on the beach with cousins. She looked so pretty
and friendly, someone you'd like to meet at a
dance or take to the pictures.

Small boys avoid big sisters but mine in age
against all the odds in that battle with her
body proved that grace could win.

'Daddy's Girl', I drafted these lines for you on
the warm stones of a Mediterranean
beach, on our father's birthday.

John's war

Among the things her children had to deal with after Norma's death was a cache of letters John had written to his mother during the war. Their daughter Kathy had it and she offered it to me in case it should be useful to the writer in the family. I said I thought I could use it for fiction; but I found I couldn't. This material was in no sense my own, and I could not truly escape from reality into fiction. I would have to have engineered a version of myself in a story that interested me but that I had not 'lived', and I would have been constantly conscious (I thought) of an artificiality – something fake or false. (This may mean no more than that, at that particular time, I was not in what I think of as 'fiction mode'.) So I turned them into the non-fiction narrative which follows.

There were a few other things came with the letters – photographs, souvenirs, and the wallet John was using in his last years. His mother's letters had not been kept, so I was only able to divine what she wrote from his responses.

The letters are by a young man aged from eighteen or nineteen to twenty-two or twenty-three. His style is quite fluent. He has no trouble filling a page – in fact he's good at running on even when he has next-to-nothing to say. There are variations in tone, but the predominant one is jaunty – and with that goes a tendency to rhetorical flourishes: 'As it is only 9 p.m., Mum, I have decided to wield the old pen in your favour' – that kind of thing, only wield is spelled weild. In fact though his spelling is mainly correct there are a number of words consistently wrong: villiage, arround, adress, souvineers, cheif, consentrate, sandwitch. Etc is always ect. He recons this or that is likely. He thinks a woman who takes his eye in Tel Aviv is ellegant. John's secondary schooling had been brief, and what skill he had in accountancy came only from an army course done during the war. But he's neither stupid, nor lost for words; he can construct sentences, and tell a story.

There are letters from camp in New Zealand and from the ship en route; but the bulk are from Egypt first, then Italy. I soon recognised that they fell into a pattern: first the greetings, the explanation and apology if more than a week has passed since his last; then news of what he's been doing. Next come responses to her most recent letters; often then a brief discussion of the war, how well it's going for the Allies and how badly for Hitler, with assurances that it will soon be over and he and his mother will be together again. He mentions the promised Second Front often, becomes impatient when it seems not to be happening, and then celebrates in June 1944 when he hears it has come in the form of the Normandy landings. Finally come the farewells (usually protracted over at least half a page), nearly always with the final formula, 'God bless you, darling [or Mum], from your loving son – John.'

Somewhere in all this, which will run on for anything from six to twenty pages, there is very often an assurance to his mother about his wayward younger brother Max. Max is also in the NZ Div. in the Middle East, and John saw him often enough to report to their mother, usually that 'Max is 100%', that 'Max is having a good time', often that 'Max means to write' and only doesn't get around to it because 'he says nothing much happens to him and he hasn't got anything to tell you'. Sometimes there's mention of Max's drinking – but only to say how much less he drinks now than he did at home, how he's 'quietening down', how the two brothers have a plan to start up a country store together, and how well they intend to look after their darling mum when the war is over.

John's own news, including his location, is always under the censor's eye, and therefore described only in general terms. Sometimes you know where he is because he writes on letterhead paper from somewhere like the YWCA at Maadi, or a hotel in Rome. Other letters have only his name, rank (corporal, later sergeant, then staff sergeant) and unit at the top of the page, and you have to guess from contents and from letters before and after (he always dates them) where he may be. They are the letters of a young soldier, provincial, insular and in many ways still innocent and ignorant. It's as if the troops in those days travelled inside a cultural cocoon, in which the narrowest of national prejudice was sanctioned and unquestioned. He uses the language of the common soldier in which ordinary Egyptians were 'Wogs' or 'Gypos' and Italians 'Ities', even once 'greasy Ities'. They were all thieves, liars and cheats, purveyors and eaters of awful food. Though he describes poverty and filth it is in a tone that suggests the fault is their own. That they steal seems almost in his mind unconnected with poverty – or anyway the connection is not made, or not allowed as an excuse. They steal parachutes for the silk, tents for sails on the Nile, even army blankets not just for warmth but to make suits of clothes. They steal tyres, equipment, 'anything that moves and isn't screwed down'.

A partial explanation for the frequency of these complaints in his letters is his role in the army. Early on he was assigned to the SIB – Special Investigation Branch of the Military Police. It was described as a base job, meaning he never saw action, but was on call night and day to deal with what was often petty crime, especially the theft of army property and army food. So like every cop, I suppose, he developed a thoughtless blind spot about the causes of crime and the reasons for telling lies. Egyptians were not allies exactly and Italians had been enemies; and if you add to that an insular upbringing in an isolated corner of the British Empire, a lot found in these letters can be understood. But I think also that he is telling his mother what she wants to hear: he knows the illiberal note will be appreciated. He is on the right side of the law and they are not.

When he describes his encounters with petty criminals I imagine the man I knew. He was by nature courteous and kind; and there are stories in which his basic humanity shows through. For example a New Zealand soldier sees a musical instrument in a shop window he knows is his and was stolen. He gets into an argument with the shopkeeper, the local police are called in, and soon Sergeant John Datson of the SIB as well. The shopkeeper has a docket showing that he bought the instrument from another dealer. Sergeant Datson wants the local police to take the matter up with that dealer, or simply leave it alone, but see that the instrument (he doesn't say what it was) is handed back to its rightful owner. The local police just want to arrest the shopkeeper and prosecute him for receiving. John argues, insists, and in the end gets his way. The instrument is restored to its owner, and John has a friend, a shopkeeper called Angel who invites him home for a meal.

To his mother he is not complimentary about the food Angel offers him – marrow stuffed with seasoned rice, followed by watermelon. This is his way of flattering her about her own cooking; but he can't conceal that he has enjoyed the visit, and Angel is only the first of several who cease to be 'Wogs' in the letters and become 'my Egyptian friend'. There is a photograph of one, very civilised he looks, in Western suit and tie and with a neatly trimmed moustache. John refers to him as 'Fatty', but the name on the back of the photo shows his real name was Fathy Yehia.

After one of these visits there is a glimpse of the Kiwi abroad unimaginable now. He writes, 'Here you don't get spaghetti in tins like we do at home, Mum' – and goes on to tell her that it comes in dry sticks which are then boiled until they go soft, and served with a tomato or other sauce, and a sprinkling of pepper and cheese. He describes the difficulty of eating the stuff, how he tried to wind it around his fork but it kept falling off, and in the end he was eating 'with my chin in my plate' as his hosts were doing, which he considered bad manners but unavoidable. This was in Egypt. Later in Italy he encounters something he calls 'paster-shooter'. I puzzled over this and decided it must be a confused combination of the words 'pasta' and 'prosciutto'.

But he's taken for rides in 'Fatty's gharry', his friend wearing suit and fez, and enjoys the feeling of riding high, and of social consequence; or he takes a taxi for thirty piastres from the camp and charges it, and a meal in Cairo with his friends, to his unit as 'expenses', noting this in the letters as a small personal score against the war that has put him in this foreign, and mainly undesirable place. The main entertainment in camp is drinking and smoking, with the first fifty cigarettes, called 'V cigs', supplied free by the army; and movies in which the stars seem to come always in pairs – Bob Hope and Dorothy Lamour, Abbott and Costello, Fred Astaire and Ginger Rogers. There is a boxing tournament, concluding with a demonstration bout by the world champion, Joe Louis, touring for the war effort. There is also a musical show by the aging but still famous Bebe Daniels.

There were times when he was able to behave like a tourist. He went by train to Tel Aviv and on to Palestine where he visited all the Jesus sites, recording them like a true believer for his Presbyterian mother – Pontius Pilate's Hall, the Garden of Gethsemane, the Stations of the Cross, the place of crucifixion, the sepulchre. When he gets to Italy he spends a few days in Rome, tours the ancient sites, and also the Vatican with appropriate signals of shock and disapproval at 'oppulence and synicism'.

Right through the whole three and more years of letters the dominant theme is anxiety about his mother – her health, her loneliness, her dislike of her workplace (she's employed on the counter at George Courts department store in Karangahape Road), her fears for her two soldier sons, her worries about money. He makes detailed arrangements for her to receive two shillings per day from his pay, the maximum amount permitted without cutting out the one shilling and sixpence per day she receives from the government as the dependant of a man in the forces overseas. Then a good deal more of his pay (most of it in fact) goes into a savings account in Auckland to which she has free access; and he is constantly urging her to raid it whenever she needs to. Though the amounts sound small by the standards of now, when her pay from George Courts (probably about three or four pounds) is added, and the fact that she is letting one of the spare bedrooms in the house for ten shillings a week, it's hard to see why she had reason to complain.

He repeats the details of these arrangements again and again, responding to letters which must have combined confusion and complaint. She must still have been in her forties at the time, so hardly a confused old person; and I found it difficult to resist an impression that John had been played upon and exploited by a demanding and unreasonable mother. The nearest he goes to reproaching her is to remind her of the poverty and distress he is seeing everywhere. 'Even though you had a hard time you didn't have half as hard a struggle as most of these poor beggars. Compared to them you are in paradise.' John himself, meanwhile, though full of anxiety about her health (asthma in particular) is himself in and out of hospital two or three times with bouts of dysentery.

As he travels more widely in Egypt, and sees and describes more, a background picture builds especially of labour in the countryside.

The bargeman leans on his pole and walks with it, pushing, from bow to stern, then trudges the length of the barge, trailing the pole, and begins again, on and on. Donkeys vanish under the weight of cane they are made to carry. An ox walks around and around, hour after hour, turning a wheel that brings water from a bore into the irrigation channels; and likewise two small boys working a corkscrew apparatus that brings up river water. Harvesters wield sickles, and winnowers use broad forks to toss the cut stalks up into the breeze separating the grain. Ploughs drawn by two donkeys work the stony fields. 'Bints' carry water in stone jars from wells. Camels lope by with (he records) 'long-suffering faces'. Perhaps they made him think of his mother.

'Non ti scordar di me'*

There is a story from his childhood John told me once, and referred to from time to time, with enough feeling for it to have remained with me vividly. It happened when he was seven or eight. Every day, punctual and regular, their father got home in time for the evening meal (called 'tea'), and if it wasn't raining the boys, John and Max, were allowed to walk down to Dominion Road and wait across the street from his tram stop. On this night they waited . . . and waited, until their mother came and waited with them. Tea was ready, had been ready for some time, but no father.

She took them back to the house and they ate their meal together. There was no phone in the house, and in any case nowhere obvious to call, even from the phone box at the end of the street. The father's meal was still waiting, keeping warm for him in the oven, when the boys were put to bed.

Next morning there was still no father – nor the morning after that, nor any of the mornings that followed, ever. From his

* 'Don't (you) forget me'. There's a lovely version of this song, readily available online, sung by Pavarotti.

workplace the mother learned that he had been absent all of that day when he didn't come home. The police were called in, enquiries spread far and wide, friends and neighbours were contacted, a small item appeared in the daily paper headed

MAN MISSING

Puzzling Disappearance of Mt Eden Resident

No message or explanation came. Had he committed suicide, or run away? No corpse was found and it was assumed he must be somewhere in the country, or in Australia, with a new identity, perhaps with a new woman.

John's mother claimed she had never had any warning that anything was wrong. She'd thought they were a happy family, and was puzzled, baffled, distressed. Her own mother came to live in the house with them and look after the boys after school, while she took the job at George Courts to support them all. They were now always short of money, and their mother was always deeply unhappy – worse than a widow, lacking a mate yet still officially married; talked about, pitied, depressed and ashamed. For the rest of his childhood John lived in the shadow of an absence.

From that time on the role of head of the house was pushed on to him. He felt more and more that he was responsible for his mother, had to work at pleasing her, making her happy, promising her a better future; had to discipline his wayward sibling, work when he could, and leave school early to support the family. It had become the central fact of his life.

Was that, then, why, when he came of an age to be called up for army service he chose a role that gave him a base job – so that his mother would not need to be worried that she might be deprived of her main support? Or did that happen by accident? This is one of the details I don't know. But there is one particular and quite untypical eruption of anger in the letters that seemed to me, when I came upon it, significant.

By the time John arrived in Egypt Montgomery and Freyberg had Rommel beaten. Italians had surrendered in huge numbers and the German forces were exhausted and close to final defeat, but there were still a few battles to be fought. Some kind of push required more New Zealand troops and John asked to be included. All his best mates were being sent, and he wanted to be with them. Permission was denied.

His anger in the letter which reported this was immense. He had been told he was too useful right where he was and couldn't be spared. So this was his reward for doing a good job – to be denied the right to fight alongside his mates. If it had been possible to 'resign' from a war, he said, he would have done it.

Yet somehow within this angry letter there was, or seemed to be, an unspoken recognition that he was in the SIB precisely in order to stay alive; and so the anger, which seemed unreasonable, read to me like a reproach to his mother. It was not a direct reproach, perhaps not even a conscious one; but that was how it struck me. He was complaining to his complainer that she had denied him the experience of a lifetime, one for which he would gladly have risked not only his own life but her happiness and security.

He was able to write nothing about strategic matters; and for the most part he avoided talk of wounds and death. But after this final military push he reported sending a photograph of the grave of one of his mates to the lad's mother, and later receiving a tearful letter of thanks from her. He visited a distant cousin, Frank, in hospital. Frank's right hand and half his arm had been blown off, and John had written, since Frank couldn't do it himself, to the father explaining what had happened and assuring him that his son was in good spirits and recovering. He reported that his old friend Shorty, though still in hospital, 'seems to be shaking less and is getting his speech back'. In a copy of the *Weekly News* he found pictures of three school friends who had been killed.

I should not give the impression that these letters were only and exclusively dutiful. He looks for her replies and complains when a long time passed without any. He describes the scramble for letters when mail arrives, how each soldier takes his away and reads it alone, two or three times; then how they merge again into a group, exchanging news; and the feeling of disappointment when there's nothing. Often he tells her about imagining what he calls 'the homestead' seen from the street, going through the gate and walking up the path around the house to the garden at the back; looking through the back windows and seeing her in the kitchen. I've seen this 'homestead', a small wooden bungalow with corrugated-iron roof, down a side street off Dominion Road. I search the sentences in which this daydream is described looking for irony. There's none. He meant it. He was homesick.

In another letter from this period he asks her to send a good photo of herself so he can keep it in his wallet, in 'the place of honour close to my heart'. When she's reluctant to do this because she thinks of herself as 'old and ugly' he tells her she is his 'pin-up girl' and reminds her of a time when he took her to a dance and they pretended she was his girl.

But when he applies to be returned home 'on compassionate grounds' because his solo mother is ill, I'm sure he does it for her, not for himself; and though he expresses regret when he receives the expected NOT GRANTED reply, my feeling is that he's relieved. Already he is in Italy, missing friends in Cairo but making new ones. To leave now, before it – the big IT in his and so many lives – was truly over, would not have been welcome.

And in Italy there are the beginnings of a change of tone. It doesn't happen suddenly. There is still evidence of what I've called the uneducated provincial. He notices infants and small children with pot bellies and wonders what they are being fed, not seeming to know that he is observing a major indicator of malnutrition, even starvation. Though Italy has surrendered he still blames the Italian population for supporting Mussolini; but his pity is aroused too. He describes a small boy with a wounded leg, both parents killed, living at the police station with nowhere to go, nothing to do. John wants to help him but says it's like when you're kind to a stray dog and it follows you. How do you then drive it away? So he does nothing except give small handouts, attempting to remain impersonal, and feels bad about wanting to give him a hug. He describes raids on families for repossession of stolen army property, the women wailing and throwing themselves about, the men silent, grim – and his own feeling for them which he's not allowed to express.

He was based first at the camp in Bari where he took a course on the law as it would apply to their work in Italy. Unspecified tasks sent him twice to Naples and once, with three mates, south to Brindisi. On the way back they camped by the sea, swam, and slept, two on the tray of the truck and two on the hood. He was learning something of the Italian language. In the New Zealand Club in Rome he slept in a bed, the first in many months, with a mattress and sheets. He had his twenty-first birthday, received a cable from his mum, and celebrated with a haircut and shampoo, and then tea and cakes at the club at Bari.

As the war moved, grinding on and stalling in its drive northward up the boot of Italy, he moved with it but always in the rear of the battles. Late in 1944 he arrived at a small town, Senigallia, just north of Ancona and east of Florence on the Adriatic coast, and set up his office there. Suddenly there was a change of mood. He was happy; he had a good office, comfortable quarters, friendly people, and said he would be content to see out the war right there.

The army had chosen a rather grand and abandoned villa for local SIB headquarters, and John was to have, both as office and sleeping quarters, a big room on the first floor with a balcony looking down to the sea. Though 'banged about' by the war, with bullet holes and cracks in the walls, this was, he told his mum, 'officer's quarters', too grand for a sergeant, or even the warrant officer he was about to become; but he was not complaining. He was only holding his breath, afraid it was too good to last. Directly below his balcony there was a steeply terraced garden with a small landing stage and swimming platform. Why the owner had abandoned the house was unclear, but for the moment it was appropriated by the Allies, and Warrant Officer John Datson was in charge. He was in walking distance of the village, and a mile from his regiment's camp. He was fixing up a real bed for himself, a big one with a mattress. 'This is the best war I've been to yet', he joked.

In the gatehouse a family who had been the villa's household staff remained. They seemed to see it as their role to continue duties as if nothing as inconvenient as a war had happened. They overlooked the gate, checked the identities of those who wanted to enter, and acted as guards. They cooked and cleaned for John and his small staff. A major, in charge at the New Zealand camp a mile away, had authorised this and saw to it that they were paid. Gina, the young daughter of the family, spent mornings in the villa cleaning and polishing. She was a pretty, bright-eyed, singing kind of girl, and she and John struck up an instant rapport. She had little English and he less Italian, but each was trying to learn the other's language, and it was surprising how much they were soon managing to pass back and forth.

From Gina John learned that her brother Gianni had been missing almost two years and it was thought he must be dead. She wept as she told it and was hugged; but soon she was smiling again, bringing flowers for his desk. They sometimes swam together when the weather was calm and the waves not beating on the rocks down there. When John noticed there were no perceptible tides he tried to explain to her how in New Zealand you took note of high and low tides, and how they could make swimming possible at some times and not others. It seemed she had never heard of such a thing, couldn't imagine the sea rising and falling except as waves; but the failure to understand made them both laugh. They went for walks together in the evenings. At first her married sister, Ada, came too, uninvited chaperone. But soon Ada gave this up, whether because the family had decided he was 'safe', or because they didn't really care what happened, he didn't know.

In John's letters to his mum Gina was mentioned often but for a long time not named. She was 'the young girl', even 'the nice piece here', or 'the little piece'. At first he made it sound as if she was hardly more than a child, and that he was quite indifferent to her; but that tone quickly vanished. Soon she was appearing as 'my little girlfriend', pulling apart an old sweater of his for the wool which she would knit into something new. She was darning socks, mending shirts, doing his washing. In one letter he reported 'My little friend here has been busy this past week knitting a very pretty pink scarf, which upon completion she displayed for my approval. Then she told me she had knitted it for my dear old Mum.'

On 28 April 1945 he writes, 'I have my little girlfriend in here and she wants me to tell you that she is returning to NZ with me when the time comes, so you will have to buy yourself an Italian dictionary. She is a great kid.' Later in the same letter he seems to take fright at the boldness of this and refers back to it as a joke – not to be taken seriously. But it is a joke that's repeated a week or so later.

Once he reports that brother Max has come to visit and found him in his bedroom with his 'girlfriend'. The last thing Max has said to him on leaving is, 'Be careful!'

I puzzled over this letter, in which, as he goes on, he tries to suggest a misunderstanding by Max of an innocent situation, and to make a joke of it. Why, then, mention it at all? Not, surely, because he was afraid Max, himself famously miscreant, would tell her. I could make sense of it only in one way: they were lovers now, he and Gina, and he wanted his mother to guess, but did not want to tell her. In the context of all these letters, dutifully written week after week, all designed to assure her that he was still her dependable support, now and in the future, I think he wanted, in effect, her permission. He wanted her to recognise what was happening and to say it was all right. Yes he could bring this girl home. Yes he could marry her.

There is no sign that any such message came back. Possessive and complaining, his mother must have responded only with a frosty silence. And then, while John worried, and tried to think of ways to confront his Presbyterian mum more directly with this Catholic prospect, Germany surrendered and the war in Europe was over.

He described how eagerly he'd waited for this, thinking when it came he would be 'drunk for a week'. Now he was puzzled to find he felt nothing – only irritable and deflated. Next day he took Gina to swim at a beach where they found hospital patients celebrating and taking turns to ride on a donkey. The future hung over them like a cloud across the sun.

It was then the order came to move on, not homeward but north to Trieste. Gina was anxious and, with her whole family, shed tears. John promised he would return; and the day was saved by the reappearance of the long-lost brother. Gianni had been wounded and a POW in Egypt, his identity somehow lost in the system. So under cover of this new storm of family emotion, but himself wrenched and wretched, John climbed aboard the last truck in the convoy and trundled north towards Trieste. In his letter home he wrote only, 'I did it hard leaving.'

The letters show that he did return to Gina as promised, but only briefly. After Trieste he was ordered south again and did some kind of heroic diversion in a 'borrowed' army truck from Lake Trasimeno to the coast. There, he tells his mother, he met up with Gina and promised once again that he would come back. 'I lied to her and told her that I would return knowing damn well that I couldn't. I didn't like doing it but it was the best way. To be honest with you, Mum, if she had been a NZ or an English girl I would not hesitate to marry her, but there it is – the fortunes of war.'

This is certainly franker, closer to the truth, than he had been before with his mother. Maybe I read too much between the lines of these letters; but isn't he, here, giving her once again, and more clearly, the opportunity to release him from his bond – to say, 'If that's how you feel, my boy, do go back to her. And if you find it's what you both want, bring her to New Zealand'?

Once again there is no hint from him subsequently of any such reply; and since her letters were not kept, there's no way of knowing what her reaction was. The question of why her letters were not kept, and the circumstances in which they were lost or destroyed, remains unanswered.

So it seemed I had taken all there was to be had from that cache of letters and photographs. I looked again at the photographs, most from Egypt, but a few from Italy, able to add, from knowing that country, the colour which the black-and-white prints lacked: the dark green of the pines and blue of the sea; the yellow and ochre walls of village houses; the grey-green of olives and pale green of vines. There were a couple of John too, looking rather Italian himself with his tanned face and thick dark hair, handsome in his battledress, quizzical, his circumflex eyebrows raised as if one question remained, never to be answered.

But there was one other item in the box I had not looked at – the battered wallet he had used during I don't know how many of the last decades of his life. It contained very little, only things you would expect to find in an old man's wallet. (This was the prior-to-bank-cards period.) But in the innermost compartment there were just two items. One was his military ID for Italy which explained that the carrier was 'un agente della Polizia Speciale Investigative, Neo Zelandese, 2 N.Z.E.F.' The other was a photo of a young Italian woman, a small studio portrait. She is wearing a simple black top and a single string of pearls and looking, not at the camera but down, smiling at the bunch of roses she is holding. On the back she has written 'Non ti scordar di me – Gina'.

6. Life and Death in Liguria

Pound as currency

When P. E. Bishop in *Choice** reviewing my last academic book, *Pound, Yeats, Eliot and the Modernist Movement*, said 'In explaining why poets read *The Pisan Cantos* with such admiration, Stead surpasses both Hugh Kenner and Donald Davie', he or she placed me for a moment with the two critics of Modernism I most admired – for their ability to bring clarity to complex literary-critical questions, and to write accounts which were readable, interesting, even exciting, making you want to read on. I met both men, Davie at the Savile Club, a meeting I've described in *You Have a Lot to Lose* (p. 312), and Kenner first in 1958 when he was a young lecturer visiting Bristol, and then approximately forty years later in Rapallo. They were both brilliant, both eccentric, and both resistant to the fashion for literary theory that occurred during their (and my) lifetime, preferring, as I did, intelligibility to jargon and mystery. Kenner, profoundly deaf from childhood and his speech consequently affected, was in his critical writing given to

* Journal of the American Association of College and Research Libraries. (Clipping kept but no date.)

overstatement and blind (or at best partially sighted) loyalty – but his *The Pound Era* is a great story brilliantly told, and in scholarly terms comprehensive and dependable. Davie was a sober-sides Yorkshireman, temperamentally conservative, and caught between the conviction that the British literary establishment did not sufficiently appreciate and honour Pound, and that the Americans did not sufficiently recognise what a threat his poetic theory and practice represented to literary, and therefore to social and political, order. Davie was born into a Baptist family and became (frying pan to fire) a devout High Church Anglican; and Kenner was a Catholic convert: so I assume it was that desire in them for an ultimate Authority which put them temperamentally at the disposal of authoritarian Ezra.

But what was there in me that was likewise drawn? Only, I'm afraid, the aesthete. I recognised and responded to the aesthete in Ezra and rejected most of the rest. But this was not just a taste for Beauty with a capital B; it had also to do with Energy with a capital E – with Action, and the Action was verbal, was words, their variety and richness, their syntax and grammar, their capacity to make sentences and structures, to run on, tell stories and to make sense and nonsense. It was language – the talent which alone makes us distinct among the animals.

I advocated reading Pound's *Cantos* fast, not stopping over what you did not understand; because what was 'difficult' about it was not, like the difficulty of Donne and the Metaphysicals, or even of Shakespeare at his most dense on the page, something you needed to linger over and 'nut out'; it was, rather, a set of arcane facts and anecdotes which were part of Pound's weird creation of a history; it was, at least in part, 'Fake News' on a grand scale. You could take for granted that it meant something, and the *Annotated Index to the Cantos of Ezra Pound* could tell you what it was – but you did better to ignore the *Annotated Index*: take it that it *meant what it said*, and enjoy instead the man/the language in action, the display, the *poetry*!

I was not suggesting the reader of Pound should be indifferent to anti-Semitism or anything similarly toxic if it reared its head; but mostly the *Cantos* is a mix of history and memory. It's an assembly of many facts, often like a box room or storage space full of old furniture, much of it unpainted and broken. Sometimes they seem to be suggesting conclusions most readers would prefer not to draw; but the *Cantos* I was able to recommend wholeheartedly (*XLVII* for example, or *XLIX*, or *The Pisan Cantos*) are not for the most part, or perhaps for any part, evil or deplorable; they are just mysteriously and erratically beautiful poems; and in the case of *The Pisan Cantos* they are the record of a man in a cage, literally for a time, and then, no longer caged but still confined against his will, looking back on failure (his own, society's, humankind's), and contemplating death as he watches the world around him – the ant, the birds on the wire, the prison guards – going about its business.

He is like a war poet who fought on the wrong (the losing) side, sending his despatches from the front. And for the time he was in the US military detention centre at Pisa, awaiting transportation to Washington where he was to be tried for the capital offence of treason (an American citizen who had broadcast for an enemy in time of war), he had the great benefit that he was deprived of access to the books and libraries he had been in the habit of raiding in the course of writing his *Cantos* thus far. This, I suggested in my book about him, was the (blindingly simple) explanation why *The Pisan Cantos* stood out plain from all the rest: because he could put into them only what was immediate and present and concrete, or what had been processed in memory and thus reduced to essentials. I regarded this as my contribution to Pound studies, quite as simple and *right* as my perception about Eliot's composition of 'The Waste Land' had been in *The New Poetic*, but not destined to earn me the same kind of acknowledgement because there was not the kind of universal interest in Pound that there had been in Eliot in the 1960s.

WHEN POUND DIED IN 1972 THERE was a cartoon of the Prime Minister of Britain, Edward Heath, holding a newspaper with the headline, POUND DEAD, and preparing to jump off a building, and someone shouting from below, '*No no Prime Minister – it's only the poet*'. The pound sterling was seldom stable or secure, but it was a more dependable currency than the Pound Ezra, whose literary fortunes fluctuated wildly, and could only be described as 'up' for very brief periods. He made sure of that himself, always finding new methods of self-harm. It was Ezra who jumped off high buildings to his literary death, not once, but repeatedly throughout his life. He was mostly famous because he said he was, or asserted loudly that he ought to be. The worst self-harm was his romantic attachment to the Strong Leader – Mussolini in the first instance, but by extension Hitler, and Franco too; and with that went his anti-Semitism and the associated commitment to Douglas Social Credit. Social Credit would cure the world economy which was being destroyed by the 'usurocracy' of Jewish bankers, and only strong authoritarian leaders could bring this to an end.

Ezra's monumental self-importance took him to Washington just before the start of World War II seeking a meeting with the President so he could put Roosevelt straight on these matters of international finance and keep America out of the coming war. He met a few senators and congressmen, but was rebuffed by the President who consequently became, in Pound's letters and later in his broadcasts from Rome Radio, Jewsfeldt and even Stinkie Roosenstein. Mussolini on the other hand agreed to meet (just once for half an hour) this somewhat famous American poet-admirer, and became, by telling Pound he found the *Cantos* entertaining (*divertante*) at once a man with a brilliant and penetrating mind. The fact that he played the violin made Mussolini 'an artist' too: a genius and an artist – Italy was in good hands!

So Ezra Pound was not only, from my point of view, politically unacceptable, socially dangerous and morally indefensible; he was also, in many of his actions, a fool. And yet he was capable of great penetration and sharp recognitions in literary matters, and there were moments of exceptional beauty among the litter and waste of his poetry. He had been a significant figure in the development of literary Modernism – an early discoverer, promoter and (in effect) publisher of James Joyce; the man who turned Eliot's 'The Waste Land' into a viable (and great) poem; and an inspiration to many younger poets who were excited by his dictum 'Make it new!' and by the brilliant intelligence that burned in so much of his literary-critical writing. He excited writers and artists because his focus was more on the process than on the product, the writing desk than the published outcome; more on the studio where the work came into being than the gallery where, finished, it was displayed.

Only a small coterie of academics wanted to study or teach his work; but I had to take note of the poets who insisted on its importance. Eliot, who had profited by Pound's advice, had dedicated 'The Waste Land' to him as 'il miglior fabbro'; and Robert Lowell after reading *The Pisan Cantos* said there was 'no poetry since Thomas Hardy so moves the heart'. In 1950 George Barker said that contemporary English-language poets were more 'profoundly indebted' to Pound than to Yeats or Eliot. Such testimony had to be taken seriously.

To me Pound represented a challenge unmatched anywhere else in my literary studies: how could you write about this man in a way that acknowledged both sides of the contradiction – the brilliance and the wrong-headedness, the genius and the fool, without letting either side wipe out the other? Oscar Levant said: 'There's a fine line between genius and madness and I've erased it.' It's a good joke; but if you imagine Ezra saying it, you might have to take it as a statement of fact.

For Pound everything came back to language and language was unstable. It came in through the ear, in different accents and with different emphases, and every word or phrase carried with it the shadow of other sounds, other meanings, a different history, another language. So verbal structures were like social structures – a set of conventions, a tragic-comic pretence at permanence and stability which might at any moment break down. They were buildings that creaked and swayed when the wind blew. Pun, *double-entendre*, wordplay, verbal shiftiness, represented the universal comedy of our insecure hold on order. And I think this was a recognition much more available to an American of the early twentieth century than to a European. Ezra's assertive 'Amurkanism', which caused lips to curl and eyebrows to be raised, had an intellectual basis. A man could walk on water but only so long as confidence – which meant health, vital energy, testosterone – lasted. Pound lived on after those vital energies and juices ran out. Those were the last sad years of his long silences, out of which he emerged only rarely, usually to say his life had been a failure, his work 'botched', and that he 'could not make it cohere'.

Pound's philosophical base was scepticism; its principle was uncertainty, indeterminacy; and his talent was correspondingly lyrical, not epic. His great error was to propose solutions to the world's ills and attempt to project them on an epic scale. He was the boastful egotist-only child, showing off to Mummy and Daddy, getting above himself but too much loved to be told he was being silly.

I met the Pound challenge head on; and in the course of that engagement I made good friends, not least among them Massimo Bacigalupo who lived in Pound's Rapallo and was Professor of English and American Literature at the University of Genoa. He had – and has – unequalled credentials, both academic and family/personal, for the study of Pound – an Italian but with an American mother, son of Giuseppe Bacigalupo who was Ezra's physician in Rapallo and whose German mother, Elfriede, was likewise doctor to the poet. Elfriede's husband, Massimo Ruggero Bacigalupo, was Ezra's pharmacist who is described in one of the canto drafts from 1943:

> and on that day
>
> stood Massimo, before the doors of his pharmacy
>
> with Corrado the oculist

The present-day Massimo, who has his own teenage memories of sailing with Pound in the family yacht, *Vagabonda*, lives in (or more precisely in the hills above) Rapallo, the town where Pound lived from 1923 to the end of the war, and to which he returned after thirteen years' incarceration in St Elizabeth's Hospital for the insane in Washington DC. This confinement had been not so much a defined sentence for a particular crime but rather the only way the American authorities of the time could devise to evade the embarrassment of hanging a celebrated American poet for treason.

It was in Rapallo that Pound had gathered around him, in the years before the war, a constant wife, English Dorothy, a constant lover (mistress, as she would then have been designated), American Olga Rudge, and two constant parents, Homer and Isobel, after Homer retired from the US Treasury. The battle of wills between wife and mistress was to go on for decades, the wife in their seafront apartment, the mistress up in the hills above the town at Sant'Ambrogio, reached on foot by a steep *salita* through olive groves and informal gardens and vineyards with, looking back, views over Rapallo and the Bay of Tigullio.

In Rapallo Ezra played to the hilt, in the decades between the wars, the part of 'il signor poeta', to be seen often along the seafront wearing a large hat and cloak or cape, speaking Italian fluently but with a harsh American twang. Ford Madox Ford said Ezra played tennis 'like an agile baboon' and he played it a lot in Rapallo telling his partner, usually Giuseppe Bacigalupo (who was to become one of Italy's best players) to keep out of the way except when he, Ezra, missed a shot.

Dorothy, who must have been the major source of the very little income they had, was daughter of Olivia Shakespear, now famous in literary annals as the lover who relieved the young W. B. Yeats of his virginity. Dorothy is reputed to have said 'Some cook – I do not', so their main meal of the day was eaten out, usually at the Albergo Rapallo which Ezra called his HQ. Olga Rudge did not cook either, but it's said that Ezra was talented in the kitchen when he put his mind to it. Unlike her loquacious husband Dorothy spoke only enough Italian to get by doing the shopping and exchanging civilities with neighbours. She accepted, but not, it seems, happily or with good grace, the fact of the mistress, and that Ezra's life was lived, as he says in the *Cantos*, 'between a door and a door'.

When Olga became pregnant Dorothy disappeared from Rapallo for a holiday which seems to have included a cruise on the Nile; when she returned she too was pregnant. The father has never been named – only that it was not Ezra. When the child was born Ezra and Dorothy were both in Paris; but it was Ernest Hemingway, not Ezra, who took her to the American Hospital for the delivery. No one has suggested he might have been the father, but he remembered that occasion and referred to it in a letter to Dorothy twenty-five years later: 'Remembering the taxi ride out to the hospital at Neuilly and how you finally told me it was time'* – which puts him in at least a trusted, if not necessarily an intimate, relationship with her. It was Hemingway who taught Ezra boxing, while Ezra taught Hemingway fencing; and since no one (so far as I know) has advanced a documented theory about who might have been the father of Ezra's son, I offer Hemingway as a fictional progenitor. But Ezra was there to fill in the necessary forms at Neuilly accepting legal parenthood of the boy who was named Omar (a variant on the name Homer) Shakespear Pound – 'note the crescendo', Ezra said, a good joke but in fact the names were chosen because Ezra's father was Homer, and Dorothy's family name was Shakespear.

I suppose Dorothy might have said, 'Some people bring up their children. I do not' – because once the boy was born she took him to England and handed his upbringing over to her own mother, Olivia, who in turn seems to have handed him on to others.

Almost a year prior to all this Ezra had followed Olga up into the Italian Tyrol where their child was to be born. I have never seen

---

* *Ernest Hemingway: Selected Letters 1917–1961*, edited by Carlos Baker, Simon & Schuster, 2003, p. 742, letter to Dorothy Pound dated 22 October 1951.

any explanation for Olga's choice of the location. It seems rather like something in myth or fairy tale, or like the rejected baby in Shakespeare's *The Winter's Tale* abandoned on a wild shore to be discovered and brought up by shepherds. The baby was a girl, at first named Maria Rudge (they should have called her Perdita), and at once handed over to a peasant woman in the same hospital who had lost her own baby at birth and was therefore able to nurse Olga's. This woman and her husband were offered 200 lire a month to foster the child; the house they lived in was vetted and considered satisfactory, and Ezra and Olga left. Thereafter, as Maria (subsequently Mary) records in her memoir,* the child grew up speaking Tyrolean German in a household of many children, believing the adults she called Mamme and Tatte were her parents, but visited each year by an English-speaking couple who took her on a summer holiday to Venice, where they lavished affection, gifts and the English language on her, with much additional instruction, and then returned her to the mountains. This couple were Ezra and Olga. It wasn't until towards the end of World War II, when Italy was being crushed to pieces between the Allies and the Axis, that Ezra made his heroic dash – tramped in borrowed and ill-fitting boots, hitch-hiked, rode the rail-cars – up into the mountains to tell his daughter the truth, that he was her father, Olga, to whom he was not married, her mother, and that there was a wife, Dorothy.

By this time the Germans had appropriated Ezra and Dorothy's apartment on the Rapallo seafront and, having nowhere else to go, they had moved in with Olga at Sant'Ambrogio; so an uneasy situation was made worse. Mary describes the household as 'pent up with two women who loved him, whom he loved, and who coldly hated each other' – which seems not unlikely, but Olga denied it to Pound's biographer Humphrey Carpenter, telling him 'we were all civilised people and behaved accordingly'. Dorothy as usual said nothing. When US forces first appeared in Rapallo and the

* Mary de Rachewiltz, *Discretions*, Little, Brown, 1971.

Germans retreated, Ezra was arrested by partisans who handed him over to the Americans, thus lifting him out of what Mary describes as a domestic battle zone and her mother insists was nothing of the sort.

Hollywood again?

I have described in *You Have a Lot to Lose* how the Stead family in 1972, returning to Menton from Venice, first wandered through Rapallo hoping they might catch a glimpse of Ezra Pound; and how twelve years later Kay and I with daughters Margaret and Charlotte returned there and located Pound sites – the apartment he and Dorothy had occupied on the seafront, the *salita* up to Sant'Ambrogio, and the house there now called the *Casa Ezra Pound* which had been Olga Rudge's and figures in the *Cantos* as 'Circe's Ingle'. By that time I knew the main lines of the biographical story and was well advanced with my Pound Yeats Eliot book, so was a more knowledgeable guide than in 1972. We had also found the little Giardini Ezra Pound, with its cannons and frog fountain and one enormous eucalypt, all in sight of the old fort; and nearby, overlooking the Giardini, the somewhat derelict hotel *Villa Cristina*, which the family later called *El Dumpo*, and would be the model for the hotel *Villa Vittoria* in my novel of that name.

Straight after that 1984 tour with Kay and the daughters I had made Rapallo an important one of the shifting European locations visited by the mysterious and unnamed narrator of *The Death of the Body*. Now, several novels later, and following visits there which included an Ezra Pound conference where I first met Massimo Bacigalupo and Pound's daughter Mary, the town was to be the starting point, and in a way the central focus, of a new novel.

The idea for *Villa Vittoria* was to include a Pound character. I called him Sterling Grant, an American poet and Mussolini supporter, some years dead when the novel begins, and most famous for a long, never-ending poem called *Historia*. Sterling Grant's former mistress, Albertine Marshall, is to unveil a bronze bust of him in a piazzetta modelled on the one named after Pound, in sight of the hotel *Villa Vittoria* in a town called Tigullio, clearly Rapallo renamed. The old Fascisti who have remained loyal to their defeated cause but don't display themselves often, would be there to honour the name of their American poet-comrade; but there was to be a total ban on photography. The story opens with the unveiling of the monument, and a young British journalist, Miranda Frayn, in search of a scoop. Hiding herself in the somewhat derelict hotel *Villa Vittoria* she succeeds in getting forbidden shots of the unveiling and of Albertine Marshall, and finds herself pursued by people who want to prevent her shots getting out into the world. She is helped to escape by Steve Jenson, an American academic, lecturer at London University's Bentham College, a Sterling Grant scholar who has gone to Tigullio to see the unveiling. There are sparks between them, so here is the 'love interest' – but he has a current wife or partner, so there is (in terms of the mechanics of fictional plot) 'the obstacle'. Back in London Steve is stalked and harried by dangerous people wanting to identify and track down the photographer he was seen with in Tigullio.

Steve's partner, Jean Kinleith, also a lecturer at Bentham College, has previously been married to Bruno Strawson, a character I modelled partly on Christopher MacLehose. She's still half in love with him (a plot convenience, if Steve and Miranda Frayn are to be lovers). Her two children, Pete and Paula, are Bruno's, and she still looks to him when there's any sort of crisis, rather than to Steve who is clever but less dependable, less solid. Bruno is thoroughly British, a man of honour, engaged in work Jean was never permitted to know much about, except that it is dangerous and secret. Bruno is a former paratrooper. During their marriage she supposed his work was with MI5 or MI6; but for her own safety and that of the children, she was not told, and just had to accept that he was often away on assignments. So the marriage broke up and now she lives with Steve, but still really cares more about the father of her children.

Villa Vittoria is essentially a thriller, my one shot at the genre, and did not, as I had rather hoped it might, take off and sell in tens of thousands – which it might have done if Roger Donaldson's interest in it, and his attempts to raise the cash needed to make a big-budget movie, had succeeded. Since making his first movie *Sleeping Dogs* from my novel *Smith's Dream* Roger had established himself as a dependable Hollywood director, and his list of movies with major stars was impressive. His interest in *Villa Vittoria* was serious, and he involved me in the project. He suggested I write the screenplay, supplied me with the computer software Final Draft that does the job of setting the script out as required on the page, sent me screenplays he had directed, including *No Way Out*, a thriller in which Kevin Costner and Gene Hackman had been principals, and was influential in getting me paid by the New Zealand Film Commission for the job. When a second draft was near completion and he was liking what I was making of it, he got me over and I lived for a week or so in his house in Santa Monica (only a mile or two away from Cal Bedient), completing the task.

Roger also brought into the project the London-based New Zealand movie producer Finola Dwyer,* who engaged a second and I think a third scriptwriter, and gradually I had a sense of watching my movie sailing away from me, fading as it went. It was a disappointment but not a huge one. I had read William Goldman's *Adventures in the Screen Trade* which prepares a writer for the fact that a very high proportion of such projects go a certain distance down the track towards an actual movie and then fall over, most often for want of money. I had enjoyed the experience along the way. Like all such movie-making ventures, involving, as they always do, someone taking an option on a novel and paying for it year by year – and in this case including the writing of a screenplay

* Finola's movie *Brooklyn* won an Oscar in 2015.

for which I think I was paid $25,000 – I had not been working for nothing, or even for peanuts. Hopes of big payouts came to nothing; but a more-than-working wage had been received along the way – and I was learning all the time, encountering new people, new human situations, new 'material'. Other such 'adventures in the screen trade' would follow, including one for *My Name Was Judas*, which has gone tantalisingly close, and at the moment of writing still hangs in the air undetermined.

There was also a poem that sprang from my sojourn with Roger in Santa Monica, and anything that produces a poem is, on the entirely inward and otherwise unintelligible scale of literary reward, pure gold.

Hollywood*
(for Roger Donaldson)

In winter sun
we lunch by the pool
in a garden

of oranges and lemons
palms and olives
where the

chill of desert shadow
signals
snow in the mountains.

Spring, you tell me
will flower purple
in the courtyard

---

* The form is thirteen-syllable triplets – one I used often at this time.

and in high summer
only the drift
of mists up from

the Pacific
will temper hot winds
down from the hills.

All day with our script
we play the game of
put and take

each 'Say we do
this' sending me back
to the keyboard

to the mysteries
of 'slug line', 'cut to'
'action', 'fade'.

Evenings
we watch classic movies
suggesting 'Say we dos'

for tomorrow.
My novel's shrinking
under our hands

into scene-and-speak
the rest dropping away
like ripe

olives on the path
to your front door.

Last night I dreamed

those giant letters
high in hills
spelled GOLLYWOG

and the tall palms
running seaward on Sunset
were fountains.

'Will our movie be made?'
I asked the ocean
and heard

clear beyond wave-break
the budget
whistle in its cage.

The Bacigalupos

Professor Massimo Bacigalupo has the kind of civility and sophistication we English speakers describe as 'European', meaning it as a compliment, something we can't quite match but might like to. Unlike many Italians who tend (as we do) to think that one language is enough, he is fluent in English and German, his manner polished, gentlemanly, somewhat formal, and yet with an ability to get up close that English stiffness inhibits. You might be asked to meet him on the seafront and there find yourself invited simply to walk – that is the point of it, the *passeggiata*, side by side, even arm in arm – and chatting: a stroll in the open air and a conversation. No need for coffee, or a drink or snack, though these may come later. There may be something Massimo wants to talk to you about – or nothing in particular. You are friends, meeting in a public place, enjoying fresh air and the views, getting to know one another better. The word 'ceremonious' seems too grand; and yet there is something of ceremony about it, a feeling of form, of formality.

Like his grandfather Massimo, this Massimo also married a German – Angela, an elegant and charming ballet dancer he met in New York when they were both staying at International House, he on a Fulbright scholarship working on a movie, she on a visit as a dancer with the Berlin Opera. They have two sons, at least one of whom, Lorenzo, has followed a family tradition into the medical profession. They have a small yacht, and Kay and I have been out in it a number of times, and swum off it in the Golfo di Rapallo. Most times it was plain sailing in beautiful weather; but Kay remembers one occasion when the wind came up suddenly, the sea responded, and I was threatening to be sick over the side while Massimo, with one hand on the tiller, went on reading aloud to us the poems of Eugenio Montale. The yacht we sailed in was *Vagabonda III*, but there had been *Vagabonda*s *I* and *II* before, and Pound had sailed with the family in the first two. There is a 1962 or '63 photograph of Massimo in the yacht, a teenager in swimming shorts side by side with a very distinguished-looking, cheerful and white-bearded Ezra, with nothing of the shaggy and bewildered look that clouded his last years in Venice.

Massimo opened a Pound conference in 1993 in Rapallo's beautiful municipal *Salone*. A few days later he and Angela invited me to have lunch in their garden with Pound's daughter, Mary de Rachewiltz. It was a beautiful summer setting, high in the hills, under a rattan screen among olive trees, with views down towards the town, or eastward towards Sant'Ambrogio where Mary's mother Olga Rudge had lived. I told Mary how much I admired her autobiography, *Discretions*, as a piece of writing, and she said that was unusual – most who spoke to her about it saw it only as a scholarly resource. She had subtitled it *Ezra Pound, Father and Teacher*, and I told her I had given it to my daughter Charlotte on her seventeenth birthday ten years before, and that I had that copy with me now and was going to ask her to inscribe it for Charlotte.

After the lunch Mary drove me back in Massimo's little Fiat and we were hurtling down the steep hills towards the town, Mary driving exactly as I imagine Ezra would have, headlong, reckless, when she remembered that her book had not been signed. She pulled at once over to the side of the road and on the Pound principle, mentioned by Hugh Kenner in his paper that morning, that most things requiring to be done can be achieved within twenty-four hours of recognising the need, she took the book in which Charlotte had written 'Charlotte Stead, 14 December, 1983', and wrote 'Thank you Charlotte for getting your father to read my "old" book. Mary de Rachewiltz, Rapallo, 14 July 1993.' It was a misunderstanding that Charlotte had made me read the book, but that hardly mattered – I had a typically odd and picturesque Poundian memento to return to its owner who was already shaping up to be a writer herself.

In his paper to the conference Hugh Kenner mentioned the gum nut Pound had picked up as he was marched down the *salita* by partisans. He was expecting to be shot but was in fact handed over to US troops. That was the beginning of his incarceration, first in a wire cage in the US military detention centre where he began writing *The Pisan Cantos*. Kenner explained that the gum tree was an Australian eucalypt and said he did not know why it should be found in Rapallo. As a Mansfield scholar I was able to tell him when we talked later that blue gums were considered to be helpful to the breathing of TB sufferers who came to this region for escape from the cold winters further north; and that when I had spent most of a year in Menton in 1972 two of my children, following the example of their French peers, used to find a gum nut in the colder weather, stick a fingernail into it and put it on the schoolroom heater so the air was suffused with the smell of eucalyptus. Also that the golden mimosa which is made such a feature of Mediterranean France, and which most French seem to believe is native to the region, likewise originates in Australia.

I reminded him of his visit to Bristol long ago and we talked about Charles Tomlinson, the only living British poet he would take seriously. He knew I didn't agree, and thanked me for my review in the *TLS* of his recent collection of essays, *Historical Fictions*. The review he said had begun looking like 'the kind of hatchet job' he was used to receiving in the UK, and finished by 'turning itself on its head'. I had indeed begun by deploring some of his worst excesses and inexplicable partisanship, but concluded:

> It is a form of high scholarly entertainment, spiked with small pertinent narratives and off-beat facts. He is the most readable of living critics and the one I should least like to be without.

Ezra had kept the gum nut as a symbol and memento of his escape from death, and when he died in Venice in 1973 it was buried with him.

MY MEETINGS WITH MASSIMO IN RAPALLO have been scattered over a period of more than two decades and I'm no longer sure when one or another of them occurred, but certainly over that time I learned not only a lot about Pound of a kind that is not to be found in the published scholarly and critical books; I learned also about the Bacigalupos and their extended family.

In 1996 Karl Miller asked me to review for the *LRB* the two-volume *The Clairmont Correspondence*, the letters of Claire Clairmont, half-sister of Mary Shelley who had an affair with Byron and a child to him, and possibly also a child to Shelley. This review* involved me in research into that extraordinary set of Romantic aristocrats and middle-class intellectual rebels whose adventures were pulled up short by the drowning of Shelley in the Bay of Spezia – so I was taken back into the same physical region of Pound and of the Bacigalupos. Massimo knew and

---

* *LRB*, 22 February 1996, reprinted with a postscript in *The Writer at Work*, Otago University Press, 2000, pp. 271–81.

introduced me to the current owner of the *Casa Magni*, the house once occupied by the Shelley group, including Mary and Claire, and their friends Edward and Jane Williams. Byron had been in the region too at the time, and had done one of his heroic swims, six kilometres from Portovenere to Lerici. It was from the *Casa Magni* that Shelley and Williams (a young naval officer) set off for Livorno, with an English boy as crew, in their two-mast sailing boat the *Don Juan*. On the return trip one of the sudden and violent storms the Mediterranean is known for blew up and their boat was swamped and sank. Unlike Byron, Shelley could not swim. All three were drowned, Shelley with a copy of the poems of Keats in his pocket.

A road now divides the *Casa Magni* from the sea which in Shelley's time beat up below the terrace on which Jane and Claire sat playing their guitars and singing while Mary lay indoors recovering from a recent miscarriage, all waiting for sight of a sail that would bring the two husbands back to them.

On the same research adventure Massimo and I used various points of reference that figure in the contemporary accounts to work out as nearly as we could the place on the beach at Viareggio where Shelley's body was cremated. The cremation was achieved using an iron frame constructed by Shelley's friend Edward Trelawny. Leigh Hunt was present; so was Byron, but it seems he couldn't watch, and stripped off and swam away before the body was consumed by the flames.

It was on a similar venture into that region that Massimo and I hunted for the site of what had been the US military detention centre, some distance from but in sight of Pisa's Leaning Tower. Here Pound was held in one of the wire cages intended for men condemned to death, but was later moved to more comfortable quarters and allowed to use the dispensary typewriter for his poems; and it was during the months of incarceration there, awaiting transportation to Washington for his arraignment, that he wrote *The Pisan Cantos*.

Massimo and I were on a country road with only farmhouses, fields and barns round about, and as we stood there looking for signs of a military encampment a local woman came along the road. When we told her what we were in search of she said we were in exactly the right place, though all structures had been taken down and the land returned to farming. She had grown up in this neighbourhood, had never moved from it, and had vivid childhood memories of the sounds that came from the camp, American officers shouting military commands, and the crunch of boots marching along the road.

Conversations about Pound shaded over frequently into Bacigalupo family matters and there was one story that particularly gripped me because it was so full of echoes and ironies. I heard it in bits and pieces, and then more completely when Massimo lent Kay a copy of a book written by his half-sister, Eleanor Erickson.*

As a twenty-year-old playboy medical student and tennis champion Massimo's father Giuseppe, known to friends and family as Bubi, was told by a girlfriend, Clara Orazi, visiting Rapallo from Rome, that she was pregnant to him. The year was 1932. Bubi must have reported this to his mother Elfriede, the German-born doctor in Rapallo, who seems to have gone into action at once, making arrangements for the young woman to be sent to live with one of her friends in Germany until the baby was born. In Germany Elfriede's friend was not able to take Clara at once so she was sent first to the friend's friend, Erna Uhlenbrock and her husband Friedrich. Throughout the pregnancy Clara waited in hope of a letter of concern or just a fond word from Bubi, with whom she was deeply in love, but none came. His mother had sent him to Siena ('far from the temptations of the Riviera' Massimo told me) to get on with his medical studies. Clearly she did not want

* Eleanor Erickson, *So They Will Not Forget: An Autobiography*, AuthorHouse, 2006. In this account she calls her foster parents Mutti and Vati rather than by their names, so my account will slip into referring to them thus.

him burdened so young with the cares of parenthood, and neither did he.

Meanwhile the Uhlenbrocks were kind and loving and invited Clara to stay on with them. Since there appeared to be no hope of marriage, Clara intended to hand the child to nuns to be brought up by them as an orphan, or adopted out; but when the baby was born the Uhlenbrocks, who had two grown-up daughters of their own, offered to take the baby. It seemed the best possible outcome, and Clara accepted.

The baby, Eleanor, born in 1933 in the year when Hitler took power in Germany, was to grow up believing that the Uhlenbrocks were her Mutti and Vati, and that she was German. German was her language from birth, and she experienced the war as a Berliner, feeling herself loyal to the Fatherland, and regarding her Vati's rages against Hitler and the Nazis as an inexplicable and more and more dangerous embarrassment which she had to help her Mutti to conceal.

Sometimes for the child there were intimations that she was different. Why was her surname Orazi on school records when Mutti and Vati were the Uhlenbrocks? It was an Italian name and an embarrassment to the child. She was possibly eight when her blind uncle, saying goodbye after a visit, embraced her and she thought she caught sight of something yellow under his lapel. Jews had to wear the yellow star – but the uncle was Mutti's brother, which would make her mother a Jew. That could not be so, and she decided it must be something he had to wear so people would know he was blind.

As the bombing in Berlin grew more intense, and every night they had to trudge down five flights of stairs to the air-raid shelter, her father moved them out of town to a small village; but then there was a problem about ration cards (food, clothing, almost everything was by now strictly rationed) and, mysteriously, Mutti had to spend all week in Berlin, coming to the village only in the weekends.

In 1946 when the war was over a letter came addressed to her as Eléanora Orazi. This triggered an explosion of mother–daughter emotion which led to some of the questions that had been suppressed being asked and answered. Eleanor was told who her real parents were. After that revelation she learned over time that the woman she loved as her Mutti was a Jew and had been protected at first only by the fact that her father, her Vati, was Aryan, a Catholic, and had won the Iron Cross in World War I. Meanwhile Mutti's two older daughters by a previous marriage had escaped Germany, one to England, the other to America.

It was only now, after it had happened, that Eleanor learned how the web had closed on her Jewish Mutti, and how narrow her escape from the death camps had been. A bribe of one hundred thousand deutschmarks had been paid by Vati to an SS officer with a promise that his wife, who was soon to be 'picked up' as a Jew, would not be sent to one of the camps but would survive. They had no choice but to pay the money, take this on trust, and hope it was true. So Mutti had been taken with a group of Jewish women to Oranienburg, the closest (35 kilometres) concentration camp to Berlin. There they were kept in one large room for more than a day, during which one by one, with long gaps, their names were called and they were given a slip of paper indicating where they would go next. After many hours there was only Mutti and one other; and then only Mutti. When her name was called the slip of paper she was given revealed that she was classified as *arbeitendes Familienmitglied*, an Aryan category which meant she was free to go.

After the war Eleanor immigrated to the United States, taking Mutti with her.

For me hearing this story the ironies were huge, and the parallels extraordinary – not least Eleanor growing up with German-speaking Mutti and Vati, and Mary with Tyrolean German-speaking Mamme and Tatte, both of them believing as little girls that these were their parents and this was where they belonged – and then discovering as the war came to its grisly end, that the truth was quite otherwise.

And then there was the Jewish factor, and Pound the anti-Semite. It seemed clear that Massimo's family must have been supporters of Mussolini – probably not enthusiastic Fascists, but passive accepters of the status quo. Their dealings with Pound were extensive, but mainly medical. Had they heard his broadcasts from Rome Radio, and later from Milan? Probably not, but (sailing with him for example, playing tennis with him, in social encounters) they must have heard that sort of stuff direct from the man himself. When I asked Massimo about this he said his father thought Pound 'half-crazy, an innocuous eccentric'.

Massimo reminded me that Jews were a small minority in Italy and well assimilated – which was true; but anyone who has read novels like Giorgio Bassani's *The Garden of the Finzi-Continis* knows that Italy's enforcement of anti-Jewish laws after 1942 was no small matter, either in the numbers deported to the death camps, nor in the impact. In a paper about the American poet Robert Lowell's relationship with Pound, Massimo quotes Lowell writing to Ezra, 'I love you, laugh with you . . . Still I have no mind for your gospel, and don't let us talk about Jews. I have several on my family tree, and . . . but let's drop it.'* I imagine that is how Massimo might have responded if he had been old enough to engage with Ezra on the subject.

Postscript:
Pound conferences were held at different locations and one I attended in July 1995 took place in Brantôme, chosen because Périgord, the region of the troubadour poets, figures so importantly in Ezra's life and writing. It was there I saw – the whole conference saw – Pound's opera *Le Testament de Villon* performed in one of the immense caves in the wall of rock that looms above the town, which

* Massimo Bacigalupo, 'Robert Lowell and Ezra Pound in Washington and Rapallo', *Robert Lowell in a New Century*, Camden House, 2019, pp. 96–104.

is itself built on an island formed where the river Dronne divides into two parallel streams. It was a fitting setting for a bizarre event.

It was in Brantôme I met again an American academic, Professor Gail Holian of Georgian Court University, Lakewood, New Jersey, previously met at an earlier Pound conference in Rapallo. Gail, now in charge of a department, invited me to visit and deliver a public lecture there. Travel costs and accommodation would be covered and I would receive a fee. The arrangement offered was generous and Autolycus, now seeing everything as potential 'material', accepted.

The story I called finally 'The Name on the Door is Not Mine'* had begun using material from my month or so, years previously, in Edmonton as the University of Alberta's 'Distinguished Visitor'. In that first section the famous (fictional) Canadian poet Alban Ashtree is supposed to have died (an appropriately alliterative death) in an avalanche in the Austrian Alps. In a later addition to the story I had brought my travelling academic, Henry Bulov, home to Auckland where he begins to make a name for himself as an international expert on the work of Alban Ashtree. It was a narrative that still needed a resolution, so now, in the course of the visit to Lakewood, New Jersey in winter, once again this story would be what I described in letters to Kay as 'my knitting'. The narrative that began in a white landscape of a North American winter would end similarly. Alban Ashtree emerges from his faked death, but only to meet in secret the academic who has promoted his work, confirming and even extending its fame. The story is really a comic-satiric view of academic success and literary reputation. The continuity of the fame, which the poet wants and the academic needs, depends on Ashtree remaining dead, while Bulov continues to write about him; so poet and academic come to an agreement which will keep the name alive and the poet dead.

Once again as in Edmonton I made shameless use of place and people. Gail Holian and her partner of the time, and even Gail's

---

* The title story of *The Name on the Door is Not Mine*, Allen & Unwin, 2016.

elderly mother, are all in the story pretty much as they were in reality; and the ride by limo into New York, taken as a birthday present for the mother, happened as in the story. But fiction is fiction; people that begin in fact seldom remain there, static. They shift, like 'facial recognition' images, altering as the narrative demands. They declare themselves, especially in speech, and every one becomes an aspect, an emanation, of the author. Each one is as much me as him/her self. And of course the lotto ticket (did Ashtree cheat them out of the big prize which should have been shared?) and the poet who agrees to 'die' so his work may live, were inventions, parts of the satire on academic and literary lying and faking. It's the story of Henry Bulov, a less than top-class academic, and how he makes his way in that world by typical and largely harmless kinds of deception.

But there was an additional truth that had no place in the fiction but has a place in this present narrative of Pound and the Bacigalupos. The very capable and rather lovely Gail Holian thought I should visit Yale while I was in the region; so a dinner was arranged for me at the university and there I met Omar Pound, Ezra's legal son though (and this was not to be mentioned in the presence of the man himself who valued his Pound entitlement) the biological son only of Ezra's wife. I have floated the suggestion that the real father might have been Ernest Hemingway, but Massimo dismisses this, believing that Omar's (now the late Omar's – he died in 2010) father was probably an Egyptian diplomat Dorothy met on a Nile cruise when she took off from Rapallo on hearing that her rival was pregnant.

My meeting with Omar was affable and he greeted me as someone agreeably affirmative about, and expert in, Ezra's work. He gave me a copy of a collection of his own poems, *The Dying Sorcerer*, suitably inscribed. They were not at all Poundian poems – more like the work of an uncertain Imagist, but with momentary fond and sad memories of a childhood spent in England.

7. The Writer at Work – 1990s

The *Listener* letter

It was not supposed to be known, which meant everyone in the know knew, that when I was very young, and long before Maurice Shadbolt and I were friends, he had published a story in the *Listener* and I, in collaboration with Kay and with Frank Sargeson and possibly also Janet Frame, had written a letter to the editor saying (more or less) what an awful piece of horseshit it was. When Stephen Stratford was interviewing me for his 1990 'Why the literati hate C. K. Stead' article in *Metro* he asked me, twice, whether I had written it, and my answer, twice, was no. If he had asked again and I had said no a third time a cock might have crowed and Maurice might have been crucified. The reason for this lie was that thirty-five years had passed and I couldn't even begin to explain this event without implicating Frank who was now dead. But on the other hand when Conrad Bollinger asked me the same question I replied in the affirmative with a ringing sonnet which, since it didn't say who was intended, would only (except again to 'those in the know') be meaningful as a general statement, not as a particular and personal one.

> 'Did you write that sharp-tongued letter?' Yes, I wrote it
> Two decades ago, because a story in a journal –

How can I explain? – simply, it went over my nerves
Like a note off-key, like the goodwill of a salesman

His foot in your door. Why quibble about one story?
But that voice has gone on sounding until now it's known

And honoured and echoed through all the echoing rooms
Of this high house of Culture you and I

Are committed to – and still to my ear, Conrad,
It's false, factitious, fabricated, vain.

April is our *helden* season when the new toi toi
Ride into heaven and the old men march again.

I no longer write such letters – nor disown them.
Petitions from the faithless, they lie in the lap of the gods.

But 'the *Listener* letter' was like T. S. Eliot's 'that corpse you planted last year in your garden – has it begun to sprout?' It sprouted again and again. By the early 1990s I thought I'd smelled the last of it, but then Maurice himself dug it up, using it to illustrate how, right from the beginning of his career, he'd faced adversity and malice. He described it as his 'rough introduction to the literary life', a 'bruising initiation',* and loaded the blame unfairly on Sargeson, whom he maligned ('a vain, preening and rather paranoid man') while conceding that a small part of the blame fell on 'a youthful acolyte' who 'served as a hit man'. Monte Holcroft, editor of the *Listener*, on the other hand, emerged with honour.

I would not have been made aware of this if Michael King, in the role of the 'sneaky one', which Janet Frame and I had assigned to him when he was writing her biography, had not brought it

* *One of Ben's: A New Zealand Medley*, David Ling, 1993, p. 192.

to my attention. It was when he accused me of advocating 'the ethnic cleansing of New Zealand literature' and I threatened him, and *Metro*, where he had said it, with an action for defamation, and demanded an apology and retraction. These were duly given, and Michael wrote me a note saying his apology was 'sincere, not just a formality' and that the 'phrase in question had leapt out of the word processor as I was polishing and invigorating for *Metro*'. But he said he didn't know why I'd picked on his comparatively innocuous piece when others had said things 'of a much more defamatory nature' about me, and gave as an example 'Shadbolt in his forthcoming autobiography' which Michael had seen in proof.

This prompted me to write to Maurice, and a quite amiable and worthy exchange followed in which I acknowledged fault for a lot that had gone wrong between us since those days of early friendship in London, and told him how I had come to respect him for 'keeping on' and never allowing himself to be put off his chosen path, and he assured me that no harm was done to me in his forthcoming book.

The subject of the *Listener* letter was complicated because Frank had been the driver, I had written it, and Kay had signed it using her old Henderson address; and Holcroft, Frank's real target, had clipped the last sentence or two, pretending in a footnote that in this he was protecting Maurice from worse when in fact he was removing the part that criticised him for lack of editorial taste. I summed all this up best from my point of view in a letter to Maurice which said:

> I'm not going to be very Frank about the letter of 1955, but it's worth saying that in that year FS and Janet and Kay and I formed, for a brief time, a wonderful and slightly deranged quartet, Frank 53, Janet an adolescent 30 or 31, CKS 22 and Kay 21 – so of course Frank dominated, but it was full of magic and rudeness and good reading and bad taste and malice and poetry and paranoia and wit – and tremendous fun. There were

Friends and Enemies. None of us knew you. All knew, or knew of, Holcroft, who was by Frank's definition an Enemy; and the truth about the letter to the *Listener* will never be known unless its full text is discovered. Holcroft did a very clever thing by cutting off its last sentence and giving the impression that he was protecting 'Maurice Shadbolt' when he was in fact protecting himself. Not that that's an excuse for the letter – but then who would have thought it would be remembered even four weeks after it appeared, let alone four decades? I, at least, had not the faintest notion that we were already living in something called 'literary history'. Had I known I would have been better behaved.

S. S. and the SS, and Karl

One who was never unconscious that he was living in literary history, in fact making it, was Stephen Spender whose possibly most famous poem (read at his funeral by Ted Hughes) began 'I think continually of those who were truly great'. I've written a number of times about Spender.* One was particularly difficult because it was to be for Alan Ross's *London Magazine*. I'd had lunch a number of times with Alan, and sometimes with Spender too, at their favourite Italian restaurant, Piccolo di Venezia, a meal always accompanied by a bottle of Lambrusco, a sparkling red Alan favoured. Stephen had so many enemies (who did not know him personally but knew that for one reason or another he was deplorable) and so many friends who knew him well, knew his faults and failings because he made confession almost his speciality, all of whom (as his biographer records), at least liked him very much, or loved him. I didn't know him well enough to be called a friend, but what I did know I liked; there was something

---

* 'Stephen Spender – Inside the Great "O"', *The Writer at Work*, pp. 138–45; and 'Big Spender and Little Matthew', *Shelf Life*, pp. 429–36.

innocent and loveable about him, as well as picturesque and posh, famous and faintly ridiculous. And there was about his poetry the feeling that it was on the edge of being what it was not, major, the work of a truly important poet. His life was like that too; he mixed with the 'truly great' as well as thinking about them continually – but was not himself one of them. How could I make something of this perception without being as frank about it as I can be now?

I did it first with an anecdote. I had been in Germany, in Tübingen, with a Scandinavian student called Svenja who took me to the little garden overlooking a river and under the tower where the poet Hölderlin, because he was mad, or thought to be, had been incarcerated for thirty-five years and where he had continued to write poetry. The vines that covered the walls and base of the tower were turning orange and gold as were the trees that covered an island in the river. We had already been to a nearby tavern, a single ancient room with crooked wooden beams, for a piece of the local onion pie and a drink of the frothy local Swabian wine that tasted like a cross between wine and cider. After that we had crossed a bridge over the river to the island and there, under big trees sending down showers of leaves, Svenja had pointed out to me a huge statue erected by the Nazis representing a nineteenth-century composer of folk music. Out of his bronze pockets and from under his bronze coat emerged small armed men, soldiers, showing that the might of Germany sprang from its folk tradition.

I was puzzled by the feeling of strangeness-and-familiarity that crept over me as I experienced this place, until it all came together in the notion that I was inside a poem by Stephen Spender, 'one which, like the very best of his poems, has never been written'.

And then, having planted that small explosive device in the piece I was writing about him I escaped into anecdote, but allowing myself a glance at 'I think continually of those who were truly great', describing it as a Wordsworth in Shelley's clothing, and observing that 'To press too hard on these images, to require of them an exact logic (how can an hour be a sun endless and singing?)

is to undermine the quality peculiar to Spender the poet.' They make a kind of 'half-sense', I suggested, 'which must be completed by the reader'. 'In Spender's most authentic poems the reader's complicity is won or lost by eloquence.' And then back once again to the big picture, the literary world in which he figured always and so importantly, a sort of ambassador for poetry itself as well as a spokesman for free speech. Curnow read this piece and wrote to me 'here is that metaphysical magic of yours [. . .] the piece of Stead's mind that lends itself to another writer. I suppose that's the secret of real criticism.'

Around this time I was walking in a London street with Christopher MacLehose and we were stopped by Christopher's friend, the Liberal peer Mark Bonham-Carter, who wanted to show us a little book he had just acquired. He put the book down on the nearest car bonnet which at once set off its alarm; but Bonham-Carter, undeterred, simply moved on up the street, away from the racket, and tried again. The book was the list of people, drawn up by the German SS, of those who were to be summarily dealt with when England was invaded; and there, among the names marked for death, in black German Gothic, was **Steffan Spender**. It seemed to mark out his importance – that even the potential invader should know about him and want to be rid of him. What his son Matthew's book *A House in St John's Wood* (2015) would reveal is that Stephen had anticipated this and had a suicide plan, one which as a somewhat serious daily swimmer I understood and could take entirely seriously: if the Germans occupied England he would simply swim out to sea until he was so far out that even if he lost courage and changed his mind he would be too exhausted to be able to get back and would drown.

In October 1992 Kay and I were to occupy the Spender house in Loudoun Road while Stephen and Natasha retreated to their getaway in Provence, *Mas-Saint-Jérôme*, to escape what she called 'a besiege' by journalists that followed a new biography that was somewhat more frank than the family welcomed about Stephen's bisexuality. Natasha had responded to this not on the whole unfriendly account of Stephen by writing a sort of rebuttal in the *TLS* which only succeeded in making matters worse. So now we were to guard the home front while they retreated to the white hills of Maussane-les-Alpilles and the beautiful garden she had created there.

Only recently I came upon a notebook I was keeping at this time and it casts another light on this couple whom I had got to know better when my old friend Barry Humphries married (his fourth wife) their daughter Lizzie who inherited her father's statuesque and blond-blue-eyed good looks. Barry and Lizzie appeared not unwilling to support Natasha in her determination that she and Stephen should be seen as a conventionally happy heterosexual couple; and it would only be when the Spenders were both dead that their son Matthew's book, *A House in St John's Wood*, would disclose, in a kindly and loyal but truthful way, how 'willpower' on his mother's part and 'good manners' on his father's kept up this pretence, while Stephen from time to time fell in love with this or that male acquaintance.

The recently discovered notebook has an entry:

> 14/10/92 We are now in the Spender house. The night before we moved in I had supper with them – 'Snackeroodles' Natasha called it, though it turned out to be melon first, then beef with cauliflower and rice, and then, when N said 'What next? Just silly old fruit?' Stephen asked for zabaglione, which N obligingly whipped up. Meanwhile S and I had begun with g & ts and had drunk most of a bottle of Bordeaux given them by Valerie Eliot. (N had drunk only a thimble-full.) The zabaglione tasted strongly of brandy – and there were chocolate biscuits with it, and coffee. (Snackeroodles?) The beef was rare and tough and one thought about mad cow disease; but we all sawed away vigorously and chewed and sawed and swallowed and asked for more. They told me there

> were squirrels in the roof and a man was coming to drive them out and cut branches of a tree that gave them access. Next day when Kay and I arrived America, the cleaning lady, told us the man had found no squirrels in the roof and the tree was duly trimmed. That evening at sundown I looked out of the bathroom window and there, silhouetted against the red sky, were two, then a third, then a fourth squirrel, racing around the trimmed branches, chattering madly, going to the outermost points trying to discover what had happened to their road home. They had gone out for a day's work and come home to what was, no doubt, their winter retreat in the roof, to find themselves evicted. Bosnians. A natural tragedy.
> 16.10.92 Last evening I found Stephen's notebook-journal for Jan 1962–June 1963. He had cleared out two drawers in his desk for me to use, and the journal was among things stuffed into drawers on the other side. Probably most of it went into the published journals but it added flavour to read them in the original holograph.

The house had been rented by the Spenders for about half a century and had probably been protected over those years from significant rent increases by the Fair Rents Act. It was in a state of disrepair and internal disorder – the problem being one a person of my present age understands, being much less a failure of orderliness by the occupants than of their having acquired too much valued stuff over too long a life. There was what must have been an extraordinary archive of papers downstairs in a small room next to the large kitchen where meals were taken. This room contained nothing but cabinets, some of them glass-fronted, all their doors bulging, some appearing to be held closed with something like sellotape. It was a bibliographer's happy dream and nightmare all in one. In the rest of the house the books in the many bookcases were two deep, and on the upstairs landing there was a five- or six-foot-high pile of books in no sort of order, completely covered with an Indian rug. There was also an alarm system wired (I discovered when I made a mistake with the access code) to the local police station. The paintings were notable and valuable – I think a Picasso, certainly a Rouault near the front door and a John Piper in the bedroom. The bathroom had been decorated – painted – by Matthew the sculptor son who had written a very good book, *Inside Tuscany*, about his property there which the Italian director Bertolucci had used as the scene of one of his movies.

It was a happy chance to be the occupiers and I had my sixtieth birthday there.

The notebook entry of 16.10.92 quoted on page 162 concludes:

> Karl Miller has resigned very publicly from his editorship of the *LRB* with an article about it in the *Guardian*. I rang Mary-Kay yesterday and she confirmed that the paper will continue and she wants me to go on writing for it.

Karl had disagreed with Mary-Kay Wilmers (their disagreements in the *LRB* office were loud and legendary) over something relatively trivial and failed to agree. Karl reminded her that he was editor and his wishes had to prevail; she reminded him that she was owner of the paper (said to be losing money hand over fist, and she bore the losses bravely). He wrote her a letter pointing out that the etiquette of journalism is that the editor not the owner is responsible for what the paper prints, and offered his resignation. It seems he didn't mean it except as a warning that if she tried to overrule him she might lose him. She accepted his resignation.

It was a terrible blow to Karl, worse because in this same month his tenure as professor at UCL came to an end. He wrote his article about it in the *Guardian* and then regretted it. He reverted to the subject a year later in his 1993 book *Rebecca's Vest* (pp. 167–68) where the pain was acknowledged:

> I'd had enough practice at this sort of thing to be prepared for what happens when you stop doing what you have been doing, with a will, for a long time. What happened this time, however, has been worse, and grief is the only word for it I can think of.

'Material'

In the European summer of 1993 I was back again – in Rome, in Rapallo, in London and Paris, and then in Dinard in Brittany, still in pursuit of 'material' – the people and places for this novel *Villa Vittoria* that was giving me so much trouble; and at the same time trying to sort out my affairs with publishers – Christopher MacLehose with whom relations were back on track after an interruption; Faber, for whom I was writing 'A Note on Absences' for my *South Pacific Short Stories*; and (more cheerfully) Paul Otchakovsky-Laurens whose publishing firm POL produced that year a classic French-style plain-cover edition of *The Death of the Body*, renamed *Je ne suis pas ce corps* (*I am not this body*), a title I regretted not having used for the English edition. Paul also arranged for publicity shots to be taken of me in Paris settings, and for the novel to be discussed on a Paris television programme, *Le Bateau livre*, devoted to books.

So five or six years after its publication in English, France appeared to be taking to *The Death of the Body* enthusiastically. Allen Curnow was receiving news of this from his brother Tony in France and wrote, 'What a welcome your two French reviewers give you between them – DOB has made its conquest of Gallic mind and taste – "le coeur des choses" – you deserve to be pleased!' A review in *Le Nouvel Economiste* by Gilles Plazy (13 August 1993) began 'Le Néo Zéalandais C. K. Stead a de l'intélligence, de la sensibilité et de l'humeur' . . . and ended commending 'ce roman fort bien mené et joliment pervers' (this finely managed and delightfully perverse novel).

In Dinard I stayed with Caroline Forbes on a farm I think she (or perhaps her mother) owned, though she lived mostly in a modest terrace house in Hammersmith. I'm not sure at what point I made the decision but it was here in rural France *Villa Vittoria* was going to end. I liked Caroline very much – a woman in her late thirties with one son to a Japanese man she had married during a brief time in America and had since divorced. The son was out of sight, probably at boarding school. Caroline was a professional photographer used by Harvill, and one of her shots of me was on the back jacket of *The End of the Century at the End of the World*. When I think of her I remember being told this or that was 'not right' – said with a downward tilt of the chin and a frown. More often than not it was herself she was reproaching. But there was also a lot of fun with her; a lot of laughs. She said she distrusted charm but was charming herself.

I had to show her how to chop kindling; but on the other hand I could see she had done mighty work clearing a field of nettles and brambles to make a vegetable garden. She had spent some of her childhood with her maternal grandparents, the Earl and Countess of Stradbroke. The grandmother was the daughter of the Duke of Westminster, but none of that vast wealth came her way, and the Stradbroke lands were entailed, so they considered themselves poor. Her father, a naval man, left her two sweaters when he died. Her mother, who was Christopher MacLehose's close friend before he married French Koukla, was Lady Penelope. Caroline had the accent that goes with the family silver and I imagine is less easily lost. She gave me a jeans jacket that had belonged to her grandfather the Earl and for a few years afterwards I kept it at Karekare and wore it there. She had done a BA in English at York University and had a boyfriend there who later tracked her down via *Burke's Peerage* and, when refused a re-entry into her life, wrote rude comments in a visitors' book when an exhibition of her photographs was showing at the Lyric in Hammersmith.

Caroline taught me to make a Spanish omelette in a heavy iron pan with a lot of olive oil, the potatoes, green peppers and onions cut up small and cooked in deep oil, the eggs beaten a little, not too much, and added to cook (I think – Kay thinks not) slowly – then allowed to cool and eaten cold next day. She smoked guiltily, always breaking a bit off the cigarette before lighting it, and taking only half a dozen puffs and stubbing it out. In cafés with her I learned to order *citron pressé* – pure squeezed lemon which came with large amounts of sugar to be stirred in, according to taste. I can still see the sugar grains swirling in the pale greenish liquid on a very hot day and remember the sense of a coolness-to-come that prickled like rain on the roof of the mouth.

Caroline told me about a novel, *Naomi* by Jun'ichirō Tanizaki, in which a mature man falls in love with a girl thirteen years his junior. He begins as her benefactor but gradually falls under her spell and in the end is totally abased. Caroline lent it to me (or Miranda in one or another draft of my novel lent it to Steve) and I (or he) read it in the cornfield and found it painful, distressing as the man's love is exploited to make him a slave. Caroline said she recognised how wonderful it would be to be loved like that, but also how corrupting.

Our friendship was brief and vivid, and I invented scenes for the novel and was later unsure whether they happened or were merely fiction. Did Caroline say she would need not less than five years of my life or she would have none of it – or did I invent that for the character of Miranda?

Adieu, S. S.

Seventeen July 1995 was a Monday and I was in Paris on my way to the Pound conference in Brantôme, my notebooks and my head still full of endless tiresome changes of mind and direction about the novel that would be *Villa Vittoria*, when I heard the news that Stephen Spender had died of a heart attack the day before, exactly one week after I'd had supper at a Piccadilly restaurant, Le Caprice, with Stephen and Natasha, Barry and Lizzie. When I got to Brantôme Barry had called daughter Charlotte (living in London at the time) to ask where he could reach me, and she rang to tell me that Barry was hoping I would be at the funeral. I sent cards to Lizzie and Natasha saying how shocked and sorry I was, and rang Barry to tell him I didn't think I could abandon the conference for the obsequies. The truth was I really wanted to see that Pound opera performed in a cave (not a good choice on reflection – the funeral would have been more interesting).

A week or so later, on the brink of returning to New Zealand, I rang Barry for a farewell chat and he said how good it was that we'd all been together at supper with Stephen just a week before his death. He said he hoped I'd taken notes of everything that was said. I replied that yes I had of course, but evasively, feeling guilt that I might have failed in a duty.

'That amazing revelation about Hitler and D. H. Lawrence,' Barry said.

I didn't remember but agreed it had been extraordinary. And then after the call was finished and I was reproaching myself, the story came back to me – not about Hitler and Lawrence but Hitler and Hugh Walpole. Walpole had been in the habit of going on summer walking tours in Germany, and some German friends had said their friend Adolf was rather anxious and unhappy at the moment and would benefit from an outdoor adventure. Would Walpole consider taking him along as a companion?

So he did, and they got on reasonably well. Hitler walked mostly in silence but now and then could be enticed into conversation, and could be entertaining, especially doing imitations of his enemies. This was probably in the late 1920s, but Stephen said he had met people who had known Hitler much later and they too said his mimicry was clever and funny, especially of Neville Chamberlain.

Did I have nothing else to report about Stephen's death? There is nothing more in that notebook – clearly I was nobody's Boswell, though I suppose it would be fair to say Spender was nobody's Dr Johnson. What I had recorded at this time was something quite different – a (to me) delightful *Paris* moment:

> 23/7/95 Last evening about 11 p.m une rencontre dans la rue Mabillon (auprès de l'église St Sulpice) – both of us impatient – 'Allez, Monsieur '– 'Allez-y' – 'No please, après vous'– with a middle aged man who, when I looked up, was . . . *Marcello Mastroianni!* The star of Fellini's *La dolce vita*, my favourite movie! I felt my face break into such a look of recognition, smiling as if I'd known him for years (as indeed I had). He smiled back, recognising my recognition and accepting it as the compliment it was meant to be – and accepting now my insistence that he go first between the two parked cars. Nothing was said or needed to be.

But the notebook is mainly crowded with lengthy frustrated accounts of plans and false starts in a novel that had been going faster backwards than forwards.

Fathers and sons

Kay and I were to see more of Karl Miller in the years that followed his departure from the *LRB*; and he was less the grumpy overworked editor-professor and more the wry and very funny Karl, the man I'd always known was there, but demanding too much of himself and everyone around him. Now he was free to write his own story, which he did up to a point. He always came to my book launches when they were in London (three at New Zealand House), and we sometimes had a meal at home with the Millers, or (our shout) at a restaurant. Jane was Jewish, professor at the London Institute of Education and sister-in-law of the famous opera and theatre director Jonathan Miller (no relation to Karl). She had written an autobiography in which she mentions Karl as seldom as he mentions her in his. This was not an indication of any kind of estrangement – far from it; but in her case the family self, and in his the professional self, not the spouse, was subject. Nonetheless she does dedicate hers to Karl; his is dedicated to no one.

There was a supper at 26 Limerston Street when the short story writer and literary journalist Francis Wyndham was also present. He had brought a video of a movie about Lucian Freud in which Wyndham, whom Freud had painted a number of times, figured; and we sat (I'm not sure why) on cushions on the floor and watched it.

There was another occasion, after a book launch, when we were travelling with Karl and Jane in a taxi to a party at the house of Christopher MacLehose whose formidable wife, Koukla, we agreed, meant no harm but had a manner that made you uncertain whether you should have accepted an invitation. Karl said he always had to repress a strong inclination to say, as the door opened, 'Good evening Koukla, I'm sorry I'm here.'

Justin Paton, editor of *Landfall* in 2001, thought of asking Karl to review my *The Writer at Work*. I would never have suggested it, nor expected Karl to agree to do it, but he did,* adding remarks also on my novel of 1999, *Talking about O'Dwyer* which, he pointed out, revealed Stead (contrary to one popular view) to be 'far from indifferent or hostile' to the Māori contribution to life in New Zealand. It was a review in a tone I was unused to seeing in anything about myself, in *Landfall* or anywhere in New Zealand – by no means agreeing with me on everything, but so relaxed and accommodating.

> In the course of a lecture of 1993 at the University of Otago [Stead] said that he hadn't 'really set out to be contentious on this occasion', but had possibly slipped into it. This brought a smile, all those thousands of miles away [. . .] In London too, as in New Zealand, he is known to have been contentious. And in the Otago lecture, which occurred towards the end of the heyday of the delusional barrenness of literary theory, he'd only a moment before said that literary theory had

* 'Talking About Stead', *Landfall* 201 (Autumn 2001), pp. 176–79.

> been 'like an auto-immune reaction, the cells of the body of literature attacking and destroying themselves'.
>
> It's good that he has been contentious, willing to risk offence for good reason.

In this review Karl allows himself a personal aside in parenthesis:

> Perhaps I should also declare that in an introduction to this book he describes me as abrasive in the sense of 'dour'. Scots people, even those who are as dour as budgerigars, get used to being called by that name. Stead remarks here that he is not thought, by those who know him personally, to live up to his reputation. This is true of Stead. And I keep saying it of myself.

He discusses seriously, and with reservations about it, what he calls my aestheticism – my resistance to moralising in literature and literary criticism, likening me to two of my academic contemporaries in America, Helen Vendler and Harold Bloom, both in trouble, as I had been, for declining to bend aesthetic judgements to match the requirements of the race/gender ethic. I was happy with all of this because it was a necessary discussion which could never reach a final and 'right' conclusion, but needed to continue as long as we took literature seriously; and the positions I take now are probably nearer to Karl's than they were in the book he was reviewing. What pleased me even more was that in 'this engrossing book', he said, 'the foreign reader discovers [...] what it has been like to be' a New Zealand writer, and 'to be this one in particular, a Kiwi agonistes.'

Karl also wrote a cover blurb for the Carcanet edition of my *Collected Poems, 1951–2006*, and two years later a beautiful little book came from him on my birthday. I had no idea he knew what my birthday was or why he should notice it this year or any other. It could only have been an impulse, an affectionate one, inscribed 'Happy Birthday Karl from Karl, October 08'. I had known it pleased him that we were both Karl with a K (we both felt Carl would seem less strong and that the K had a whiff of Marx about it); also that he thought of us both as 'outsiders', though his distance from what we conceived of as the 'centre' when young had been measured in hundreds of miles, mine in thousands. As I'd said about him in my poem for his seventieth birthday

> Scholarship Scot
> among the Simons at Downing
> you took
>
> bookish London
> by the back door
> making space for yourself

so if he was still removed from that (so conceived) 'centre', and still an 'outsider', it was only in the mind. To me he *was* the centre, and I was still where I had put myself and meant to remain, at its Pacific periphery.

When Karl died in 2014 Neal Ascherson remembered how the young Karl had treasured George Barker saying of him 'That boy! He's got a tiger in his loins.'

> I think he felt Barker had put the tiger in the right bit of him. Not so much sexually, though that implication was a nice bonus, but determination to do what it's in you to do. A tiger in the head or a tiger in the typewriter would not have rated.

He also remembers (something that seems to me to catch his subject's bizarre jokes perfectly) Karl behind his desk at the *New Statesman* greeting him with, 'Hullo Neal. I'd offer you a cigar but I've only got six left.'

Mary-Kay Wilmers remembered him as literary editor of the *New Statesman* when she was junior editor:

> He was a charismatic figure, tall, fair, slim, nattily dressed, flirtatious and a little wayward – a head-spinner. But severe too. You minded your words and that was part of the attraction. When he gave me a book to review I thought my life had met its moment.*

She concluded 'I'd like to think this is still very much Karl's paper.'

THREE BOOKS ABOUT THREE FATHERS I had known were published by three sons in three years – Matthew Spender's *A House in St John's Wood* in 2015, *Fathers* by Sam Miller 2016, and *My Father's Island* by Adam Dudding 2017. Matthew was the sculptor who had lived in Tuscany most of his adult life since running away from home with Maro (whom Natasha had never liked), the daughter of the artist Arshile Gorky. In the introduction to his book Matthew describes racing back to London immediately upon hearing news of his mother's death, and seizing the diaries and papers that would be the substance of his book – the most interesting and best written of the three. I noticed from his opening pages that the squirrels were back in the roof at Loudoun Road, and that some kind of order had been established in the little room next to the kitchen that housed the archive. In this on the whole affectionate account of his parents' marriage Matthew re-establishes the Stephen who was the good father and loyal but not faithful husband, and whose deviances from sexual fidelity were always with a male – the Stephen, in other words, who began his public literary life as companion of the notably gay Auden and Isherwood. He also reveals that his mother appears to have had an affair with the thriller writer Raymond Chandler, though whether it went beyond sheets of paper to bed sheets is unclear.

---

* This, and Neal Ascherson's memories of Karl, were published in the *LRB* in the issues immediately after his death.

Sam Miller's book is a warm account of his relations with Karl whom he refers to throughout as 'my father' but reveals that he learned only as a teenager, and from his mother, that his biological father was Karl's friend and fellow amateur footballer Tony White. Karl, it seems, knew about the circumstances in which this came about, and accepted it, but possibly did not know that the relationship was twice resumed. It's possible that it was a fact that operated as an excuse for his own infidelities, which I sometimes heard talked about in London but are only hinted at and neither confirmed nor denied by Sam.

There had been one thing in Karl's *Landfall* review of *The Writer at Work* that had struck me as odd. He spent a paragraph on my mention of Pound and his wife each having 'a child with an extramarital partner'; and followed this with mention of my essay about Claire Clairmont's child to Byron and possible child to Shelley. This is right at the end of the review, and concludes with some less than perfectly clear observations about my 'forbearance in relation to the vagaries of poet parents and poet spouses, and to other aspects of the ambiguous privacy of writers' – a forbearance he seems to link tentatively with 'aestheticism'. It's not important to try to tease out exactly what Karl meant there; only to observe that when I read this book by his 'son' I felt I knew why elements in my book of essays had pulled him somewhat off course into a thicket of ambiguities, and why he had preferred to stay there rather than explain.

The third of these books told of how our literary editor Robin Dudding, much admired by the New Zealand writing community, grew over the years, in his domestic dealings with wife Lois, five daughters and one son, into a morose tyrant. During this same period Robin was known to those of us who had dealings with him as usually genial, a keen table-tennis player on his outdoor table at Torbay on the North Shore, but more and more dilatory, agonisingly slow to make decisions and always failing to meet his deadlines. I gave offence by writing an entry about him in some kind of international directory and describing him as an excellent editor but 'saurian'; and Adam Dudding quotes me as saying, when he interviewed me for his book, that Robin was heroic but 'you can't go on being heroic in slow motion'.

I had one direct experience of this growing moroseness when I acted as my own publisher for two small collections of poems. I offered him a new short story for *Islands* on the understanding that he would see that my new book was reviewed. I didn't ask for favours – just a review. I thought I was doing what publishers did to promote their books, but he bridled; and when I said it was an understanding he would have to agree to if he wanted the story he told me that if I 'continued to behave like this I would be finished as a writer in New Zealand'. I bridled back and told him *Islands* needed me more than I needed it. I sent the story to the *Literary Review* which published it.*

In better times Robin had published a long poem of mine, 'Scoria',† a section of which was a recollection of the sounds of the domestic hens I was in charge of as a child, their clucking, their peculiar drawn-out caw that seems to signal nothing in particular but sounds like the languid complaint of a layabout, and their cackling, when an egg is laid, that might be outrage or panic, as if no such thing has happened to them before.

> Bk bk bk bkaa bkaaa
>   bkaa bkaaaa
> bk bk bk bk
>   bkaa bkaaaa
> bk bk bk
>   bk bk bk bk bk
> lay language

---

* 'A New Zealand Elegy', first published in *Literary Review*, Edinburgh, December–January 1979–80, and later in *Five for the Symbol*, Longman Paul, 1981.

† *Collected Poems, 1951–2006*, pp. 130–42.

                    your waking
subsiding (bk bk bk)
to the languid / discontented
kaaaaa
        kaaaaaa
        kaaaaaaa.

Robin had needed no translations for this poem's 'lay language'. I always said I spoke Chook better than French, because I had learned it in the right way, by ear – and in fact its orthography had had to be invented only after it had been learned as language. Robin could read it, and could recognise my account of the ritual of insemination – the rooster as matador – with the enthusiasm of one who was himself a keen breeder of bantams.

As the matador's cape concealed the steel
so the spread wing in sunlight
                        or a black shield
green in sunlight
the black knight strutting and shining
green in sunlight
under the red comb she goes down for
            as under a cloud
            as under a fiery banner
            crouching
to the packed soil
beyond the bean rows
black on black glinting
green in sunlight
                        shuddering
a moment only
                        ruffling
and back to
      picking and scratching

picking and
        scratching
it being important to scratch the packed earth
to the left and the right
    with thighs big like a peasant's
    under heavy skirts
importantly
        to the left and the right
picking in the scratches

But none of us knew (or I did not) of the darkening shadows on the home front in Sealy Road, Torbay, where poverty and neglect was leading to anger, squalor and embarrassment. It's the saddest of these three father/son stories, though once again the son is loyal and admiring of the father he is nonetheless putting on record in an unfavourable light.

When Robin died in 2008 the death notice said the funeral would be at Schnapper Rock on the North Shore. When Kay and I arrived at the crematorium chapel someone recognised us at the door, welcomed us warmly and said we should sit up near the front. We were not keen but were led forward and given prominent places. Then as we looked around we began to wonder why the chapel was not full of familiar faces. I became alarmed and asked the person beside me whose funeral this was. The name was not Dudding and we escaped just in time. Outside we found a notice directing us to the cemetery itself, and there on a hillside under trees was the freshly dug grave, the Dudding family and many familiar literary faces gathered around, waiting, we were told, for some Dudding aunts who were (like an issue of *Islands*) seriously late. But they arrived in two taxis and we heard a speech or two and sang old songs and ballads as Robin's wooden coffin, with fruit and flowers on the lid, was lowered into its green grave. This was followed by a celebration of his life at the local yacht club; and somehow Kay and I finished the day on the veranda of the writers' centre on the side of Mt Victoria in Devonport, with poets Chris Price, Greg O'Brien and Jenny Bornholdt (the first two had been students in my creative writing class and Greg had married the third), watching boats coming and going on the moonlit water. These were homely occasions for which I wrote a homely poem:

Waving Goodbye
to Robin

The working port is a sheet of noisy light
across the harbour. Greg thinks he hears men's voices
shouted above their fork-lifts, drifting
over the autumn water. Floodlit on the hill
the Museum stands to attention. Eastward
light and shadow scout's-pace the Waterfront Drive.

Kay and I and Chris, Greg and Jenny –
today we watched our editor Dudding let down,
fruit and flowers on his plain-wood coffin,
while we sang to trees and sky those arcane ballads
he liked to croon – 'Clementine', 'Yellow Bird',
'Cockles and Mussels' – a life remembered, rich
in songs and daughters, books and chooks and friends,
fruit, vegies, flowers, never quite in tune.

Some shadowy tug or fishing boat chugs by
discreetly, puttering over the silky water.
Summer is always ending. Five good friends
on one veranda now, we're looking across
to the brilliant city as if that were our past
and we at the rail, sailing out, waving goodbye.

8.
Who Would You Trust?

Villa Vittoria is published

We were still in the dark ages before children were born with a small electronic device in (usually) the right hand and the compulsion to click on it with one or both thumbs morning till night; and when novels were printed on paper and reviewed, bought and read as books. So there were many reviews of a new novel and these offered their likes and dislikes, and their reasons. The author always hoped the nicest would be seen and believed: these said (more or less) that he was one of our finest writers and had produced another gem. Naturally he clung to his preference for these; but he learned slowly to discriminate. There were some you could (and should) trust even if they didn't flatter; and others whose praise was undiscriminating, uncritical, even on occasion meaningless. At its simplest, the ones you should listen to proved their worth by being well written. Karl Miller's headline about 'The Age of Spite'* was not wrong – the literary world was full of it, and it was important that it should be recognised and ignored, walked around rather than confronted. Some sensitive writers (Craig Raine for example) did not read reviews – the experience was too painful. Craig's wife Li (Ann Pasternak Slater) read them

* In his *Guardian* piece about his loss of editorship of the *LRB*.

for him and told him whether he should or should not take a look. She'd advised against his reading my review of his *History* in *The London Magazine* though I had thought it quite admiring. Maurice Shadbolt claimed not to read them but I never quite believed him. Denis Glover said if you were wise you didn't read reviews, you measured them.

I read them, even though it was sometimes painful, because curiosity was so powerful. But when I now go through the files of reviews of *Villa Vittoria* I'm struck by how many there were in those days, and that though I may complain about my reception in New Zealand being often hostile, they are predominantly affirmative – even welcoming. The novel was 'hard to put down', 'a fascinating new direction for this superb writer', 'vintage Stead', 'should not be missed', 'in a class of its own when it comes to good sex and intelligent dialogue', 'elegant'. No there were no reasons for complaint and more than enough for celebration.

Damien Wilkins, who in 1992 had suggested that my novel *The End of the Century at the End of the World* hated itself for not being a poem, cited *Smith's Dream* and *The Death of the Body* as precedents.

> *Villa Vittoria* is perhaps his best-made novel. [. . .] Genre stuff maybe, but done with a light touch and a sure sense of timing, and always kept slightly and enjoyably off-centre by the author's own, well, *quirks of intelligence*. It feels recreational, but then C. K. Stead like Roland Barthes never dodged commitment to pleasure.*

Dell Panny in her book about me says 'Copies produced in Britain sold so rapidly that the book was out of print in five or six weeks with the next consignment still reprinting.'† I'm not sure this is accurate. I don't believe that there was any separate British edition.

* *Listener*, 8 March 1997.
† *Plume of Bees: A Literary Biography of C. K. Stead*, Cape Catley, 2009, p. 163.

I think copies sold there would have come from New Zealand, and would have sold out quickly because the number sent would have been small. If there were any British reviews I didn't see them. Penguin New Zealand was now on its own, and the Penguin imprint was no longer truly international as it had been when *The New Poetic* went into Pelican, or my Mansfield *Letters and Journals* appeared as a Penguin Modern Classic. In losing Harvill as my publisher I may have gained attention at home; but I had lost it in the wider Anglophone world and would be glad soon to get it back, whatever the cost at home.

That, then, is a glimpse of the making and publishing of what was in fact my seventh novel. It was as though I had gone in pursuit of material, of 'life in the wild', and had come back having given and received wounds, but with a trophy – a story which, if Roger Donaldson's luck had been better, might have been that big-screen movie he wanted it to be. The 'getting it right', the wrestle recorded in two notebooks, had been Jacobean (Henry rather than King, Jamesian, but perhaps both). So many alternatives were tried and rejected. I'd told Allen writing it had seemed like bending iron bars or shifting heavy furniture, but in the end it seemed, at least to the author, well told and worth doing. The dying Brasch reading *Smith's Dream* had asked his journal, 'How can I take Stead seriously after this?' Would his reaction to this one have been any different? I doubt it. This was (to use the word Wilkins settles on) 'recreational'; it was the game of literature, but played at a level that was beyond Brasch – beyond him to recognise that it did, and how it could, take itself entirely seriously and yet be 'fun'.

And meanwhile the other-and-overseas literary life, the more or less real one, involving Karl and Stephen and Caroline and Barry and Massimo and their milieux – London, Paris, Brantôme, Rapallo – and the histories those places and people brought with them into the story, or into its flavour, its tone, the note it struck – all of this, all of these, had been engaging me, keeping me on my toes, wearing me out. I look back on myself at that time, writing that book, meeting and engaging with those people, with a mixture of astonishment, pleasure, and not without twinges of guilt.

The Singing Whakapapa

This novel came before *Villa Vittoria* and was only published in New Zealand and Australia. I wanted to make use of the story of my great-great-grandfather, John Flatt, my earliest forebear in New Zealand, who came as a catechist (unordained cleric) with the Church Missionary Society arriving in the Bay of Islands in 1834 together with William Colenso. Of the two it was Colenso who was to be famous in our history – printer of the first Māori translation of the Bible, and recorder of the events leading up to and including the signing of the Treaty of Waitangi – while Flatt receded into an obscure corner of the annals from which it was my intention to rescue him and bring him into the light.

My grandmother Caroline Karlson (née Flatt) was John Flatt's granddaughter. She remembered him well and it was she who told me about his conflict with the Church that had first employed him and then sacked him. It was the question of why the Church Missionary Society had refused to re-employ this young man who was so keen to return to New Zealand, and how he had succeeded in making his way back without the Church's endorsement, that I wanted to make the crux of my novel; but I determined to (I suppose) complicate the narrative by having a central contemporary character, in some ways like myself, but a not wholly successful academic historian, Hugh Grady, undertaking the research that would give him the answers he sought about his forebears. At the time of my writing this novel Kay was still working in the New Zealand and Pacific section of the University of Auckland Library, so I had a ready researcher on hand, able and eager to scour records of the CMS and anything else that would cast light on that bit of our past. Kay became my 'Jean-Anne', the character in the novel who acts as Hugh Grady's assistant. But

Jean-Anne was Hugh's daughter, the offspring of his long-ago affair with her now out of sight mother Lydia – so in writing this novel I was also using my own affair with Jenny North which produced no offspring but has been recounted in *You Have a Lot to Lose*. Some of Jenny's letters to me had been kept and I used them in the novel; and in a farewell letter just before her death, Jenny wrote 'thank you for Lydia [her name in the novel]. I took her, and the use of my letters, as A Fitting Tribute'. This then was a novel unfolding family matters near and far.

I decided that I would impose a stylistic rule on myself in the writing: there would be no direct speech, no dialogue – none of that drifting into the default mode I was always warning myself against and called 'conventional fiction'. This was a considerable imposition; and I acknowledge that dialogue, which I enjoy writing especially when there's an element of discord or debate, can be crisp and brilliant. But I wanted this novel to have the virtues of narrative prose at its best; and also to avoid the wholly implausible representation in detail of what characters out of the past had said to one another, and what they had 'thought', in unrecorded moments and encounters. It was a hard rule to keep, and I lapsed now and then into brief direct speech exchanges, but only very occasionally, and on the whole *The Singing Whakapapa* achieved the kind of prose I was hoping for.* I began with a subject, or two subjects, and a stylistic principle and stuck to them; there would still be discoveries and invention along the way, but the path ahead was plain.

Some considerable time after the novel had been published, Tony Axelrad had retired from his work with the International Tribunal on the Yugoslav war, and he and Pat had moved to Norfolk. Kay and I visited them there and one day we all went by car in search of the village of Methwold in the surrounding countryside.

---

* 'Of our best-known novelists only Frame and Hulme write as well.' Kai Jensen, reviewing *The Singing Whakapapa* in *Printout*.

It was in this region that John Flatt had learned farming. In the Methwold churchyard many of the falling-over and derelict gravestones had been stacked along a stone fence surrounding the precinct of the church. Among these was a considerable number with the surname Flatt, some from the eighteenth century before John Flatt left, some from the nineteenth after his departure. As we walked back to the car Tony, whose forebears were Jews from Eastern Europe but had come to London via Scandinavia where they had acquired the name Axelrad, said, 'At least you know who you are.' It was an interesting observation, because I don't think I gained any particular and personal sense of 'identity' from those gravestones. John Flatt was one element in the genetic mix, English, Irish, Scots and Swedish, of which I was composed; but the sense of identity, despite, or perhaps because of, the mix was almost entirely Pākehā New Zealander. We had been here long enough for me to be confident of that, and to have lost any significant sense of blood connection with any one of several possible 'homelands'. There was, perhaps, a romantic attachment to the idea of my Swedish grandfather, and a feeling that it was his genes predominantly that had made me not only a writer, but the person I am. But the other connections, though very important, were intellectual and came from education and reading. My grandmother after all was the one who boasted that she was 'a real Pig Islander' by which she meant that, though born in 1871, she was the child of parents who were both themselves born in Aotearoa.

John Flatt had been appointed, on the basis of his farming knowledge (combined I suppose with the necessary dollop of piety and missionary zeal), to go as an agricultural assistant to the Bay of Islands mission; but he had found he was not welcome there. The Rev. Henry Williams and the Rev. Richard Davis were establishing their own little empire in the Bay, acquiring (without CMS sanction or knowledge) as much land as they needed from local Māori. They had ample workers and did not feel they needed an expert 'assistant', especially a young eager newcomer who might act as a spy. So Williams had sent Flatt on to the mission at Matamata, across the Kaimai Range from Tauranga, to work under the direction of the Rev. Alfred Brown, whose mission had been established under the protection of the local chief, Waharoa.

This part of his story has been told not only in the novel but also in my first volume of autobiography.* Waharoa's tribe, Ngāti Hauā, was threatened with attack by Te Arawa of Rotorua and it was decided that for the time being it would be safest to close the Matamata mission. Flatt was leading a group of young Māori over the Kaimais to the safety of Tauranga, and they stopped to camp for the night near the falls. A meal was prepared and eaten, prayers were said, and they retired for the night, the young Māori to a raupō hut, Flatt to his tent. In the early morning there was an attack by an Arawa raiding party. Alerted by their dogs, the group who had been sleeping in the hut ran off into the bush and escaped, but a young woman, Tarore, was killed outside John Flatt's tent. There are two or three vivid and horrified accounts of this event in Flatt's letters and reports. Tarore was killed 'with a small axe'. The top of her head was taken, and also her heart – trophies of a 'first kill' in a warrior engagement. Also taken was a flax kete around her neck which contained Colenso's printing of the Luke Gospel in Māori. Flatt himself, protected by the tapu that was accorded to the missionaries at the time, was stripped of everything but a shirt and his horse, and sent on his way to Tauranga.

At this point the story enters legend, and Flatt fades, or vanishes entirely. It was said that Tarore's copy of Luke converted the Arawa to Christianity and therefore to peace, and that thereafter there were no intertribal wars. War now, if it happened in Aotearoa/New Zealand, would be between Māori and Pākehā. So in 1977 the Māori Queen, Dame Te Atairangikaahu, had Tarore's grave identified and rededicated, with a picket fence, a white wooden cross, and a headboard saying 'Tarore [with details of her age and

---

* *South-West of Eden*, Chapter 7.

date of death] whose Māori gospel of St Luke brought peace to the tribes of Aotearoa' – no mention of John Flatt nor the brutal manner of her dying.

I REMEMBER PROFESSOR RAEWYN DALZIEL telling me 'I've read your novel, Karl' – by which she meant *The Singing Whakapapa*. Her tone was reproachful.

'And?'

She told me she preferred to get her history from the documents – which was what I thought I had done; but I concede there must be many more I had not looked at.

In the novel Tarore is outside the tent when she is killed because she has been inside it with John Flatt. There were two reasons for this apart from the convenience of fictional plot-parallels within the novel itself. The first was that there had been, at that time, such a fuss in the Anglican missionary community at the discovery that some of the young missionaries had been indulging in (hetero- and homo-) sexual adventuring with the natives, that it was decided all unmarried clergy, ordained or not, should be sent home to England to find themselves wives. Flatt was one of the number sent home for wiving. It was plausible, even likely, that he had been one of the guilty. The second was that when Kay and I climbed the Wairere Falls on the track across the Kaimais Flatt's group would have taken from Matamata to Tauranga, we could see the piece of beaten-flat ground on which the raupō hut had been built, and then there was nothing level enough for the pitching of a tent until quite a distance up the track. It was by no means conclusive; and in telling this part of the story in *South-West of Eden* I did not repeat what was only a fiction writer's guess. But it was hard to see how Tarore was killed (as Flatt reported more than once) 'outside my tent' if she had not emerged from inside it.

So in resurrecting Flatt I suppose I had also blackened his character in the eyes of the Church – and perhaps also (for all

I know) in the eyes of his family which I believe is quite extensive. Fiction is fiction – and one has perhaps greater responsibility when the characters have the names of real people. To me it remains more than plausible, and in no way a black mark on his character. He and Tarore were both young, and if there was sex between them in fact (as in the fiction indeed there was) let's hope there was also love – because it was an indiscretion which appears to have cost him his job. When Kay and I looked into this part of the record there was a half-page missing where an explanation for his not being reappointed would naturally have been offered. That the CMS would not have wanted any more reports of such behaviour made public would explain this excision. Better to remove him from the record and refuse him the chance he wanted to return to New Zealand than have another blot on the record of the Anglican Church there.

What is indisputably on record is that John Flatt's evidence to the 1838 Select Committee of the House of Lords set up to look into 'the State of the Islands of New Zealand' told of direct purchases of considerable blocks of land from the Māori by the missionaries – including Henry Williams and Richard Davis; and that this led, by a long slow process, first to Davis (protesting that all he had ever wanted was to 'live and die for the benefit of the heathen') being forced to move on from the large farm he had made his own to more mundane service in Kaikohe, and second to Williams being dismissed from his role as Archdeacon at Waimate in 1854. He was reinstated in 1869; but the shadow of the thousands of acres he had kept remained, and still hangs over his name. From time to time, even up to very recent years, the Anglican Church reaffirms his worthiness in a way which seems only to confirm the doubts. His compromise is representative of the Anglican Church in New Zealand. How could he, and they, deplore Edward Gibbon Wakefield and the New Zealand Company as colonists, while themselves profiting by the purchase of large tracts of Māori land?

Flatt's evidence, which was cited also by Wakefield, was made possible by his having been one of the unmarried mission-clergy sent home to find a wife; and it appears that it was while in London he was told he would not be reappointed to the mission. Perhaps it was as a direct consequence of that unwelcome news that he agreed to give evidence to the House of Lords hearing. He told his story in the mildest of tones, explaining why their many children meant these men – Williams for example with his 22,000 acres (later halved to 11,000) – were in dire need of land for the future of their families. It was like a 'turned' Mafia novice explaining to a police tribunal why certain murders, though regrettable, were necessary.

My novel gives an account of how he made his way back to New Zealand with his new wife, and his difficulties making a life for himself, first in the Bay of Islands, then in Auckland (Parnell, indeed) as a gardener. An encounter with Henry Williams on the foreshore at Paihia is recorded somewhere among Flatt's papers. He was in debt at the time, and desperate – and cheeky or foolish enough to ask Williams for a loan. Perhaps he asked tongue in cheek, knowing he would be refused. Who can say? What is clear is that Williams declined angrily and suggested that 'some of his rich friends in London' might buy him a dray. The dray was a class put-down; and the 'rich friends' in London a reference to the Wakefields.

But both the novel and the volume of autobiography about my early years had left out of the mix my other great-great-grandfather Martin McDermott, who had passed himself off as a Presbyterian Scottish settler.*

The issue of the moment

... when *The Singing Whakapapa* was published was Māori–Pākehā relations. When in New Zealand was it not? In the debates of the 1980s and '90s I had not stepped around it, but I had not stepped warily. I had given offence, sometimes suggesting there was a Pākehā side that deserved to be heard, that was in no sense anti-Māori,

* See Chapter 4, p. 80.

and that I was trying to give it an educated voice. This had put me sometimes in unwholesome company and in places I would prefer not to be; but I thought it was enough to be (so to speak) pure in heart, well-informed and with a clear conscience.

As I took *The Singing Whakapapa* around the country the debate travelled with me. Some (usually Pākehā) told me I had no right to that title; no right to use a word representing something that was sacred to Māori. I don't remember what I said in response but it would have been staunch, unapologetic. I claimed Aotearoa/New Zealand as my whenua. I did not have, or want, another. My family were well-established here and they were my whakapapa.

I seemed to be harried especially by Kim Hill. I had (and still have) the greatest regard for her as a broadcaster – admire her exceptional intelligence, her wit, her sense of humour, her grasp on complex subjects and her ability (in those days when she was on the *Nine to Noon* weekdays slot) to knock off a book a day (more, I'm sure, than her bosses required of her) and speak of them lucidly or ask comprehending questions about them. But she was very proper on the issues of the day, and seemed to have picked up out of the Wellington air that I was not. Maybe she'd had to share an elevator with Victoria's journeyman of literature Roger Robinson and caught his chill. Maybe there'd been a lunch with Lauris or a briefing from Fiona. Or (more likely) she had just read every word I'd written on the subject of Māori–Pākehā relations and thought it wasn't always quite what a right-thinking person would say.

I remember especially an interview with her in Wellington when she was pregnant and had dyed her hair bright red. She pressed especially on the question of whether we were or should be 'bicultural'. I had argued that ours was essentially a monocultural society, but with a second (and in effect secondary) culture of immense importance. One could argue that it should not be thus; but that was (then) our present reality. Once lost in this contentious thicket Kim challenged me about the relative value of Māori culture compared to the inherited European one. On this I didn't know how to equivocate without lying shamefully. I had read my Anne Salmond and my Judith Binney and could beat about the bush with the best; but if pressed, and Kim pressed, I would not pretend I thought other than that the inherited European culture with its several languages, written record and long history back into classical antiquity had to be richer, more various, demanding and rewarding than a tribal one evolved by a very small number of people, with its insularity (a thousand years cut off in one place), its lack of a written record, and lack of any significant technology (the wheel, pottery, iron).

As Kim pressed harder I pushed back. I was not saying Europeans were superior to Māori – not at all; I was speaking of two cultures which anyone in New Zealand might partake of, and their relative richness.

She didn't relent; wasn't going to let me off lightly. I wanted to say 'Lay off, Kim. This doesn't have to be said.' But she pushed, and I said it. I said Māori was a stone-age culture. This was true; but I knew how unacceptable it was.

I was invited to talk about *The Singing Whakapapa* at The Elms, the mission house at Tauranga to which John Flatt had fled after the murder of Tarore. It was their Open Day, 19 November 1994, and Kay and I went together. Tauranga and the region round about was Kay's territory. She had spent childhood holidays there on farms owned by her grandfather and uncles at Ōmokoroa and Pahoia; and we had often taken our children there for holidays when her mother and aunt lived at Maungatapu. When we had a meal in a restaurant a young man approached our table and asked was I C. K. Stead. When I confirmed that I was he turned to Kay and said, 'I'm your cousin, Colin Stewart.'

The group that came to hear me at The Elms was pretty much the kind of audience a writer gets at book festivals, with a slightly clerical or biblical emphasis, and a larger than usual number of Māori. They seemed well-disposed. I doubt whether more than a few would have read the novel they were to hear about. There were some preliminaries in which a random group, but including of necessity the visiting speaker himself, were dragged to the front and coached into performing a sort of haka. I did not shine: in fact I failed dismally and grumpily. I have never been able to get past the idea that sticking your tongue out, far from representing noble and fearsome defiance, was how an otherwise helpless child expressed dislike and anger.

So I began on the wrong foot but was confident on the subject of my novel and was soon back on the right one – but not for everybody in the hall. A large middle-aged impressive-looking Māori man got slowly up from his seat as I began to speak and moved conspicuously to the aisle and down to the doors at the back of the room where he stopped, with his broad back to me. It was more impressive than just walking out. There he was with his back to me.

I'm not sure why I wasn't disconcerted by this, but I wasn't. I carried on. I had a good story to tell, and it was about this area, had happened hereabouts, involved more Māori than Pākehā, was dramatic involving a murder – or, if you could see it that way, a brutal killing in a tribal war. And then, for the biblically disposed, there was the Luke Gospel in the flax kete, its peaceable effect on the Arawa, the fact that Tarore's father Ngakuku said he asked for no utu and wanted the Rev. Brown's assurance that his daughter would go to heaven. I don't remember whether I said it was part of the story as I had told it in the novel that Tarore had been in Flatt's tent. Possibly not. But I did take the story back to London with Flatt, and recounted how he had given his evidence to the House of Lords of CMS purchases of Māori land. The CMS had in effect sacked him, and his evidence, I said, was 'a bit of Pākehā utu'.

It's not usual as a novelist to tell the story you want your audience to read, but the circumstances here were unusual and it seemed the right thing to do. I was watching those shoulders at the back of the room. It was as if he'd been waiting for the right moment, waiting for me to say something really offensive so he could make a final dramatic exit. But as my discourse continued

I thought the shoulders relaxed. Can shoulders listen? These had been hostile shoulders. Now they were listening. And when I used those two Māori words – Pākehā utu – and everyone laughed, he turned around smiling, and sat in the nearest chair.

In the early part of the novel there is a lot about the missionaries, protected by the tapu of the great chief Waharoa (who had told his people that each of the cabbages in the mission garden was his own head), but living in an atmosphere of spying, random killings and the constant threat of utu and attack. There were many precarious negotiations, a lot of fear, courage and praying; and often an uncertainty about whether what was said to the Rev. Brown by Māori was seriously meant or a joke. Were the missionaries believed about the saving powers of Jesus Christ, or were they mocked? And did even the chief know the answer to that? While Māori life went on and an attack on the pā seemed imminent, the missionaries were a distraction and should not get in the way. Eternity had to be set aside.

As Brown noticed Waharoa ordering more flax to be harvested, which was sold for the purchase of more guns, he warned the chief that if he died fighting in a tribal war he would not go to heaven. Waharoa replied that this war was necessary; but when it was over he would 'believe, and go to heaven like a British soldier'.

Looked at objectively from the perspective of a rational humanist, what's revealed is two interacting patterns of irrationality, one (the Christian) impinging on the other, the Māori, which was resisting but not altogether successfully. The missionaries report horrors – most notably the eating of human flesh; but more random (sometimes potentially comic) things, like four rangatira listening to the bugs in the walls of Brown's raupō house to learn whether or not it was destined to be burned in the coming conflict – and when Brown runs after them to learn the verdict he's told, oh yes, it will be burned to the ground. Or, more grimly, the tohunga telling a Māori mother that she and her baby are ill because she ate off a tapu cloak, so to survive she must strangle her baby – which she does – and then suckles her dog to relieve her swollen breasts.

16. Karl thinks this was taken by Marti during a memorial occasion at the Sargeson House, 14 Esmonde Road, Takapuna. (Fibro background and plastic cup would seem to confirm.)
Courtesy of the Gerrard and Marti Friedlander Charitable Trust

17. *(Above)* Lunch in the Bacigalupos' garden above Rapallo. Karl with Angela Bacigalupo (left) and Mary de Rachewiltz (daughter of Ezra Pound). Photo by Massimo Bacigalupo, Professor of English and American Literature at the University of Genoa.

18. *(Below)* Ezra Pound returned to Rapallo in 1958 after his twelve-year incarceration in Washington. He is seen here soon after, with the then teenage Massimo Bacigalupo, in the family yacht *Vagabonda*.

19. Covers of UK and US editions of *The New Poetic*, clockwise from top left: the original Hutchinson University Press hardcover, 1964; original US Harper Torchbook (paperback and hardcover), 1966; the Pelican edition, 1967; Continuum paperback (London and New York), 1998, with Seamus Heaney's quotation about the book; Continuum reprint, 2005; Athlone Press (University of London) edition, 1998; University of Pennsylvania Press edition, 1987; Pelican 1969 paperback reprint; and the Hutchinson University Library 1975 reprint (centre).

20. (Above) Karl with Jadranka Pintarić at Dubravkin Put, Zagreb, 2007, the occasion described in the poem 'Speaking in Bronze' and site of the important statue of the writer in the prize-winning story 'Last Season's Man'.

21. (Left) The brilliant Croatian publishing pair, editor Jadranka Pintarić and translator Ljiljana Šćurić.

22. *(Above)* Audience for poetry in the Carlos Vieco Theatre, Colombia, July 2007 – colourful, enthusiastic and politically engaged – part of the International Poetry Festival in Medellín, the city also known at the time of the drug wars as the world's 'murder capital'.

23. *(Below)* Karl with poets and posters at the 5th Festival Mundial de Poesía, Caracas, May 2008.

24. *(Above)* With Kevin Ireland, for a book launch at Time Out Bookstore, Mount Eden.
25. *(Below)* Karl with Tessa Duder and Witi Ihimaera welcoming Árpád Göncz, writer and President of Hungary, to Auckland in 2000.

26. *(Above)* Karl on stage in 2012 when New Zealand was 'Guest of Honour' at the Frankfurt Book Fair.

27. *(Below)* Lunch at 37 Tohunga Crescent, 30 September 2017, after the University of Auckland Curnow Symposium celebrating the launch of the Curnow biography and *Collected Poems*. From left, Kay, Mac Jackson, Charlotte, Jan Kemp, Michael Hulse, Nicki Jackson and Paul Grimshaw. Photo by Karl.

28. *(Above)* Karl with Allen Curnow after the launch of Allen's last collection of poems, *The Bells of Saint Babel's*, March 2001.

29. *(Below)* Janet Frame in hospital receiving a blood transfusion, and reading Karl's *Listener* review (headed 'John Alone') of Vincent O'Sullivan's biography of John Mulgan, 2003.

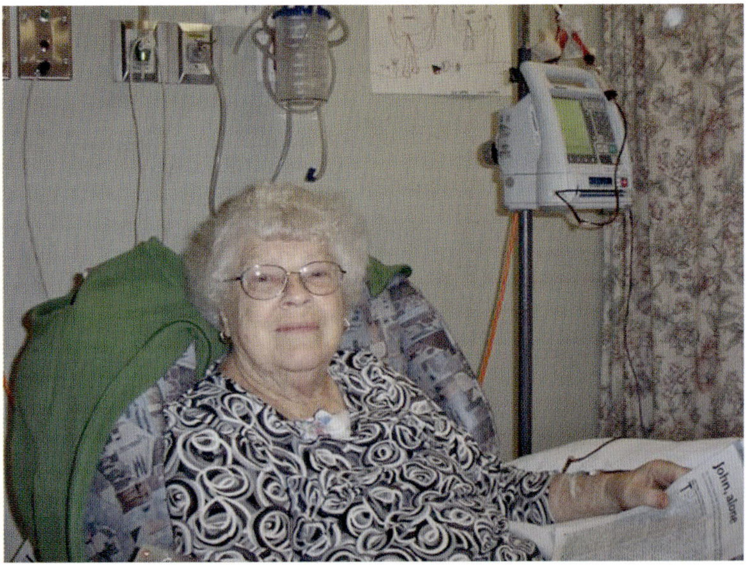

But why were such things more absurd or outrageous than telling Māori that they will go forever to a lovely place when they die, but only if they believe that a child born to a virgin far away and many moons ago was executed, came back to life, and rose physically up to heaven where a god (who was his father) welcomed him? – and that only this sacred person can get you in to that lovely place? All you had to do was believe his story – or say you did. To someone not brought up a Christian from childhood it must have seemed at once too easy and too unlikely. But the Māori's own social context encouraged them to believe things which no rational mind would accept, so why not? It was only another level of superstition to take on board.

It's unlikely I would have been so clear, frank and specific in my scepticism. I was speaking to what was, after all, a Christian gathering; but my tone would have implied it. Certainly it would not have been a tone that gave more credibility or honour to the missionaries than to the 'heathen' they were out to convert. For that reason, at least, the shoulders did not exit, and their owner returned them to a seat where they remained until the end. 'This Professor joker' (they might have said) 'seems OK. At least he's a straight-talker!'

I received a letter of thanks from 'The Elms Historic Family Home Preservation Trust Inc.' on notepaper which still featured a little picture of the unprepossessing Rev. A. N. Brown in its top left corner. 'Jinty Rorke (Mrs)' reported that they'd had 'a great many positive comments about how much [my] talk was enjoyed'; the attendance had been four times as many as last year's Open Day, 'which was most gratifying' – etc. And copies of my book had been bought in reasonable numbers.

Postscript:
Soon after the publication of *The Singing Whakapapa* and my 1994 visit to The Elms I received a letter:

Dear Mr Stead

I have just finished *The Singing Whakapapa* & want to tell you how much I enjoyed it.

William Fairburn was my great great grandfather – my great grandfather was Edwin – you mention him in your book [. . .]

Some years ago I met in Blenheim the Rev Sidney Flatt and he showed me a magnificent Bible with all the family tree written up. He also told me an interesting story of when he attended an Anglican Synod and when he ran into the Rev Williams he was 'cut dead' – so old animosities carry on even through second and third generations!

Best wishes for 1995 and more books please

Yours sincerely

Diana Gunn

I knew that the Williams family had continued clerical down the generations, but it was news to me that a Flatt had made his way back into the Anglican fold and even achieved the ordination that had eluded our forebear John; and it was of special and piquant interest that the old animus still smouldered. It seemed to confirm, and to ratify, the story I had been telling.

In spring 2019 a publication from The Elms, sent me by my nephew Jim Datson who lives in the Tauranga area, records a visit to Tarore's grave on 19 October to commemorate the 183rd anniversary of her death. Ngāti Hauā kaumātua Jay Gillett had been present and there was a short speech by Archbishop Emeritus Sir David Moxon. It seems from the report there was no mention of the manner of Tarore's death, nor of the presence of John Flatt when it happened – only of the flax kete, the Luke Gospel and its peace-making magic – in the words of that older inscription that 'brought peace to the tribes of Aotearoa'. That is how the Anglican Church likes its history written – an almost colourless wash, soothing to pious middle-class eyes which find the light of truth harsh and unwelcome.

9.
The Pākehā Poet and the Tangata Whenua

Voices

I'd had to establish that now, free of the university, I could be a novelist – write novels more or less at will. *Sister Hollywood* was published in 1989 and *The End of the Century at the End of the World* in 1992; but in between came the poem commissioned by Minister of the Arts Michael Bassett to celebrate our sesquicentenary year 1990 – one hundred and fifty years since the signing of the Treaty of Waitangi – the same historic moment he had tried to mark by purchasing the London flat for our writers. Michael commissioned only a poem, thinking possibly of Curnow's 'Landfall in Unknown Seas' written for the centenary celebration of 1940. I could have provided that and taken the money. Instead I wrote a book of poems, drawing on our history over the whole period. It involved research, family, memory and the sheer opportunism of poetry; and I wrote the poems in a style that set largely aside the experimental elements that had gone into my poems in the preceding two decades. This was because I thought they should be public poems for a public purpose, available, accessible, possibly even for use in schools – poems that working journalists, and teachers hungry for easy access to our history, could read and make sense of. If they should be thought technically unadventurous by the avant-garde, it was not for the avant-garde they were being written. If Ian Wedde and Alan Loney looked at them, they looked away again. Even Catullus and the double-margin form I used for him was on leave. It was, you could say, my style of the 1950s; but these were serious exercises in the craft of poetry. Of course there were complaints that I was being favoured by Bassett. He replied that he'd chosen well and that the outcome proved it; but I remember the launch in his office in the Beehive – a nice occasion but with some sour faces that couldn't resist 'being there' but felt honour-bound to make their disapproval of this shameless example of 'cronyism' apparent.

The book was nicely made by the Government Printer (soon to be flogged off cheap, like so many government-owned entities, by the Roger Douglas clique of which Bassett himself, alas, was one) – a hardcover of fifty-five pages with a purple jacket, with fifty poems at irregular time-intervals between 1820 and 1990, each in a different and quite specific voice/persona, the last in my own voice, a summing-up written 'At the Grave of Governor Hobson' in the Grafton cemetery where some of my forebears, both Flatt and McDermott had been buried.*

At some point I made a set of notes to explain my sources for these anecdotes/snapshots/exemplary moments. They could have been published together as a single book. It would have been ideal for the classroom; but I was nervous that explanations would get in the way of the poetry, as if the poems could not stand on their own with the virtue of poetry irrespective of 'the facts'. There was also the thought I had offered more than once in writing critical reviews, that primates in zoos had been observed to like their lunches better when they were hidden and had to be hunted for. Readers value more what is difficult; having, so to speak 'cracked the code', they can compliment themselves on their cleverness.

---

* Some of the graves latterly moved to make room for a motorway down Grafton Gully to the port.

I was intensely aware of the collection representing a step back in terms of poetic technique, and nervous of the critical reproaches I might get for this, an irrelevant consideration that should have been ignored. In a note at the end of the book I said I had

> allowed myself to raid biographies, autobiographies, letters, journals and then make my own use of them, sometimes sticking to the facts, sometimes altering them. I suppose the equivalent is historical fiction, where the writer lays claim to historical accuracy but not to veracity in detail. [. . .] I was looking for personalities that were typical, and for events and circumstances that seemed to represent more than themselves, and could even, at times, seem to carry symbolic overtones – the whole thing to be cast in somewhat formal verse structures appropriate to semi-public poetry.

The writing took about six months and did not proceed chronologically but ranged over the 160 years covered, finding subjects, developing them, moving backwards and forwards, working especially on the more formal ones (mostly sonnets) which observed rhyme schemes so that they were present but not obtrusive – did not, for the most part, ring loud and clear on the ear but were there for the technically appreciative eye. In that sense these were poems for the connoisseur and the poet. When the Christchurch *Star* gave them an approving review on one page and on another a full spread of sample poems with accompanying illustrations this was flattering and great publicity, but the samples looked like blocks of prose, showing that whoever had prepared the page had been a journalist interested in 'content', not a critic appreciative of form.

The hunt for subjects had been difficult because of what was for me a rule of literary life, a simple fact about poetry, that it dealt in the concrete not the abstract, in the particular not the general. The collection as a whole might be read to illustrate larger realities, but could attend only to small ones, and one at a time – singular, particular, the fact. So for example I wanted an item about that greatest of triumphs in our sporting history when, within an hour or two at the Rome Olympics, New Zealand had won two gold medals in athletics, itself the golden code and the one on which the original Olympic Games was founded. I would have preferred to have focused on Snell, our greatest athlete ever; but where was the point of focus? My friend Don Smith, whose great athletics year was 1958 when he beat the European champion, came from Oxford to represent New Zealand in the 800 metres at the Rome Olympics in 1960 never having heard of Snell (nor of Arthur Lydiard). Training with the team Don had helped by holding the stopwatch while Snell ran repeated 200-metre sprints – five or six in quick succession all at speeds that would have done a sprinter credit. Reflecting on this afterwards Don said, 'I'd never seen anything like it. He was a force of nature.' But that was Don's story, not mine, and I couldn't find a poem in it – or anything else about Snell except that he was 'a force of nature' – and (as I was) a MAGS old boy!

On the other hand there were two things about Halberg (apart from his withered arm, damaged in a football accident, which he tucked into his chest making his running style appear slightly lopsided). One was that he made his break in the 5000 metres final with three laps still to run; the other was that he'd told Maurice Shadbolt he'd made a visit to Greece two years before the Rome event, had prayed there to the gods of Olympus, and that they had promised him success. Without that assurance he would not have made his break when he did – so soon that none of his competitors went with him, none believing anyone could sustain that pace for the three circuits still to be run. They thought he'd made a miscalculation and gone too soon. But Halberg knew he did not have the power of Snell, he was not 'a force of nature', and in a sprint for the line he would have been beaten by others in that field. If he was going to win gold it had to be from the front – and it was, and he did! And there was that dramatic end when, after crossing the line, he collapsed on his back – so much more real, less staged, than John Walker's arms-above-the-head crossing the line at Montreal in 1976.

Each poem in the series had to be in the first person by someone located somewhere significant in our history. This one, then, had to be Murray Halberg in his own voice:

Rome 1960 The Athlete

Two years ago on a visit I prayed to the gods
of Olympus. They listened. They promised victory.
After that came Auckland's steepest roads –
Mt Roskill, Waiatarua, Waitakere.

You learn to push through pain as through a mirage
and keep on pushing. Specs ran with me, and Peter.
Arthur kept at us – always for greater mileage.
A three-lap sprint to finish five thousand metres

is the greatest distance the human mind can travel.
They let me go. Only a man who'd been told
by the gods to do it would break so soon in a final.
The crowd was my rainbow. There at its end lay gold

and my own body, discarded, sprawled on the track,
watched, so it seemed, from above, and wearing black.

Yeats says 'a line will take us hours maybe',

Yet if it does not seem a moment's thought
Our stitching and unstitching has been naught.

For me the satisfaction in writing a poem like the Halberg one was not in the material. The material was important – essential – but it was shaping it to its form that was the art of poetry. It was what I think of as a 'hard work poem' (as most of Curnow's were, and Kendrick Smithyman's – whereas Baxter's, even in formed stanzas with rhymes, seemed less effortful, more 'natural' like Keats's 'leaves to a tree'). The rhymes were all in place, but unobtrusively, so readers who were not poets would not notice them until the final couplet when the rhyme declares itself.

There's an artificiality about rhyme which I had mostly wanted to avoid in recent years as I tried to get closer to common speech (what Wordsworth calls 'the real language of men'); but it was good to confirm I could still do it, as I'm sure abstract painters are reassured to find now and then that they have not lost the art of draughtsmanship and accurate representation – or contemporary classical musicians, that they can still strike off a melody that takes the ear by surprise and won't let itself be instantly forgotten. These were public poems and dressed for the occasion, slightly formally.

There were seven formal sonnets on the subject of the Treaty of Waitangi – the first in the voice of a very young Māori woman to whom the whole process means little or nothing. She is thinking about kinds of prayer – the kind recommended by the tohunga and the kind recommended by the missionary; but really she is more interested in remembering the sailor, 'blue-eyed, freckled, his skin tasting like salt', who has given her a knife.

Then come two in the voice of 'the Printer' Colenso. In the first, February 5th, he reports the rivalry between Catholic Pompallier and Anglican Williams, and the chief Kemara wishing the Governor 'good health' and telling him to go home. Colenso is anxious about Williams' translation of the document and whether the chiefs, if they sign, will understand it. In the second, February 6th, he asks the Governor whether he thinks the chiefs 'understand what they cannot read', and Hobson replies that they 'must heed the missionaries' good advice, as Heke will'. He orders that blankets be given out as gifts to those who sign, and declares in Māori 'Now we are all one people'.

Next comes a settler who does not like the implications of a treaty which might deprive him of rights to land he has bought direct from local Māori. This is followed by one in the voice of one of the chiefs who thinks about what is happening but doesn't speak his thoughts aloud. He is uncertain about the whole business, nostalgic about the old warrior days which he thinks are coming to an end, but is not certain he wants them back. The last two sonnets are in the voice of Governor Hobson, who has been warned by an old Māori that he may not live much longer. In the last he is anxious to get the whole process done before either the French, or the Wakefield company in Port Nicholson, gain an advantage.

I'm not sure how successful these seven are as poems; and as history they certainly need explanatory notes; but I'm not aware that anyone has attempted to subject our 'founding document' to the rigours of verse. If the seven reveal anything it's that the official view of the Treaty which we've now settled for and even made mandatory, is a subsequent concoction. At the time of the signing it meant different things to each of the participants – which is why it was largely forgotten in the nineteenth century, and only revived as a contract of 'partnership' in the second half of the twentieth. The sequence is not as challenging to the idea of the Treaty as my other poem about it* which teases Claudia Orange (who pronounced Treaty Treedee) and explains it to an imaginary visitor puzzled by the tone of spooky reverence in which he hears it discussed:

It's a shibboleth
I tell him
a jackup that went wrong
a royal present
an exploding cigar

* 'Treasure Island', *Collected Poems, 1951–2006*, p. 289.

It's a mantra
a midden
a mistake
a line from an old song
come back to haunt us.

It's a heaviness in the limbs
a very private
very secret
boredom.

When I call her at the library
'Kia ora Kay'
I say
'Kia ora Karl'
she replies
then we go out
to an Italian
meal or a movie.

This is much more sprightly, less dour and serious than the sonnets, and more characteristically CKS of that period; but the seven sonnets are in their own way subtly, and perhaps more radically, subversive.

In *You Have a Lot to Lose* I say the more you write the better you get at it, and that you reach a point where you can make something of nothing and eloquence of almost anything. This is an exaggeration, but it contains at least a half-truth; and there were a few poems or passages in the sequence that did seem to achieve eloquence. One is John Flatt's waking in his tent on the morning that Tarore is murdered (though Tarore is absent from the poem):

Dogs bark me from sleep. Pale light through an open flap.
Grass swish. Twig snap. Whispers – and now this hush
a thread in the book of my dreaming – a threat?

I wake to myself – John Flatt, crossing the Kaimais
from Matamata down to the Bay of Plenty.
The forest lifts dark arms to that billowing light
expecting song. Why are its choristers silent?
Fear won't dispel this well-being of my waking.

Another, '1908 – the Actress', is derived from the autobiography of Ngaio Marsh and written in her voice:

On the river it seemed it was always late afternoon,
summer, and quiet. Our oars clunked in their rowlocks,
willows trailed green streamers on a perfect surface
reflecting our drifting through suburban gardens
in lovely hats, as if all life were a poem
composed in Edward's England and enacted
dreamily here at the farthest reach of Empire.

Oaks, playing fields, the spire of Christchurch cathedral,
and the Port Hills – I could see it all from a tree
behind our house. How thrillingly more-than-English
our visitor declared! But when I looked to the north
across forty miles of the Plains on a clear day
the Southern Alps stared back, white in the sun.
To see so far – it was frightening. This wasn't England.

It was then I decided everything was unreal –
everything but the theatre. It was all theatre,
and they in far places, the great executors
of the world's will – they didn't know they were players!
The Alps spoke to me, beautiful, hard and cold
against that blue which goes up and away for ever.
I answered as I could, in the language of Shakespeare.

I like the idea in this that there's something in the colonial situation which gives us, or gave us when Ngaio Marsh (Allen Curnow too) was young a sort of removal from 'reality' – which would explain her commitment to theatre (and to the theatrical/formulaic unreality of the murder mystery genre) and on the other hand Allen's at times almost frantic insistence that there must be a 'reality prior to the poem'.

The collection received mostly generous attention around the country; but best, most complex and judicious was by Kevin Ireland, who began (how could he not at that time and for the *Listener*) with reflections on what a peculiar choice Bassett had made, offering this (in effect) laureate commission to one who 'has not had a good press lately'.

> [Stead's] feet-on-the-ground efforts to procure an overseas pied-à-terre for New Zealand writers have been misinterpreted. His latest novel has not received from local reviewers the excellent notices it was given overseas. His cool contributions to such hot issues as education, gender, race and the Treaty of Waitangi have been attacked with no recognition of their sincerity or of how they have, at the very least, helped raise the level of the debate.
>
> However the choice of such a controversial and deliberately contentious writer to be the state-paid laureate of the 150 years of our nationhood, and therefore presumably to impose a sort of official decorative seal on it, has to be considered a pretty eccentric gamble on the part of the minister or his advisers.
>
> In the event *Voices* turns out to be an agreeable, well-written and dignified work. The writer has faced up to a difficult assignment, cautiously and intelligently, and the minister has got his money's worth.

Not a word about cronyism, or Tonya Harding! Kevin and I knew one another only slightly in those days – I'm not sure he had yet returned finally from his two decades of living abroad. He did not pretend to like everything about the collection:

> The burden of Stead's laureateship imposes the same detectable strains that were apparent in Allen Curnow's centenary reflections. Fancy and humour are casualties [. . .] But the extraordinary overall achievement of *Voices* is that, in spite of its status as an 'official' pronouncement, it is so readable. Its easy formal structures and simple language complement each other, and help gracefully to make it 'civil' in every sense. Of the many accomplished poems in the book, the outstanding concluding work, '1990: At the Grave of Governor Hobson', should not escape special mention. It is full of echoes of the text that precedes it, assured, allusive, satisfying. A terrific note to end on, and an anthology piece if ever I saw one.

The *Listener* then quotes the whole of this poem; and it was to appear as the last poem in Bill Manhire's 1993 anthology, *100 New Zealand Poems*. Here are the last two of seven ten-line stanzas:

> Last night, yellow as butter, an outsize moon
> sailed over the ridge of Parnell. In Emily Place
> it picked the obelisk out that marks the place
> where you laid the first stone for the first St Paul's;
> it gilded the six-lane highway, once a track,
> where you used to lead your Lila and her schoolfriend
> Harriet Preece, and lift them over the ditch;
> it laid a lily of light on 'this beautiful spot
> on the slope of a wooded valley looking to the sea,'
> once yours and, given to the city, yours again.
>
> Let today be all the days we've lived in New Zealand:
> stench of whale meat, a rat cooked on a spit,

morning boots frozen hard, the southern Maori
ravaged by measles, rum, Te Rauparaha;
wars in the north, gumfields, forests falling
to ruminant grassland, cities climbing like trees;
and everywhere this language both supple and strong.
You didn't start it, Governor. As we do, you fashioned
what time, and the times that live in us, required.
It doesn't finish. These verses have no end.

Māori – and Mr Smiler

It sometimes seems to me that the Pākehā who are most reverent, cautious, nervous about Māori issues, the ones most likely to 'hum and sway', are the ones who know them least well. If your life has brought you often enough in contact with Māori they seem a natural part of your social and emotional environment, and not an aspect requiring special treatment, tiptoeing around in fear of making a mistake. To be truly Pākehā you must have Māori in your consciousness, part of your life, even if it isn't always a bit you feel entirely comfortable with. In my own life there was the Māori first cousin, and his mother the colourful Auntie Trixie, Uncle Don's first wife, who used to wrestle my somewhat proper (but rather pleased) mother to the floor in an excess of exuberant affection. Cousin Donnie lived with us while Uncle Don was away at the war, and went to Maungawhau School with my sister Norma and me.

Later there were the two of Norma's children who had Māori partners – so now there are Māori great-nieces and -nephews; and I have described in Chapter 5 how the Māori element played its part at my sister's death and obsequies. When I was made Poet Laureate, 2015–17, that branch of the family coached me in preparation for the marae ceremony and awarding of the tokotoko at Matahiwi marae.

Māori figure in my fiction – not only the nineteenth-century Māori of *The Singing Whakapapa* but the twentieth-century World

War II of the Māori Battalion who are so important in *Talking about O'Dwyer*. In *Voices* again there is '1849 The Settler' based on experiences of my great-grandmother Annie Flatt (née McDermott) related to me by my grandmother, including

> Last year the local hapu took my husband.
> They told him, 'Eat and grow so you will make
> good kai for us.' After two nights they laughed
> and let him go – told him, 'Long pig, run home!'
>
> Two days ago a war party stopped at our door –
> took pork from my kitchen. I couldn't speak.
> Naked, beautiful men – by now they may be dead,
> or eating the dead.
>
> Light dances on the water,
> sharpens the headland's edge and the far horizon –
> a brightness that speaks to the soul. Home is the dream.
> I fear for myself, longing for a sail, and letters.

There is the British soldier in an assault on a pā during the Taranaki wars; and then '1864 The Warrior' remembering the siege at Ōrākau:

> Not the taste of peach but its hard wrinkled stone
> to suck on, bite. It's so quiet in this grove,
> the autumn air so still, peach leaves, apple leaves
> falling. I think the dead come to me here –
> the woman lost, her child, my uncle, cousins.
>
> Three days they shelled us, stormed, sapped –
> we drove them back. What was it made two hundred,
> facing two thousand, so resolute for death?
> Those Tuhoe, mad for battle, put us here.
> Rewi kept us. 'Ka whawhai tonu ake!'

Chewing raw kumara, licking dew from grass,
counting bullets – and then, by daylight, the breakout!
Orakau seemed to hold its breath as we came,
not running, one body, women at the centre,
warriors at the front. My heart thumped in my throat.

Eyes shut among the peach trees I see them again,
their bayonets ready. Only Death could stop me.
He was busy with my friends – I got away.
The Pakeha cursed – and praised us. Was it worth it?
Is life worth it, e hoa? Ake! Ake!

None of the poems in *Voices* was quite so grimly bloody as one, 'The Hand',* that went into a sequence I wrote later, *King's Lynn and the Pacific*, about earlier British encounters with Māori. And none was quite so militant and threatening as one written in response to the police closing down on the Bastion Point protest.† But I think '1860 The Pakeha-Maori' in *Voices*, based on the conclusion of F. E. Maning's *Old New Zealand*, is at once the toughest, truest and most profound statement on the subject, because most deeply and equally based in both cultures:

I know that talk: 'It's time to drive the British
into the sea.' No, I don't take it lightly.
Those who say it mean it. A Pakeha-Maori
I say 'God save my Queen', and then I wish

my tribe success. I know that men must fight.
Pakeha in me says, 'We can take New Zealand
but only if we get our strategy right.'
Maori answers, 'Our ally is the land –

---

* *Collected Poems, 1951–2006*, p. 356.
† '4 April 1986', *Collected Poems, 1951–2006*, p. 209.

we will drag their mana down, and the white Queen's law.'
I think who wins is right. I salute the victor.
It's long since Lizard Skin, old warrior chief,
his death-bed eyes burning because he foresaw
this conflict, gave to his kin these words I offer
to both sides now: 'Be brave, that you may live!'

It was Keith Sinclair's *History of New Zealand* in the early 1960s which had corrected any lingering primary school memories of *Our Nation's Story* with its bland account of our history and of Māori–Pākehā relations. And Keith's poetry had also given us some of our turbulent nineteenth century, including Thomas Kendall's sexual adventuring that had so distressed the CMS. Keith had also given us a poem about Ihumātao which became such an issue in 2019.*

Also in the 1960s Māori began to appear in significant numbers among our students, including a certain Mr Smiler (students in those days were Mr or Miss, or occasionally Mrs) who would later change his surname to Ihimaera and emerge as Witi, the first twentieth-century Māori to publish significant fiction in English. Witi was shy, handsome and rather smooth – a quite different and socially polished person compared to the rough-hewn boilermaker Hone Tuwhare who was doing in poetry what Witi was to do in fiction: giving it a Māori voice, though neither of them had grown up speaking Māori and only learned some late in the day because of the significant public roles they were assuming. Hone, a serious Marxist-Leninist trade union man, who took inspiration from the poetry of R. A. K. Mason, seemed to have the scars of being Māori – not the noble chief but the social underdog. Witi had none that were visible at least to me; and insofar as there were scars one can say in retrospect it's more likely they were a result of knowing, or suspecting, he was gay in a

* See Keith's collection *Strangers or Beasts*. It contains notable attempts to incorporate his historical subjects into poetry – particularly 'Waitara' where he sets up a dialogue between the settler and the chief in 1859 and then brings the story forward to a gloomy guilt-racked 1948.

Māori society which made him think that would be morally wrong and even disgusting.

Witi was a natural writer, fluent though careless, leaving the work of bringing his manuscripts up to publishable standard to others – most often Michael Gifkins, who half resented that he was not allowed to claim publicly the credit he was anything but silent about in private. Witi altered the landscape of New Zealand writing just by being there and doing what he did. It wasn't all well done, but it was important because it was a sign, a signal, a symbol. There was a hunger for these two, Hone and Witi, especially among the intellectual and academic community, painfully conscious of wrongs that could never be righted, and of imbalances that could be corrected but only over time. No one was going to give up even a quarter acre of private land that might have been wrongfully acquired; but there were pieties and required guilt rituals which were never one hundred per cent sincere.

Witi prospered because he was talented and because he was necessary. But one unit of a foreign language was a prerequisite for a degree in arts at Auckland, and that was Witi's stumbling block despite successes in (from memory) English, history and anthropology. Māori had been accepted as a foreign language unit* but Witi, despite his background, didn't manage it. Later he carried his Auckland degree units over to Victoria where there was no language requirement, and completed his Bachelor's degree there. Along the way came employment in the Department of Foreign Affairs, marriage, two daughters, postings to Canberra and Washington, and by the 1980s he was established both as a significant New Zealand fiction writer and as our consul in New York. It must have been at some time in this period that Witi and his wife separated and he came out as gay, and published

* But only after a battle with the old guard, especially Professors E. M. Blaiklock and Olly Keys, who asked 'Where is the literature?', which the anthropologists answered by bringing in a pile of Māori dictionaries – signifying, I suppose, an oral culture.

the novel *Nights in the Gardens of Spain* in which the gay central character is Pākehā.

My few meetings with him were always amiable and easy, with an element of uncertainty at least on my side, probably on his too. I am more than usually pale-skinned, tending in childhood to freckles, and I remember once when I had been in the sun a lot and was untypically tanned Witi commented on it and put his bare forearm alongside mine, as if to show me what a *real* tan looked like. It seemed a sort of Māori joke, emphasising difference, but friendship. There was something simple, direct, authentic about it – as there was about his earliest work before he developed a tendency to overwriting and the grandiose:

> Sometimes, late at night, I'd hear Nanny crying because she was lonely. I'd creep softly down the corridor to her room and brush her tears away with my hands.
>
> – You're too old to cry, I'd growl her. But she'd keep weeping.

'I'd growl her' is like that brown arm alongside my paler one.

After I left in 1986 the university advertised a chair in English. They had an associate professor, Mac Jackson, excellently qualified to deal both with New Zealand literature and with Eng. Lit. back to Shakespeare (on whose work he was an internationally acknowledged expert). To move Mac up a grade into a personal chair would have been the prudent course because it would have left my salary largely untouched for an appointment much needed further down the scale. Instead, urged by the English Department's best hummers and swayers, a new chair was advertised. There were applications from Jackson, Vincent O'Sullivan and Peter Simpson, all of them much better qualified than the man who got the job, Albert Wendt, who had a second-class hons MA, not in English but in history from Victoria. Further, since Wendt at that time was not a New Zealander but Samoan, a case had to be made to the Department of Immigration that there was no New Zealander available who was qualified for the post – an extraordinary and blatant lie. This was the beginning of the university's attempt to match its teaching with the social and political realities of Auckland's increasing population of Māori, and the favoured destination for migration from the Pacific. The effect was to alter significantly the emphasis Bill Pearson, Allen Curnow and I had given to the study of New Zealand literature in the English Department. What Alex Calder would call our 'settler literature' had had its brief moment and was to a large extent gone – relegated, an episode. Witi was soon brought in to enhance the effect, and before long was designated 'Professor of English and Distinguished Creative Fellow in Maori Literature'. That BA from Victoria had taken him to the top. If a second-class degree in history could get you a chair in English, why not?

Inadvertency – and beyond

One of my first tasks for Karl Miller was to review Witi's big novel, *The Matriarch*, for the *LRB*.* In one of his early stories Witi had written of being hustled and pestered by people wanting him to be militant, and of his determination to resist this pressure. Now eight or nine years had passed since his last book and he had emerged with a novel that was full of Māori militancy and the sense of wrongs to be righted. I wanted to do it more than justice but my notes before writing the review show it was difficult, and sometimes impossible, to be upbeat. As an exercise in the art of fiction it was overblown and badly written; as history it was often inaccurate and partial. In my review I tried to separate truths from half-truths, and half-truths from untruths.

> Looked at in detail the simple image of New Zealand history as a kind of slow rape is a half-truth. [. . .] But in broad terms

---

* *LRB*, December 1986; and *Kin of Place: Essays on 20 New Zealand Writers*, Auckland University Press, 2002, pp. 330–37.

> it has to be accepted: we may have killed with muskets (sale of, more than use of), with European diseases, with money, with intermarriage – even with kindness. Whatever the means and the intention, and however the indigenous people may have collaborated in their own downfall, history has rolled cruelly over the Maori race. Today they are disproportionately the urban proletariat, the unemployed, the disaffected. From their 10 per cent of the population come 50 per cent of the inmates of New Zealand jails. Everyone must know there is a problem, which full civil rights and equality of opportunity has not been sufficient to overcome.
>
> [. . .]
>
> The novel repeatedly, and in the end tiresomely, asserts the stature of the matriarch. The language ('amazing', 'breathtakingly stunning', 'an incredible beauty', 'a blinding presence', 'charismatic', 'extraordinary', 'astonishing') becomes florid as if with the effort of conjuring into being a greatness that has no foundation in fact, nor even, perhaps, in the imagination of the novelist. At no time did I really believe in the greatness of Artemis. Worse, I was never entirely persuaded that the novelist believed in it either.

My review then quoted a rare passage which seemed to come direct from Ihimaera's childhood. I continued:

> There, momentarily, is real life – and you might say there also is the motive and the justification for indignation, rhetoric, myth-making. But the curtain closes and we are not shown anything like it again. It simply remains in the mind a measure of all the rest – so much more direct and true and powerful than all that windy, badly-written stuff about the matriarch with her magic, her poisoned spider and her recitativo.

Witi published his children's story *Whale Rider* in 1987, and *Bulibasha* in 1994. In 2009 came *The Trowenna Sea*, and with it the announcement by the Wellington-based New Zealand Arts Foundation that Witi was to receive one of its annual awards, with a prize of $50,000. But a review in the *Listener* by Jolisa Gracewood at just this moment revealed that the new novel had sixteen significant passages taken unacknowledged from published work by other writers.

The first reaction was protective, and self-protective. Witi said the thefts had been 'inadvertent' and he apologised for them. The publisher said the book would not be withdrawn but a new edition would be published with the due acknowledgements. The university said it was looking into the matter, and then almost at once that it accepted Witi's explanation and apology. The Arts Foundation agreed and announced that it would go ahead with the award.

Far from closing down on the controversy these soothing oils only troubled the waters further. There were complaints from academics and teachers that so much of their time went into warning against, and policing, plagiarism, this bad example from a senior academic deserved a real sanction rather than excusing. Peter Wells blogged his outrage that the book was still on sale and achieving best-seller status by infamy. Professor Keith Sorenson, some of whose work had been used in *The Matriarch*, questioned the appropriateness of the Arts Foundation award, and said the university's reaction had been inadequate. As the matter went international an American academic said that Vice-Chancellor Stuart McCutcheon's reaction had been typical of a 'very provincial university'. When the *Listener* added a further six examples of petty theft from published sources even Vincent O'Sullivan broke his vow of silence and said plagiarists in literature were like drug cheats in sport. The *Herald* published a scolding editorial and a cartoon by Emmerson which showed Witi riding a whale marked PLAGIARISM, the whale reflecting, 'Come to think of it Whale Rider did have Orphan Annie meets Dr Dolittle about it.'

By now the amount of detected 'inadvertency' had grown quite large. In reaction to all this Witi bought back 1800 copies of the novel, no new edition was published, and the author retreated into a silence with his now tarnished Arts Foundation award; and then, after a year, gradually re-emerged as the episode faded from sight. He showed commendable fortitude in this, but was helped by new success. The movie of *Whale Rider* was soon in the forefront of the public mind and the shadow of Witi's bad deed retreated to the rear – half-remembered, but mostly forgotten. He was back on his feet because he was necessary. He was our representative Māori fiction writer. New Zealand needed him, our literature needed him, because without him it was only (to borrow Alex Calder's phrase) the settler's plot.

Postscript:

In the 2018 Auckland Festival I gave the lecture that is sponsored each year by the University of Auckland, and I concluded by giving an account of an exchange with Witi. Recently he'd had an interview in the *Herald*'s *Canvas* magazine in which he described himself as a secondary school boy in 1959 reading a story by Douglas Stewart about a young Pākehā who is invited into a Māori village and stays the night with an old couple in a flea-infested whare. 'The whole story is very dark,' Witi tells the interviewer, 'and the descriptions of the Maori are very demonic, as if these people have invited him for some sinister purpose. This was anathema to me as a Maori because I never thought of our marae as full of fleas and people who would take advantage of strangers. I threw the book out of the window and was caned for it. I made a vow that if I ever became a writer I would write a book about Maori people that would be an antidote to these kinds of stories and it would be placed in front of every school child in New Zealand.'

I was struck by this for several reasons so I read the Douglas Stewart story and emailed Witi:

Kia ora Witi

Your interesting piece in the *Canvas* sent me in search of that Douglas Stewart story, which I probably hadn't read before. It's interesting – much less sensitive to Maori feelings than any writer now would be, but possibly more honest, do you think? The Maori community he's writing about must have been almost half a century before any you would have experienced, and at a time when Maori were at a low ebb. It feels as if he's reporting it just as he experienced it, and is puzzling out why the old couple appear to want him to stay. The fleas are a mystery. Could Maori have been partly immunised against them by constant exposure? Kay's grandmother remembered walking into an abandoned Maori whare on land her husband had bought at Omokoroa wearing a white muslin skirt and when she looked down it was black with fleas.* The old woman in the story keeps promising to do something about the fleas but doesn't get around to it. When the narrator leaves he writes them a very nice apologetic note; and the tone overall is not disrespectful. More than anything puzzled – which might be an accurate reflection of the (intelligent) Pakeha view of Maori at that time.

Of course none of us learned much of NZ history and nothing of NZ Lit. – so we were all colonised; but you were doubly colonised. And I can see how a Maori boy would have been offended by the story – or perhaps embarrassed by it – embarrassment seems more likely. But I found the bit about your throwing the book out the window and being caned for it and resolving to write a book about Maori people that 'would be placed in front of every school child in NZ' all rather improbable – a case of gilding the lily. Of course you *have* done that, and you fully deserve every accolade it has brought you

* Witi omits this sentence when he includes this exchange in the book he was copy-editing at the time – *Native Son: The Writer's Memoir*, Vintage, 2019, pp. 220–21.

– but the idea that you foresaw your own success is positively Shadboltian! Am I wrong to be such a sceptic?

Witi replied almost at once:

Kia ora Karl,

What was really uncanny about your email today was that it arrived as I was checking the final publication draft of my next memoir, Native Son – at the point that I refer to the Douglas Stewart story. [. . .] So . . . I wonder if I could include your email in the memoir to give an alternate view of Stewart's story and to allow me to hint at the whole idea of the writer as an unreliable narrator?

[There was more, personal interchange – and then . . .]

Thanks for writing to me Karl! I really appreciated it.

Nga mihi mahana,

Witi

The bit about himself as the 'unreliable narrator' seemed to confirm my suspicion about gilding the lily. I replied:

Kia ora Witi, and thanks for your prompt reply. You are more than welcome to use my e-mail.

[There was much more in this exchange – about the memoir I was writing and about swimming, and about Witi having been a student in Curnow's, Pearson's and Stead's classes at Auckland University – and then I concluded . . .]

Kay and I both admired and enjoyed *Maori Boy* so much and we're looking forward eagerly to the sequel.

Nga mihi nui

Karl

My lecture quoted these emails and concluded:

> What I want to suggest about this exchange is that for me, at the age of 86 and looking back over quite a long writing life, it does have the feel of a step forward – something that I don't think could have happened half a century ago – because at that time there was no Maori writer with the ease, confidence and fluency Ihimaera displays; and I suppose equally at that time I would not have been so at ease exchanging ideas with a Maori writer in potentially sensitive areas.
>
> Literary history is sometimes seen as the measure of history on the larger scale: political history, social history. Ezra Pound called writers 'the voltometers and steam-gauges of their time'. Ihimaera it seems to me might be seen as the Maori version of Curnow's 'child born in a marvellous year' who 'will learn the trick of standing upright here'. I can't make claims for myself, and we are neither of us perfect on paper or in public; but let's hope we're both 'standing upright here'. If we are, it's a small matter but more than gossip: it's some kind of historical marker.

This made a good and affable end to a festival event – and I think it's at least half true.

10.
The Curnow Factor – His Last Two Decades

The transition

Cross-crescent relations with the Curnows were good – especially when I was in my Curnow-designated role of his 'Critic', which involved reading each new poem when he felt it was finished and ready to be offered. It was a role I embraced with pleasure – they were such good poems! We also met socially and were in and out of one another's houses, invited to one another's parties and dinner parties. At first Jeny talked of having babies but none appeared and she contented herself with attempting to be stepmother to Allen's three children – not altogether easy because there was family sympathy for and loyalty to the abandoned Betty. It appeared to be a good, successful second marriage, though I'm sure Jeny had from time to time to weather the 'abominable temper' of which even those who knew Allen only casually saw occasional brief but fearsome flashes.

I wondered how they were going to manage in conversations with friends because Allen had been so dominant with Betty. In those days, when I was a student and Kay and I visited the house in Herbert Street, Allen would run on with one of those monologues he was famous for and after four or five minutes Betty would interject with a small contribution. Allen would flinch and flick the trail of hair back from his brow and say in a pained voice, 'I was *talking*,

Piggy.' (Piggy was his nickname for her; for Jeny it was 'Little one'.) There must have been a tussle for supremacy. Jeny was not going to be so easily silenced; but it soon became apparent they had resolved this crux, not by taking turns, but by each grabbing a guest from the company. If it was just the four of us, Jeny would grab Kay and Allen would grab me, and the conversation (sometimes) or monologue (often) would continue unbroken.

Jeny was very protective of Allen's reputation, and of their image as a happy couple. It was almost a 'branding' exercise. Betty, though something of a toff in Christchurch terms,* had been a picturesque untidy Bohemian, well-portrayed in the Rita Angus and Louise Henderson portraits; Jeny was very middle class. Her house was always immaculate, and she liked to appear with Allen in good clothes, 'looking smart'. I suspect in this, as in so much else, Jeny was more to Allen's taste than the Bohemian Betty had been. Jeny had a mantra 'We are very private people'; but Allen was also a very public person and as the years went by he became more and more protective of his image, never going out on a limb (or not alone), never putting a foot wrong. He always made it a condition of granting an interview† that he must see, and adjust if necessary, the copy before it went to press; and more than one interviewer has talked about an answer given to a question that had not been asked, or a particularly favourable review cited by the interviewer who in fact had never seen it.

Our relations were more than cordial. I knew Allen counted on my opinion of his poems, and that possessive Jeny did not altogether like, though she respected, this reliance which had begun when I was still an MA student. It was like a certificate of quality control. I was always careful, sensitive, discreet, knowing I could easily spoil this rapport and not wanting to. I did not need

---

* I heard Allen say to Keith Sinclair at a party (this was before the break-up of the first marriage) 'Betty's a Le Cren, you know.' Keith's reply was 'What's a Le Cren?'

† Interviewers included Peter Simpson, Mac Jackson, Gordon McLauchlan and Steve Braunias.

him but I valued him, and valued the relationship in which the mentor had become something different, something neither of us had quite expected. Mostly I just confirmed what he suspected already, that the new poem was brilliantly successful. Now and then I would first affirm the success of the poem, and analyse why it succeeded so well, and then would say if there was something I thought perhaps was not up to the quality of the rest, and even suggest how it might be corrected. In these cases he usually made a change, but seldom the one I had suggested.

There were very rarely neighbourly disagreements, but there was one which simmered for the most part out of sight. The Curnows' property across the road and up the hill from ours was home to some healthy pōhutukawa, which grew from insignificant when we first moved in, to more than significant over the years. Allen (I think Allen and Jeny together) noticed and mentioned with something like a guilty wince the lines in 'Walking Westward'

> the moon
> this moon
> this very moon and no other
> moon of 15.2.76 making over Hobson Bay
>   its universal statement
> sailing over pohutukawa
>   that shade our house in the mornings.

Nothing, or nothing more, was said; and the trees went on growing. I think it was Kay who mentioned some years later that they might be trimmed without harm to themselves and with benefit to the neighbourhood, which was met with the Curnow stone stare and the Jeny reproachful glance. Later again, when I knew Allen, unless prompted, was reading nobody's poems but his own, I published a little exercise in irony in a collection called *Straw into Gold*. I concealed it among Catullus pieces, but it was really in an early Pound-prosy manner:

Honoris Causa

Cornificius
whose 'mighty pohutukawa'
tower over the suburb
earns praise for his stout defence
of the native flora.

This is one honour
he might have had to forego
if their shadow condemned his house
to damp and darkness in winter.

Since it falls however
exclusively on his neighbours
he is able to enjoy
the acclamation
with a clear conscience.

The damage done by tree-shadow was exaggerated for comic effect; and none was done to the Curnow–Stead poet–critic collaboration.

Over the decades we interacted not only in Parnell but at Karekare on the beach and in one another's baches on Lone Kauri Road which Allen was turning into a significant location on New Zealand's literary map. Karekare figured more often in his poems than it did in mine; but that wild west coast got into my fiction – particularly *The End of the Century at the End of the World*; and I remember finishing at speed the writing of *All Visitors Ashore*, which had nothing at all to do with the west coast, in the little hut at the top of our section which looked all the way down the Karekare valley to the ocean.

Sometimes I went on the family expeditions; other times Kay took the children on heroic treks through bush walks along dangerous bluffs and into valleys while I went on writing in the hut. We all swam constantly out there, trudging up and down the mile or so of unsealed road from bach to beach. One of Charlotte's short stories is a childhood memory of an adventure with Oliver, and Don and Jill Smith's son Matthew, on a walking track we should have checked before letting them go on it without adults.* Oliver had studied the map and assured us they would be safe. They got back unharmed, but we later reproached ourselves for parental carelessness when we walked the track and discovered its dangers.

I finished my 1982 collection *Geographies* with six poems in a style Allen and I were both experimenting with at the time, the poem divided usually into stanzas but with no punctuation apart from occasional full stops. It was Allen who initiated this, and he justified it as a way of making his syntax declare itself and show its importance. Glover didn't like the practice at all, and neither did Alan Ross (editor of *The London Magazine*). But Allen wrote to me (echoing Marlowe's Dr Faustus) ''Tis syntax, syntax, that hath ravished me!' It was an element no less important to me, because I had always been more interested in the on-running momentum (and complexity – and consequent necessity for grammatical dexterity) of syntax than any other poetic element – than metaphor or image for example. Two of this last block of six poems were tributes to my two mentors, Curnow, then Sargeson, the Curnow opening with three non-stop unpunctuated stanzas, the Sargeson with four.† The Curnow was called 'A poem called "The Weather in Tohunga Crescent"' and began

> Up in the night to free the cat that
> slept in the cupboard among towels
> and got locked there look out and it's
> moon all over and stars the big

* Charlotte Grimshaw, 'Pararaha', *Singularity*, Vintage, 2009, pp. 70–88.
† *Collected Poems, 1951–2006*, pp. 180–82.

ones not so much points as small
beautiful orbs and the bay of course
glass echoing moon echoing stars
over and above so if the gulls squabbling

for standing room would just stop
and the crickets lay aside their
bows a moment you might hear it
the music of the spheres.

(The gulls did squabble all night for space on the structure housing the sewer pipe which in those days crossed Hobson Bay.)

It was at this time that Allen was writing the poems that went into the collection he called *You Will Know When You Get There*, and poems were going back and forth across the crescent. One was called 'The Weather in Tohunga Crescent' – hence the title of my Curnow tribute. Our two books, Allen's and mine, were both published by Auckland University Press in 1982, and his was dedicated to me. (My later collection, *Between*, was dedicated to him.) Allen's title poem, and three others, 'The Parakeets at Karekare',* 'Dialogue with Four Rocks' and 'A Fellow Being', are west coast poems, the last being nineteen extraordinary pages of vivid serio-comic social and economic history, centred on the figure of F. J. Rayner, a Canadian with a fortune gained by marriage to a Chicago meat-packing heiress, he a dentist specialising in 'electricity', who recognised in the west coast kauri forest a means to vastly increase his wealth. It's a poem I described as 'buoyant, its affirmative tone making it a marvellous light and shade pair with Allen's Italian masterpiece, "Moro Assassinato"'. The sequence is predominantly comic, but it ends on a serious note. This alien creature, businessman, entrepreneur, doctor of dentistry, exploiter of everything in sight people no less than trees, this unstoppable North American whose

---

* There is a discussion of this poem in my *The Writer at Work*, pp. 45–48.

'soul' has been invoked in a tone of irony bordering on derision, is in the end found to be 'a fellow being', somehow reincarnated in the poet who is giving him another west coast life:

> your life-cycle and mine
> humming the hymn of it's finished
> to the tune of it's just begun.

Also in this collection is 'Organo ad Libitum', an extraordinary extension of Curnow's range, a poem which leaves behind so much, the small snobberies and vanities that sometimes get a toe in the door of his lesser poems, and 'ad libs' on an imaginary organ, prompted in the first instance by the funeral of Kath Allison (bursar at Auckland University in the 1950s and '60s), but becoming a fantasy, a 'trip', a cavort, involving a semi-blue movie seen in Paris in which nuns poison their mother superior and dance naked singing 'La Mère est morte!', swinging on the bellrope. Along the way this poem takes us on a visit to 'Sam Butler' at Erewhon, and to the controls of an airliner that crashes on Mount Erebus in Antarctica. It is a poem that reveals the Curnow mind naked, and the quirky talent surprising even itself, teasing out finally Schopenhauer's idea of palingenesis (which had also been hinted at in 'A Fellow Being') – the dead soul going nowhere but where it was already, to be restocked with itself, so that the new known might have a faint but scary shadow of familiarity and anything might bring with it a hint of *déjà vu*. But the poem had to come back (before the funeral organist closed his console) to Karekare where it was being written:

> and it's the same wave
> spirits you away
> out to sea while the
> biodegradable
> part picks up its heels
> recycles all its

degradations

fresh

wreaths every time and

no resurrections.

With the back and forth across Tohunga Crescent went letters, explanations, discussion, analysis. In March 1988 he sent me a poem, 'The Pug-Mill', together with thanks for 'a tremendously enjoyable party' in which we'd introduced the Curnows to two visiting Swedish writers, Inge and Lars-Olof Ahlstrom. Of the poem he says, 'I suppose this is my way of trying to climb Ben Bulben's back, without W. B. Y's genius of splendour in nostalgia. I hope I haven't done it once too often. I wonder if (all unconscious – I only thought of it afterwards) I've adapted the grammar of your last line in your last poem.'

My poem had been one called (using the title of a Margaret Drabble novel) 'The Radiant Way' and had ended

Anyone tape-talks
and it's history. I tell him, 'Believe in your books.'

'The Pug-Mill' ends

They are asking *Where-*
ever have you been? I tell them *Helping Mr Prisk*.

Here is part of my response to the new poem:

> I try to get around the word, but really my reaction is that 'The Pug Mill' is 'beautiful' – I think (strange) because Mr Prisk (good name!) seems almost underground, while the sun is shining up there – he seems like a gnome out of German mythology – a character for Wagner. He is also you making poems ('so long / as there's a next there's no last') [. . .] You are

> yourself as the child watching yourself as Mr Prisk – something which connects at once with yourself in 'Continuum'.

Allen was pleased:

> ... I can't say how glad I am that you like it so well – & esp that you like its opening which worried me but I could think of no way to change it.

It was in the same month (March 1988) that I sent Allen a complete copy of the about-to-be-published collection *Between*, telling him I wanted it to be dedicated to him. I knew how very little Allen now read of contemporary poetry (though not allowing this deficiency to inhibit his engagement in the ongoing Modern/Modernist debate). Now that I am the age he was then (eighty-seven) I understand this reluctance better; but I accepted it as a 'Curnow fact' and did not expect *Between* to be read closely. Nevertheless his reply showed he had done his best with it:

> I'm proud of your Dedication, indeed I am! I read (or re-read) nearly everything yesterday – too fast of course but your poetry comes 'of itself' at more than one 'speed', and exhilarates more than most poetry does. When you open the throttle I trust the driver (like that Neapolitan taxi) and forget to feel scared. Can always slow you down and see so much more. If I had to find the distinguishing word it would be Candour though it's a poetic quality and there can't be just one word for it. I'm on much better terms with your Catullus than I once was – he's so amazingly versatile – and in that fine Postscript you seem to take off the mask without dropping it, as if holding it in the hand.
>
> It's a rich collection, the way it insists on 'this world', both geo- and theo- – but not without an eschatological shiver.

I puzzled over this because though well-meant and sincere, it was clear he had tried not to say more – or not too much more – than he meant. I knew how my talent for smooth surfaces encouraged fast glides and consequent failure to read depths; and I made perfect sense of the word 'Candour': I was overt where Allen was covert. I suffered (Damien Wilkins had said of my fiction) from 'a surfeit of lucidity'. I had grown up (as Allen had) in a time when T. S. Eliot had declared that modern poetry had to be *difficult*. I remembered how when I first knew Kendrick Smithyman, and he used to show me poems, if I seemed to understand a new one at once he would take it back and rewrite it. As a poet I was out of key with the time, in that my inner anxiety was always that I might not be understood; Allen's (like the early Kendrick's) was that he might be understood – or understood too soon, and exposed – 'naked on the beach'. He liked to be explained by 'his Critic'; but not so it sounded easy.

Although Allen exerted considerable effort not to behave as if he was *il miglior fabbro*, I was never in any doubt he believed that, as poet, he *was*. And I should say that I was always honoured to be his designated 'Critic'. Jim Baxter long ago had warned me it was important for a younger poet not to be overborne and submerged by Curnow. But I had never felt endangered by the role. Allen knew, as I did, there were things I could do as a writer that he could not. I could not be Curnow, had no wish to be, and as far as I was concerned he was still the Master.

A brief interlude about swimming

Allen and Jeny were swimmers, as Kay and I are. When they weren't at Karekare they swam in Auckland at Ōkahu Bay, or in cold weather at the Tepid Baths. Our Auckland beach for many years has been Kohimarama, where I swim as often as I can out to the yellow buoy,* sometimes two – out to one, along to the next, and back on the

* Hence the title of my 2013 collection.

diagonal – which I've been assured, and allow myself to believe, is one kilometre. While our children were keen and Charlotte was a member of the surf lifesaving team, we stayed at Karekare often, but (a common song with bach-owners) as they grew into teenagers with interests in the town the incentive to be there diminished.

There was some but not a lot of interaction with Allen and Jeny out there. Their bach had been at first a secret (even sacred) place, where they could conduct their affair unseen, and it was as if a habit of mind (Jeny's reiterated 'we are very private people') had been established at that time and persisted. Lone Kauri Road winds up past the waterfall through deep native bush, regenerated since the days of kauri milling, and there is something about its ambience, not just in summer heat but equally in winter rain, that represents what I think of as 'the North' – my region of romance, and perhaps Allen's too, who had come to it first as a young man from Christchurch studying for the Anglican ministry.

It was their more than slight obsession with privacy that turned Allen into something of a campaigner against the local council's plan to seal the roads – first the main road to Piha, then Lone Kauri Road. Allen opposed each of these. His reason was that 'too many would come' – it would 'get to be known and become popular'. There was a meanness about this, and even a slight flavour of snobbery, as if the Westies should be kept away from what was in effect their own. My own view was practical: the sooner the roads were sealed the better. In dry weather clouds of dust flew up every time a car passed, and though the bush was a partial protection, a sealed surface would be better – as in the end it proved to be. Also, Piha was already popular, and Karekare (especially after it was recognised that major scenes from Jane Campion's Oscar-winning *The Piano* were shot there) would follow.

The Steads had had the use of the Curnow bach in 1973 when Allen and Jeny were away on leave. That was the stay which had led us to sell our section in Coromandel and buy a half-acre of bush further up Lone Kauri Road where we built our bach. So we would see and talk to the Curnows often on the beach, but we didn't swim together, and I have no clear idea of how strong a swimmer either of them was in the surf, which always held your attention while you were in it, and was often turbulent. Allen loved to swim, but also to fish, and gather mussels (for a long time plentiful until a shift in the behaviour of the sands buried the best beds) – and all of those activities, together with a sense of the history of the place, got into his poems like a rich loam. Most often he caught rock cod, and called people who suggested it was inferior eating 'snapper snobs'. (He was right – the taste, but more especially the texture, of rock cod, is excellent.) I fished there too, but not often. My days of keen fishing had been when we went for holidays with the children at Kay's mother's place in Tauranga. Fishing was associated in my mind with smoking, and when I gave up one the interest in the other diminished. I had also begun to have qualms – to feel sorry for the victim – so (illogically) preferred to eat fish someone else had caught.

For a time out there the possums were numerous. I knew it was my duty to take the side of the vegetation against them, and I even borrowed a trap and a gun and executed a few at night when (I hoped) the children were sleeping. But this could not continue; their enormous eyes and lovely soft fur won me over, and I began to feed them Vogel's bread.*

Allen was always insistent on 'the reality prior to the poem': there had to be one, and it had to be accurate, capable of being 'fact-checked'. It was a principle that would have made him, had he lived by it unwaveringly, a sort of super-realist; and you can see it in the poems often, a sort of twitch, as if he's saying 'You doubt me? But please note and be assured by the facts as I set them out.' For example

> Seven thigh-thick
> hamstring-high posts

---

* See 'St Francis at Karekare', *Collected Poems, 1951–2006*, p. 184.

embedded two
metres and cemented

in, where the side
of the road bursts

into bird space.

Exact! – but with those six lines of 'the poetry of fact' eclipsed by that last flash of the lyric imagination.

So you don't expect any lies, not in the poems. If he tells us he swims eighteen lengths at the Tepid Baths Auckland you know he means, and swims, eighteen:

and keep count. I think
sixteen, touch tiles, turn
with underwater eyes

follow the black line.
Touch, thinking seventeen, turn
thinking eighteen

and enough.

And if he says that this swim of eighteen lengths was achieved 'on the first day of his eighty- / first year', you know that this must be accepted too, without question, because this is a Curnow poem and comes with his warrant.

But if he should write (for example in a letter to Peter Bland describing exactly this swim)* 'Next morning, our usual (twice weekly) 600m swim in the Tepid Baths' there is no reason for not putting it to the test of fact and finding it wanting. The Teps (as

* Quoted by Terry Sturm, *Simply by Sailing in a New Direction*, Auckland University Press, p. 628.

they used to be called) is a 25-metre pool, and eighteen lengths is 450 metres. Poets are truth-tellers; swimmers exaggerate.

On-goings and gongs

During the last twelve years of his life I established links for Allen with the *LRB* and with *PN Review*, and persuaded Karl Miller to let me write a review article when *Continuum* was published. That article alerted Seamus Heaney to Curnow's poetry and led to the recommendation he be awarded the Queen's Gold Medal for Poetry – which he received from the royal hand itself when Her Majesty brought it to New Zealand in 1990. Allen also received in that year (as did Janet Frame) the ONZ, New Zealand's highest honour.* He wrote to me describing a dream in which he was meeting the Queen and looked down to find with horror that he was wearing dirty old brown shoes! Recently I watched the Shirley Horrocks documentary about Allen and noticed there are a few minutes about one of his 'walking-in-Parnell' poems when the camera focuses on his feet, wearing a pair of very worn and more than slightly torn or split, but no doubt comfortable, brown shoes. These were no doubt the pair that figured in his Canterbury-Anglican nightmare – such shoes for Her Majesty, Defender of the Faith!

In June '88 Kay and I had been to dinner at the Curnows' to meet Allen's close associate from Canterbury days, the distinguished political historian John Pocock, and when I wrote to thank them I sent the recently published text of my lecture on *The Tower* given

* It is commonly believed that there are only twenty holders of the Order of New Zealand. In fact, at any time the government has some special occasion it wants to mark, and a person or persons seeming to call for the highest honour, an 'Additional' award can be made if there's already a full complement of twenty. Both Allen's and Janet's awards, marking the 1990 sesquicentenary, were Additional. On the death of the recipient the medal is returned and may pass to a later recipient in the same or a similar field. In 2002 Professor Sir Hugh Kawharu was made a Member of the Order and received Allen's medal. A few years after Sir Hugh's death, I was made a Member and received his. So the medal I now hold (also Additional) was once Allen's.

at the Yeats Summer School in Sligo.* Allen wrote a very long response, slightly shocked at my questioning the great one's great poems and comparing me to Dr Johnson on the subject of Lycidas – even setting two quotations side by side, Stead on Yeats, Johnson on Milton. It took me back to the time when we had both lectured on Yeats, I to stage one, he to MA, and we used to discuss the poems in great detail in the department common room, seldom needing a text because we could usually put any of the major poems together from memory. At that time I'd suggested we write a book on Yeats in the form of letters back and forth. I thought (and still think) it could have been a major contribution to Yeats criticism, partly because our approaches were so different; and though I could see it was not an unattractive idea to Allen, he didn't like the thought of being lined up and measured alongside his junior colleague. For him they were sacred texts; he always had penetrating things to say about them, but as exegetist – whereas I was critic, not reverent when I thought the ideas foolish or that the execution could have been more elegant.

Two thirds of the way down the second typed page of his response to my lecture he writes, 'I didn't mean to run on like this. Partly it's because you open the poems the way you do.' But then, having seemed to finish, he continues for almost two further pages of handwritten postscripts, concluding 'Your final para is fine – & <u>bold</u> – it's in the major critical key.' And then a day later he apologises: 'What a towering heap of Yeatsian scrapings that was! You might feel like the lady on the *Titanic* who only wanted ice for her highball. You set me going, and on I went!'

At this time he was putting together collections of recent and past poems in arrangements that consistently frustrated the reader interested in chronology. I understood the wish to have the best poems the first the reader encountered, and the last too, leaving a favourable impression; but books of poems can't be counted on to

---

* Reproduced in *Answering to the Language*, pp. 29–46.

be read like books of fiction from beginning to end, and the effort (on which he spent so much time and anxious thought) produced collections which I thought were more confusing than useful. It was a quirk of his, a peculiarity, a needless anxiety that *if only* the right arrangement could be struck the *true* worth of the collection would be revealed. Only when asked, I gave advice. For the *Selected Poems 1940–1989* I wanted as many of the early sonnets as could be fitted to the planned space, and identified those I thought could perhaps be dispensed with if there had to be a reduction. On this subject I wrote:

> I would rather see the sonnets *in*, and 'An Abominable Temper' *out*, if it came to a choice. I think the one weak point since 1971 (I haven't of course said this in my *LRB* review) is the whole Abom. Temp collection most of which I think you could leave out if you're pressed for space.

My suggestions were mostly accepted, but (he wrote) 'I think I have to be pig-headed about "An Abominable Temper". Perhaps family piety blinds me, but if so, so it must be.' At least he was leaving out a couple of (I thought) unpleasant poems that went into that rather hasty collection of 1973 – the refusal to read at a Baxter memorial, and the poem about the uncomprehending 'unfortunate young woman'.

The Curnows travelled a lot in these last years of his life, and so did we after I left the university in 1987, so our communications were as often intercontinental as cross-crescent. So much was happening to us both at this time – Allen's multiple gongs and multiple collections and selections; my *Voices* for 1990 and *Sister Hollywood* (in 1989) – and we were both reading and commenting on one another's work. The London flat controversy was also going on at this time and got into our exchanges back and forth. In my admiration for his new poems as they emerged I was always entirely sincere, though often irritated by his ego (as he might well have been by mine). In my note congratulating him on the Queen's Gold Medal I said:

> How happy and glorious! I feel as if, on the subject of 'Curnow', the world has been slowly catching up with me since I first read him forty years ago. I can now rest on his laurels. Next stop Stockholm? I'd like to think so.

The Stockholm thought pleased and excited him, and I sometimes thought he imagined I had connections there that might advance his cause. I didn't of course; but I had tried to persuade the NZPEN to nominate him for the Prize.*

It was a quite exceptional act of diligence for Allen to have read my *Sister Hollywood* at what was a busy time for him; and possibly the sense of having exceeded his duties brought out a burst of something like irritation. It certainly brought out what was in no sense a surprise to me – I knew this aspect of his character so well:

> I forget who questioned the 'credibility' of your Arlene. If anything all too 'credible' for me – nothing like that to bother this reader – perhaps rather, that I didn't manage to like her as well as the story seemed to expect. Is it perverse of me to find her a girl on the make, much tougher and a better survivor than either hapless hubby or wimpish Jesse (though that's not quite right). Not an easy story to forget. [. . .] The recreation of that whole L.A. ambience is marvellous and also relieves me of any wish I ever had to know it better.

* Unsuccessfully because our PEN wanted Frame to be New Zealand's nominee. I wrote the letter on her behalf several times. I knew a fiction writer, especially one with Frame's history of obstacles overcome, was a more likely Nobel Prize winner, and I made our recommendations warm and even fulsome; but I thought in fact that Curnow would have been a more deserving Nobel Laureate.

It was so absolutely 'true to form' for Allen to characterise a young woman struggling against odds, and succeeding in a tough male-dominated world, as 'a girl on the make' – and not to like and admire her. I didn't tell him that Antonia (Byatt) found Arlene 'inspiring'. I replied:

> Arlene 'a girl on the make' – yes I suppose that's one way of describing her. I admire her, enjoy her – probably because I put so much of myself into her. My grandmother, a charitable woman, would have said she was 'on the go' [meaning energetic, purposeful].

In the last couple of years when he was putting together what was to be his last book, *The Bells of Saint Babel's*, there was a strange intense acceleration of our exchanges. I remember feeling the strangeness at the time. There were fulsome compliments going both ways across the crescent and at the same time a sense that each was more than faintly irritated by the other. I liked very much – as much as ever – the long thin poems of the *Bells* . . . collection as they appeared one by one; they were Curnow 'on form' – no loss of power or penetration. I let him know – not brutally, but why at all? – that I didn't much like his pantoum 'For Peter Porter at Seventy'. He and I were the two NZers in a collection, put together by Ann and Anthony Thwaite, of twenty tributes to Peter on his seventieth birthday. Allen's was I thought Whim Wham on hard labour. But his want of another book was desperate so this pantoum (and the connection it registered with Porter) had to go into what he was now calling the 'exiguous new collection' – and he may even have been pleased with it.

On the subject of his 'Fantasia and Fugue for Pan-Pipe' I asked, 'Isn't it, not "two thousand years and a bit", but two thousand years minus 33, since Jesus called out in a loud voice?' Perhaps because to acknowledge my question was right might have meant a revision, he preferred to explain it as no problem at all:

> I decide that Christ's Nativity and Crucifixion are a single event, so one doesn't need to allow for those putative 33 years of his incarnation and earthly ministry. I think I added 'and a bit' more to cover any calendrical anomalies.

This was the language of the man who had trained for the Anglican ministry, and with some DIY theology – but '*putative*'? Heresy, surely! However, he later changed 'and a bit' to '(rounded out)'.

In August 2000 we were all four, poets and wives, at the New Zealand Book Awards and Allen received the 'Lifetime Achievement Award'. I told him I was glad – 'absolutely your deserving' – and that I was touched to have been mentioned in his speech. He replied:

> It helps me past that 'terminal' touch in 'lifetime' to know you are glad they made that award, and can give me a pass for my rather messy speech. Remembering (would I forget?!) your remark about Mr Prisk was a lifeline.

If my own news about festivals ahead and behind, and recent reviews of *Talking about O'Dwyer* by Peter Porter and John de Falbe, are added into the mix, together with exchanges about how to read and review Les Murray, and whether the Ogilvie biography of Denis Glover deserved praise or blame, there is something hectic about these interactions. We launched *The Bells of Saint Babel's,* Allen's last book, in March 2001 on the deck of Elizabeth Caffin's house in Northcote. I made the speech and was able to say it was fifty years almost to the day since I'd first seen him – enrolment day March 1951, I an eighteen-year-old 'fresher', he a thirty-nine-year-old journalist newly arrived from Christchurch to take up a lectureship. It was at that launch that one of the very few photographs of us together was taken. He inscribed my copy 'for Karl – always somewhere in earshot', knowing I would at once recognise the source, Yeats's

> Pardon, old fathers, if you still remain
> Somewhere in ear-shot for the story's end.

In that shot of us together he doesn't look as though 'the story's end' was close, but he probably had an inkling that it might be.

The story's end

In what was to be (though I didn't know) my last letter to Allen (dated 18.8.01) I responded to the news that Bounce (the Curnow's dog that had followed after Towser's death) had been run over and killed in Brighton Road.

> Your note reached me c/o Margaret and I have to say first how sorry we both were to hear that Bounce had been run over. Not that one could converse with Bounce – he was much too nervous to speak to strangers. I used to toss him the odd remark as he bustled about and he always looked appalled and veered away as if I had uttered a solecism or (more likely) a threat. On the other hand his welcomes to your house tended to excess (I liked all that racing around and yapping with ears flapping). He was quite distinctly *there* in the neighbourhood and in one's consciousness. There was a time when I thought you had developed an eccentricity – or worse: you were to be seen from time to time at, or inside, your car sounding the horn at short intervals and looking displeased. It was some time before I recognised that this was a way of summoning the wandering pooch home. We do both send our sympathy.
>
> We arrived here [Saint-Maximin, near Uzès] yesterday after adventures *en route* from Nice airport, which included a (new) hirecar (Renault Eurodrive) with an almost empty tank sealed and locked by the electronic device which would unlock everything but the tank. Mechanics swarmed over it on a layby on the autoroute and finally we were towed off the autoroute

and through a wood by an unbelievably sweaty bandit who spoke not a word of any language, Kay and I jammed beside and behind him in his cab, Kay convinced that we would soon be strangled and robbed and left among the pines. But this, as it turned out, was a way of getting off the autoroute without going 20 kms to the next exit and back; and soon we were at the Renault works at Fréjus where a repair was done and we were able to motor on. [. . .]

I passed your good wishes to Karl Miller at his 70th birthday party at Faber and he returned them. Kay was in France so I took Margaret. It was quite a party. Karl's speech was masterly – witty at first, and then very moving when he shifted from himself as the occasion of the occasion to Ian Hamilton who had organised it (and the anthology of poems and prose tributes) and couldn't be there because he is ill – dying in fact, Karl told me, of cancer. Seamus Heaney, slightly drunk and very jolly, told Margaret that after his inaugural lecture as Prof of Poetry at Oxford some years ago I had told him that his lecture had been shaped like a condom.

I told Allen that at the forthcoming King's Lynn Poetry Festival there was to be a final session in which each of the poets would choose to talk about and read from a favourite twentieth-century poet. My choice was Curnow, and I had with me *Bells . . .* and *Early Days Yet* from which to read.*

For the next three weeks or so Kay and I were in Saint-Maximin with two of our oldest friends, Jill who had been with Kay in the third form at Auckland Girls' Grammar, and Don who had been with me in the MA class of 1955. They have floated in and out of these memoirs; and after I left the university Don had stayed on as Professor of English, which was still his role. They had been with us

* Allen's reply to this was dated 8.9.01 – so just three days before what we would all come to know as 9/11, and a fortnight before his death. It went astray in the post and only reached me back in Tohunga Crescent (where it had been written) in December.

just a fortnight when I decided they should see Natasha Spender's garden at the *Mas Saint-Jérôme* near Maussane-les-Alpilles. The drive took us across the Rhône through Beaucaire and Tarascon. When we got back to Saint-Maximin someone turned on the TV and the screen revealed what looked at first glance as if there had been a nuclear attack on America. It was September 11th – 9/11 – and our alarm was increased, as the nature of the event became clearer, and the Smiths remembered that their partially sighted daughter Caitlin was supposed to be in New York at that moment. It was some hours before they received an email confirming that she was safe. She had been proceeding with her white stick in the direction of the Twin Towers and had wondered why the crowd – larger and larger, more and more agitated as the minutes passed – seemed all to be running the other way, until someone turned her in the safer direction, away from the mayhem of the burning skyscrapers, from which, so far away, we were watching bodies hurtling through the air to escape the flames and crashing to their deaths.

Later it was considered insensitive to show those deaths; but at the time, TV cameras were focusing narrowly on one figure after another at or emerging from a window, and then following its flight – almost it seemed slowly, the drop was so huge – all the way down to a shield protecting ground level from anything that might fall from above. Even with the cameras turned away, focused on the crowd and the panic, those hideous impacts went on sounding – *bang, bang-bang, bang*.

Again and again, with the rest of the world, we watched replays of those two airliners flying like deadly spears into the heart of each tower; and then, after some hours, first one building, then the other, tottered, subsided and collapsed in upon itself. Was Allen watching too – or was he already unconscious in hospital, his body wired up and sending messages that the failing heart could not go on beating much longer?

Life went on. We took a breath with everyone else and continued enjoying France, completed our holiday while watching the world

– meaning for the moment America – from a distance. We drove to Menton with the Smiths on 23 September (a Sunday – the best day for being on the roads in France, because trucks are banned) and stayed at the Hotel Edwards, modestly priced and conveniently placed. It was there that phone calls reached me from New Zealand to say that Allen had died. We both talked to Charlotte and then Oliver, both in Auckland, and to Margaret in London. I was asked to write an obit for the *Independent* and agreed. The same request from the *Daily Telegraph* had to be declined. It was only when we got back to London I managed to speak to Jeny. She was distressed but in command of herself and we had one of those murmuring exchanges of necessary and consoling nothings. I wrote my obit on Margaret's laptop, lacking reference material but trusting memory, and met my deadline.*

I spent the last two days of that month at the King's Lynn festival. My choice of Curnow for the '20th Century Icons' session now had a special resonance. It made Allen a presence in that festival as he had never been in fact. And then it was back to London for the dinner Harvill put on as a launch for *The Secret History of Modernism*.

I'M NOT SURE WHEN I WROTE 'His Round' but I think it was two or three years after Allen's death.

His Round
Allen Curnow 1911–2001

'Home' for the boy had meant
somewhere between England

* Jeny would point out four insignificant errors of fact and add that in the 'so-called blank period, late 1950s–1972' Allen wrote two plays. 'Reasons for not publishing in this period are complex.'

where God was still living
and the ground under his feet.

As a man he wrote of islands,
talked tides and distances,

and seldom bought his round.
Not Prospero, but like him,

he made words work and had
'an abominable temper'.

His project was to catch
the heron's deliberation

lifting itself over mangroves,
or on that opposite coast

the careless way a gull
could be tossed in an updraft.

These were his annotations
on a world that exceeded

all it could say of itself.
He fished for the brown cod

and had a name for those
who thought it inferior eating.

He summoned his dog by car horn,
looked hard into sunsets,

and called himself 'an old man
who wouldn't say his prayers.'

Stubborn, still owing his round,
he was towed at the last

headlong into the westerly,
tottering, leashed to his Dog.

In *Talking about O'Dwyer* the two boys, Mike and Frano, are much taken with the thought that 'God' is only a word – in fact dog spelled backward. This seems to suck the power – the immanence and eminence – out of it; and it's an idea that hovers somewhere around a number of poems in the collection I called *DOG*. So in 'His Round', the Dog Allen is leashed to could be the Anglican God with whom he had partly, but I thought never completely, severed company. He had always said his funeral service would be the full Anglican job (which I could not quite disconnect in my mind from 'the full English breakfast') because he found all the alternatives unsatisfactory or (more usually) distasteful.

I read 'His Round' on the radio, and Jeny phoned me immediately after the broadcast to say she had been driving with the car radio on and when she heard my reading announced she had pulled over to listen. She had been deeply moved, to tears she said, and was ringing to say so. But later, when she read it as a published text, her view of it changed: it was quite unacceptable. I thought her first reaction had been the right one. She had heard the feeling in the poem and had known that it was affirmative – positive and loving.

Our relations which had been pretty good were now, not cool, but wary. When she heard in 2003 that I was to give the annual 'Curnow Reading' at the Going West Festival she wrote asking me please not to read 'His Round'. 'I – and the other Literary Executors' (i.e. Elizabeth Caffin and Tim Curnow) 'find it capable of untrue and unpleasant interpretations. The other poem about Allen is lovely.'

I wondered whether it had crossed her mind to imagine how Allen would have responded if the widow of Mike Joseph had asked him not to read 'Dichtung und Warheit'. Mine was the same. She was away overseas so would not be present to be offended. I ignored her request and read the poem.

What she found objectionable of course was the statement that Allen 'seldom bought his round'. This was a fact known to everyone who knew him even slightly. He was famous for meanness. Terry Sturm, who wrote the biography, had heard so many stories that confirmed it; but Terry, watched constantly by Jeny, would have agreed with her that this should not be 'that kind of book'. It was to be a literary biography of a great poet, not a record of disrespectful and unsubstantiated gossip. And yet that famous refusal to acknowledge debt or obligation I saw as an essential aspect of a very large character – the man who had told Terry he would not have his poems 'pawed over by his inferiors' on the New Zealand Literary Fund Advisory Committee. His ego, his arrogance, had to be there in the record, in *my* record, or it would not be the man I had known.

In 2011 when the hundredth anniversary of Allen's birth was coming up I wrote a poem about him* in thirteen-syllable triplets which I offered to the *LRB*, and Mary-Kay published it to match the date. I also read it at the Frankfurt Book Fair that year as part of a ceremony for the handing over of guest country status from Greenland to New Zealand, and spoke of Allen as 'New Zealand's greatest writer'.

Postscript:

Tohunga Crescent

Across the street the Allen Curnow house
sold and garden-tidied and refurbished,
respectably letting as 'AirBnB'

* 'The Gift', *The Yellow Buoy*, Auckland University Press, 2013, pp. 97–99.

is home to wild parties, and just once
a riot bringing cop cars, a paddy wagon,
pepper spray and more than one arrest.

Always there's rubbish at the roadside when
the random tenants leave. Tonight by morepork
and moonlight while the neighbour cats patrol

I'm watching Jeny walk in her ghostly gown
smiling and weeping, and here comes Allen alert
with a new poem needing to know at once

what I will make of it – but as I read
he seems to slide away among the trees
all darkness and displeasure. There's a light

down at the Bay – that's Graham with his spear,
full tide at midnight, and the water still
holding itself for something new to reflect.

Morning will disclose the pohutukawa
know it's December, time for spectacular blossom –
and Jeny's ambiguous tears have left me anxious

about those flashing lines of Allen light
seen and forgotten like the spell of weather
just gone you hadn't known might be a blessing.

11.
Croatia, and 'Last Season's Man'

1996 and beyond

In Chapter 1 I write about my novel *Talking about O'Dwyer*, and about the Māori Battalion, Crete, Dan Davin and Oxford connections, Rob Dyer and his father Col. Humphrey Dyer who was part model for the character of O'Dwyer – all these, but only in passing about the other element in the story, Croatia, except to say that while Kay and I were living in Oxford we were invited to Zagreb for the launch of a Croatian translation of *All Visitors Ashore* which had been discovered by two extraordinary editors, Ljiljana Šćurić and Jadranka Pintarić. Croatia became part of *Talking about O'Dwyer* because my Māori soldier Joe Panapa, who is destined to be shot during the Battle of Crete by his commanding officer Donovan O'Dwyer, is married to a woman of Croatian descent who lives with her family on their vineyard in Henderson, the West Auckland location where Kay grew up. O'Dwyer has been living since the end of World War II in Oxford, which he chooses to see as the working out of a mākutu put on him by the family of the soldier he shot. The novel begins with O'Dwyer's death; and another New Zealander, Mike Newall, an Oxford professor of philosophy two decades younger than O'Dwyer, is prompted by the funeral, and by a dinner at his college which follows, to begin 'talking about O'Dwyer' to an old retired don, Bertie Winterstoke. By this device a structure for the novel as a whole is established: it will range about in time and space, but will keep returning to this extended conversation, in which the younger (but not young) Mike Newall tells the story the novel is unfolding.

I'm not sure when these diverse elements came together in my mind as one story; but I know that I was so vividly struck by the Zagreb book launch, and by the atmosphere of that place so sharpened by the war which the break-up of Yugoslavia had brought about, that I felt there was fiction here waiting to be written, and that I had to go back in search of it. So the old story I had been living with since my student years, about how my friend Rob Dyer's father had shot one of his own Māori Battalion soldiers and had been cursed for it by the soldier's family, seemed now to want to find a 'way out' for itself partly via the tale of a more recent war. The Māori soldier, Joe Panapa as I called him, has married into a Dalmatian* family; and Mike Newall has grown up as their next-door neighbour and their son Frano's school friend. After Frano aged about eighteen is killed (or kills himself) on his motorbike, his mother, Ljuba, who has now lost both the men in her life, husband and son, returns to her family in Croatia only to be caught up in the Yugoslav war of the early 1990s. Her house is destroyed and for a time her whereabouts are unknown – so Mike Newall, who has kept contact from Oxford with her family in New Zealand, undertakes to go looking for her.

It was those two remarkable women, Ljiljana and Jadranka, who made it more than possible for me to enact Mike's role and make the discoveries I would need in order to write this part of the novel. They encouraged the project and made it easy to achieve. I had only to find my way back to Croatia the summer after that book launch and they would look after me, provide accommodation, take me

---

* As we used to call them when I was young – i.e. from the Dalmatian (coastal) region of Croatia.

about, show me things, translate for me and explain what was going on around me. They were excited by my fiction and were glad to think they might have a part in the telling of a new story, one that would include the part of the world they called home.

The character of Ira in the novel is a contraction of Ljiljana and Jadranka, and a good deal of what happens in Chapter 3 is a direct account of my experience when I returned to Zagreb and stayed with Ljiljana and her aunt. The description of the apartment there is exact – four floors up in a concrete Soviet-style building with no lifts, with windows looking down to a main street, Šubićeva, where trams clank and bell by, and with a balcony looking inward to a courtyard into which the sun did not penetrate and in which the sounds from the other apartments – happy, sad, angry, tearful, singing or shouting – constantly echo.

Later in the novel, Chapter 16 and beyond, the same visit is used again, or used further, not all of it 'what happened really', but place especially, and the mood of time and place, a direct record of Croatia in the precarious state of immediate-post-war tension. I drove all the way down to the coast with them in Jadranka's noisy Škoda, passing first (only 50 kilometres from Zagreb) through farming areas where more than half the houses were burned out, blackened and pock-marked by shells, crops and grazing animals largely abandoned, and where I was warned, when I wanted to take photographs, not to stray far or linger long because there might be a landmine, or someone (a 'mad Serb' for example) among the trees with a grudge and a gun. Now and then there would be the sight of a family trying to hang on and eke out a living as before, or a child looking lost and forlorn.

We went up over some mountains and came down again to the coast and to a small town, Zaton, on an inner waterway of astonishing beauty where the relatives of one or the other of my two companions gave us meals and drinks of traditional welcome. All of this would go into the novel – and not least an evening of beautiful, often sad singing by an all-male klapa group in traditional black and white, against a background of fishing boats and still, moon-reflecting water. The elderly widows who entertained us had been peasants who married partisans during or after World War II, and had been good communists under Tito, so were by no means fanatical supporters of the new order, but content now to be loyal Croatians. In this they were like Ljiljana – though she was more sophisticated and better educated.

Ljiljana's father had been a diplomat and she had been, as a child, a Young Patriot, about to earn a medal for excellence of some leftist kind when Tito died and the old order began to fall apart rendering such honours meaningless. Her parents had been killed in a traffic accident when she was twelve, and after that she had lived with her aunt in that apartment which I could see was rather grim and unlovely, but had a fascination for one who had lived most of his life (consciously) on one side of the Iron Curtain and now felt he had crossed over into what was left of the other. In Croatia at that time there was still a strong lingering flavour of the old Marxist state, with its workers and its nomenclatura. Like the character of Ira in my novel, Ljiljana had had a lover killed in the siege of Dubrovnik.

Jadranka, though quite as much a product of communist Yugoslavia, was a more typical Croatian. She came from a middle-class Catholic family and although (unlike Ljiljana) mostly silent on political matters, she was sometimes fiercely, even passionately, nationalistic and anti-Serbian. The new dispensation, in other words, seemed to please her more than it pleased her friend.

It was down at that beautiful coastal area that I was lodged in a room in a stony village with all windows open to the summer night, and listened to those echoing sounds recorded in the novel – the giant snorer, the rooster crowing at the moon, the regular chiming of a grandfather clock in a nearby house, the occasional clatter of goat hoofs on the cobbles below, and just now and then the extraordinarily loud 'HEE-HAWING' of a donkey, lamenting (I suggested) the size of his ears and the weight of the loads he would carry tomorrow. The three of us had been drunk that night, partly an effect of those welcoming meals which were always accompanied by local varieties of spirits and wines, and partly of our three-way fondness – an inebriation which had reached a peak when Jadranka had gone down on her knees on the stones to a wayside effigy of the Virgin and had prayed – fervently and in tears. Long after this exotic time was over Jadranka would write me one of her very rare letters, apologising for that moment, but in a way that told me she remembered it rather than that she regretted it, and perhaps hoped that I did too.

On the way back to Zagreb from the coast and the town of Šibenik we seemed to avoid the mountains crossed on the way south and took a more direct route through the area of the Krajina, where the small towns seemed largely deserted. When I asked why this was there was a silence until Jadranka explained that the people there had been mostly Serbs and had 'just gone away'. Ethnic cleansing? I didn't ask the question nor, if that was what it was, how it had been achieved.* But I discovered only later that when Croatia had declared its independence from Yugoslavia the Serbian population who predominated in the Krajina region had declared an independence of their own, which Croatia had not accepted and the matter had been settled by force.

In the years that followed, Jadranka, whose English was less than perfect, wrote seldom, Ljiljana, constantly, and there were many letters between us about linguistic matters, about her delight in the sly jokes she found hidden in my texts, and the subtleties she perceived in my use of the language. Her English was fluent and her intelligence exceptional.

* The term was used to describe what happened a great deal during the Yugoslav war, sometimes by lethal enforcement, at others by 'persuasion'. It was in the air at the time and explains why I considered it seriously defamatory when Michael King said I had advocated the ethnic cleansing of New Zealand literature. These were the matters which the International Tribunal in The Hague that Tony Axelrad worked for had been set up to deal with.

> I realised the other day that if someone had asked me about the narrator in *All Visitors Ashore* I would have answered without a moment's thought that it is written in the first person. I was really surprised when I remembered that it isn't – somehow it feels as if it is. I think you have managed to produce a narrator's position that defies definition there. [. . .]
>
> If I caught a goldfish, my wish would be that my story [she was thinking of writing fiction] ends up with the compactness of *All Visitors Ashore*, but I suspect even goldfish aren't what they used to be, and you said that you didn't think even you could do something like that again. The one I have in mind when I think of plagiarising is *The End of the Century* . . .

In my reply I said I was writing the movie script for *Villa Vittoria* with help from our cat Zac, and I added:

> I do feel you must write your novel. Don't worry about the difficulties. Just do it. And 'Plagiarise' of course! – except that it's not plagiarism. Every writer must be helped by other writers who have gone before. That is the nature of the 'tradition'.

When *Talking about O'Dwyer* was published in English Ljiljana went to work to translate it into Croatian for the same Zagreb publisher:

> I am now slowly re-reading it – and as always the depth and density of your sentences drives me crazy with envy. And the wit, needless to say. On another level – I think it will be appreciated in Croatia, because even though you don't actually take sides, it feels as if you do through the relationships with Croatia. [. . .] Apart from the main story, it was really fascinating both to see a reflection of oneself and the transformations made to serve the story, to see how you do such things.

> And what you did with my idea of two people talking about (do you mind me saying it was my idea?) I'm so glad you used it and what you did with it is so far beyond me – amazing.

We kept up regular exchanges about 'everything' – mostly books, and the subtleties and difficulties of the translation process; but her letters were also personal, confessional, and I seem to have adopted the role of adviser, the older man, anxious for her. This was often about online dating, still relatively uncommon and quite unknown to me until then – and I urged her not to do it. Her argument (which I have heard so often since) was that it was no different from meeting someone in a bar. *Totally* different I insisted – pointing out that tone of voice, eyes, body language, even aromas, were subtleties that words on the page could not convey, or could misrepresent. I also wrote:

> And there's something (to me – please forgive my frankness) *dingy* about it. I would rather be free-standing and alone than have to resort to the back-streets of the internet.

In reply she told me I had never been alone. 'You could not possibly comprehend the scope of my loneliness and the lack of available/interesting men.' Later she would follow an online 'lover' all the way to America, marry him there, discover that most of what he had told her about himself was untrue and that he was a lifelong alcoholic.

Ljiljana was intellectually brilliant but also deeply neurotic – subject to eating disorders and panic attacks. There is a moment in *Talking about O'Dwyer* when Mike Newall, walking about the city at night with Ira, orders ice cream 'because it was the only food she would let him order for her; and even then she only stirred it around in its dish and licked small amounts off her spoon. Before long her cigarette would be alight and the ice cream pushed across for him to finish.' That was typical. It seemed she could eat most of the meal her aunt cooked for us at midday (and no doubt the aunt knew her fads), but almost nothing else; and I don't know how she survived on that drive to the coast. I thought she must have had secret supplies which she raided in the night. Otherwise it was cigarettes and liquids.

Ljiljana told me in more than one letter of the wish to kill herself which she said invaded her every month. I had no way of knowing (and didn't ask) whether this was to do with painful menstruation, or, on the other hand, the fact that the arrival of a period meant there would be no child, or just a way of saying it came quite often and regularly. I do have a recollection that there was an e-message saying she was arranging to look after a refugee child and that this seemed intended as therapy. It reminded me that there had been a similar episode in Katherine Mansfield's life. In both cases the child was soon abandoned, or the idea set aside.

Through most of 2000 Ljiljana was translating *Talking about O'Dwyer*, sending me detailed questions and enjoying herself, and I was making progress with the novel that would be *The Secret History of Modernism*. 'The new novel', I told her

> . . . is not only strange and terribly LITERARY (and therefore probably unsalable) but also somehow intransigent. It has a personality of its own, goes its own way, and is not altogether nice or ingratiating.

The English version of *Talking about O'Dwyer* was launched in London at New Zealand House in May 2000 – one of those rare and somewhat lavish occasions when I felt in charge of my life – that I'd made a good launch speech to memorable people, and was pleased, or not too displeased, with myself.

Ljiljana always insisted that Jadranka was 'the real intellectual' and a force in the publishing world of Croatia, but because of her difficulties with English there was never the same kind of rapport. To me she always seemed mysterious and beautiful. It was like my old overt-covert paradigm: Ljiljana was overt, Jadranka covert. Sometimes on our adventure together we had joked about Jadranka's mistakes in English, and she appeared to enjoy these – perhaps even worked on them to make them funnier. On that drive south, going over the mountains before reaching the coast, we'd stopped at a restaurant which, though it had had one large hole blasted in its side and another in its roof, Jadranka insisted would suit me well because it specialised in 'ships'. It took a moment or two to discover that by 'ships' she meant 'sheeps' – i.e. mutton. Best was her explanation that a ruin had once been 'a house for middle-aged knits' – by which she meant it had been a castle occupied by knights of the Middle Ages.

It was Jadranka who wrote to tell me that Hrvoje Božičević, the publisher who had put on the lavish Zagreb launch of *All Visitors Ashore*, provided the top-class restaurant meals and wines, the expensive hotels, chauffeur-driven cars and lovely random gifts, the man who (with his wife) wore such stylish clothes and expensive fur coats, had put the company deep into debt and was in trouble for having tried to exploit his close friendship with a grandson of the President, and with the President himself, Franjo Tuđman. The name Božičević remained as the publisher, but Hrvoje (his first name, which Christopher MacLehose and I shortened to Roy) was gone. As a consequence of that upheaval Jadranka had lost her job. 'So I have to work on some other jobs to support myself because as you know I'm alone on the Earth.' She signed the message 'Pusa' – with a kiss.

2007

In May 2007 I made a ten-day visit to Croatia for the launch of Ljiljana's translation of *My Name Was Judas* (*Zvao sam se Juda*). So much happened in those ten days it seems in memory a much longer period – organised by Roman Simić who was pretty much in charge, or at least the live wire, of the new publisher, Profil. By now Ljiljana was living in America, married to one of her internet lovers, and probably already divorced; and though she had done this translation, I had lost contact with her – which may explain why Jadranka was to tell me it was untypically rough and careless and had given her as editor many hours of work bringing it up to standard.

I see from my appointments diary that the morning of the day I was to leave New Zealand, 8 May, Kay and I had our usual swim at Kohimarama. That evening I flew off to LA where I spent a few hours in transit, and then flew straight on to Munich and Zagreb. Although I was going for the launch of the Judas novel I'd been warned that *Talking about O'Dwyer* (published in Croatian as *Makutu*) was also creating considerable interest, so I should be prepared to talk about it. I read it on those flights, and wrote in a notebook I was keeping:

> I had forgotten most of it and read it 'as a novel' – anyone's novel. It has a faintly desperate wisdom which I quite liked, and a lot of wit. The character of Winterstoke is good. I think it's a novel I can be satisfied with, but it does put quite a strain on the reader's patience and attention, because it moves about so much in place and time. Only a literary reader would bother, probably.

The notebook continues:

> Roman Simich met me at Zagreb. He is very young – or appears to be – pleasant and enthusiastic. I asked to be left for the rest of the day – it was mid afternoon – slept for a bit, and then found a good restaurant and had a kind of goulash – bean soup served in one dish with a ladle and in the other, two largish slices of cooked meat. I assumed one cut up the meat in the bowl and ladled the bean soup over it. Anyway that's what I did and it was excellent – with a glass of red wine followed by coffee.

I have been drafting some poems, ideas for poems, first in transit in LA and now here. Spirits are OK without being UP, and waves of exhaustion wash over me, with feelings of wanting to get it over and get home.

[. . . After a day of literary meetings]

Still tinkering with poems. Moments of jet-lag gloom but not too bad. Tonight is the launch.

13/7/07 Judas launch last night after a day of walking about, sleeping, preparing my readings, and faint apprehension. It all went off well I think. Sometimes I was momentarily inarticulate – but mostly fluent. The atmosphere was full of respect (preceded by quick TV and radio interviews) – I have a very literary fan-base here, especially among writers. The panel was Roman, Milan [I'm not sure who this was] and Jadranka who took turns asking me about the book. Jadranka talked about knowing me, and about our trip to the coast which got into *Talking about O'Dwyer* (*Makutu* here) and said she might be in the book. This is apparently asked a lot ('Did it happen?') and she refuses to answer but doesn't seem to mind the question. I think people suppose she is Ira and we were lovers, which was not the case. I had a meal with her afterwards and liked her very much – so vivid, such a mobile excited face, such a clever woman and so strong and serious as well as funny. She came for me today at 5 p.m. with her friend Mia who translated Judas's poems and we went to a sort of teahouse in woods and took tea and talked until it was time to go to the launch.

I have a photograph the friend Mia took of us on that occasion which reminds me of the magic Jadranka had for me, the covert woman who had continued to occupy a small bright corner of my imagination since we'd first met in Zagreb ten years before. This was one of those times when anything that happened to me threatened (or promised) to be a poem. So,

Speaking in Bronze*

for Jadranka Pintarić

Spring has come early to Zagreb.
The market tables are scarlet with strawberries,
the town woods are in full leaf.
On the wide veranda of Dubravkin Put
the melancholy waiter serves us English tea
with a look of regret that says
'This is what you ordered, but our coffee is so much better.'
The statue of the writer with the unpronounceable name
watches us pass on the path that was once his own.
His house was there among trees
and his heart was in the city.
Life was serious then, every word counted.
There was a world to be saved, or set to rights.
'Where did it all go wrong?' he seems to ask,
speaking in bronze.
'Why did I die too soon?'

The morning after the Zagreb launch I was driven almost 300 kilometres to Zadar, down on the coast where it was to be launched again. I was set up briefly in an apartment and looked after by the local librarian, Mladen Masar, who gave me a tour of the town with many reminiscences of the time when it had been shelled by the Serbs from the hills above. Mladen ('Think of Bin Laden', he told me, and add an 'M') I learned was the same age as Roman Simić, thirty-five, and they both were fathers for the first time of one-and-a-half-year-olds; both feeling sensitised to the world by the new reality of parenthood. I knew what he/they meant, though I had to look back more than forty years to remember it.

---

* The statue of the writer with the unpronounceable name will be another element in the story 'Last Season's Man' which will figure later in this chapter.

In the few days I was there I walked to his office each day to keep up my exchange of emails with Kay, swam in the mornings, gave a talk in English on 'post-colonial literature' to university students ('with extraordinary fluency, even, possibly, eloquence' my notebook reports), gave a reading in a bookshop and managed to catch on TV the movie of A. S. Byatt's Booker winner, *Possession*, with Gwyneth Paltrow in the star role.*

In the same year, 2007, the firm of Božičević (now without big-spender 'Roy') had published a translation of my novel *Mansfield* with the title *Srce nema ništa s tim, Katherine* (*Your heart's got nothing to do with it, Katherine* – which comes from the text) – so that was another subject to be discussed in these bookshop encounters and newspaper interviews.

The apartment I was occupying was one kept by the local authorities to be occupied by a foreign writer willing to live there for a month at the city's expense and write about Zadar. There was a suggestion that I might have the residency at some future date if I was interested. Back to the notebook:

> A nice lunch with Roman somewhere on the Lungo Mare (seafront) – seafood and white wine. He has published two collections of his own short stories. He rhapsodises about parenthood and agonises about the novel he has been trying to write. Tells himself it should be different now he feels the vulnerability of parenthood. I told him he must stop fussing in *abstract* about what sort of writer he should be. He should assume he is a person of sensibility, talent, acuity, sympathy etc and write what pleased and satisfied him. If there's something

* *Possession* was a novel I had talked over often with Antonia when she was writing it, and had even offered a solution to a problem – that a letter from one character whose correspondence would not be found until late in the story needed to be discovered sooner. 'Make it a *draft*' I had suggested. She had done that – and I was delighted that this solution, and the word 'draft', had survived even into the movie script.

> wrong with it, *fix it!* Agonising was just a way of not getting on with the job. He is full of feeling and anxiety and lack of clarity. He may do something terrific – but probably not. He had been to see his twice divorced and re-married mother. His 54-year-old father joined us briefly, fresh from the tennis court.

And all the time the natural world was coming at me, especially in the early mornings, and was somehow turning itself into poems with a Keatsian ease I found strange and exciting, as if I had been invaded and occupied, not by a foreign Muse but by a better self.

In that moment . . .

In that moment when the morning swallows
dash and skitter across the terrace
and under its shallow roof
there are flashes like the kingfisher's wing –
a blue as vivid but not as dark.

They have a lot to say in so short a time
and then are gone
over the roofs and down
among the vines and olives.

A visitation,
a blessing which takes no account
of who might receive it,
it has the ease, the indifference
even, you might think, the disdain
of perfect art.

My Name Was Judas had its Zadar launch (it went well – even better than in Zagreb I recorded), followed by supper with Mladen and Roman, and next day the mysterious 'Milan' drove me back to Zagreb, where I gave a radio interview at 12.30 and one to a newspaper at 1.15, and had to cancel an evening reading because I had talked and read too much and lost my voice.

Next day I was to return to New Zealand, and Jadranka drove me to the airport after a long walk by the lake and lunch. She gave me a tiny earthenware dish with a picture of a city under snow and a small angel hovering above. I gave her a copy of *All Visitors Ashore* with the poem I'd dedicated to her ('Speaking in Bronze') handwritten in the front. We hugged our farewell, as if neither expected to see the other again, and regretted it. I flew straight home, Zagreb, Munich, Hong Kong, Auckland. That notebook ends:

> A day later came a message from Jadranka to say that an hour after leaving me at the airport she had heard that Ljiljana had committed suicide in America. This is a huge shock – to both of us.

And of course one should have known: no one who thinks seriously, 'once a month', of killing herself should go to America. It would be so easy just to pop down to the nearest gun shop and buy the weapon and ammunition, like buying cigarettes, or milk.

A week after getting home I began a verse letter to Jadranka about Ljiljana. It took ten days and thirty pages of drafts to complete.* It was a form that had been relatively common when I was young – there were examples by both Curnow and Baxter. I had addressed a youthful one to Rob Dyer, and one to Frank Sargeson from Australia. It was the reverse of those poems that had visited me so deftly in Zagreb and Zadar, eight stanzas each of eleven lines; no less a poem than those visitations had been, but certainly not arriving 'as the leaves to a tree'. It was what I called a hard work poem, Curnow's kind. I kept exchanging versions of it with Alan Roddick whose advice, as so often, helped. Here are the final two stanzas:

---

* 'A Letter to Jadranka Pintarić', (i.m. Ljiljana Šćurić), *The Yellow Buoy*, pp. 24–27.

vii

That was ten years ago, and those were chapters
you edited, she translated – and now I forget,
or I'm uncertain, which things happened 'really'
and which were 'fiction'. In America she married
and soon divorced. You remained in Zagreb
where the war fades like a scar, sometimes forgotten.
Renzo Aboré sings to the lost child
in the ruined house, and three adventurers
drive on forever, south, towards the sea.
Everything is unreal. Lonely, exhausted,
she buys a gun and writes her farewell letters.

viii

Last month in Zagreb, my newest novel launched
in her translation, you drove me to the airport
in your new Renault. There, we hugged goodbyes
maybe for the last time. My gift was a poem,
yours a small bright angel in porcelain
to guard my flight. As I crossed the Alps to Munich
you took the call from dark America.
She'd wanted no regrets and no farewells
and asked to be forgotten. Our dead may ask,
and we are free to refuse, at least till Time
which does our forgetting for us, has its way.

Auckland, June 2007

2010

Place has always been a hugely important element in my writing, both fiction and poetry. Places are like people, with personalities, associations, histories, 'sounds and sweet airs'. Shakespeare says the poet's pen can 'give to airy nothing a local habitation and a name' – but for me Curnow is right to give the 'reality prior' precedence over the 'airy nothing'. I can't at the moment find the drafts of a story, 'Last Season's Man', that was to give me the most extreme rewards and punishments of any single item I was to write: on the one hand (abroad) the honour of winning the world's largest short story award and £25,000; on the other (at home) brickbats and outrage.

It began with my wondering about Jadranka's piety, her bare knees on hard stone in the moonlight at Zaton, as she knelt before a wayside effigy of the Virgin. It was a moment Ljiljana and I, knowing Jadranka's rejection of her childhood faith, called theatre. I had visited the Zagreb Cathedral with Jadranka; and also the flower-filled tunnel-like space in the old town, the Kamenita Vrata, between two ancient buildings, which had become a shrine daubed with pious graffiti and stuck over with small religious icons in marble or brass, each representing someone's prayer. Then (another element in the story) there was our tea at Dubravkin Put in the town woods, with its statue of the writer; and finally the waterfront at Zadar with organ pipes sounded by the movement of the waves. All this – together with the historical moment of Croatia's emergence from Yugoslavia as a modern nation – was the mix. I suppose it was wrong to dismiss Jadranka's prayer to the Virgin simply as theatre. But what did she pray for so fervently? Supposing it was the death of an enemy, or (even) of a friend – Ljiljana for example. And supposing the fr/enemy subsequently died. That thought was the kernel.

The story is set in the theatre world before, during and beyond Croatia's war with Serbia. A young, handsome successful playwright, Tomislav Buljan, writes a devastating article in a much-read newspaper dismissing the work of an older rival, Mario Ivanda. Ivanda's reputation, already in decline, sinks further and he, though no longer a practising Christian, relieves his hurt feelings by praying to the Virgin for the death of the man who has done him such harm. To his surprise Buljan is soon diagnosed with cancer, and makes it known publicly that he intends to fight it. The fight is long and unsuccessful, and when he dies, Mario, who prayed for this death, becomes convinced that it can't be the end of the story. He is no longer a believing Catholic, but like most of us he's superstitious. His prayer must have been a sin and he will be punished for it.

In Croatia's war of independence he shows exceptional courage because he is expecting to die and knows there's no use in trying to save himself. He survives, and as the nation becomes more sure of itself his reputation as a playwright begins to recover; but still he waits for the blow to fall. When he finds himself, after a few chance encounters, obsessed – in fact deeply in love – with Buljan's widow, Vesna, he sees this as his punishment. He visits the Virgin (in whose powers he still does not really believe).

> Two wretched days later he had to be in Zagreb, and there he found time to call on his friend the Virgin. He bought her a larger, more expensive candle, lit it and placed it where she could see it. 'So this is my punishment, Holy Mother? I am to be in love with the wife of the man I killed. The woman I can never touch.'
>
> Her smile as she looked down at him was faint, enigmatic, but he believed she was answering 'Yes'. Her sense of humour was subtle, but the pain she was inflicting was real.
>
> On an impulse (so much now was impulse) he went into the confessional. After the usual preliminaries he said, 'Father, it is a long time since my last confession. No doubt I have committed many sins, but I am here because I killed a man.'
>
> Even through the heavy grille he felt the priest's excitement. 'How did you kill him, my son?'
>
> 'I prayed to the Virgin that he would die of a painful disease, and that is what happened.'
>
> There was a sigh, perhaps of relief, more likely of disappointment. 'You did not kill him, my son. Only God decides who dies and how they die.'
>
> 'But I prayed to the Virgin.'

> 'That has nothing to do with it.' The priest's voice was impatient and had lost its authority. Mario felt a rush of amusement.
>
> 'Ah Father, if even you doubt her powers, who is there left to speak for them?'

Slowly Mario overcomes his feeling that he must not tell Vesna of his love. He takes courage from a scene in Shakespeare's *Richard III* where the crookback hero-villain seduces the wife of the man he has just murdered. Soon they are lovers, then husband and wife. In their last decade together before Mario's sudden death (a smoker's heart attack) he becomes the new nation's most famous playwright – so we are brought back to the beginning of the story when a statue of Mario is unveiled in the presence of his widow Vesna who smiles and says only 'I hope so' when the Minister of Culture refers to him as 'immortal'.

Now the ceremony is over, the crowd has dispersed, and an unnamed narrator approaches the bronze figure.

> It was Mario as I had known him. I felt I was looking into his eyes, and into his soul.
>
> 'Old friend,' his effigy said, 'you must know there is no Justice. That I am here and Tomislav is not is neither right nor wrong. The Universe is indifferent and does not love us. Everything is Chance.'

The tone of the story is comic, but like most literary comedy it has an entirely serious undertone. Jadranka's knees on the stones were 'theatre' in the sense that no one – not the Virgin Mary, not God, not the Stars nor Fate – was listening, and none of her gestures would have consequences, any more than the flowers and the little plaques and sad graffiti in the Kamenita Vrata, or the forest of candles in the cathedral, would bring anything about or change anything. We all tend to be superstitious and to indulge in propitiatory behaviours.

Those of us who take sufficient notice of the universe as it is progressively discovered by science know not to think of this as anything more than a human quirk – the habit of an animal with language and the wish to be in control of his fate.

But there was another element in the writing of this story. In 1994 I had myself been the subject of a clever article, 'Leading with his chin', by a brilliant younger writer, Nigel Cox, in a magazine called *Quote Unquote*, more or less dismissing my work to date and saying I had achieved nothing significant since leaving the university to write full-time. It was not the kind of analytical piece you could call 'literary criticism', but rather journalism-with-malice. Kay had gone down to Unity Books in Auckland where Nigel Cox worked and berated him. He had 'joined the rat-pack', she told him, and he should be ashamed. If she had asked me, I would probably have said don't give him the satisfaction of knowing I'm upset; but she didn't ask, and I'm grateful for that support – which incidentally both Nigel and his wife Susanna admired.

But a year or two later it had been made public that Cox had just been diagnosed with serious cancer. He had a lot of support, pity for a hugely promising career threatened with an early end, and great sympathy when, after protracted illness and failed hopes, he died in 2006. I knew nothing at all about the details of his death. In having my fictional character Tomislav in effect rebel against the advancing cancer and assert that he was going to live, I had in mind Ross Stevens who had seemed to refuse to accept what was coming. If there was any similarity to Cox's last days, that was by chance. And I knew nothing at all of Cox's wife – though I would get to know her later as a consequence of the fuss over my story. But the connection was made between Nigel's death and my story, and there was outrage in Wellington. I had (it was said) wished him dead, he had died, and now I was dancing on his grave with a story about it. The fact that the prize was so large, and so internationally significant, made my crime worse. If I had won a little local prize it might have produced a little local outrage. But this was big, and so was the anger.

There had been more than 1100 entries from around the English-speaking world and the whole process took time; but in the end I was in a short-list of six and summoned to the UK for the prize dinner which was to be held at Corpus Christi College in Oxford during the Oxford Literary Festival. I left on 20 March after swimming that morning with Kay, and with Tony and Pat Axelrad who were staying with us. The few days in London were hectic with interviews about the award and photo sessions, a sound recording of my reading 'Last Season's Man', and, off to one side, an interview with Professor Donald Singer about the Hippocrates Prize for Poetry and Medicine which I had won that year.*

I stayed with Margaret in London and took her as my guest to the dinner. TVNZ had sent their UK correspondent, Lisa Owen, to interview me in London and to be there with a camera team at the dinner. It was a Friday night, so Saturday morning in New Zealand, and once the dinner was over and the prize-winner had been announced, a link was established with Kim Hill in Wellington. She congratulated me on 'a triumph' and asked a few routine questions about the story, and then said, 'I understand your friend A. S. Byatt was one of the judges.'

I thought I was used to Kim's technique of keeping a nasty surprise in reserve until her subject had begun to relax and then hitting him with it (she was known in our family as Kill Him) – but this came as a shock. What effect could be intended except to suggest that this was how I had managed to win such an important international prize? I replied that Antonia was one of six judges and the only one I knew personally, and that they had said their decision was unanimous.† I could also have said I knew what a scrupulous woman Antonia was, and that being her friend would

---

* Another £5,000 – it was a record year for our joint UK sterling account!

† The judges were Andrew Holgate, books editor of the *Sunday Times*, Matthew Evans, former chairman of Faber and now chairman of EFG Private Bank (funder of the prize), British fiction writers Nick Hornby, Hanif Kureishi and A. S. Byatt, and journalist and popular linguist Lynn Barber.

not have improved my chances in any way. It was best left, but it was a breath – a bad breath – of New Zealand. Did she have a motive?

The *Sunday Times* published the story in its magazine that weekend, and in the book pages an interview with me as a seventy-seven-year-old 'decked head to toe in blue like a merchant sailor', survivor of a stroke five years before which had rendered me briefly dyslexic, but from which I was now completely recovered – except that my signature had changed and no longer looked like my own. The *Financial Times* liked the stroke story and ran it with the headline 'Author who beat stroke wins £25,000 Sunday Times prize'. That stroke had been the subject of my Hippocrates Prize-winning poem, 'Ischaemia', written in the voice of Catullus as survivor, so not irrelevant.

I flew back non-stop, arrived late on the 29th, in time to farewell the Axelrads who next day were heading home to Norfolk. Soon after that the shit hit the fan. My story, I began to hear, had been a cruel revenge on Nigel Cox. The first to reproach me directly was Fergus Barrowman, Nigel Cox's publisher and close friend. He sent me a message saying he had asked Stephen Stratford to put Nigel's article about me back up on the website that *Quote Unquote* had now become, so readers would be given 'the backstory'. He said 'Last Season's Man' was an abuse of Nigel and Susanna and their children and he was sickened by it. He would publish a poem of mine he had already accepted for *Sport*. After that he would not have to bother with me again. I replied:

> Good god Fergus! Certainly spare yourself any further dealings with me. But are you incapable of reading fiction as fiction? Feelings have their origins in events; but the 'story' is entirely a fiction, and the message is entirely benign.

I suppose Fergus's reaction was not altogether surprising, given his closeness to Nigel; but re-reading the story now, and imagining how it would have appeared to those neutral judges in the UK, it still strikes me as full of charm and cleverness and humour, and that the word I ended with to Fergus was right. There was no malice: it was 'benign'.

But the outrage continued, especially in Wellington but spreading outward, abroad, and has been referred to at intervals since, always as another example of my bad behaviour rather than of my good writing. I remember being harried by a highly indignant person on the *Listener* staff demanding to know how and when and why I wrote the story, clearly looking for replies that could be used against me. On the other hand the wronged widow, Susanna Andrew, sent me a message which quoted Milan Kundera's *The Curtain*: 'A nation's possessiveness towards its artists works as a small-context terrorism, reducing the whole meaning of a work to the role it plays in its homeland.' Her feelings were clearly mixed – how could they not be? – but this, and an acknowledgement that the fuss was 'provincial', seemed to me supremely enlightened coming from the only one who might have had an excuse for feeling aggrieved.

Cathy Galvin, the deputy editor of the *Sunday Times*, warned me to brace myself for something that was coming at that end (Kiwis abroad taking their cue from home).

> I would advise doing nothing. It will blow over. It is more than possible to keep your long stride. I am sorry this is happening but I know it is out of proportion. You wrote a story. It had a one in a thousand chance. It made it against the odds. It is its own troubled but bizarre gift and seems to have a life beyond its few thousand words – and its own dark humour. When you feel like writing something about it, it will be worth reading.

In reply to Susanna I told her if I was bruised that was no fault of hers and I was grateful to her for her sympathy. I said it should have occurred to someone that it was a story by the author of *My Name Was Judas*, that it asked whether there was or was not Divine Justice, and gave the same answer.

The story could be said to have ended where it began, in Croatia, translated and published in one of their major papers, where, Roman told me, there were some who claimed to recognise the people in the Croatian theatre world on whose lives my story was based.

Risk

I have written of Frank Sargeson's satisfaction at finding himself doing what he felt was his best work in his seventies. I turned seventy in October 2002, and what are, or may be, my three best novels, *The Secret History of Modernism*, *Mansfield* and *My Name Was Judas*, were published in 2001, 2004 and 2006. During the same decade came four new collections of poems, *The Right Thing* (2000), *Dog* (2002), *The Red Tram* (2006) and *The Black River* (2007) – all of this rounded out by my *Collected Poems, 1951–2006* published in 2008. In 2013 when I was eighty came what might well be my best single collection of poems, *The Yellow Buoy*.

Two thousand and ten when I won the big short story prize was my seventy-eighth year, and Roman Simić was organising a 'Festival of the European Short Story'. I was invited, and a bonus would be that I could have that one-month residency in Zadar. I was in two minds about this. I had embarked on a new novel, *Risk*, which I thought should be my last (there was in fact to be one more after *Risk*). I had written a whole draft of it and was now rewriting it from the beginning. A condition of the residency was that the recipient would write and publish about Zadar in a way that might help promote its image. I was always conscientious about such 'understandings', especially when they included money; and I was well into the new novel. Could both – the novel and the terms of the residency – be satisfied? I thought they could and planned accordingly.

I think the idea for *Risk* had come when I heard Margaret's husband Guy Clayton (a Kiwi banking lawyer with Morgan Stanley in London) talking about the scenes of chaos on Canary Wharf when Lehman Brothers collapsed and the square was full of young (and not so young) professional people coming down with their cardboard boxes full of papers and stationery having been told to clear their desks and go. After I embarked on the writing Guy took me to see the trading floor and told me a few stories which helped me with background.

So I had embarked on a story about a New Zealand lawyer who remembers fondly his young years of an OE in London. When his marriage breaks up, he decides to return there and try his luck in the great capital. At perhaps forty-five, he would be a much younger man than I was at the time of writing; and the actual time, the particular years, of this adventure was critical to the story, because I was interested in writing about the late 1990s up to about 2009 – the lead-up to the invasion of Iraq in 2003, and the gradual faltering and failing of the banking system with its collapse in 2009.

The rewrite of the novel was already under way, and the visit to Croatia would be fitted into it to satisfy the conditions of the Zadar residency. So my character was now Sam Nola, with Croatian forebears, and with relatives still living there. His first visit would bring him to Zagreb during the war of independence from Yugoslavia; and he would return for a conference, representing the bank he now worked for in London, Interbank America.

This plot element had one weird effect which strikes me much more clearly now than it did at the time I was doing it. Sam's association with a distant Croatian cousin, Maja, is very similar to the one between and Mike and Ira in *Talking about O'Dwyer*; and Maja, like Ira, is a mix of characteristics derived from Ljiljana and Jadranka – though Maja is a rather more old-style communist, and her car is an East German Trabant rather than a Russian Škoda. So our central character sets off once again to travel down to the coast in time of war; but in this second version of the story they don't get all the way and are cut off and turned back by fighting in the region of the Krajina. When he comes back for Maja a few years later he's told by her aunt that she's dead. But the similarities are so close, if someone else had written it I might have had to complain of plagiarism. Can an author plagiarise his own work? This overlap of source material still gives me a feeling of embarrassment, as if I have caught myself out in at least a clumsiness if not an authorial crime.

Kay dismisses this anxiety. Every novelist, she says, if you look under the surface is writing the same novel again and again. 'Think of Henry James. That experience was important to you so you reused it.'

And I have to say that when I look at *Risk* piece by piece and follow its narrative line as it moves with Sam from France to Sweden to Croatia to New York to Berlin, but coming back always to London which is its centre, always keeping abreast of a world in the grip of two headlong deluded leaders Bush and Blair, hell-bent on war in Iraq while the banking world totters towards collapse – and yet all this arriving as the story of one Kiwi abroad on his mid-life OE/crisis – it strikes me as at the very least a thoroughly professional novel, comprehending, and finding ways of containing, difficult matter and making a unified story of it. I had always said I wanted the big picture – as background, necessarily, but so much more important than passing the butter and falling in love. I was not really interested in writing domestic fiction. What was the point of fiction rather than poetry if it didn't use its full reach? There had to be history – and that was what I was giving it here.

There's an interview with Ian Wedde in the Shirley Horrocks documentary about Allen Curnow where Wedde says that at a certain stage in a successful writer's life there's such confidence and competence, whatever's offered to readers has to be accepted without quibble: the right to do whatever he or she wants has been earned. It doesn't mean it's all equally good; but it's all part of that particular writing life. I feel *Risk* is that kind of a novel – probably not as good as the three that preceded it, but earning those affirmations that came in due course and in large number, including this:

> A few chapters in and I found myself in the grip of an artist ... Readers of [Thomas Piketty's] *Capital* will find this a companion piece.

Risk's method might have been unconventional, even eccentric; but it had found a way to take on the big subject of the world as it was in that decade, both political and economic, in a way that could convince even the *Financial Times*!

I was booked to fly to New York for a PEN Writers' Festival in April 2010 but cancelled, uncertain I could go on coping with so much coming and going, so much jet-lag. I reached a summer total score of 123 visits to the yellow buoy on 5th May, and left for Croatia on the 21st. I did my duty in Roman Simić's Festival of the European Short Story, which involved a good deal of moving about, with appearances in Zagreb and Rijeka, and then settled for the few weeks of the residency in Zadar, a city which in that month was redolent of the linden flower, both colour and fragrance. But the town authority had changed its mind and the apartment was no longer the one I'd occupied for a few lyrical days three years before. In messages to Kay I referred to it as 'my Soviet squat'. I remember now only that it contained a large constantly day-and-night-noisy refrigerator which I called Tito because it must have dated from his time. There were no romantic moments of the kind I had marked with new poems in 2007. This was a prose venture. I swam and I wrote, walked to the library to keep up daily contact with Kay, and relieved loneliness by going to an open-air theatre where I saw movies like *Robin Hood* with Russell Crowe and *Sex and the City* with Sarah Jessica Parker, bizarrely dubbed in Croatian. I met and had waterfront dinners with Kay's nephew John Laurie and his new Serbian wife Ksenija Obradović, who were touring and keeping their Belgrade number-plate out of sight for fear of being recognised as 'enemy' and vandalised. And I met (as one of the writers at Roman's Festival of the European Short Story) the Hungarian writer László Krasznahorkai, whose name and appearance I borrowed for my novel. He became the mysterious 'businessman' and hedge-fund manager André Kraznahorkai whom Sam and his boss Reuben rename 'Hawkeye of Hungary'. Hawkeye has spent his early years as manager of the Red Star swimming pool in Budapest, studying Marx's *Capital*, but only with a view to escaping to the West where the rich get richer and the poor poorer – and since the fall of the Wall he has achieved this.

Despite its focus on politics and banking, *Risk* still gives poetry a foot in the door in the form of Tom Roland, the trader who is secretly a poet visited in a dream by the dark figure he calls *Monsieur le Noir*, who gives him half a poem early in the novel, and returns later to give him the other half. There is an odd fact here worth recounting. Tom Roland's poem, 'Banking on feathers', was a revised version of one I had written and abandoned as unsuccessful way back in the 1960s. It had been influenced by, even modelled on, poems in a collection, *Songs* (1959), by Christopher Logue. In his later years (he died in 2011) Logue had become best known for a series of brilliant and powerful poetic dramas, collected as *War Music*, based on Homer's *Iliad*. Kay and I saw at least one of those plays at the National Theatre in London and I got to know Logue when I read with him at King's Lynn. He was a good friend of Craig Raine's. In the opening pages of *Risk* Sam arrives back by air from Nice with his recently discovered daughter Letty, and they are to have dinner with friends at the Polish Club in Kensington. They are delayed because their bus from the airport is abandoned in a field by an angry immigrant driver; and when they get to the club their Oxford friends, Charles and Ghita, are being harangued by Jake Latimer, 'an actor with an actor's voice', about Bush and Blair:

> 'We're being lied to every fucking day. They have self-correcting software, if they gap for a moment and type a truthful statement it inserts a 'not'. Tony Blair can't do a shit that's honest.'

This character with his angry political rave was closely modelled on Christopher Logue, and the event on a real dinner at that club – so Logue is present in two forms in *Risk*, as poet (through Tom Roland's poem), and as political activist/ranter. It's a novel he might have enjoyed, especially for its politics.

The novel had already been well under way before I arrived for the Zadar residency, and now my character, Sam, was despatched first to Zagreb then to Zadar, for a banking conference, where I contrived a series of topics for discussion signalling, to any who might wonder how I knew so much about the banking world, not only the influence of Guy Clayton, but what a regular reader (or raider) of the *Financial Times* I had become. Putting Zadar into the mix that was *Risk* meant I was fulfilling my undertaking to give the town an appearance in my fiction. I probably finished the writing of that second version later that same year when Kay and I were living again at Saint-Maximin. It appeared from MacLehose in 2012, and the following year in Croatian as *Rizik* from the publisher that still bore 'Roy's' name – Božičević.

But how do you end such a story? Sam at the end is free. Ruth, currently the woman in his life, has just become a widow, and though her husband's fortune has gone down the banking drain her own, inherited since the death of her brother, has exploded by one of those 'shorting' miracles that the collapse of 2009 made (rarely but dramatically) possible. Sam has been sacked, along with most of the staff, by Interbank America, but he has had his 'Rastignac moment',* determining that he is now ready to take London on again and win – which we assume Ruth will help him achieve. It's at this 'last moment' that the said-to-be-dead Maja reappears, solo, as free as he is, and apparently ready, if it's what he wants, to become a new Dalmatian immigrant among her relatives in New Zealand.

So the reader is left with Sam's dilemma: will it be London so full of excitement and promise, or New Zealand offering 'something

---

* As at the end of Balzac's *Père Goriot*.

different, something nobody counted on'? I remember Christopher MacLehose saying of course it will be London. Kay, on the other hand, was quite as sure it had to be New Zealand. It's only now, looking back, that it occurs to me what I had done was re-create my own dilemma of the late 1950s. Each reader would make Sam's choice for him.

South-east of everywhere

I was at the Frankfurt Book Fair in October 2011 as the New Zealand writer deputed to accept the handing over of a scroll signalling that we were to be 'guest nation' for the following year, and I used the chance on the podium to commemorate Allen Curnow's hundred years and to read the poem I'd written for that occasion which had been published in the *LRB*.

So a year later, October 2012, I was back, this time with a large contingent of our writers and publishers, New Zealand as the guest nation with a beautifully designed water pavilion displaying who and what we were in the world, and with the clever slogan 'While you were sleeping' referring to how the time zones placed us relative to most of the Western world – (south-east of everywhere!). I had a number of sessions, one of which was the launch of *My Name Was Judas* in German translation and a discussion about it with Katharina Bielenberg from Harvill. Margaret was there as publishing director of Atlantic Books and she and I went together to a dinner for our amiable Deputy PM Bill English, who had graduated in English from Victoria and told me he regarded me as a piece of New Zealand's family furniture.

On 17th October, my eightieth birthday, I was in London to record an interview on the BBC *World Book Club* programme with Harriet Gilbert, answering questions from a studio audience and from people calling in from around the world.* It was an hour-long

* It was recorded on the 17th, broadcast on the 19th, and is still available on BBC *World Book Club*.

session, in effect an overview of how *My Name Was Judas* came about, how it works, and the various ways in which its further implications (especially in terms of faith) might be seen. Kay, Charlotte and Margaret were in the audience.

So two novels, *My Name Was Judas* and *Risk*, were intertwined with the occasion of my turning eighty. And it was also at this time that I was completing the collection *The Yellow Buoy* which would be published the following year, both in New Zealand and the UK.

Postscript:
In February 2020, writing this memoir, I found an old e-address of Jadranka's and sent her a greeting saying I hoped she was well and prospering. After many days a brief reply came back:

> I don't know what to say . . . my English is even worse than it was because I haven't used it for 10 years . . . I have feeling to have lived several lives. I will never forget you and Ljiljana, but you belong to an ancient time . . . better than today. Most of the time I'm depressed and just live like a zombie. I'm OK with that. I'm so glad that you are still writing! Love, J

12. Hitler and So On

Marti

Marti Friedlander never wrote a personal memoir, and when she did put together a *Self-Portrait* it took the form of a recorded and edited monologue with Hugo Manson, apparently with little recourse to documents.* I have a very accurate and detailed memory, but I know how wrong one can be, when depending on memory, about 'the facts of the case' – so let me begin with one example. Marti tells Hugo that when the Baron Philippe de Rothschild was visiting New Zealand she suggested he should meet Karl Stead, and that as a consequence the Friedlanders and Karl got together with the baron 'at a café on the Shore'. She describes an evening somewhat spoiled when I brought up the subject of Israel and Palestine and the baron and I had 'a heated discussion on the subject' while Gerrard and Marti 'kept out of it'.

In fact Marti had nothing whatever to do with my meeting the baron. She was not there when it happened,† and her account is sheerest fantasy. Charles Brasch wrote to me on 22 March 1970 to tell me his friend Jocelyn Harris had written from Boston to say

* Marti Friedlander with Hugo Manson, *Self-Portrait*, Auckland University Press, 2013.

† If she had been, there would be Marti pics of me with the baron, and Leonard Bell, who looks after her files, confirms that there are none.

the baron would be in Auckland while his wife had heart surgery at Greenlane Hospital. Rothschild was a literary man as well as a famous vintner. He had translated Elizabethan poetry into French and, Charles wrote, 'longs for someone congenial to talk to'. Would Kay and I meet him? As a result of that we spent an evening with him at the Mon Desir Hotel, where he was lodged, talking about many things, mainly but not exclusively literary. The baron ordered a local wine, tried it, said to the waiter, 'Give it to the cook!' – and ordered something excellent from France, probably one of his own Mouton Cadet. I didn't altogether admire this showmanship; and I took critical note of the fact that he said at one point about 'the Arabs' that they were 'such uninteresting people' – the sort of racist dismissal a sophisticated and educated Jew should be the last to utter; but the evening passed pleasantly and he invited us to visit him at his winery in France when we were in Menton on the Mansfield fellowship the following year. We did not discuss Israel/Palestine at all probably because it was (despite my later firm views on the subject) something about which at that time I knew next to nothing and had no opinion. We talked especially about Andrew Marvell whose poems he had translated, and whose 'To His Coy Mistress' and several other shorter poems I was able to quote. I reported back to Charles and he replied 1st May:

> Thank heavens it wasn't a wild goose chase! I felt a trifle hesitant asking you to look up Baron de R. and am relieved that he was worth meeting. Thank you for the kindness.

When Marti's book was published in 2013 I wrote to her explaining that she was quite wrong about this meeting, and got no reply.

I have a measure of how ignorant I remained of the Israel/Palestine issue even for a time after it had entered the domain of general knowledge and public argument. I was heading home from the university some time in the 1970s when something stencilled on a wall caught my eye and I only began to think about it after it was far behind. I thought I had read FREE PLASTICINE! What did this mean? Something to do with kindergartens or pre-schools? I looked for it next day and it read, of course, FREE PALESTINE! After that I stopped skipping the columns in the *New Statesman* that dealt with the subject and over the years became convinced that terrible wrongs were being inflicted on the Palestinians. They were being dispossessed of their long-time homeland, and the world was turning a blind eye to this out of feelings of guilt at and responsibility for (as it has come to be known) the Holocaust. Worse, when anyone tried to make a case for the Palestinians, they were at once labelled anti-Semite. So anti-Semitism and the Nazi extermination of Jews in World War II were becoming a defensive wall behind which wrongs committed by the Jewish state were being hidden.

The Holocaust was a particular horror for people my age (and Kay's). We had been about eleven or twelve when the death camps were discovered. Day after day we saw images and read accounts of cruelty and murder on a scale that seemed almost beyond belief. We had grown up knowing 'the Germans' were 'the enemy'. Now they seemed to be exposed as uniquely wicked (though of course that too was something that would have to be unlearned – they had been wicked, but not uniquely so). It made the US conversion of post-war Germany into our ally against Russia one of the many things about the Cold War that were hard to swallow.

So in the immediate post-war years, when the state of Israel was established, it seemed entirely (as in *1066 and All That*) 'a Good Thing'. The least the world could do for the race that had been so harried and discriminated against and slaughtered was to give them what they wanted, a state of their own in a region to which they had ancient ties.* One did not know about, or give any thought to, matters like the rights of indigenous Arabs driven out

* The cynical anti-Semite Ezra Pound had said in one of his pro-Fascist Rome broadcasts, 'Give 'm Australia'.

of their homes in the conflict of 1948. What I remember clearly was a feeling of approval of the general Labour-leaning and egalitarian flavour of the new state. The fact that the politicians always had open collars and no tie was their declaration of escape from authoritarian and stratified Europe, and a mark of worth. The idea of the kibbutz seemed virtuous too – and we learned from an approving press how they were 'making the desert bloom'. I don't mean that all these favourable impressions of Israel were wrong or groundless; but they did leave out a few essential elements. I remember saying to Mike Joseph in the English Department common room in 1967, when the Six-Day War had ended in triumph for the Israelis, how good it was to have a war over so quickly and with an outcome one could celebrate. That was in the days of my FREE PLASTICINE misreading.

From time to time, as I learned more and my opinion became clearer (and harder), this subject was touched upon and quickly skirted with the Friedlanders. It was apparent that Gerrard was particularly militant on Israel's behalf; Marti less so. I always had the impression that Marti's Jewishness was more profound than Gerrard's. His father was Jewish, his mother Gentile. Marti believed both her parents had been Jews; but the significant shaping element in her life had been infancy and childhood in a London Jewish orphanage, and the closeness there to her sister. Gerrard's Jewishness had the feeling of an ardent political commitment; hers was (or seemed) more like a notion of self. It was not of the synagogue and strict observant kind – I'm sure she didn't care whether pork was or wasn't eaten; it was more an aura and an identity. She looked Jewish. She was and wanted to be Jewish – and 'Marti'. In conversation, and in talks about her photography, she named herself often as if she saw herself from the outside, still the super-clever little sister in the Jewish orphanage. One might see her any time of the week except Friday evening which was always set aside for private observances, the lighting of a candle, perhaps the reciting of a sacred text and a phone call to her sister in London.

I suppose food came into it too, but these were the hours when one would not expect to meet.

Marti and Gerrard had met in London when he was there on his Kiwi OE. They embarked on a tour of Europe by motorscooter, and she returned with him to New Zealand. They had married in a synagogue in London, which was possible (Marti records) because Gerrard's mother had converted to Judaism. Marti adored especially his good looks, inherited from his mother, and liked to joke that he was her 'blond and Aryan' Jew. Gerrard was endlessly critical of and superior about New Zealand, condemning us (always with good reason of course) as socially primitive (the six-o'clock swill, no wine in restaurants, no weekend shopping, wharfies who 'didn't work in the rain', an indifferent arts scene). Marti agreed; she was bored and irritated by New Zealand as she found us in the 1960s, and yet was fascinated and set about capturing what we, on the inside, didn't see, or hadn't thought worthy of record.

There is a photograph on p. 76 of Marti' s *Self-Portrait* of a ravaged hillslope with a new road going up to what look like recently built houses, and the land closer to the camera cleared for further development. There are seven cars, five parked, two in motion, and no people except in the foreground, a family of four, mother, father and two children, climbing the hill on the newly made pavement towards the houses. There are what appear to be 'For Sale' signs on two of the sections. There is some washing hanging out to dry, but as yet no gardens around the houses. It's a picture of Becoming rather than of Being; but this is it as it was when Marti put it on record – with a barrenness and ugliness she hated. Who else would have dreamed of photographing it?

As a couple Marti and Gerrard were always in two minds about New Zealand; and Marti finishes her piece about me in her *Self-Portrait* saying, or implying (again not totally without reason), that so was I. But I was *of* it, and had chosen to remain so – that was the difference.

Marti was quick-witted and shrewd, never lost for a word. Gerrard was much slower in conversation; and it occurs to me that though he had no trace of a foreign accent, English must have been his second language – born in Germany, both parents German-speaking, taken in infancy to Palestine to escape what the Nazis were doing, and then on to New Zealand as settlers. He must have learned to be an English speaker in a New Zealand primary school. His father was a doctor/dentist who couldn't afford to retrain in medicine as New Zealand required, but was able to set up as a dentist. At some point the family (with two children – a third was born here) moved to Henderson, West Auckland – to 'Loomis', Maurice Gee territory – but also Kay's. Gerrard's father Bertholdt was Kay's dentist when she was at secondary school; and it was Bertholdt who told Kay's mother that her false teeth were 'awful', and made her a new set.

In later years the subject of Israel and the Palestinians did once or twice erupt into argument between us – mainly with Gerrard; and on p. 164 of her *Self-Portrait* Marti gives an account of one such. If my behaviour on that occasion was as she describes it – Karl shouting and 'powerfully articulate' and Gerrard '*that* upset' – I apologise to her ghost and to Gerrard wherever he may be at this moment. The alcohol would have been to blame for the volume; the lucidity which Gerrard found so daunting would have been all my own. The conviction and intellectual substance would have come from intense general reading – but also, in particular, from the Palestinian writers I had met at the Eaglereach retreat before the Sydney Writers' Festival of 2003. They were so civilised, so patient and long-suffering; and I think in particular of Ghada Karmi and Raja Shehadeh. Kay and I visited Ghada at her house in London and read her books *In Search of Fatima* and *Return: A Palestine Memoir*; and we had read Raja's books, *When the Bulbul Stopped Singing* and *Occupation Diaries*. It was not possible to talk to these people and to read their books without feeling deeply the wrongs the state of Israel had inflicted on them. As I said once in a message to Gerrard, attempting to explain how we felt, this was one of those international moral/political issues – like that, indeed, of Jews in Germany in the 1930s, like the Spanish Civil War, the Vietnam War, apartheid in South Africa – that required every serious-minded person to take a stand, to speak out; and if he cared about the future of the state of Israel and wanted it to have one, he would join other Jews around the world in urging compassion and restraint – and above all *comprehension* – on Israel in its dealings with people who were, comparatively, powerless.

Marti dates the end of our friendship from that party: 'It was devastating for us to lose such a long and intimate friendship.' But it's not true it ended. Gerrard's sulk was serious and fairly durable – and we certainly never discussed Palestine (or even Plasticine) again; but there were later Sunday brunches, usually with Marshall and Prue Cook, on the Friedlanders' Brighton Road veranda looking out over Hobson Bay; and we crossed paths with Marti constantly. She was always summoning me to some corner of Parnell where suddenly the light was perfect, or the background was right, or there was some spare film in her camera, or too long had passed since she'd last got a good shot of me. As late as 2009, three years after the 'end-of-our-friendship' quarrel, I gave an illustrated talk at the Gus Fisher Gallery about being Marti's subject. Marti was there in the audience and she wrote afterwards:

> I was so moved by your talk on Saturday, getting it all together must have been quite a task – but it was just wonderful to see all those images of you and the family over the years. It is quite a story of friendship and love, and I thank you so much for talking as you did with such affection, and humour too. Just wish Gerrard could have been there, I know he would have been delighted. [. . .]
>
> Again, thank you so much. Being part of your Family over the years gave us so much joy. Gerrard is recovering reasonably well, but with his zest for life I know he will be fine.

Wish I could have taken that picture of you walking with Charlotte yesterday. I was on my way to see Gerrard.

Love

Marti

So why Marti in her *Self-Portrait* chose to make so much of that bad moment at a party remains a puzzle. I had written (without naming them except as 'Jewish friends') something on the subject of our relationship and differences,* but in an entirely conciliatory tone. The friendship had not ended, and her pics of me kept pace with my aging until only a year or two before her death in 2016.

Back then

After Kay and I returned to Auckland in 1960 a young Jewish colleague, lecturer in philosophy, Edward Kamara, brought Marti and Gerrard to visit us at our flat in Masons Avenue in Herne Bay. Edward was lodging with Dr and Mrs Rosenbaum whose daughter Eva had been my good friend during student years. Eva was like Gerrard, one the Nazis had categorised as a Mischling, with a Jewish father and an Aryan mother; and like the Friedlanders, the Rosenbaums had escaped Germany to Palestine, and then come on from there to settle in New Zealand.

In Palestine Eva's father had an affair with a local woman and his angry wife, encouraged from home by her Aryan family who had not approved of the marriage, decided to leave him and return to Germany – where of course her social standing would be improved by divorcing her Jew. But at home she began to have doubts and regrets, finally changing her mind again and returning to him in Palestine from where they moved on to New Zealand. All the trauma and uncertainty of these childhood upheavals were in Eva's background. For her as for Gerrard, English must have been a second

* *Book Self*, pp. 318–19; an entry dated 20/9/06.

language – and she had memories of speaking not only German as an infant but also Hebrew. There was no accent at all, but whereas his speech was always slightly hesitant, hers was so fluent it didn't sound quite real. Every sentence was grammatically perfect, sometimes syntactically complex. Often there would be colloquialisms and these would seem to be in quotation marks. I am probably exaggerating, but only to give what I think is a true impression. It was hard not to notice and be impressed by Eva's formidable monologues; but the longer one continued – and they often continued many minutes – the more I felt I was listening to something different under the surface of what was being said, something that was saying in a language I did not speak, 'I am one of Hitler's victims.'

Eva and I ran the student literary society for a couple of undergraduate years, and we were in the graduate section of the Auckland Teachers' College in 1954. She belongs in this chapter because, like Gerrard, she was to play a small part in the evolution of my novel *The Secret History of Modernism*.

I wrote to her (she didn't use email) early in 2001 telling her I had finished a novel and that it

> . . . includes a Holocaust survivor (or child of) for which I raided your memories, and the Friedlanders', and books. [. . .] So thank you again for your help. There's very little in it you will recognise as specifically yours, except perhaps atmospheres; but there is one scene where a fearful mischling child is left minding the luggage on a railway station platform while his mother is taken away and asked for her papers – and this derives from one of your reminiscences.

At that first (1960) meeting with the Friedlanders at our Masons Avenue flat Marti was exceptionally lively, a breath of London, flirty, opinionated. She and Gerrard were living in Tirimoana Road, Henderson, next door to the Gees, and they invited us to a barbecue where I remember I had a serious conversation with

Maurice Gee ('Moss') about whether one could or could not take the other Maurice (Shadbolt)'s fiction seriously. I was inclined to say not really; Maurice was anxiously unsure.

I think Marti was pregnant at this time or soon after. If so, this was her only pregnancy and quite late in its term the baby died in the womb. It was a major tragedy in her life – that and the fact that she didn't ever manage to be pregnant again. Over the next decade she loved to photograph Kay pregnant, and with her babies as they arrived, and the babies themselves. I still have on the wall of the Lockwood where most of my writing is done an enormous blow-up of baby Charlotte. Marti took it for a Family Planning poster, which was to have the text MAKE EVERY CHILD A WANTED ONE.

The next time I recall Marti after that barbecue was when we had moved from Masons Avenue (where Marti and Gerrard were to build their second house) to our little rented two-storeyed house in Maunsell Road – and here Maurice Shadbolt figures again. His first book, *The New Zealanders*, had been published – a text I knew well because I had read it for him and commented on it in London before it went to the publisher. It was a Saturday morning and Kay and I were amusing ourselves with comic readings of his florid passages when Marti arrived and at once began bossing us into position for pics. One of these is my favourite of the two of us together. Kay is looking lovely; she is wearing one of my sweaters and has her arm draped casually over my shoulder as she looks down at the book I'd been reading from – *The New Zealanders*.*

After the loss of their baby Marti and Gerrard went back to London for a year or two, leaving the young dentist-poet Alan Roddick and his wife Pat occupying the Tirimoana Road house, and Alan as locum in Gerrard's practice. It was at this time that Alan and I got to know one another and to exchange poems – a friendship and an exchange that continued after he departed for life in the South Island, and continues even now.

---

* See *You Have a Lot to Lose*, facing p. 93.

30. Karl and Kay swim at Kohimarama most days from mid-October through to early June.
Copyright NZ Herald/Brett Phibbs

31. *(Above)* Marti Friedlander and Kay visiting Kay's sister Olwen in Hamilton, early 2000s.

32. *(Below)* Karl with writers at the Eaglereach retreat, New South Wales, including Aminatta Forna (front left), and Palestinians Ghada Karmi and Raja Shehadeh (third and fourth from left).

33. Karl with Marti, two or three years before her death.

34. Kay and Karl at 37 Tohunga Crescent, with paintings by (from left) Jenny Doležel, Colin McCahon, Louise Henderson and Gretchen Albrecht behind (partially concealed), and their own grapes on the table. *Copyright Stuff/Patrick Reynolds*

35. *(Above)* Forty years after graduating PhD from Bristol University, Karl receives from the same university an honorary doctorate in letters, with, from left, son-in-law Guy Clayton, daughter Margaret and Kay, 12 July 2001.

36. *(Below)* Karl's investiture at Government House, Auckland to the Order of New Zealand, with, from left, daughter-in-law Virginia, son Oliver, Kay, son-in-law Paul Grimshaw and daughter Charlotte, 6 February 2007.

37. Sarah Maxey's brilliant design for the jacket of Karl's collection *Dog*, using the words in his poem 'Psalm' ('Every Dog has his day / but this one taketh the Prize . . .') to make the image of a dog.

38. Karl after receiving his tokotoko as New Zealand Poet Laureate at Matahiwi marae, with Kay and their three children, 2 April 2016. *Copyright Chris Szekely*

When Kay was pregnant with our first child we bought (for £3,250) a small and rather run-down house in Tohunga Crescent close to Hobson Bay. It was to be refurbished many times over as the family grew and has remained home for us ever since. Marti was in and out of there often. She says in her *Self-Portrait* that she and Gerrard 'became part of the Stead family' and this is true. We went to one another's parties and dinner parties. Sometimes the Friedlanders were there for our Christmas celebrations, and later for family weddings. When they moved from Masons Avenue and built their new house on Brighton Road, we were virtually neighbours. We knew one another in the way siblings do, 'with all our faults'. I admired Marti's photographs because they captured aspects of our society no one else looked at – conventional suburban, rural shanty, outback Māori, protest, intellectual and cultural, music and the arts; and because she could talk about it so well, explain her thinking and intentions so fluently. One of her most remarkable sequences, done with Michael King and published as *Moko*, was of old Māori women with the moko done in the old way with the chisel. If those faces had not been captured by Marti's camera they would have been lost for ever.

I don't know what Marti thought of my writing. I doubt that she read much of it. I think she just knew I was 'significant', liked the public figure I cut and liked recording it, and enjoyed my company. But she liked also the family and to be part of it; and during those early years when the loss of the baby threw her life with Gerrard into all kinds of turmoil, she confided often in Kay.

Over the years Marti seemed to pop up everywhere I went, photographing me addressing a protest rally, marching in the street, giving poetry readings in Auckland, a lecture in Wellington, being the 'writer' in London, the Mansfield Fellow in Menton . . . My joke was that if ever I climbed Everest or got to the South Pole, Marti would be there demanding I adopt this or that posture. She says there are not many pics of me smiling: that's probably because I was always under instruction from this impatient dominatrix-of-the-camera-lens. She was inclined to be pompous about how 'sensitivity' was needed in our dealing with our fellow human beings. She would roll this out like a sermon at intervals; but she was herself anything but sensitive. Socially she was much more of a ruffian than I was – but then I didn't grow up in an orphanage. Nonetheless we always seemed to like and admire one another. I had the feeling when I ran into her in the street that we both *rose to it*. Our voices became louder. The pitch, the intensity, even the sense of there being a challenge, lifted perceptibly – as if we were on stage. Each probably thought the other preposterous, but clever and good company.

The Friedlanders were living in their London *pied-à-terre* in 1972 when all five Steads (the children now aged eight, five and almost two) arrived by sea on our way to Menton where I was to take up the Katherine Mansfield fellowship. Gerrard helped me organise the transfer of the huge amounts of luggage we travelled with in those days, ship to shore, and then on board the train that would take us to Paris.* Marti said she would come and stay with us in the summer.

Our transit through Paris was effected with the help of the Goodyear family (Alan was with the New Zealand embassy in Paris) and I have described in *You Have a Lot to Lose* my first view of the Med and our arrival in Menton. Marti arrived to stay as promised in the summer and took many photographs, including of the music festival where Théodorakis and his band, exiled from Greece by the Colonels, performed music from the movie *Zorba the Greek* which Oliver had become obsessed with before we left New Zealand. Kay's mother was also staying with us so Marti had to bed down on a couch in the sitting room, and to mollify her for not having a room of her own, Kay assembled a perfect French hotel breakfast, with croissants and French bread, and coffee with hot milk in a separate jug, and brought it to her in bed. Marti declined this offering, saying

* The carriages rolled on to a ferry in the night and then off again in France.

she didn't eat breakfast – which wasn't true; but it meant (as often with Marti in prima donna mode) there were prickles to be skirted.

At the Mansfield memorial room she photographed me (and I her) both inside that rather stark concrete blockhouse, and out in its little garden.* She took some colour shots of me at my desk, working at a very busy and worked-over manuscript, and with just one book visible on the desk – an edition of Catullus. Two of these appeared in the *Listener*.

Back at the flat we had a boules set acquired when the Goodyears came through at Easter and taught us the game. The metal pétanque balls are very heavy and one was lying near to the edge of the table. Something dislodged it – it rolled, teetered, and fell on to Marti's foot. There were howls of pain and a lot of drama. Later Kay and I asked one another how it had happened. We had both thought, but suppressed the idea, that five-year-old Charlotte might have set it rolling. Fortunately there was no hint that Marti had had the same idea.

In Charlotte (now Grimshaw)'s collection, *Singularity* (2009), there's a story called 'The Olive Grove'. A New Zealand family of five are living in the South of France near an olive grove, and they're visited by the parents' friend, Javine. There is a certain suppressed hilarity between the parents, and the mother, Beth, says the father, Per, spoils her sleep by making too many jokes at bedtime. Javine is blonde, French, and not physically like Marti; but the story clearly derives from her visit. The child, Emily, doesn't altogether like Javine who seems to flirt with her father. Javine is telling Emily that she shouldn't just colour in squares and triangles and oblongs; she should be creative, make her own pictures – and Javine does one of a cat.

> 'We make our own picture, see. Not other people's lines.'
>
> Silence. The scratch of the pencil. Emily gave the ball a tiny push. Down plunged the heavy object – *thud*.

---

* *You Have a Lot to Lose*, facing p. 197.

> Javine gasped. She screamed. Emily shrank down, quick-small in her chair, clenching her fists. Javine crumpled, making a strange sound, grrrrnnnnnnn.

We have seen in the story little Emily grow very attached to a young policeman who is assigned to keep people from watching football matches from the olive grove without paying. Now the family are in town, with Javine nursing her bandaged foot, when they come upon a group of policemen bullying and beating a young Nord Afrique. The parents are outraged, and Emily is distressed because the nice cop – the one she likes so much – is one of the beaters. The parents are uncertain what to do, but Javine surges forward and berates the police in French, threatening them with a formal complaint to their superiors. They become hesitant, and their young victim escapes.

We had seen in fact a young North African beaten by French cops, arrested and forced into the boot of their car and driven away. There had been no heroic intervention. But it seemed to me extraordinary all those years later when the story appeared that the five-year-old had seen and remembered so much, and so accurately – both Marti's theatrical tendencies, and yet her formidable sense of the rights of the underdog.

One of the things that might have accelerated over the years any sense of a gap between us was the Friedlanders' defection from support of, and voting for, the Labour Party – not (which would have been entirely comprehensible) because of Labour's brief and disastrous leap into Rogernomics, but because Phil Goff had shaken Yasser Arafat's hand, and Helen Clark had spoken sympathetically of the Palestinian cause; and I sometimes suspected that in her account of the quarrel which 'ended our friendship' Marti had really been thinking of one that had happened on the subject of loyalty to Labour, and that she'd chosen to make the issue Israel/Palestine because she didn't want their defection from the ranks of Labour supporters to be widely known.

Marti was like a number of women writers I have known who had been able to establish themselves while supported by a working husband. The Friedlanders always seemed to have a lot of money. They travelled widely (in later years always business class), to Israel as well as to Europe, drove expensive cars, built themselves a beautiful house in Herne Bay, and a few decades later another (Sargisson-Cook designed) in Brighton Road. And there were some decades when they owned a flat in (I think it was) Redcliffe Square in London. Marti always had the best cameras and excellent darkroom equipment, and was not employed except with occasional contracts. So there was a great deal that happened because of Gerrard's cooperation, which flowed on to others, including to me. Marti always sent me a selection of the best (often large) prints of any photo session, of myself and of the family. She never charged, and always insisted I was free to use them for publicity. All she asked was that she be acknowledged as the photographer. I am immensely grateful – to them both – for that, though I know it felt at the time, to them and to us, just the way friends behave towards one another. They received copies of my books of course; and I think she liked being my photographer as much as I liked being her subject.

Hitler's nose

In February 2000 I wrote to Ljiljana Šćurić that I was

> struggling to start a new novel – two starts, two stops. I'd given it up, but now, this morning, decided that on Monday I should begin one more time and try a different line of attack. The idea seems to have taken hold, but so far I haven't been able to make it work. It's a question of finding a method, but more of striking a note.

This was the novel I was to call *The Secret History of Modernism* – a title Allen Curnow liked but I would come to think had been a mistake, because it suggested a new academic work by the professor. My idea was to begin with a writer in later middle age who is intending to write about his younger days as a postgraduate student in London, but is suffering a bad bout of 'writer's block' – as I was myself for the first time since I'd aspired to write fiction. To overcome writer's block by writing about it was the idea – and at a third try after those two failures, it worked.

For some pages I entertained my character, Laszlo Winter, with ideas of how he might spend his time if he should stop writing. Thus engaged (and, I hoped, amusing my readers) I began simply to enjoy entering the character of witty Laszlo. So I wrote myself into his story which was to be (of course) partly my own. This opening chapter is called 'Hitler's Nose', and in another February 2000 message I wrote:

> Last evening Kay and I had drinks with a German whose life had overlapped with ours at various points. There had been so many casual overlaps and yet we had never really sat down together in the same room and talked. It was a very strange encounter, meant to 'catch up' on ourselves. He has a pointed nose so like Hitler's I couldn't stop looking at it. Then we left him and went to a restaurant in Mission Bay and sat on a terrace overlooking a street busy and noisy enough to be somewhere in Italy, looking out on a sea calm enough to be the Mediterranean. It was a good way to end a week in which I had achieved nothing but bits and pieces. Sometimes I think I might retire as a writer; but when I haven't got work under way I feel weightless, and even seriously depressed. (Writing of course is a kind of insanity.)

This was the trigger of my opening chapter – and when the novel appeared the German, Gerhardt Trabing, far from being upset, was delighted to claim having had a hand (or a nose) in its conception. In my mind he had become part of the big picture – in the same category as Israel Getzler and Otto Bergmann, the German Jew and the Wehrmacht soldier who figure in *You Have a Lot to Lose*. Ger (as he asked us to call him) told us that as a child he had been recruited into the Hitler Youth. His father had been a trade union secretary and therefore frowned on by the Nazis; and Ger had become aware that his father now feared him. He had never had any reasons to traduce his father; but he looked back with shame on feelings that the Hitler Youth had given him of importance and even power over his dad.

Chapter 1 of *The Secret History of Modernism*, 'Hitler's Nose', involves Laszlo, his third wife Louise, and their meeting with Otto Stiltz, who had been very briefly married to Samantha (Sammy) Conlan, the great love of Laszlo's youth. The connections are intricate. There is clearly much plot-work to do, much to be unravelled. But re-reading it now what strikes me at once is how the novel, surreptitiously but clearly in this chapter, declares that its subject is only apparently personal, domestic, close-focus, and that in reality it is occupied with the big picture, with the history of the century that is just ending as the writer embarks on his task. And then, having established that priority, that clear intention, it brings itself down to what is the centre-point of my (i.e of Laszlo Winter's) world. He and Louise are at Mission Bay in Auckland:

> Afterwards we walked along the beach holding hands. It was too hot for hand-holding but Louise insisted on it. Being French, she liked always to make *un joli tableau*.
>
> We looked at the people, Pakeha and Maori, Asian and Polynesian, promenading, talking, sitting on the grass and the sea-wall, eating takeaways, playing guitars and singing. Beyond the beach, on the town side, the pohutukawa-topped cliffs were flood-lit; across the water, the dark shape of Rangitoto loomed; and between, the moon made its white-footed way over a summer-night sea. I was happy. I loved it all, and I loved Louise. This was my comfort zone. I didn't want to break out of it; but the thought was there somewhere that I might have to if there was ever to be another book.

In Chapter 2 we jump back at once to London in the 1950s. Laszlo is a postgraduate student from New Zealand, deeply attached to a young Australian, Sammy Conlan, who in turn is in love with a married Jewish-Australian journalist, Freddy Goldstein. Chapter 3 gives us Sammy's back story, which I had 'borrowed' from several Australian women I'd known, probably more from Penny Nelson than any other, though some of Kay's experience of employment in Armidale also went into it. Freddy (Friedreich) has a Jewish father but has inherited the blonde hair and blue eyes of his Aryan mother – my debt to Gerrard on whom the character is loosely based. But Freddy's back story is the one I took from Eva Rosenbaum's family. His parents have escaped Nazi Germany and reached Australia via Palestine, where the father has had an affair with a Latvian flower-seller – causing the mother to go back to her Aryan family, though on reflection she relents and returns to him. So when married Freddy is having his affair with Samantha he refers to 'the sins of the father' and says she is his 'Latvian flower-seller'. Freddy loves Sammy but he does not want to leave his Jewish wife. That in a way is the 'domestic' crux of the plot. Laszlo loves Sammy who loves Freddy who loves (more or less) his wife: very conventional, very tedious, as most of real life is; but feeling and action have their springs in the big picture.

At intervals Laszlo Winter reflects on his own practice as a writer telling his own story. This for example:

> This narrative, myth, or fairy-tale, this history of the century just finished, had been the story I knew best, went on learning, and had to tell myself over and over in my writing, each time with a different emphasis. It was in a way my dreamlife, because it's only by dreaming (though the dream is founded on the facts) that reality is grasped. 'Tread softly, because you tread on my dreams.'
>
> And strangely, it was the second half of the story, the half I'd been part of, that could sometimes seem less significant,

> less interesting, less momentous – a long aftermath rather than a dénouement. It was as if the twentieth century had ended when it was only half done, with the bullet in Hitler's brain, the opening of the Nazi death camps, and the dropping of two atom bombs. Since then we'd all been in school, trying to learn the lessons, squabbling about what it all meant and where to go next, not quite daring (thankfully) to let our biggest mistakes repeat themselves.

But (I could have continued) we had all been living with the consequences – the grief and the nightmares, the shaming and blaming, the quirks and inherited neuroses. That's how it seemed to me when I surveyed my Jewish friends: they were living under that cloud of past events, not able quite to escape from it. We were all – but they particularly were – the inheritors of 'Hitler and so on'.

In the London of the 1950s Laszlo and Sammy get on with their life as friends. He teaches a call-girl in a neighbouring bedsit, Heather, about Shakespeare – because she's interested, wants to know, likes his stories and the way he tells them. Heather pays for these 'lessons' in the currency of her own profession. Sammy, meanwhile, works for a magazine editor, Marx MacLaren, a Scot I modelled on Karl Miller. Marx has an assistant, Wilma Marienbad modelled on Mary-Kay Wilmers. It's a pretty accurate though slightly cartoonish account of the *LRB* office, moved back in time, and I had a cheerful message about it from Karl ('I have had a very agreeable time reading your new novel') to which I replied I was glad he had

> not taken offence on behalf of the Scots, nor of editors, nor of anyone who might be thought to bear any resemblance to Marx MacLaren. Thank you for that. I'm sure anyone who saw herself as Wilma Marienbad would not be so forgiving.

At intervals we return to 'the Goldstein story' which has episodes not wholly derived from either Rosenbaum or Friedlander histories

– though they might have been, coming as they do from German Jewish escapes from the Nazis in those years before and during World War II. In the end, the Goldsteins are safe in Australia but that history is a weight on Freddy, making demands of him, influencing him and determining his choices. At last Sammy herself is freed of her 'first love'. Slowly Laszlo has replaced Freddy in her affections, but he doesn't know and she doesn't say. By now she is pregnant to Freddy and in love with Laszlo, a conundrum she resolves by marrying Otto Stiltz, the man with Hitler's nose whom she will very soon divorce.

Now we are back in 'the present' – right at the end of the twentieth century, and Laszlo, as in the first chapter, has established, after a gap of many decades, email contact with Sammy. She asks him whether he knows where Freddy can be found, because she thinks he should be told that he has a son – and grandchildren too – in Australia. Laszlo finds him in a retirement village in Tauranga, a widower, watching birds through binoculars from his deck. He receives Sammy's news calmly and sends his love. The subject of Israel and Palestine comes up, and he tells two stories, one about a Jewish family evicted from their apartment in Berlin in the 1930s, a second about a Palestinian family evicted from their apartment in Jerusalem in 1948. He doesn't quote Auden because he's not a literary man, but it's as if the novel is quoting for him the famous line, 'Those to whom evil is done do evil in return.' I attributed to the character of Freddy Goldstein, in other words, an even-handed view of that subject which I doubt his model was capable of.

At the front of the novel there is a 'special thanks' acknowledgement to Gerrard Friedlander and Eva (Rosenbaum) Reid. I had made use of their family histories and felt that, without being at all specific, the debt should be acknowledged.

But what was 'the secret history of modernism' – that probably unhelpful title I'd stuck with? Late in the novel Sammy writes to Laszlo about the thesis she had tried to write on that subject:

> I decided it had something to do with tossing out the nineteenth-century Romantic idea of beauty – dismissing it as soft and sentimental. The new art and literature would 'burn with a hard, gem-like flame'. The new blade would cut through the butter of the past. There would be a new discipline in writing and in thought, and also in social and political life. It was going to be all steel and sinew and will. Like most *avant garde* ideas this had its own logic and its own truth. But undiluted it was poison.

The reception

I have been chastised for quoting favourable reviews but they are part of the story and there are sometimes lessons to be learned. Readers in New Zealand mostly seemed to enjoy *The Secret History of Modernism* and to take, perhaps from something witty and insouciant in its tone, permission not just to enjoy, but to take it all more lightly than the author intended. Lawrence Jones in the *Listener* thought it was a Citroën or Porsche, a 'classy vehicle'. I suppose I was on top of my game. But should one seem to be 'at ease' when, however lightly, 'touching upon' the Holocaust? There was no (or not very much) evidence of authorial angst: I could not have called it *Mein Kampf*. Even John de Falbe in the *Spectator* urging people to read it described it as 'challenging, fun, urbane and brilliant' – which did not quite match its darker 'content'. Iain Sharp in the *Sunday Star-Times* took it seriously enough to say it was my 'wisest and most assured novel'. But the best reviews came from Ireland. Rosemary Goring in the Dublin *Sunday Tribune* described it as 'fiction of the highest order, gracefully intelligent, emotionally probing, politically sharp', and thought its 'antipodean perspective' was 'a healthy, and at times astonishing, corrective to European self-centredness'. And then there was Eileen Battersby in the *Irish Times*:

> Stead's handling of this student life of uncertainty and confused sexuality is far more graceful and humane than V. S. Naipaul's sour handling of similar material in his recent novel *Half a Life*. *The Secret History of Modernism* is as subtle as Jane Austen and as fatalistic as Thomas Hardy. [. . .] a minor miracle of a novel.

Even with such great reviews there is always uncertainty. I often said – and meant – I thought this was my best novel, or anyway my personal favourite; and I took huge reassurance especially from the Dublin pair. But in the back of my mind there was nervousness about the Holocaust subject. The only time I discussed the novel with Marti she said very little – so little I couldn't be sure she'd read it – and there was nothing in what she did say that removed the anxiety. There wasn't much from Gerrard that helped either – though he did say he liked the mention that New Zealand's medical fashion for circumcision in those years had made it a great destination for a boy who was a Jewish refugee. I'd felt I had to cite the cases of Eva and Gerrard because they lent an element of authenticity; they authorised my telling this story – but of course they didn't really. They neither approved nor disapproved.

Part of me was indeed Autolycus, the 'snapper-up of unconsidered trifles'. I had trespassed and taken what was not mine to use. It was the kind of opportunism Henry James says or implies is the fiction writer's business – which is not to say he would have approved of this example.

Ann Thwaite wrote to me in February 2002 about her enjoyment of the novel, and the strong conviction parts of it gave her that they had 'really happened'. I replied:

> No, I invented the bit about the dungeon under the sandcastle – and the visit to Christina Stead, and the encounter with TSE – and many other things readers imagine must have happened 'really'. It's strange how when writing fiction one knows that something is 'as if it really happened' by a feeling that comes

> over one about detail. When I wrote that scene with the Jew's exchange with the little boys and their sister, and the Jew racing away embarrassed, I knew this was 'real' – as if I had for a moment slipped down a funnel into history. I felt exactly the same about the moment outside the High St Ken tube station when Laszlo has his first conversation with the call-girl Heather – the 'business' about how to hold the cake and who should hold the umbrella: it just jumped out at me as REAL. One wants that all the time but it only happens sometimes.

Marti and the *Champs-Élysées*

The Steads and the Friedlanders tried hard to steer clear of the prickly Israel/Palestine subject, but Marti's strange reversion to it in her ad libbed *Self-Portrait* shows how it lingered for her. Sometimes it came up inadvertently. In April 2002 at a time when the strife was becoming particularly violent and the IDF was hitting Palestinian targets with their usual lethal efficiency, the University of Auckland conferred its promised honorary doctorate on Allen Curnow who had died too soon to receive it in person. There was a ceremony and readings. Marti and Gerrard were in the audience, and Marti wrote afterward reproaching me. 'You and Kay were less than friendly on the evening of the tribute. Perhaps you were just surprised to see me at such an event, or is it something to do with the situation in Israel and Palestine?'

I replied:

> Why would either of us have been surprised to see you that evening? You were among friends – and I was touched that you told me I read well. If it seemed we didn't talk to you it must have been because you are (not surprisingly) in a state of heightened sensitivity about what is happening in Israel and Palestine, and reading (misreading) negative signs where they don't exist. It was one of those literary occasions where so

> many people we know, many we haven't seen for a long time, are all together in one place, and attention gets pulled this way and that. It should have occurred to me (but didn't at the time) that you might be looking for a bit of friendly reassurance, and I should have given it. I'm sorry I didn't.

In reply she told me that if she 'had been feeling less distressed about events at the moment I would not have been so over-sensitive'. Then she told me that she had once asked

> a friend of ours who had been in Auschwitz, Rabbi Hugo Gryn, how he managed to remain sane during his time there. He replied that it was Hope, that marvellous ingredient of life that we all call upon in times of grief. So Gerrard and I cling to that in our sadness at the escalation of violence, that perhaps some sanity and wisdom will prevail.

I felt that citing an Auschwitz survivor was like going to a Higher Authority which made any answer impossible – but that's how it was dealing with Marti.

WERE THE FRIEDLANDERS (in Auckland terms) Westies? Gerrard had spent a significant part of his childhood in Henderson. His father's practice was there and Gerrard never quite escaped from it. They bought their first house in Tirimoana Road, and though their second and third were in Herne Bay and Parnell, I think the Henderson practice was maintained. Gerrard once did a repair job on one of my teeth there.

But Marti's interest in painters, especially Don Binney with his Te Henga (Bethells Beach) connection, and Colin McCahon with his at Helensville, Titirangi and French Bay, pulled her westward. Dick Scott involved her in photographing the orchards and vintners of the Henderson Valley before property prices had begun to squeeze them out. She was not one to plunge into the surf – I never saw her in a bathing suit, not even in Menton; but that wild west coast had to become part of her consciousness as it was part of ours. So at some point (I think in the 1970s or early '80s) Gerrard and Marti bought a section at Karekare. It was just above the car-park on a ridge that continued up to become one of the tracks north towards Piha and beyond. Further up that ridge and overlooking Karekare was the house belonging to Harry Turbott, head of Auckland University's Town Planning Department; and also, in later years, the fine architect-designed house of mayor of Waitākere Bob (now Sir Bob) Harvey.

Somewhere in sight at that time was a hump of sand under which those of us who had been visiting Karekare long enough knew sat the old rusting loci that had once pulled kauri logs on rails over the rocks and along the foreshore to be loaded at Whatipu. That was a fading part of the story Allen Curnow had revived in his 'A Fellow Being' sequence about the Canadian dentist and kauri plunderer F. J. Rayner. Just below the Friedlanders' section was the old schoolhouse that had been lifted in a flood from further up the valley and deposited where it was now, restored and reblocked, and occupied by Owen McShane and his wife or partner Jenny Parkinson. Owen was a remorseless intellectual of somewhat extravagant right-wing economic opinion, an unstoppable neo-libertarian monologist. He used to write letters to the paper and sign them as Director of the New Zealand Centre for Resource Management Studies. He had a grand letterhead for this, giving the impression that it was a large and authoritative organisation. In fact it was only Owen. Jenny had a nice singing voice. In the family I used to refer to her as Madame Butterfly and to Owen as Thinkerton.

I remember Marti pointing out that whichever way you came to Karekare – down the Cutting or the longer route via Lone Kauri Road – brought you to that car-park. There your wheels had to be abandoned and you proceeded on foot to the vast black-sand surf beach, to do your swimming or sunbathing, or your fishing from the rocks. Several streams gathered together at this point and had to be forded or waded on the seaward side of the car-park, or crossed on the road bridge and skirted through Pohutukawa Glade. Equally, you arrived there on foot if you came up from the beach or from any of the main tracks – the Zion Ridge, the Pararaha Valley, the beach track from Whatipu; or from any of the northern tracks. This was the coastal region Curnow's poems had colonised, making it his own and by extension ours; and McCahon and Binney had done the same in paint.

I could see why Marti was so excited. When their bach was built, she said, they would be sitting above the *Champs-Élysées* of Karekare, or indeed of the west coast. For a time they rented a little house further up the ridge, I suppose to acquire the Kiwi habit of the bach for holidays and weekends. But it was more the idea than the fact that was exciting. Slowly it faded, the rented place was dropped, and nothing was built on their section. When I asked her about it once, and reminded her of her idea of the *Champs-Élysées* of the West, she seemed to struggle for an answer and then said, 'Oh you know me darling, I'm a city girl.'

Marti died in November 2016 and was buried at Waikumete, the West Auckland cemetery not far from Henderson where she'd made her start as a Kiwi. The service had a kind of starkness which Kay liked but which to me had the grim black-and-white feel of Marti's earliest New Zealand photographs. In a charming, quite small chapel (probably not the right word) shaped like a Star of David and built all in wood that had the familiar (to me) feel of a Lockwood about it, the coffin was draped in plain black and the Kaddish was read in Hebrew by the rabbi and then in English by Len Bell. As the coffin was carried out and the crowd followed no great distance to the graveside, Roger Horrocks told me that his wife Shirley, who had made a wonderful documentary about Marti (and another about Allen Curnow), had grown up in a Jewish family and that one of the horrors of her childhood had been this ritual of burial, with the sound of the clods thudding down on to the coffin.

Marti was duly lowered into the ground and Gerrard stood a moment with the shovel, his capped head bowed as if in prayer and farewell. Then he looked up and to his right and said, 'Oh is that Kay?' Kay was in the crowd – but it was Charlotte who was in his line of sight, and his mind had leapt back several decades seeing the Kay of younger years.

It seemed to be the role of the men to follow Gerrard in sending a shovelful of earth down into the grave, which I couldn't quite bring myself to do, though I could imagine Marti saying in her smoker's contralto, 'Come on Karl, you can do this for me.'

She had received an honorary doctorate not long before her death and Kay had written congratulating her and telling her how well deserved it was.

> I am so sorry you are ill. You are in the thoughts of all of us. So many memories since our first meeting in the little flat in Masons Avenue with Edward Kamara. How exotic and what a Londoner you were. Do you remember Menton? And the time you and I went to Hamilton to see Olwen and we missed the bus at Huntly and had to hitch a ride with the Evangelicals? And Tirimoana Road, next door to the house where I had spent so much of my childhood. And later all your photographing of the children – such wonderful photographs. You have enriched our lives, dear Marti. Much love to you, and to Gerrard (whom I remember even further back as a Grammar boy).

That message was sent on the 3rd of November and Marti died eleven days later.

Postscript 1:
Twice (2007 and 2011) staying at the Bogliasco Foundation's Liguria Study Center Kay and I were assigned an elegant and spacious room one floor up at the front of the villa, with a balcony looking out

through pines and cypresses to the sea. All meals were provided, lunch and dinner superbly prepared and served (we were waited on) to the seven or so fellows with their partners around one big faultlessly laid table. The company were mostly American – artists, writers, musicians, academics – and the conversation was civil, clever, entertaining. There was much good wine but not too much. We were well-fed and nice to one another. I enjoyed it all, far as it was from the 'real world' where poverty and want predominate. My job was to write well and I worked hard at that, accepting the fellowship as an earned reward.

But there was one relationship I formed there that was especially memorable. It was with Benny Morris, the Israeli historian. I got to know him well, liked him, and played ferocious table tennis with him every day after lunch. Benny was known as the historian who had written the truth, which others had evaded or glossed over, in particular about the 1948 Arab–Israeli war which had established the state of Israel. Because I had heard just that about him I expected to find Benny deeply sympathetic to the sufferings of the Palestinians. He was not. Where wrongs had been done to them he recorded those truthfully and admitted they should not have happened. But he did not consider (for example) the removal of 700,000 Palestinians from their homes and farms wrong or a war crime. Without ethnic cleansing, he argued, the state of Israel could not have been established, and the wrongs done to the Jews by the Holocaust meant the world owed them a homeland.

So here I was still in the region of the Mediterranean, still confronting the intractable and interminable consequences of World War II. At the time there was great anxiety in Israel about Iran and the possibility that it might soon be able to manufacture a nuclear weapon. Benny thought the US should put an end to this possibility at once. But the facilities were said to be deep underground – that might require something huge mightn't it? Even nuclear? The means, Benny said, would be up to the US President; what was important was that it should be done. I didn't press him on the means. I had learned with Marti and Gerrard not to venture too far into the sacred territory of Israel's relations with the region to which it claimed ancient rights.

After we had returned home Benny sent Kay a copy of his classic study *1948: The First Arab–Israeli War*, which he had inscribed 'For Kate and Karl – fond memories – Benny'; and I sent his wife Leah, who loved poetry and admired the work of Elaine Feinstein, a copy of a book of her poems Elaine had inscribed 'For Karl – of course I remember Toronto',* which I reinscribed for Leah. Kay read and annotated Benny's book (I let myself off) and marked a passage on p. 65 as 'Benny's Credo'. It was a passage referring to UN Resolution 181 (II) calling for the partition of Palestine into two sovereign states, one Jewish, the other Palestinian, and ending the British Mandate on the territory. On this subject Benny had written:

> Though the Arabs could not, or refused to, see it, Resolution 181, besides geopolitically redesigning a sliver of eastern Mediterranean coastline, was an emphatic ethical statement, one of those crossroads in history where morality and realism come together. Or as one Jewish historian later put it: '[It was] Western civilization's gesture of repentance for the Holocaust [. . .]' Viewed in the longer span, the vote represented humanity's amends for two thousand years of humiliation and persecution – both by the Christian and Islamic worlds – of the Jews, the world's eternally stateless people, the world's eternal minority.

Kay's comment on this reads, 'This is intellectually, and possibly semantically, untenable. Does "humanity" include or exclude the Palestinians?'

---

* In *You Have a Lot to Lose* (p. 314) I describe how I missed Elaine's reading at Toronto and was then unintentionally prevented from hearing her read in Cambridge by the formidable drunken duo of W. S. Graham and George Barker.

Postscript 2:

There were many notable friendships made at Bogliasco but perhaps the warmest was with a gay couple, Willard Spiegelman and Ken Bleeth, very civilised Eng. Lit. academics, Willard a well-known American essayist. When he sent us his next book* we found he had included Bogliasco – and us, 'Karl and Kay Stead, the two wisest guests' at the Study Center.

I put Willard and Ken into a sequence of poems I wrote there,† a sonnet-tribute to them, but also to us:

> There they go again, the American couple
> Willard and Ken, a long way out
> from the pebble beach, heads full
> of books and history (including
>
> their own) – treading water, talking.
> Like us, they've been together
> decades, no doubt had their
> times of turbulence, or when careers
>
> pulled them apart – but survivors
> and still afloat. Willard sets off
> towards Nervi, stops and waits
> for Ken to follow – two greying heads
>
> against the Mediterranean blue
> with the sun's blessing, and mine.

---

* Willard Spiegelman, *Seven Pleasures: Essays on Ordinary Happiness*, Farrar, Straus, and Giroux, 2009, p. 196.

† 'LIGURIA', *The Yellow Buoy*, pp. 46–57.

13. High Octane

The poem vein

In a message to Craig Raine of 24 February 2002 I wrote:

> Last Thursday I wrote some dialogue that might be the start of a new novel I have been hesitating towards for weeks and months, reluctant until I was sure the poem vein had run out, and reluctant because a novel's harder work even than teaching literature. But there it was, a start (maybe). That night I dreamed my hair had come back. It was red – but vivid, more orange than red. I didn't mind the colour at all. Kay tried to trim it at the front because it was falling over my face. My only worry was that no one would believe it was real. They would all think it was a wig. I guess that's a Reverse-Samson dream.

'The poem vein' had lasted five months. In that time I must have written most of the poems in *Dog*, including the sequence 'At Wagner's Tomb' which sprang from our visit to Bayreuth to hear the *Ring* cycle one more time and visit the Wagner house, *Wahnfried*, with its garden where Richard and Cosima are buried. *Dog* also included the sequence 'King's Lynn and the Pacific', the consequence of my receiving the King's Lynn Poetry prize, awarded one year to a poet who comes back the following year as King's Lynn Laureate, bringing a sequence of poems he or she has written about King's Lynn and its relations with a foreign country or port. I was the fourth recipient and I decided to do 'King's Lynn and the Pacific', about two famous local sailors, James Burney and George Vancouver, who had both sailed with Cook, and one of whom, Vancouver, was famous later for explorations in North American waters.

The Wagner sequence was somewhat esoteric – poems for Wagnerians. But the King's Lynn sequence, though I had set myself syllabic forms which could be complicated and demanding in execution, was more open and available. The King's Lynn Festival produced the sequence in paperback and hardcover, the latter a particularly handsome small book with broad pages. Between these two sequences in *Dog* there were twenty-three occasional poems, including an elegy for my beloved cat Zac, 'Cat/ullus', ending

> Zac the radical,
> Zac the bed-crowder
> the window leaper
> the lateral-thinker,
> Zac the head-first rat-eater
> is dead,
> is 'laid to rest',
> has met his match.
>
> Frater, ave (etc)
> *Black Zac*
> *Zac the Knife.*

There were two elegies to Allen Curnow, the one Jeny had been affronted by ('His Round') and the version of Catullus 65 dedicated to Allen which she'd thought 'lovely'. There was the poem I'd written for Karl Miller's seventieth birthday; and a sequence, witty and now and then obscene, called 'Creation etc' which hovered around traditional notions of the Christian universe, all either ironically explored or gently deplored in the name of what can only be called Reality as it is understood in the twenty-first century. This is where the book's title comes from, because I was keeping alive the idea the two boys in *Talking about O'Dwyer* were fascinated by, that 'God' is only a word, dog spelled backwards and signalling no reality external to itself. And the book's brilliant cover illustration by Sarah Maxey was the text of the poem called 'Psalm' written in thick black ink in such a way that it formed the shape of a dog.

Every Dog has his day
but this one taketh the Prize
therefore buy Him a deserving collar,
feed Him and walk Him.

His Yap in the high country
driveth home the sky-flocks,
his clattering Feet
are the claws of the pelting rain.

A distant quake is his Growl
in the deserts of Kadesh,
his Whine warneth Lebanon's leaves
of the burglar Time.

Dog the heavens call him
whose Bark and Bite alike
shall be praised for ever
in the temples of man.

So much, then, comes down to language – and to style. The language and style of the Psalms are preserved here, but it is dog rather than god that is honoured. The New English Bible had retranslated the traditional text to be plainer and (it was claimed) more 'accurate', but at the expense of beauty which, to a non-believer, was the real (and immense) value of the King James version; and I had made this point in an earlier collection, *The Right Thing*, with a poem called 'Even Newer English Bible', an ironic rewrite of the 23rd Psalm ('The Lord is my caregiver so I'm OK').* Now in *Dog* I offered 'Even Newer English Bible 2', another ironic rewrite, this time of the Lord's Prayer:

> Big Daddy-in-the-Sky
> your PR's good –
> we're backing you to win
> down here as you won up there.
> Please feed us
> and go easy on us
> as we go easy on
> those other bastards.
> No honey-traps –
> we want to stay out of trouble
> because you've been
> the Big Cheese always
> and likely to remain so
> for the foreseeable future
> amen.

'For the foreseeable future' was twenty-first-century science's equivalent of 'for ever and ever'.

Though these were meant to entertain, they were entirely serious, and the sequence ends with a rhyming run through the philosophers

---

* Which I now discover Arc, who published the UK edition of the collection, removed! There must have been someone there who baulked at such blasphemous levity.

struggling towards a truth that keeps eluding them, ending with Stephen Hawking unable to take them further than the present boundaries of human knowledge:

> I dreamed I met a man in space
> he had a brain and not much face
> he used a small machine for talking
> it said his name was Stephen Hawking
> I said 'I know that Space is bending'
> he quacked 'It's worse than that. It's ending.'

But the poem preceding this one in the sequence is less full of itself, slightly mournful, but not nihilistic, and still ends alone with poor old dog:

> vii *Dogma*
>
> Stillness came to the garden –
> so many greens!
> and it occurred to him without beauty
> there would not be much to speak of,
> much to love.
> A face, stars, islands,
> a vastness
> of darkness and light,
> a few wrenching bars –
> these made sadness possible,
> compelled regret.
>
> Last night
> straining to make his ears
> attend to the silence
> he heard it in the distance –
> a dog barking,

and then a half-asleep voice
(his own) with laughter in it:
'Dog, are you there?
Good dog. *Dog*!'

The next novel

But what were the lines of dialogue mentioned in that message to Craig Raine? It must have been the opening scene of my novel *Mansfield* in which I have Katherine and T. S. Eliot coming away together from a dinner party at Jack and Mary Hutchinson's home in Hammersmith. They had indeed found themselves together at that event, Tom without his wife, the very weird Vivien, and Katherine without her partner, the very unctuous John Middleton Murry. I knew a lot about both of them, and on that basis was able to invent their conversation.

So I was embarking on a different kind of novel, one that would not draw, except in the sense that every piece of fiction does whatever its 'subject', upon my own personal experience. There would no longer be a man at the centre of the story of whom reviewers could say 'Stead is writing about himself – *again!*' They would not suggest I thought myself Mansfield, or a woman – and yet that too would be at least half-wrong. I felt confident writing about Katherine, not simply because I had studied her so closely and knew her work, both fiction and non-fiction, so well. More than knowing a lot *about* her, I felt confident I could *become* her – in the same way I had *become* Emily Summerscroft in my first serious piece of fiction, 'A Race Apart'; and just as I had *become* the unnamed female first-person narrator in my story 'A Fitting Tribute'. In *All Visitors Ashore* I had confidently assumed the voice of Cecelia Skyways – so successfully I had been accused of invading Janet Frame's privacy. Female first-person narrators, or simply a POV that switched to a female character, appeared at intervals throughout my writing – which was why I had never accepted the feminist dogma that only women could write about women.

Eight of fourteen chapters in the novel as it emerged would be Katherine's – her POV – and if there were to be problems I didn't see, as I embarked on it, why there should be. But I didn't tell anyone what the subject of this new novel was to be. Kay knew, but no one else – not until I told Margaret Scott in November 2002 when it was well under way:

> I'm writing a novel with Mansfield more or less at its centre – so of course the *Notebooks* [which Margaret had transcribed] are very important. And the letters. And Alpers etc etc. It's surprising. One discovers much more clearly the difference between fiction and biography. Fiction must always be particular, up-close, dramatised; it can't skim, summarise and guess as biography can – it must always *know* – yet it can leave huge gaps which biography can't. One discovers how much is NOT known about KM – and it's in those interstices that fiction can pitch a tent, so long as nothing that is put there contradicts what is known. It's something new for me and I'm enjoying it. It will cover only a few years – roughly 1915 to 17. The technique I'm using is to shift the central consciousness about from chapter to chapter. [. . .]
>
> I'm stuck at the moment not knowing whose consciousness is to carry the novel forward in a chapter about the Gower Street episodes and Garsington around Christmas 1916 – who is to be the bearer of (so to speak) the tape recorder and the digital camera. So much happens, so many people, so much real and fake emotion, and against the background of the Somme!

Margaret, who had given so much of her life to the Mansfield texts, was truly excited at this new project. She wrote:

> Your new novel is deeply compelling and wildly exciting. It seems as you describe it something that was ordained at the beginning of time – a necessity – and yet you are the only

> person, anywhere, at any time, capable of doing it. I have been thinking about it all the time and can see how beautifully you will bring it off.

During the next three and a half months spent overseas with Kay I was at work on the new novel more or less every day, despite the fact that we had to move about so much.

Finally there were almost four weeks in the Axelrads' house in Uzès, where Margaret and Guy came to visit with baby Joseph and – as it happened – to experience with us the extraordinary storm and consequent flood described in Chapter 2. While in France we visited Bandol, an important Mansfield site, and the Hotel Beau Rivage where Katherine had had her first tubercular haemorrhage. Another Mansfield excursion of these on-the-move months had been one to Devon and Cornwall with our old Bristol friends, Robin and Elisabeth Marleyn, with whom we hunted out the two adjoining cottages at Zennor where Mansfield and Murry lived with D. H. Lawrence and Frieda, and where Katherine recorded the beating Lawrence visited on his wife.

The point of being in Europe so long was partly to be in easy reach of Margaret with her first baby, partly to do those visits to Mansfield locations, but also because I had three festivals to attend, inconveniently spaced – Manchester (June), Edinburgh (August) and King's Lynn (late September), the last being my return as their 'Laureate' with the 'King's Lynn and the Pacific' sequence. All this time I was keeping the Mansfield novel moving forward; and while in London was using the new British Library for Mansfield research – not nearly as romantic as the old British Museum Reading Room it had replaced, but more technologically advanced. A diary entry of 7 August records: 'Finished draft chapter 5 today, total now 102 pages.' In another I note that I'd thought only research would be possible while on the move but that both research and writing were continuing.

We got back to Auckland in time to organise a dinner party for twenty-four friends and family in a restaurant in Parnell (Ravel's and we took it over for the evening) to celebrate my seventieth birthday. I wrote a poem, 'On Turning Seventy', for that occasion, in time for it to go in as a last-minute addition to *Dog*:

I think it came to me in sleep
that when at Anzac dawn parades
old soldiers weep
it's not as they will say for fallen comrades

but for the young self full of sap and fire
as distant now and caught in coils of time
as one the bullets of a half-forgotten war
stopped in his prime.

For that birthday my niece, Norma's daughter Kathy, gave me a beautiful wooden box carved somewhere in the Pacific for my Swedish grandfather Christian Karlson, and with his initials, C. K., on the front. My mum had given it to Kathy who thought it should now go to the one who, as a writer, signed himself C. K.

'These are our stories . . .'

Mansfield the novel was unstoppable now; but in a way it was also responsible for the novel that would follow, *My Name Was Judas*. I remember very clearly Kay and I walking back from our morning coffee in Uzès along the unpaved road from the woods through vineyards to the village of Saint-Maximin, talking as we went about the Mansfield novel, and my saying how pleased I was that it didn't require me to write in detail about D. H. Lawrence. Lawrence was almost incomprehensible, so brilliant and so foolish, with such a vivid sense of the reality of the natural world, but such an overweening sense of his own importance and of his visionary powers. 'It would be like trying to write about Jesus,' I said.

Having said that I began to ask myself How *would* you write about Jesus without accepting even for a moment that he was the Messiah, the Son of God? You would have to give him, I decided, a companion, ideally one who shared his boyhood. And somewhere along the way, as my mind played with these problems, the thought came to me that the friend should be Judas Iscariot – someone not as remarkable as Jesus, but very clever and above all rational, clear-sighted, so he could be the measure of his friend's gradual departure from common sense, and ultimately from reality.

So each of these thoughts presented me with a fiction writer's problem – and then with a possible solution. And all the time I was saying to myself in effect Stop this! You are not the person to write a novel about Jesus of Nazareth. Why are you wasting time and intellectual energy on a novel you will never write? And yet part of me began to recognise as the days went by that I was hooked. It had begun to invade me in the night.

Jesus would have to be impressive, brilliant – this would not be an exercise in mockery or even irony. Jesus would have a certain greatness – but human, not divine. Judas would know this throughout and try to rescue him from his delusion, and from his intellectually weaker followers, those famous fishermen whose need was to believe that here was the Messiah, the Christ who had called to them and commanded them to follow, and had shown them the way to be saved in eternity – and perhaps even how they might be delivered in time from the Roman yoke. The disciples, of course, would have to represent Judas as the traitor, the betrayer of Jesus. Judas was the one who, if given a voice, would compromise the great story they had to tell the world.

So before the writing of *Mansfield* was completed I thought I knew (though sure it was a bad idea) where I was likely to go next. It must have been at some time in 2003 that I found myself at a dinner sitting beside Paul Morris, professor of religious studies at Victoria University. There had been quite a lot of wine, enough to loosen my tongue, and I found myself telling him about being obsessed by the idea of retelling the Jesus story in a new way, and how although I knew (or thought I knew) that this was not a good idea, especially for someone like myself, an unbeliever and one considered in some quarters to be 'controversial', I could not quite shake it off. Paul, who I think is a Jew, listened, nodding, not frowning or appearing to be disconcerted; and then said very calmly, 'These are our stories. They must be constantly retold.' That was all – a statement of fact. It had a wonderful effect, like a door being unlocked, a permission granted.

Essentially I wanted to retell a story everyone knew, but in a way that an intelligent, educated, rational person of the twenty-first century could find plausible and believe. Possibly I was already reading or re-reading the New Testament; and before I started writing I'd begun to be something of a biblical scholar. When there was such a specific purpose I could absorb knowledge, and retain it for use, very fast. In January 2005 I wrote to Paul Morris that I'd been reading a great deal, including books he had suggested. I was trying to keep the writing slow and the reading fast and finding it difficult.

> What is useful to the fiction writer is the amount that is NOT known, and the degree to which the experts contradict one another. I intend to have a closer look later at some of the huge books of commentary on the Gospels – questions like, for example, whether anyone has a theory about who was the 'Disciple whom Jesus loved', referred to a number of times in the John gospel. And who was the naked youth who fled from the Garden when Jesus was arrested.
>
> One has to absorb so much and then make it vanish, so there is a bland clear simple fictional surface, as if a man of that time wrote it, and took for granted (and therefore seldom spelled out) all that he knew. [. . .]
>
> I'm no longer sure about the trip to Israel. Marti Friedlander wanted to come with me and hesitated, I think, only because we differ so seriously about Palestine which understandably makes her nervous. Not that I would confuse the two or cause

> her embarrassment. But while the novel runs on on its own, perhaps travel won't be necessary.

I soon had my explanation for how the 'betrayer of Jesus', who in one of the Gospels hangs himself in despair at what he has done, survives to tell in old age the story as he lived it up to and beyond the time of the crucifixion. There are two quite different biblical versions of how Judas dies, so neither can be called authoritative or definitive – and in fact the life stories of the men and women close to Jesus are full of vagueness and contradiction. His mother, for example, is often represented in painting as present at the crucifixion, but only one of four Gospels says she was there.

My Judas would be the loyal ally and schoolfellow of Jesus, and would foresee where his friend's increasing belief that he must be the Messiah was leading, and try to warn and protect him from the Roman wrath. In this he would fall out with the other disciples, and would not corroborate their accounts of Jesus before or after his crucifixion. Among other things, he had to provide an explanation for how the body of Jesus disappeared from the tomb provided by Joseph of Arimathea. This, when I came to it, I thought the most important (because so entirely likely) correction to the story as told in the Gospels.

At each stage of the 'oft told tale' there would be revisions to be made; but these often came easily, not only because I was a fiction writer and used to 'making things up', but because the original versions are, many of them, simply implausible. You have to have 'faith' to believe them. Without faith they are just parts of 'an unlikely story'.

I had made a rule for myself that I would never write about a place I had not visited, and I fully intended to visit Israel and the sacred sites. But I began the writing thinking this would just be a start before making the journey. Instead, it simply ran away with me. I don't think I had written any novel so quickly since *All Visitors Ashore* which had equally bolted, a first draft completed in five months.

Many readers found the novel especially moving in that once the element of the divine is removed it becomes a human tragedy – of a man of extraordinary powers, but deluded and misled, who finally suffers a hideous and undeserved execution; and of his friend, Judas, who fails to save him, but who has lived to correct the record. Judas is a poet, and each of the chapters ends in a brief poem, which in part repeats what has just been told, but is also a kind of commentary on it.

The last scene, of Judas with the now blind disciple Bartholomew, is in part a triumph for Judas over one of those who have maligned him; but it is also sad and beautiful. It ends with Judas's last words, his last comment on the story we all know so well – again in the form of a small poem. The 'he' referred to is the blind Bartholomew.

> This morning he
> leaves and I'll give him
> the brooch his friend
>
> the jeweller made,
> lost in that scuffle
> in the garden.
>
> Fitting, it seems
> that a blind man
> should seek the light –
>
> as that a man
> with eyes should look
> to the horizon.
>
> Our friend was
> not the Messiah, nor
> will there be one.

This is the truth
I write. It will not
hurt you. Grasp it!

MANSFIELD WAS PUBLISHED BY HARVILL and launched on 20 March 2004 at New Zealand House in London in the presence of an extraordinary collection of Kiwis and Poms, and to the accompaniment of great reviews, not least one from Alberto Manguel.* Christopher MacLehose, a towering figure in the UK publishing world, who had managed to extract the famous imprint from Collins where it began, and had published seven or eight of my novels, should have been there but was not. There was an early intimation of this when he sent me a message in April:

> Vastly looking forward to seeing you in May. Keep June 5 free in the evening please. That one will be in the garden with roses. I am, and might as well confess it now, not going to be able to be at the launch, but more of that anon. Love to Kay.

There was no explanation, and to me none was needed. He was no longer head of Harvill and would not have wanted to be in an audience listening to someone else make the launch speech it should have been his role to make.

To take the Harvill imprint over from Collins had cost money, and Christopher had achieved this by bringing together a small group of investors who would be its directors and owners, among whom he was, I suppose, *primus inter pares*, but still only one voice, one vote. He had been able to bring most of Harvill's authors with him, including Henning Mankell, the best-selling Swedish thriller writer. For a time the new Harvill imprint flourished. Daughter Margaret worked there, editing Mankell and also the

* *The Spectator*, 5 June 2004.

American novelist Richard Ford. In terms of literary respect Harvill rated high; but by the turn of the century profits were probably not good enough to satisfy the investors – and perhaps the imprint was not always breaking even. The directors were becoming restless, and Christopher was no diplomat: some thought him arrogant, and grandly careless about costs. He expected businesspeople to be realistic about a fickle marketplace, and content in bad times with respect.

They were not, and the imprint was sold out from under him, to be merged with the old Secker & Warburg imprint as Harvill Secker. Secker & Warburg had been bought by Random House, and the new Harvill Secker would be part of the large Random stable. *Mansfield* was my last novel to wear the Harvill imprint. *My Name Was Judas* would be Harvill Secker; and the new boss, Geoff Mulligan, already in charge, launched *Mansfield* at New Zealand House. He made a very good speech about it, and was doubtless a worthy man – but the absence of Christopher was to me a shadow over the launch which was otherwise a splendid occasion.*

Christopher had not been sacked. He had been given the almost meaningless title of 'Editor at Large', and an office, not at Vauxhall Bridge Road where the new owner had its offices, but at Mornington Crescent. There was a grim irony in this. Mornington Crescent was a tube station on the Northern line which figured so frequently in the BBC radio comedy programme *I'm Sorry I Haven't a Clue* it only had to be mentioned to produce laughter. For some years the station was closed, and when you went through it the train always slowed, as if in respect for the dead, giving passengers a view of deserted and semi-derelict platforms, and then picked up speed again and hurried on. To be given an office in Mornington Crescent, though probably not intended thus, must

* Christopher had wanted *Mansfield* nominated for the Booker, but Geoff had brought his own favourites from Secker & Warburg. Each publisher could nominate only two novels, and Christopher was overruled.

have felt to Christopher, and looked to his colleagues, like at least a joke if it was not an insult.

Christopher, however, did not settle retiringly into the new office and the new role. He had soon set up as an independent publisher under the (to those whose memories or whose libraries went back far enough) respected name of MacLehose, and discovered a new, and soon to be best-selling, Swede, Stieg Larsson, whose fiction would have kept any firm solvent if he had not died young with only three largely completed novels.

When my next novel, *Risk* (2012), my twelfth and the one I intended to be my last, was published, the imprint was MacLehose.

Katherine and Judas

Responses to *Mansfield* were almost exclusively literary – or literary/human – in other words to the sense of her human qualities, her wit, her indubitable courage, her erratic passions. She came to life in that novel and readers felt they knew her, loved her as a friend, and wrote thanking me for making her so real. Its publication coincided nicely with movements in England towards establishing a Katherine Mansfield society. This went ahead and I gave a 'keynote' lecture and wrote a poem for its first annual conference at London University's Birkbeck College in 2008.

Responses to *My Name Was Judas*, or those that reached me either in reviews or in the very frequent letters and direct approaches I received, were different, and predominantly to do with 'meaning' and consequences in terms of religious faith. It was a subject of a kind I'd never had before, one that the whole world was interested in. The novel began almost at once to earn advances for translation – one of 15,000 euros – so C. K. & K. E.'s London joint account, the one at NatWest we'd kept alive since 1958, and retained almost exclusively for foreign travel and living in London and Europe, was going to be more than usually healthy. An option for a movie was also taken very early and was to continue for a number of years* – the usual combination of income gratefully received but without the hoped-for bonanza outcome.

What I discovered was that there are an enormous number of people in Western society who have become adults accepting they were believing Christians, some attending church, some not, some even clergy or otherwise deeply involved in church matters, but in whom the belief factor has slowly, almost imperceptibly faded, so that if challenged with the question of how much of the necessary and central Christian story they believed as fact, as 'true', they would find it difficult to answer. Among these there were some clergy who were not able easily to slide around the question because their way of life depended on an answer, and so had agonised over it. The more radical among them were followers of Lloyd Geering, who wrote books proposing it was possible to be a Christian without believing that Jesus performed miracles and was the 'son of God', or that he rose from the dead after being crucified; even that it was not necessary to believe there was a God at all.

One of these was David Simmers who had been chaplain at the University of Auckland when I was first there as a young lecturer, and I remembered him as, at that time, very intense and serious about his vocation, telling me that he wanted to be simultaneously the preacher in the pulpit and a member of his own congregation. I could not quite grasp what this meant, but thought it might be like the teenage ego longing to be able to see itself in the mirror – 'really', as he would appear to others. It was, anyway, a clear sign of his seriousness of purpose, which he now described as having been 'naïve'. David had been a Rhodes scholar at Oxford, beating my two friends, Don Smith and John Edwards, who had been Auckland's nominees for the scholarship that year, 1956. He wrote now to thank me for *My Name Was Judas*:

---

* This was an option taken by Guy Hamling whose hunt for support in Hollywood engaged for a time the interest of Paul Schrader, famous especially as script-writer of the movie *Taxi Driver*.

> I have spent a fair amount of time and energy trying to understand the Jesus and Christian phenomenon, but the material has always seemed inadequate and puzzling. You have shown that it is possible with imagination to create a plausible story [. . .] It's a skilful and enjoyable piece of imaginative story-telling and I thank you for it.

He said he had tried to remain a Presbyterian clergyman, but had found 'doing the Sunday thing' (by which I assumed he meant the sermons) too difficult, and had taken a job as a 'government policy analyst' – still clinging to the ideas of Geering as his refuge, until 'about a year ago the Presbyterian Church's official pronouncements about same-sex partners made me so disillusioned with it that I handed in my dog-collar and now concentrate on keeping the garden tidy'.

Another grateful clergyman, Peter Wedde, wrote to me about the book and how it had moved him, and questioning a few details. I explained that the practical (fiction writer's) problem for me, wanting to tell a story we all knew, but in a way a twenty-first-century humanist would find credible, was to manage it so there could be a sceptic among the disciples. The means to this was inventing the (not at all unlikely in terms of the times) childhood friendship of Jesus and Judas, and their exposure to the teachings of the Greek- rather than Jewish-oriented Andreas; and then the later plot development, Judas's loss of his first wife and the compassion of Jesus which brings them together again. By these means we have Judas, so different from the simple fishermen, disliked by them and the one they would label the betrayer, installed among them as observer and would-be protector of the charismatic preacher Jesus has become.

There was also a senior cleric in the Anglican cathedral in Auckland who suggested we should have coffee together and discuss the book, which he assured me he had enjoyed. I'm sure he didn't suppose there was the least hope of bringing me back to the faith I'd probably never had – that was not his purpose. What he wanted was high-calibre conversation on theological and moral matters – the challenge such talk with 'a civilised sceptic' could mean. The coffee and conversation were duly had; but once was enough – probably for both of us.

But people in this 'middle state' between Christian belief and no belief had formed groups, worldwide it seemed, in a movement which they called 'the Sea of Faith', taking the name from Matthew Arnold's poem, 'Dover Beach', part of which goes

> The Sea of Faith
> Was once, too, at the full, and round earth's shore
> Lay like the folds of a bright girdle furl'd.
> But now I only hear
> Its melancholy, long, withdrawing roar,
> Retreating, to the breath
> Of the night-wind, down the vast edges drear
> And naked shingles of the world.
>
> Ah, love, let us be true
> To one another! for the world, which seems
> To lie before us like a land of dreams,
> So various, so beautiful, so new,
> Hath really neither joy, nor love, nor light,
> Nor certitude, nor peace, nor help for pain;
> And we are here as on a darkling plain
> Swept with confused alarms of struggle and flight,
> Where ignorant armies clash by night.

This was the poem which Ian McEwan's brain surgeon's daughter Rosalind in his novel *Saturday* quotes to disarm the thug who is threatening to cut her throat. She pretends she is reading it from her own collection of poems (published by Faber of course). The thug believes it is hers and finds it so beautiful all his murderous intent dissolves away.

'Dover Beach' is a deeply felt and despairing poem about the tide going out – the sea of faith everywhere retreating. It had become a rallying point to these many (I was now discovering) distressed to find themselves no longer certain what parts of their former beliefs it was possible to cling on to. They were at war with themselves, the rational clear-sighted self against the passionate, needful believer.

They had regular meetings where they thrashed out or mulled over their spiritual and metaphysical problems, and the gap which their uncertainty created. They were not to be taken lightly – and one of the reasons they liked my novel so much was that it treated Jesus with such respect, made him totally believable and (for most of the story) loveable and compelling. But it also gave the events a narrative progression which one doesn't get from reading one Gospel after another. It traces a slow change in Jesus from the compassionate preacher of love and peace to the threatening and scary thunderer of the last sermons – all of this seen through the eyes of his friend Judas, and leading to the horror of the crucifixion (which I didn't shirk) and the final tragic view of him as human not divine, asking God why he has been abandoned.

I was invited from time to time to speak to such groups. They were always nice, serious, well-meaning people, and I was well-behaved, and refrained from asking the question that their dilemma would have presented me with had I shared it – namely why, having gone thus far, not take the further step into unbelief? Why not go where common sense, and your observation of the reality around you, and the science of the twenty-first century all direct?

Of course there were also Christians offended by the book and made angry by it. One of these reviewed it for *Spanz* the Presbyterian Church magazine. She told her readers she had found it so offensive she had not finished reading it, but she still reviewed it. It was an interesting example of what the faithful (of any faith, I imagine, and every variant within) think they know, as distinct from what their sacred texts in fact record. This reviewer wrote 'we all know that in the Gospels Mary and Jesus enjoy an ideal mother–son relationship', and she was outraged that my novel represents it otherwise. In fact, as I wrote to *Spanz* in response (showing off my new skills as biblical scholar!), there is nothing in the biblical record that suggests any such fondness. *Au contraire*, Luke 14:26 has Jesus saying 'If any man come to me and hate not his father and mother, and wife and children . . . he cannot be my disciple.' And the only mentions in the Gospels of interactions with his mother (Luke 11:27–28, Mark 4:31 and John 2:3–4 – 'Woman, what have I to do with thee?') don't suggest warmth or fondness. There was a typical and quite misplaced blandness about this reviewer's confidence in a sentimental view of the mother–son relationship for which there was no warrant at all in the Scriptures.

On this same subject of the representation of Mary there was a relevant paragraph in a series of responses to the novel from my Jewish friend Eva Reid in Melbourne:

> Your descriptions of the BVM were *mots justes*. Most of the Madonna and Child paintings throughout history look like studies in post-natal depression, and the Pietas often have a resigned 'What has he got himself into now?' feel. Do you know the DHL anecdote of how he was in a village church admiring a crucifix and tried in basic Italian to share his enthusiasm with a little old woman in black who said 'Yes, but he was never good to his mother.'

So (surprising perhaps) an Italian Catholic peasant knew the Gospels better than a middle-class Kiwi Presbyterian. Eva wrote, 'Given that you didn't visit Palestine the background [which of course she knew from childhood] is most convincing.' She told me she was 'Walter Nash' on the poems that ended each chapter, meaning 'neither for not against',* with the exception that the poem at the end of Chapter 20 'is a perfect distillation of my thoughts'.

* Labour Party leader Walter Nash, when she and I were young, had famously said he was 'neither for nor against' the unions during the 1951 Waterfront dispute.

Long ago Andreas
taught us: 'The Greek
wants Reason,

'the Jew looks
for a Sign.' Is there
a Sign in the fall

of the holy
city, that our race
should abandon

its thirst for a
Messiah, its hunger
for Zion?

Honour the stones
and let them lie
where they've fallen.

Listen to wind
and wave, the language
of seasons,

and let God die
of old age, untroubled
by our prayers.

Eva added a PS to this: 'Judas's experience hearing of Titus's destruction of Jerusalem must be for every Diaspora rationalist Jew what they feel every night at the news. They would find it hard to believe it had been written by a Gentile.' She meant, I'm sure, that Jews like herself despaired at the lengths to which the state of Israel was going to establish ascendancy over Palestine and to re-create the authority and sanctity of Jerusalem as symbol – as 'Sign'.

THE SEQUENCE 'CREATION ETC' WITH which this chapter began can be used to characterise once again my 'position' on these questions, where the human mind attempts to escape gravity and its place in the world of natural things and processes:

The Annunciation

Angels are never average and seldom avenging
but was it a kindness to whisper
a victim and a victory over Death
in Mary's marvelling ear?
The light creeps crab-wise over a sky it paints
in blue-eyed blue, and it's we
cousins of the fur and the stalk must write
an End-of-Term to be delivered by
that silence behind the silence of the stars.
In the beginning was indeed the Word
and it wasn't ours. Ours will be simply the last.

Postscript:
I received a message from Harvill Secker when Christopher was leaving the firm saying that they were putting together a bound sheaf of brief messages to him by his authors. Would I like to contribute? Christopher had always called his copy-editing marks his 'squiggles' so I wrote:

To the great MacLehose
Your squiggles were invaluable
Your company incomparable.

14.
The Dark Angel and the Black River

B-LIAR

This was the period of the lead-up to the Iraq war – agitating because so manifestly a plan concocted by a President who felt 9/11 obliged him to 'do something' – which meant, by American ethics, to do something violent and lethal – when in fact there was no convenient and legitimate target. The 9/11 bombers had been Saudis, but Saudi Arabia was a US ally, and its leaders, though corrupt and unscrupulous, would not have sanctioned what their militant countrymen had done. On the other hand Saddam Hussein of Iraq was an unsavoury dictator in the region who could be said (even if it wasn't true, and it wasn't) to be secretly making 'weapons of mass destruction' – so here was a target for American force, and one which Bush's Secretary of State, Condoleezza Rice, said was 'doable'. It was neither logical nor convenient, because Iraq had been used relatively recently by the US as a weapon against Iran – but it had since blotted its copybook with an invasion of Kuwait. But an American President could not be seen to do nothing in the face of the 9/11 challenge that had cost 3000 American lives

– and reasons for choosing Iraq could be invented. This was the gunfighter mentality that governed US foreign policy, and the job for Bush now was to bring his allies into accord and accommodation – though if that couldn't be done he would proceed without them.

The UK (alas Labour – or 'New Labour' as he called it) Prime Minister Tony Blair, eager to be one of the big boys, joined forces with Bush. It was probably the most blatant and manifestly untruthful campaign of my lifetime; and distressing, as these things always are, because a large section of the population of the West, uncritical by nature and lazy by habit, either believed what they were being told about the 'weapons of mass destruction', or didn't care whether it was true or not.

There were two examples of previous post-World War II British prime ministers that Blair should have given some thought to. One was Anthony Eden, who has gone down in history for the failed military campaign, based on lies, that was meant to wrest the Suez Canal back from Egypt; and the other, by contrast, was Harold Wilson who was remembered with honour for not yielding to American pressure to participate in the Vietnam War. Blair needed no encouragement to yield to the pressure, and demonstrated a skill at lying which even exceeded Bush's own. Bush never looked as if he quite believed what had been scripted for him, and couldn't always pronounce the words. 'Nuclear' for example, was always 'Nucular'. Blair could put on an act of sincerity. It was not the act that failed him so much as the repetitions. He said the same few phrases (in particular 'weapons of mass destruction') so often they became, at first meaningless, then absurd, like a punchline in one of those BBC comedy programmes. So the protest banners began to represent him as 'B-LIAR'.

The march towards war became obvious and unstoppable, though at every stage the pretence was maintained that Iraq could prevent it. All America required of Saddam Hussein was that he acknowledge and give up the 'weapons of mass destruction' he did not have, and give up power – though to whom was never clear.

France, a member of the UN Security Council, consistently refused to accept that war was justified, and the French were rewarded with childish insult: French fries in American restaurants were renamed freedom fries; watching French movies was declared un-American; and Bart on the TV programme *The Simpsons* called the French 'cheese-eating surrender monkeys'. This was funny because everything Bart did and said was funny, not because it was deserved or apt. So we lived painfully through the months as the world moved step by step to a needless war, in which a superpower would clobber a depleted and militarily insignificant nation, only in order to make an American President look strong and feel better about himself. There were peace marches including one in London, estimated to be more than a million people, which was to figure in Ian McEwan's novel *Saturday* where the novelist's attitude to it seemed ambiguous.

For several nights and days on end after 19 March Baghdad came under continuous and spectacular bombardment, all shown on television and given a name, 'SHOCK & AWE', as if it had been a new TV programme. There had never been anything quite like it. Now the technology of the new century was providing us with (selected) images of America doing its work of war. It was like an immense fireworks display, hugely impressive, but hard to see how selections were being made (as we were assured they were) between one target and another. Clearly there was going to be a lot of 'collateral damage' – one of the many US euphemisms we were beginning to get used to.

In a very short time a statue of Saddam had been toppled in the streets of Baghdad, and Bush ('George Doubya'), wearing a battledress he had never worn in real combat, declared victory on an American aircraft carrier bedecked with the banner MISSION ACCOMPLISHED. In Iraq of course the actual out-of-sight mayhem had hardly begun and would continue for years. Some of this experience would go into my later novel, *Risk*, which also concerned itself with the global financial crisis (GFC) of 2008.

On 9 April 2003 I wrote to Phill Armstrong of Putaruru:*

> The only good thing about this war in Iraq is that it seems to be ending fast. I can't think that it will leave behind anything but chaos and discord, since the Ba'ath Party's brutality was the cement that held the two kinds of Muslim, not to mention the Kurds, together. Now it will all fly apart, like Yugoslavia without Tito.

These were political opinions I gave free expression to, as always, and we were now well into the new century when ideas travelled fast and far – opinions that did not surprise many but did upset a few, one of whom, signing himself Emile DuGrenier, wrote from Philadelphia to say that while New Zealand got on with its 'nuclear-free nonsense' America was, as always, saving the world – in this case from Muslim extremism:

> So while you sip tea among a bevy of like-minded colleagues and decry Bush the Boy as a fuck-wit, do keep in mind that civilisation is once again threatened. Like us yea, or like us nay, boorish ill-mannered slap-happy sub-educated Yanks continue to be the last hope for all you hold dear. It's my balls, my blood, and my bucks have to support C. K. Stead's freedom to be smugly superior. God bless America.

The Red Tram – and Janet

Between *Mansfield* (2004) and *My Name Was Judas* (2006), but overlapping in some degree, came another invasion of 'the poem vein' resulting in the collection I called *The Red Tram* (2004). The

* Phill was an unpublished writer who regularly sent me his work. He had real talent, though he couldn't punctuate or spell, and I once persuaded Fergus Barrowman to take something of his for *Sport*.

poems themselves are sometimes reminders of their occasions. 'Takapuna' must have been written while Janet Frame was still alive, but intended only to be published after her death. There had been talk of Janet winning the Nobel Prize for literature and when it went to J. M. Coetzee (whose work I disliked and thought hugely overrated) I wrote to her saying it felt as if we had lost the America's Cup again.

It was in reply to this message that Janet told me she had been diagnosed with acute myeloid leukaemia requiring blood transfusions to keep her alive. She joked about the 'ignoble prize', and about her 'curtailed future', and had told a reporter, who rang asking what she would do with the money if she won, that she would 'buy back the Railways', which a Labour government, in the grip of Rogernomics, had sold to asset-strippers. She sent me a photo of herself hooked up in a hospital bed receiving a blood transfusion while reading something she held so I could see it – a copy of the *Listener* with my review of Vince O'Sullivan's biography of John Mulgan. I told her how sorry Kay and I were to hear of her diagnosis, and apologised for being 'sprightly' about the Prize. We exchanged warm messages through most of 2003 and she died in January 2004. To Alan Roddick I wrote:

> The Janet business became less and less real as TV1, TV3, RadioNZ, etc etc phoned and asked more or less the same questions to which I gave more or less the same answers – so the shock (even though it was expected, it was a shock) that Janet was dead became lost and hasn't entirely returned. Slowly, through a day and a half, disgust set in – self-disgust mainly, not that one had a choice but to respond as requested.

Of the funeral I remember especially Michael King's very good eulogy; and that in my own I said that Janet had written to me once about the *embarrassment* of seeing her own words in print, and that she'd thought posthumous publication was 'the last form of literary decency'. There was a very nice joke in the printed order of service, one which might well have come at Janet's own suggestion: the hymn was 'Praise, My Soul, the King of Heaven' and in the third verse the line '**Well our feeble frame He knows**' was printed in bold. I wrote a substantial obituary in the *Listener* and that issue was printed with her face on the cover – the only time I can recall a writer being so featured.

The poem 'Takapuna' was another elegy.

So old friend you've come to it at last
(Ron Mason's line, and now an echo of Yeats!)
How does it feel to feel nothing?
No one will ask you to read, no unmarked sheet
will ever again reproach you.
You can 'become your admirers.'

Somewhere along the way your brain got sparked
but your hair stood up for you.
You wrote of shame without shame.
'Madness' was the house of your self, the house of cards
falling whenever someone opened a door.

Remember the day of our disaster?
We sat in the hut and I criticised your poem.
Clumsy, literal, your junior in years and in pain
I'd thought it was what you wanted.

There were winged things in the garden, and wilting leaves,
earth smells, compost, beans.
You sat in all your radium intensity,
in the brightness of mercury falling.
The thing you'd wanted was love!

I remember the walk home,
the glass verandah, matting on the walls,
and the view to Rangitoto.
Sea lanes were open
all the way to the World, those dark rough paths
we knew we'd have to travel.

Histories of the hive, the swallow's flight,
the archives of the ant, even an ode of Keats –
all, I know, confirm it: the thing that happens
dies when it happens.
The thing that doesn't happen lives for ever.*

2004

Janet Frame died in January, Michael King her biographer in March, painter Pat Hanly in September, and Maurice Shadbolt in October. These were all people I knew well, had been joined with in good causes, had sometimes quarrelled with – and Kay and I must have owned all of their books as well as two of Pat's paintings. Pat and Maurice were my exact contemporaries, born 1932, dead at the age of seventy-two.

A shadow had been cast over the immense success of Michael's *The Penguin History of New Zealand* (2003) when he was reported to have cancer; but the treatment, chemotherapy and radiology, seemed to be working well, and he and his wife Maria were about to take off on a holiday, I think to Fiji, paid for by his very grateful publisher, when they ran off the road into a tree. They had just had lunch and it's thought Michael may have been affected by the drugs he was taking for his illness and dropped off to sleep at the wheel. The car burst into flames and they were both killed.

---

* For the background to this poem see *South-West of Eden*, Auckland University Press, 2010, pp. 327–29.

Pat Hanly had been suffering from Huntington's chorea, an inherited condition which had made him in recent years more and more evidently 'jiggy' – spasmodic and erratic in his physical movements and unable to control them, so he could no longer paint.

Maurice's Alzheimer's disease was, like Pat's Huntington's, probably inherited (his mother had died of it) and again like Pat's was something affecting the brain cells and making it as impossible for him to go on writing as it was for Pat to go on painting. In January 2000 Maurice had handwritten a letter to me* saying he had just

> finished reading *O'Dwyer* a few minutes ago and was mightily impressed. I'm out of the running as you may know, but the successes of my long-time contemporaries make a fair substitute.

If an olive branch had been needed between us (none was) this would have been it.

Maurice's and Pat's funerals were held, a few weeks apart, in St Matthew-in-the-City, a liberal Anglican church, friendly to the arts community, famous for slightly shocking billboards and for welcoming the homeless and the dispossessed. The photograph of Pat in the order of service showed a tough guy in an ochre singlet; the photos of Maurice were reminders of what a good-looking chap he had been in his younger days. Of his several wives, the first, Gill, was there and spoke with fond regret. I was not one of the speakers – that would not have been appropriate – there had been too many rocks along the shared road; but I was there in the order of service, possibly inadvertently. The only sample of Maurice's writing it offered was from his first novel, *Among the Cinders*, a passage in which Maurice introduced himself as the writer Maurice Shadbolt at a literary party, where he and the narrator's brother Derek confront one another:

---

* Found by his biographer Philip Temple in 2020.

> Derek said literature was a serious responsible business these days, one had to be committed fully, there was no room for Shadbolt's irresponsibility. Shadbolt said where was the fun in that? Derek said he wasn't talking about fun. Shadbolt said 'Exactly.'

Derek of course was D. K. Flinders, Maurice's caricature of C. K. Stead, the humourless, serious, boring and unreadable literary critic. It seemed to me quite a good way to be both present and absent. These two deaths tore a large hole in the cultural life of Auckland.

This was the year in which both *Mansfield* and *The Red Tram* were published; and my *Letters and Journals of Katherine Mansfield*, which had been in print with Penguin Modern Classics since 1977, was reissued as a Vintage paperback in New Zealand.

I must have been now well on the way with the writing of *My Name Was Judas*, and had probably begun the long slow working through all my poems, or all I could find, with a view to putting together a *Collected Poems*. It was also in this year that Dell Panny asked permission to write my literary biography. I agreed to this, somewhat surprised, somewhat flattered, somewhat uncertain whether or not it was a good idea. Dell had long been a keen reader of my work, and had organised a kind of choric reading of my long poem 'Scoria' at Massey University in Palmerston North. I gave her a couple of preliminary interviews and access to family photographs. After a few months I began to have doubts. It was a new experience and I did not feel safe, or know what I was letting myself in for. I told Dell she could go ahead but it would have to be without my participation. She carried on, always with diligence and goodwill, and the book was to emerge five years later.

In April *Mansfield*, which had been long-listed for the W. H. Smith prize, and the International IMPAC Dublin prize, and was short-listed for the Montana New Zealand Book Awards, was also in the short-list for the $40,000 Tasmania Pacific Fiction Prize and I was flown to Hobart (with the five other short-listers) for the presentation. These occasions are only really nice if your book wins – mine didn't.

On 6 May I recorded that I had finished a first draft of *My Name Was Judas* and that it had taken me just five months.

A vascular accident

Someone in Janet Frame's *Living in the Maniototo* suffers a stroke which Janet describes with comic intent as a 'vascular accident'. My 'vascular accident', which the medical profession described as an ischaemic stroke, occurred on 11 May, just five days after I finished that first draft of *My Name Was Judas*. A devout Christian might have said I had brought it on myself with a book that denied the divinity of Jesus. If that thought crossed my mind it would only have been as a joke. But I was committed to appearing at the Auckland Writers' Festival in May and later in the year in Christchurch and then at the Poetry Festival in Medellín, Colombia, and an Ezra Pound conference in Rapallo – so the fact had to be made known and these appointments cancelled– otherwise I would have kept it to myself.

When I was sufficiently recovered I wrote (I suppose dictated) an explanation and apology:

> A week or so ago I had a migraine which turned out to be a mild stroke, though the experience wasn't mild and the consequences for a day or so seemed dire. The following day I was entirely mobile, fully articulate – with no memory loss – i.e. appeared to be unchanged. But there was some loss of vision. I couldn't subtract (when asked) 7 from 100, could not picture or remember how the streets of our suburb related to one another, and worst, when confronted with a simple text could make no sense of the words. Overnight I had become a total dyslexic – and innumerate as well. In Auckland Hospital I was seen by a succession of ever more senior doctors who seemed concerned

> to do something for NZ Lit. (genuinely – I'm grateful and they were terrific) and anxious that I might have to remain as I was at that moment, a writer who could still write but couldn't read what he wrote, nor anything else. Over the days since, however, everything has been returning to normal. There are still some unpredictable visual distortions (the clothes dryer looking much too small to hold the clothes, the sea at Kohimarama appearing a sheet of vertical rather than horizontal blue) and some impairment of vision. And reading is still very difficult. But I'm now reading again slowly, and the gaps in vision are getting smaller. The specialist now thinks I will make a full recovery.
>
> I'm now instructed to take things quietly for three months, advised not to give public readings or 'appearances', and forbidden to drive the car for six months.

There had been brain scans, interviews that were like interrogations, and plans for new medications. Kay and I were shown a scan of my brain which showed, low down at the back of the skull, a small blemish which was *it* – the stroke. The specialist thought it was more in the nature of a (metaphorical) bruise than a wound; and it seemed to be repairing itself in that the ability to recognise words was coming back. My account-and-apology was all true but it did slightly downplay the effects. When I read a newspaper, for example, my eye did not seem able to detect the edge of a column, so I found myself repeatedly reading right across the page instead of down. Reading would come back – and that European summer, when Kay and I were in Uzès, I set myself to re-read the whole of Lawrence Durrell's *Avignon Quintet* (set in the right region – the south-west of France). I completed the 1367 pages of the paperback, making copious notes in the back.

So yes I was a reader again, but I would never regain the full speed of my younger days (and even then I had never been fast); and whereas when young I had read all of Henry James's novels (James the first, James the second and the Old Pretender, as some cruel wit had described his development) I was now fine with *Washington Square*, or *Portrait of a Lady*, but the Old Pretender's *The Golden Bowl*, and *The Wings of the Dove*, which I had once read with ease and had loved, now defeated me – and I suspect would still if I returned to them. My handwriting was also affected, and my signature no longer looked like mine. I was condemned to a life of bank and book-signing forgeries. My will when I made it, whatever it contained, would clearly be fake.

But I had come out the other side of the event, left only with an anxiety about whether it would recur, which diminished over time. The dark angel that had whisked away my contemporaries Maurice and Pat had put the shadow of her wing over me, and then changed her mind. I had been afraid, not so much of death as of losing the ability to write, as Maurice had, and as Pat had to paint. Writing was what I had made, to myself and to the world (insofar as the world might be interested), my *raison d'être*. In the dark of the first few nights in the hospital I made up fragmentary poems in my head, and tried to scribble them down in a little notebook with a mother-of-pearl swan on its cover. It is hard now to understand how I could write when I couldn't read – but I did, very scratchily, almost illegibly. It was like writing in the dark – and that's what it looks like in the notebook which still exists. But they were the beginnings of a poem, a poem-sequence, I called 'S-T-R-O-K-E'. They were hardly more than language games – but with constant undertones of death and (to me) they were entirely serious:

> words have given me access
> to the inside
> of the inside
> of the mind
>
> whose mind?
> mine
> the mine of the mind

*

remember the world
when it was new?

it's old now
seventy-two

but full of reminders

*

I think
therefore I am

I think
therefore I think
I am

therefore I am
(I think)

*

stripped
disclaimed
misnumbered
unremembered
you have become
the unencumbered
whipped soul
of the noun
and the verb

Craig Raine, when he heard of the stroke, asked me to write something about it for *Areté*. I sent him 'S-T-R-O-K-E' when it was done and he rejected it because, he said, he and his assistant Adam thought it 'didn't work'.* I thought (or hoped) it did and when, a year or so later, I had finished a new collection of poems, *The Black River* (2007), I put it at the end, preceded by all the poems I'd written after the stroke happened. It was like putting the overture at the end of my opera rather than at the beginning.

The rest of the year was under the shadow of a return of migraine at intervals until the medication was corrected and they ceased. There was talk of closing my patent foramen ovale, an opening in the atrial septum of the heart which normally closes after birth but in some cases, and mine was one, remains open. The condition had been uncertainly linked to strokes, but there were possible complications in the procedure of closing it, and I decided against it. Partly because of the stroke, but also as recipient of that year's Michael King award,† and a finalist in both the poetry and fiction sections of the upcoming New Zealand Book Awards, and with *Mansfield* topping the local best-seller list, I had repeated newspaper and magazine interviews; and then Kay and I flew to Wellington for the awards. I didn't win either category, and tried to suppress the feeling that the whole distracting and disappointing business was a commercial matter we (or I) might be better without.

Mahinarangi

That October while we were in France Charlotte emailed to say 'the old surfie Bob Harvey' (later Sir Bob) wanted to make me a 'laureate of Waitakere City' of which he was mayor. This was on

---

* Kay was in England at the time and wrote to me 'the stroke poems are a kind of witness – a product of the brain in crisis. They don't have to "work" – they *are*.'

† A very generous writing award made by Creative New Zealand, and named after Michael, when he was killed, as a way of honouring him.

the basis of owning a bach at Karekare and being known there.*
I told Charlotte to tell the old surfie I was delighted to accept, and as a result got to know other 'laureates' one of whom was the jazz singer Mahinarangi Tocker. She was full of fun and mental problems and asthma, and at the few events the shared laureateship entailed we got on well. She had a very good voice and sang songs that seemed to me attractive if sometimes banal, songs that talk to real people about real problems. She said she had a good voice 'but my face isn't right'. I thought her face was fine, and so was her voice. If the words let her down sometimes, only a person like me would think so – and of course I would never say that to her. But I did write her a song, 'Black River Blues', which she seemed to like a lot, and set to music and sang.

Mahina had her manic phases when she might send me six or more emails in a day – often funny, as they were meant to be, sometimes meaningless and confusing. But she sent me recorded versions of her songs, and we had serious exchanges about them. Once she sent me a sort of poem:

> I met C. K.
> I said he was cool
> He said I was cool
> I said he's a dude
> He said nothing
>
> I write him stupid things
> He writes me kind things
> I write him stupid things
> He writes me funny things
> I write him stupid things
> He writes nothing about that

---

* These laureateships disappeared with the city itself when Auckland was amalgamated into one city.

I met C. K.
He's a hard case
He's a clever heart
He's an old fart
I met C. K.
He's no fool
When I met C. K.
He gave me a C. K. hug.

Mahina was a front person for campaigns about mental health, being open about it, accepting it without shame. Once she invited me to lunch and afterwards took me to the mental advocacy office she worked from where, she assured me, they all had hearts of gold and she loved them to bits. I describe it in a story about her:*

> It struck me as a scene out of Dickens. Just a normal office but in which the jolly ones were jollier and noisier, and the glum ones glummer and more withdrawn – normality, you could call it, but with a very broad brush. And it was clear they all loved Mahina and that she was happy there.

Her plans for what she was going to do with her setting of 'Black River Blues' sounded serious and good:

> My version of Black River Blues – I don't think it's quite finished but it's getting there. I hope it makes sense to you – a bit muddled in places cos I kept getting confused with what I was hearing and what I was needing to play or sing. I'm really keen to record properly, in the studio, with James Wilkinson – guitar, Hamish McKeitch – bassoon (nice full stops and gentle exclamations and question marks in the bassoon ideas and I've got some percussion ideas too). Oh some of your

---

* 'Anxiety' in *The Name on the Door is Not Mine*, pp. 145–51.

> words – the way they follow each other around are quite orally percussive – cool fun. Really nice to sing. I've got a dance piece to work on but it's not nearly as much fun as Black River Blues.
>
> Let me know what you think. I won't be offended if you don't like it. I'd rather know.
>
> happies
>
> marin – maharina – marinahangi – marangiiiii -----
>
> Maaahinaaaaaassssrangi Sheep Ms

She sent me an interim (slightly buzzy) tape of it with just her voice and piano. I thought her voice was lovely, and the way the piano accompaniment was composed seemed especially good:

> I think what you're doing with Black River Blues is just great. I look forward to a later stage when there will be a nice clean sound without the buzz. But this is terrific. Thanks a bunch as Frances McDormand says in *Fargo*.

At times when her own mental devils were giving her more problems than usual Mahina's messages were often quite clever and surprising, and they evoked parallel responses from me. It was a distraction from whatever work I was doing – good fun; but I began to worry when they showed signs of mania and their landscape darkened.

She told me she was fearful; her bedroom opened on to a deck, and she had pushed furniture against the doors to keep herself safe. She suspected someone was trying to poison her and had to be careful what she ate. I suggested she might like to report to the psychiatric ward that had treated her before, to receive therapy and drugs. But she wouldn't do that, she said; the rooms there were bugged *by beings from outer space*. She sent the message like that, with italics, so I would know she was making a joke against herself. But I thought almost certainly a part of her mind believed it. The problem was I didn't know who her friends were, or the name of her ex-husband, or of her doctor. If I had I would have suggested someone should check on her well-being.

She posted me a CD of some Baxter poems she'd set and recorded and promised to drop by with another version of 'Black River Blues'. I replied:

> Baxter CD arrived this morning. Thanks so much for that. We'll play it over tonight. Great to have it. Come in for a cup of tea if you're putting the tape in our box. We're in and out but mostly here.

She told me she was hearing voices; and there was one she called the Bad Voice which was *sinister* and *sometimes threatening*. I kept only a few of the flurry of messages that went back and forth at this time but there was one from her:

> I realise that you're busy with your own mahi at the moment and the apra [i.e. copyright authority] stuff can wait
>
> just that I thought of it today and told you while it was in my head
>
> and today the bloody voices are back. the one I HATE MOST is preparing to muck me up at the silver scrolls but I'm getting really good at coping with it. ha! it can't get me any more.
>
> big aroha
>
> m

I replied:

> Sorry about the voices Mahina. If they're not voices you like or want to hear, tell them 'Karl Stead says to bugger off.'
>
> Arohanui
>
> Karl

And she:

Kia ora ano

Sorry, I meant today. However my neighbour Flores is crook and so I'm going to do his washing and stuff. cuppa another time, pea?

oh and I said to the loud thoughts and especially to the nasty bastard voice

'Karl Stead says to bugger off!' and it said

'I am Karl Stead, Cunt.'

This was either clever or mad (or both) and I felt I'd been told, or discovered, that I was out of my depth. I was about to go away again, this time to take up that invitation to the Medellín Poetry Festival in Colombia I'd had to cancel when I had my stroke, but now renewed for July 2007; so I had an excuse to extract myself, to absent myself and leave her messages unanswered. It was probably not the right way to deal with this difficulty (and it did feel difficult); but I knew she had a busy full life and many others to help her.

So for some months there were no exchanges between us; and then I read in the newspaper that she had died. I'd had no warning – hadn't expected it. Remembering her fears, and those sinister voices, I wondered whether it could have been suicide, but the authorised version (which was probably right) said it was an asthma attack. Either way, it was the dark angel's wing again and another sad loss. I was glad I'd written something for her, and sad not to have a recording of her singing the version she'd planned, with guitar, bassoon and percussion.

Black River Blues

(for Mahinarangi Tocker)

Chanterez vous quand vous serez vaporeuse?

Will you sing
when you're only a ghostly thing

when your self is no more
than the squeak of an unoiled door
a creak in the floor?

Will you sing then
lyrics to furnish a room
cantos of doom?

Where will you go when you die
what will you say to the sky
as your smoke goes up the chimney
and your world has a tear in its eye?

Will you sing when you're gone away
down to the end of the ever
to row on the black river

– will you? Will you sing
when you're *not here* and *no more*
than the squeak of an unoiled door
and a creak in the wooden floor?

Craig

I have written of Craig Raine as a much-loved friend, as he was and is. But when I look at the relatively few exchanges between us I have printed out and kept (because we were now getting into the era of the email, where correspondence is continually being lost) they are full of differences of opinion, often in tones of asperity. Meetings were always fond; and I remember happy lunches and dinners where I laughed so helplessly they were slightly embarrassing to look back on. This was either the four of us, Raines and Steads together, or sometimes (later – around 2010) six, with daughter Margaret and her husband Guy. Margaret was publishing director for Atlantic Books which at that time was Craig's publisher. The fuel was often champagne – Craig the supplier; but also there was an electricity between us, the two sons of an Olive and brothers of a Norma, who had both written a version of Racine's *Andromaque*.

And yet our literary tastes were usually, and often seriously, at variance. I was never sure that he liked my poems, though he did publish a few in his journal *Areté*. And when I reviewed his long poem *History: The Home Movie* in *The London Magazine* the review was conscientious but seemed to spend too much time showing how Pound did certain things better. This poem was published in a 335-page hardcover edition in 1994 and he was paid an exceptional advance – £60,000 after his agent had turned down an offer of £15,000 from Faber. The book was touted as a 'novel in verse' (which it was not – it was really a collection of linked poems) and therefore a possibility for the Booker Prize. In my review I said as much as I could in its favour, and concluded

> . . . if architectonics does not and cannot match ambition, that fact should not be allowed to stand in the way of the pleasure and profit to be had from these poems which are consistently skilful, witty, inventive, linguistically rich and humanly rewarding.

Another difference between us was about Ted Hughes' poems. Craig was a huge admirer; I continued sceptical. But our most significant difference, one that became semi-public, was about T. S. Eliot. Since Eliot and Pound were central to my own academic studies it had seemed essential to make clear that I deplored their anti-Semitism, Eliot's in the 1920s and '30s, Pound's continuing more or less throughout his life. Craig was stalwart in his insistence that Eliot was no anti-Semite, which seemed to me extraordinary. The examples in Eliot's pre-World War II poems are gross and frequently cited. The sense not just of distaste but of disgust in these is so palpable it has its own kind of ghastly rhetorical force.

But there were also Eliot's published once but never reprinted lectures of 1933 (the year Hitler came to power) in which he said that 'reasons of race and religion make any large number of free-thinking Jews undesirable'; and also the unsigned review he published in his journal *The Criterion* of a book called *The Yellow Spot: The Outlawing of Half a Million Human Beings*, protesting on behalf of Jews suffering persecution in Germany at the time (1936). This review treated the book with scorn – 'an attempt to rouse moral indignation by means of sensationalism' – suggesting the complaints were untrue or overstated. I had written about this review in my *Pound, Yeats, Eliot and the Modernist Movement*, and said I thought its style strongly suggested Eliot had written it himself; but even if he was not the author, he had accepted it as editor.

Craig took the subject up when a review by Tom Paulin in the *LRB* (9 May 1996) cited approvingly Ronald Bush, Anthony Julius, Christopher Ricks and C. K. Stead, as believing (incorrectly, Craig argued) that Eliot had written this review. Another who had made this 'mistake' was Craig's friend James Fenton in one of his lectures as Professor of Poetry at Oxford. Craig's response was an essay called 'In Defence of T. S. Eliot' which became in turn the title of a collection of essays. This argued, not only the point about the *Criterion* review of *The Yellow Spot*, but about whether Eliot had ever been an anti-Semite – to which question Craig answered with a stalwart, and exhaustively detailed, NO. I thought it was an entirely specious essay – and also unnecessary. One could accept that Eliot had had this (not uncommon at the time) deplorable aspect to his character, and still acknowledge, write about, teach and study his subsequent work (as I, Paulin and Ricks had all done), acknowledging that 'The Waste Land' was a great poem and Eliot a major literary critic and a significant figure in recent literary history.

Craig argued that it was not Eliot who was anti-Semitic but the characters who speak in his poems. And when Eliot writes that a large number of 'free thinking Jews' in society was 'undesirable', this could be read to mean 'that Eliot was quite prepared to accept limited numbers of free thinking Jews'. So was Hitler's crime only excess – getting the numbers wrong? This seemed to me inexcusable special pleading. It was for Craig, I suppose, a delicate subject. He had inherited the chair Eliot had occupied for so many years, poetry editor of Faber, and had become very fond of Eliot's widow, Valerie, who in recent years, with proceeds from the Lloyd-Webber musical *Cats* (made from Eliot's *Old Possum's Book of Practical Cats*) had kept the firm afloat when other publishers were floundering.

When his collection of essays came out I wrote thanking him for sending me a copy, telling him how much I enjoyed them – he is in fact a fine critic and literary essayist – but saying that I regretted he'd chosen that title, *In Defence of T. S. Eliot*, because it drew readers' attention to his weakest point. I told him I had said to Kay that that essay was 'the Hutton Report on anti-Semitism in T. S. Eliot'. The Hutton Report was occasioned by the suicide of a British UN weapons inspector, David Kelly, who had secretly briefed a BBC reporter that the British government's 'September Dossier' had been 'sexed up' to make the Blair government's reasons for going to war – i.e. that Saddam Hussein had 'weapons of mass destruction' – seem much stronger than they really were. When Kelly had been exposed as the source of this briefing he had been grilled by a parliamentary committee and next day had killed himself. Hutton had cleared the government of wrongdoing and his report had been greeted by public disbelief, and outrage in papers like the *Guardian* and the *Independent*. My joke was meant to tell him again that his essay on Eliot and anti-Semitism was as specious as the Hutton Report.

Craig responded tersely in a postscript to a message about *Mansfield*:

> I take it as a compliment when you compare my essays on TSE's anti-Semitism to the Hutton Report. The Hutton Report was depressing of course, because it demonstrated that people

> are incapable of weighing evidence objectively. When Hutton didn't confirm their prejudices, everyone simply turned away from a judge they'd previously endorsed.

This response was a surprise, revealing one more serious difference between us. I had suspected that Craig might have been a supporter of the US–British intervention in Iraq, and this was evidently the case. My reply was equally terse:

> About your PS: some things absolutely require complexity and subtlety but others are blindingly simple, and in the latter case complexity and subtlety are employed as dust in the eyes, to conceal and confuse. It is, as far as I am concerned, unarguable that Eliot was, during at least two decades, an anti-Semite. It is equally unarguable that Downing Street 'sexed up' (i.e. falsified) documents and statements in order to justify going with Bush into Iraq. All Hutton's subtleties in his report, and all yours in your essay, make not a shred of difference to those two basic truths. They are a misuse of high intelligence in defence of the indefensible.

Craig's reply was short and simple:

> Dear Karl, I am SO fond of you.
> Much love
> Craig

How does one read such a response? It could be simply a snarl of the heaviest possible irony, a shorthand way of saying 'Fuck you, Karl.' But equally he *might* have meant it literally – an affirmative, and even admiring, response to clarity, and to what felt like 'tough love'.

That was the point with Craig: I could not be sure.

Postscript 1:

In a less determined vein on the subject of Eliot and anti-Semitism Craig emailed me in January 2007 saying that in an interview with Mark Lawson on *Front Row* 'I explained to him that I didn't expect to persuade anyone, I was simply seeing what could be said in Eliot's defence.'

That the Hutton Report was a government whitewash was in effect confirmed by the later (2009–11) Chilcot Inquiry which found that the Blair government had deliberately exaggerated the threat posed by Iraq which was 'minimal', had ignored its own intelligence briefings and warnings of what would happen in Iraq after the invasion, and that Blair had promised Bush 'I will be with you whatever' eight months before the assault began.

The extent of the Bush–Blair dishonesty in the lead-up to the Iraq war was exposed by the 2019 docudrama, *Official Secrets*, in which Keira Knightley plays the British whistleblower Katharine Gun who leaked official secrets exposing dirty tricks intended to get a vote in the Security Council to authorise the invasion.

Postscript 2:

From one of my laureate blogs – 14 August 2016:

> Yesterday there was a party at Craig and Li Raine's house in Oxford to celebrate the 50th issue of their literary magazine, *Areté*. Craig is editor and Li his Deputy, both retired Oxford dons (he, New College; she, St Anne's). They have four children making an extraordinary family. Craig is poet, playwright and critic, and more recently novelist too. Li, who writes as Ann Pasternak Slater, has edited the poems of George Herbert, and is known as a translator from Russian. Her background was strongly affected by her Russian mother, sister of the novelist and poet Boris Pasternak, and daughter of the Impressionist painter Leonid Pasternak whose works (including portraits of Tolstoy and Einstein) line the Raines' walls. There is about the

whole family an unusual directness and immediacy, and a great capacity for affection and loyalty. Their Englishness, which might be the first thing to strike a New Zealander, seems, at a second reading, real but skin-deep. Raine-hood, or Raine-ness, is like a nationality of its own. Walking into a party at their house, especially in summer with doors open to the garden at the back, feels a bit like walking on to the set of a play by Chekhov.

There was a crowd, both indoors and out in the garden, not many I knew though a few I recognised – Christopher Hampton, David Lodge for example. Daughter Nina was pregnant. There were two medium-to-large very affable and eager dogs, belonging to sons Moses and Vaska. Prosecco was offered and prosciutto followed by a beautiful bean soup and then an indescribably rich and wonderful chocolate dessert/pudding (depending on where you come from), a mousse perhaps, with (I think it was) whipped cream – all of this in the hand and on the hoof, a challenge but worth rising to.

I found myself talking to a woman about the dogs. She lives in Kensington and each morning before work, walks her dog in Kensington Gardens. She described to me rather lyrically the sun rising through the mist on a winter morning, and how her spirit lifts with it.

A young man told me his name was Mark and that he had drawn the feather which adorns every *Areté* cover. I told him I had always admired it.

A man half my age came up with outstretched hand, and said something I didn't catch which I took to be his name. 'It's been a long time,' he said. I didn't think I'd ever met him, and wondered whether he thought I was Michael Frayn. (In London I am frequently mistaken for Frayn.) 'You're looking good,' I said.

I sat with Li on a sofa (or couch, depending where you come from) and we talked about being 'no good at parties', a distinction we both claimed. Where was Kay? I explained she was in London, and why. Li told me I must read her just-published book on Waugh; and before I left she'd given me a copy inscribed with love to Karl and Kay.

She asked me about New Zealand's remoteness at this time of turmoil in the world: did we feel protected by distance? I could remember a time when distance seemed deprivation rather than protection, but I didn't say so. I thought of Allen Curnow's lines, 'Always to islanders danger / Is what comes over the sea', and Brasch's 'Distance looks our way' but didn't quote them. I think I said it depends where you imagine the trouble might come from.

Later Craig and I shared another sofa, under the Tolstoy portrait. We compared ailments – his gout (which I remember afflicted Ken Smithyman in his later years), mine polymyalgia rheumatica.

'Rheumatism,' he said.

'If you like,' I replied thinking it was not really so simple – but perhaps he was right and it is.

He said the painfulness of gout came from crystals of uric acid in the bloodstream, and he could feel the crystals in his ears. I told him about the American comic-strip of my childhood, *Jiggs and Maggie Everybody*, in which Jiggs often had one foot huge with bandages because he suffered from gout. People were always tripping on the foot and causing him to howl in pain.

Craig is now 72 and has been retired from teaching seven years. He's glad not to have to teach but said the idea that one should stop working at 65 or 70 made no sense in the world as it is now. He'd been taking tango lessons and told me about difficulties. He enjoyed the lessons and learning the steps, but when it came to the practice he ran into trouble. Whether this was because it was too demanding, or too demeaning, wasn't clear to me. Going out looking for tango-partners on a dance floor might be challenging at 72.

Craig asked about my Paris novel (we'd had a lunch and then a dinner together in Paris almost two years back when I was writing it) and I told him I'd abandoned it, but that recently I'd had thoughts of returning to it.

'You must write it,' he said. 'You've reached an age when anything you write will be good.'

I took this to mean that it won't be bad – that it will probably be OK, serviceable, workmanlike, publishable. I said I hoped so but thought I'd reached an age when I might expect to falter.

Kay and I are staying at daughter Margaret's house in Queen's Park, and Margaret is Craig's publisher at Atlantic Books. I told him granddaughter Madeleine (Grimshaw) was across the Park working as P.A. to the actor Jason Isaacs. Craig said Isaacs had played the part of Vittorio Mussolini in the Almeida production of his play, *1953*. This was a 20th-century updating of Racine's *Andromaque*, a 'counter-factual' (if that is the word) in which the Axis powers have won World War II. When I was very young my only attempt at a verse play was also a modernising of the Racine tragedy – a play that impressed me because of its wonderful structure, but which I found defeated me because I couldn't make its despairing love-motivations credible in a modern (20th-century) setting.

So we talked about actors and acting, and I told him about Ralph Fiennes's brilliantly comic 'as 'twere' scene in the Cohen brothers' *Hail, Caesar!*; and about his part in the movie *A Bigger Splash* where he appears with Tilda Swinton – Swinton as a David Bowie-style rock star, and Fiennes as her former lover, invading her holiday on a Greek Island. There's a scene in which he performs an astonishing, frenetic Greek dance; and later we see him capering naked around the rock star's swimming pool, initiating a fight with her current boyfriend, and (not very convincingly) killed by him.

Craig told me about an occasion when Fiennes was acting in Chekhov's *Ivanov* (also at the Almeida). Craig thought he waved his arms about too much, and possibly said so to Patrick Marber with whom he was staying at the time. Soon afterwards he was embarrassed to find himself at a large dinner party with Fiennes there among the guests. Would anyone have passed on his criticism? Craig positioned himself as far away as possible from the actor and there was no contact until the party was breaking up and suddenly, there was Fiennes looming over Craig's chair. 'I think,' he murmured, 'that "History" [Craig's long poem] is the most *beautiful* poem I have *ever* read.'

Craig acted it out: 'the moost *b-yew*-tiful poo-m . . .'

'Since then of course,' Craig said, 'I've thought he was a great actor.'

I told him about my struggle with Coetzee. He said he was outraged that the recently announced Booker long list included *The Schooldays of Jesus* (sequel to *The Childhood of* . . .) and not his friend Ian McEwan's latest.

Craig had reviewed *Disgrace* and was not surprised that I didn't rate Coetzee very highly as a writer – neither does he, and neither (he said) does Martin Amis. I have now checked what he wrote about the novel, found in his collection *More Dynamite*. Craig describes *Disgrace* as 'quite a good novel'. He analyses its moral dilemmas, finds them worthy and interesting, but thinks the novel indifferently written: 'Coetzee writes the way Fred Astaire sings – carefully competent in a narrow vocal range. (And Coetzee can't dance.)'

Craig concludes his review, 'Morally we are stretched if aesthetically we are a little starved.'

Postscript 3:
An exchange with Craig Raine, 30 September to 1 October 2020, about *You Have a Lot to Lose*, pp. 391–92.

Kia ora Craig

I've just received a TLS with your image which reminds

me I posted you last week a copy of vol II of my autobiography (or memoir, or whatever) called YOU HAVE A LOT TO LOSE, which will mostly not interest you but I felt I should send it to you with love, and as a salutation. Vol III (called WHAT YOU MADE OF IT) has since been completed and the plan is to launch it next May. [. . .]

Arohanui

Karl

Hello, Karl: Your memoir arrived safely yesterday with a bearded CKS in sandals and flares on the front. Shazzam. I read the bits about me. Very interesting. Our memories (inevitably) differ slightly. The reason for my fulsome postcard was your response to Galen's negative review – interested, calm, objective. I told Galen you were coming only minutes before you arrived. He wanted to leave immediately. But then you arrived – and were so civilised, so exemplary, so un-nettled, so *lovable*. I was bowled over.

Now I'll read the rest. [. . .] Much love to you and Kay,

Craig

I hope I haven't offended (or embarrassed) you. You did give (more or less) those reasons for fondness but I couldn't repeat them without parading my virtue – a difficulty with autobiography.

You won't want to read it all – so much of it is NZ-focussed and for NZ (literary – i.e. few) readers – though for those ('fit audience though few' – is that Keats, or Milton?) it spins along fluently and seems to be enjoyed.

There will be much more of interest in Vol III which goes from 1986 towards the (dwindling) present.

Without wanting to embarrass you (or myself) further, I do think of you always with aroha.

Karl

No. No. Not at all. And there's something hilarious about your reason for not explaining – not wanting to seem boastful. I understand that.

Usually, I don't read anything about myself. I haven't read any reviews since 1991 when I started at New College. So it was an interesting experience. I'm tempted to read your review of History: the Home Movie. But I will resist.

Instead I'll start on your memoir. Lots of it, I daresay, won't mean that much to me, but I'm interested in seeing how you set about it.

Much Love!

Craig

15. The Trick of Standing Upright Here – and There

Hons

In the years around 2007 honours seemed to pour upon me, and it felt (however it appeared from the outside) that the more I was rewarded in New Zealand the more I was also punished. My school, MAGS, had made me 'Albertian of the Year' in 2004, and now put me on its 'Distinguished Albertians' wall, neither of which should have counted for much but the schoolboy in me, who had never got his name up there for anything at all, treasured it. The City of Auckland made me its 'Distinguished Citizen' for 2007 which meant Kay and I could invite thirty or forty friends and family to the award dinner, my name would be up on another wall, and there was an enormous gold-framed certificate to hide away in a corner of our bedroom. And then (mightiest of all!) came the ONZ, which I have discussed in a footnote to Chapter 10. My medal was the one Hugh Kawharu of Ngāti Whātua had held, and before him Allen Curnow. And there were so many more readers for my books. I had often talked to small sessions at New Zealand festivals and signed books for four or five readers, while the signing queue for the famous overseas writer snaked away around the corner and out of sight. Now I had my own crowds and my own considerable snake.

On the other hand the Montana Book Awards, which I had twice won in the past when they were the Wattie Awards, now became what I called 'a ritual humiliation'. Almost, it seemed, every year for a period my books (sometimes a pair – poetry, fiction, non-fiction) were short-listed and didn't win. Mostly I thought the winner undeserving, or less deserving, which you might expect; but so did numbers of academic colleagues and literary friends who were eager to write to me saying so – which of course made the paranoia worse. Gordon McLauchlan, who had written about the disparity of arts funding as between Wellington and everywhere else (for example seven of the past ten Mansfield Menton Fellows had come from Wellington), recommended I change my name and move to the capital. I told him the price was too high. Graham Beattie, who knew how I felt and sympathised, emailed after a Montana dinner, 'But you were still smiling at the end of the evening, Karl.'

After *Mansfield* and *My Name Was Judas*, two years apart, each a best-seller in New Zealand and welcomed warmly abroad, had been short-listed and had not won, I swore that that was the last time I would attend one of those ghastly events, which were more about commerce and hype than literary quality. To many writers this would have seemed (and probably was) ungrateful and arrogant. Fortunately Charlotte and I were never short-listed together in the same year and category, and my good/bad karma did not attach itself to her. She won the Montana in 2008 for *Opportunity*.

And all this time, though it was true that if my months spent at work quietly in Parnell were added up and set against time spent overseas, Parnell would always come out a long way ahead, nonetheless it must have seemed as if I had become an international jet-setter. But family life went on, and I continued swimming with Kay at Kohimarama, out to the yellow buoy and counting. We were part of a group there (Gordon McLauchlan was a regular) of elderly swimmers, the oldest ninety-year-old Lorna, an Australian who had been a nurse with her country's forces in the Pacific in World War II, and had been captured and held several years by the Japanese – and survived.

AFTER MY 'VASCULAR ACCIDENT' KAY AND I had had our quiet time in Uzès when I worked, slowly and effortfully at first, then more quickly, and finally seeming to float, through the five Durrell novels relearning to read. Back in London, we had a supper (on what happened to be my seventy-third birthday) at the Savile Club, with Michael Schmidt (we were his guests), and with Doreen widow of Donald Davie, and Margaret. The last time I'd been in that hallowed precinct had been twenty years before when Donald and I had mulled over my Pound Yeats Eliot book. Michael was proprietor of Carcanet, the UK's largest poetry publisher, and editor of *PN Review*. Kay and I had once driven him from his hotel in Auckland across the bridge to dinner at Elizabeth Caffin's, and he'd told us he had fallen in love with New Zealand. In an email he'd said, 'If I was younger, or more intelligent and brave, I would emigrate. It did seem to me the closest I'd been to Paradise since I left Mexico in childhood.' I had reviewed his second novel, *The Dresden Gate* (set in Mexico), in the *LRB*, and though it hadn't seemed to me entirely successful the sense of place was rich and strong and remained with me. We talked about the *Collected Poems* I was putting together and he would in due course publish a beautiful 550-page Carcanet paperback of it after the Auckland University Press hardcover.

Wider still – and wider . . .

It was a twelve-hour flight from Auckland straight across the South Pacific to Santiago (Chile). I stayed one night in a hotel there, and remember only looking across what seemed to be an immense plain to snow-covered mountains. It was like landing in Christchurch, with the same sense of space, clear air and beauty. I spent a good part of the next day in the air – Santiago to Bogotá (Colombia) and then on to Medellín. That flight was like no other I had made – over vast tracts of jungle, the world's lungs we have been told, our protection against the worst ravages of CO_2; and winding through it, huge rivers, including what must have been tributaries of the Amazon itself. For most of the journey there was little sign of human habitation down there, though one supposed there must have been small settlements on the rivers, European or Indian.

Bogotá on the other hand is a city of eight million – Medellín half that. Medellín's airport is high on a plateau 40 or 50 kilometres from the central city (which is itself still high above sea level). My flight arrived there just after dark, and I had a strong impression of being on the rim of an enormous bowl of light as we made our way down into it by bus. It's a city whose beginnings date back to the seventeenth century, built on a river (or confluence of two) and carved out of the jungle which, all around and always, threatens to return and reclaim. I noticed a hospital with a sign that clearly meant 'We never close', and I thought of the city's fame, which was supposed to be passing, that it was 'the murder capital of the world', a reputation based mainly on drug wars between the Medellín cartel of Pablo Escobar and his rivals. Then there were the revolutionary (Marxist) guerrillas of the FARC, still abducting careless people who roamed too far from protected routes and pathways, and held them for ransom, or for the exertion of political pressure. By the late 1990s they were said to hold some hundreds of captives in the jungle, among them at the time I was in the country, Íngrid Betancourt, a member of the Colombian legislature who had been a candidate for the nation's presidency. They had abducted her in 2002 and in 2007 she had still not been released.*

My memory of the city itself is entirely impressionistic – the feeling that, despite urban affluence and ample 'high-rise', it was

* She was rescued in 2008, after six and a half years captive in the jungle, much of that time held in chains.

holding its own against the alien force of an equatorial climate and the Andean jungle that would win if humanity turned its back for a moment. When rain fell, accompanied by cracking thunder and lightning bolts in the mountains, it was comprehensive, nothing tentative about it; it smacked into the big leaves, challenging them, mocking their pretence at offering shelter. When the sun came out there were the colours everywhere of flowers, bright birds and flying things, insects, moths, butterflies – and heavy purple beetles that flew incompetently, crashed into things and fell, as if they were made of metal. Condors hung in the air over the barren parks where drunks and drug addicts sat, heads hanging forward, or lay sprawled in sleep. Human decorative habits tried to match nature, bold, bright, sometimes garish. The colours were matched by the noise – streets full of the cries of sellers of papaya and other tropical fruit, and of delicacies like *caracoles gigantes* (giant snails). The music of samba and rumba and salsa seemed to be everywhere, and for one like myself, whose feet and legs are permanently wired to his ears, it was hard not to break into those dance steps learned and loved in youth.

One knew that just out there, in the Amazonian hinterland, were poisonous snakes and spiders, monkeys and tigers, and in the streams and rivers, piranhas that would strip you clean. These existed in my mind like an unusable smattering of the language I did not speak or read (Spanish or indigenous) – a sense of place that was not my own nor like it – foreign, scary, exciting.

Medellín was also a city of many firearms, including some that were designed to be seen and admired (as well as feared and fired) – a silver revolver, a gold rifle, worn on the hip or carried on the shoulder through the street by security guards and bank delivery men, or just private persons wanting to be seen walking armed in 'the murder capital of the world'. There was talk of occasional gunfights in the barrios – away from the town centre where we poets were housed in the Gran Hotel. There seemed to be more priests than policemen, and the author of *My Name Was Judas* had to go into the nineteenth-century Medellín cathedral, all brick and square, very large and rather plain but with imposing stained-glass windows, and dedicated to the Blessed Virgin.

Down the long aisle
beyond the faithful
on their knees and flanked

by banks of white blooms
seven priests in green
stand at their sacred

table intoning
plainsong, one ringing
a small silver bell.

In a fine smoke
of incense, and now a
one-note tolling of

the larger bell, their
faces grow fainter,
the feeling stronger

of a force to be
feared, alien to
reason.

We read our poems at a number of smaller venues, always with good audiences, but with the promise of the big one still to come; and in the gaps were taken about in groups, or shepherded by an attendant who knew the city and where not to go in it. I asked mine about the river – I'd had such a sense, on that drive from the airport, of a vast valley through which a river or rivers must run.

He confirmed this was so but seemed to veer off the suggestion that I should see it; and since he was not fluent in English and I spoke no Spanish, I let it lapse for the moment. Then came a reading for which we were to travel to or from (I can't tell which from my notebook) Metro Estación Madera. The metro train was very modern and took us for many kilometres along the river. It seemed we were looking from the affluent side to what became more apparent was the barrios of the poor, the poverty-stricken, the dispossessed. The river was large and deep, brown and flowing fast, and the banks down to it were steep, much of them covered with ramshackle dwellings, clearly knocked together from bits of timber and corrugated iron and dangerous stuff like fibrolite. These structures clung precariously to the hillslopes, and there were places where the bank had slipped or been washed away in rainstorms taking houses with it. Everything from that side seemed to run or wash or slide down into the river which was heavily polluted; and now and then together with the junk and oil a dead animal would float by, even one that appeared large enough to have been a mule. In the worst days of the drug wars it was said the sight of human bodies floating by was common.

The Medellín International Poetry Festival had been started by Fernando Rendón (who was still in charge) as some kind of idealistic gesture towards peace and reconciliation when the drug wars and the FARC were both at their height. It was therefore not aligned politically, but committed to an aesthetic and social ideal. It was widely popular and attracted enormous crowds, but its success was not officially recognised or embraced by the Colombian government, which did not aid it, but did not seem seriously to obstruct it either. It had received in 2006 the Right Livelihood Award (popularly known as the Alternative Nobel Prize) from the Swedish Parliament 'for showing how creativity, beauty, free expression and community can flourish among and overcome even deeply entrenched fear and violence'.

We read at an art gallery, a clinic, a university, the great Parque de la Luz – and then the major reading took place in the Carlos

Vieco Theatre, an open-air amphitheatre sloping down a wooded hillside, with seating for four thousand and with every space filled. This had become an emblematic venue for Rendón's festival and what it represented. I had never had the excitement of reading to such a large, and *engaged* crowd. They listened attentively to the poem in English, and then sometimes erupted with pleasure at the translation. I read my poem about 9/11, with 'Americans falling from the sky' and its grim reflection

> and came home to it
> to watch it like a movie
> its horror, its rough justice.

They cheered. Colombia might have a right-wing elected government but the crowd here, one felt, hated, or at least deeply resented, American power. I also read a stirring one about the power of poetry itself, derived principally from reading about bad times in Eastern Europe.

> In that country
> poet spoke for people
> against the invader.
>
> Between bombings
> when sirens were silent
> poems were broadcast.
>
> When newspapers lied
> people queued for poems
> and read them on trams.
>
> Oh for such a contract
> to write only the truth,
> even to die for it –

how much better than
to be civil servant
to Propriety, our master.

Bolivarian

I was back in this Central–South American region less than a year later, this time in Caracas at the 5th Festival Mundial de Poesía. In those years Colombia was probably the only Latin American country that did not have a leftist government. The worst, or the most overt, of the United States involvement and interference in the affairs of Latin America – in Chile, in Argentina, in Central America – seemed to be over, though a great deal of CIA and secret military activity was still going on beneath the surface; and among the shining lights of the left in that region was Hugo Chávez of Venezuela. So the atmosphere I found myself in was not dissimilar to that of Colombia the year before, except that there seemed to be enormous popular enthusiasm for the present regime, especially among the working class. Poverty had decreased by 20 per cent between 2002 and 2008. The middle class were clearly divided, intellectuals approving of Chávez and his reforms, others hating the restrictions the government imposed on their freedoms, especially the freedom to travel, and to earn and spend, invest and gamble with, American dollars. My travel, accommodation and meals were covered by the festival; but when I left, my appearance fees of $1,000 were paid in US dollars and I had to have an official signed-and-stamped form proving that I was authorised to take them out of the country. This included a photograph (which I still have) of the ten $100 notes, folded so the serial numbers were visible. I was authorised to carry precisely these, not just any, dollar notes.

In a poem I called 'Caracas' there is the line 'city of vivid slogans and sad citations' and it quoted two of the slogans, 'Construyamos la patria buena' (Let us build the nation well), and, more radical and staunch, 'Socialismo o muerte' (Socialism or death). Everywhere in public places there were evocations of the great Simón Bolívar, revolutionary liberator of these regions (including Colombia, Panama, Ecuador and Peru) from the rule of Spain. The country was the Bolivarian Republic of Venezuela and Chávez its Bolivarian president; the currency was the bolivar; and there seemed to be innumerable squares and streets and fountains named after him.

The readings were arranged at a much more basic level than had been the case in Colombia, intended to reach the poor and disadvantaged, who seemed as imbued as everyone else with the idea that poetry was important, a serious aspect of education and of social life, and must be shared by all. We read to chickens and dogs, and to small groups in slums and schools, and even in a mental hospital where those among the afflicted who themselves wrote poetry joined us on stage, nervous, uncertain, but eager to offer their own work or a poem by someone famous and admired. We were taken in a minivan to deliver a reading at a small rural village. But the festival opened in the large public Teresa Carreño Theatre and ended there.

I was touched by the social atmosphere of Venezuela, felt I could share the enthusiasm which had swept Chávez to power, and consequently have never believed much of the scuttlebutt put about from Washington before and since his death. He was not forgiven for renationalising large parts of the Venezuelan oil industry that had been previously privatised – which he did to fund free health clinics, food and housing subsidies for the poor, and improvements in education. His rapprochement with Castro weakened the isolation the US wanted maintained against Cuba and displeased Washington. It seemed obvious that the economic forces ranged against the Chávez government (and there would soon be economic sanctions) were going to prevail unless he could hold on to his appearance of being in control on a path towards a more equal society; but cancer undermined him, and with him, all the good things he was aiming for. He wanted the huge oil wealth of the country to go to the people instead of to overseas investors; but unscrambling an essentially free-market egg needs more than currency reform and bold edicts, however honourable the intentions. It needed a slower pace and more subtle planning, and the whole enterprise was probably already showing signs (though not to me) of the collapse to come. One had a feeling of popular goodwill, with a partial but not insignificant current of middle-class ill will towards the Bolivarian ideal; of great hopes combined with uncertainty; so when it all seemed in the years after I was there to fall apart, I felt sad, sorry for those lovely people, but not surprised. If the Great Satan turns its face against you, you are unlikely to prosper.

One of several poems I wrote while there, or just afterwards, was published by Michael Schmidt in *PN Review*, though he said, 'This one will get us into trouble.' He meant it could be read as sneering at the poor from a position of privilege, whereas I meant it, and thought every intelligent reader would recognise it (as I'm sure Michael did) as being heavy with irony directed against ourselves – the affluent, the comfortable. I called it 'Greeneland' thinking of the novels of Graham Greene because of that irony, but also because Venezuela, with its right–left political dynamic and America's wish to influence what happened there, was a setting for a classic Greene novel.

Greeneland

Down there
in the concrete enclosure
the man in charge of garbage
is not a man. He is garbage –
looks like it, stinks of it,
is it. He has become what he serves.
His dog is his human part.
The rest is given over
to remnant and rot

> and their rendering
> to earth or fire
> so we may rise clean and clear
> in our glass containers
> to the blue of the rooftop pool
> and at night
> to dine among stars.

To be the perfect Greene novel, however, someone more prepossessing than the garbage man, possibly even a priest, would have to be a lapsed or lapsing Catholic.

I HAD ALWAYS SAID I WOULD NEVER write autobiography but now I wrote to Marilyn Duckworth that I was feeling '*blessed*' because I had suddenly found myself writing about my early years and it was happening so effortlessly I felt it had to be good. In August, the day after an angioplasty procedure had inserted a couple of stents into my coronary arteries, I was elevated to that MAGS 'Distinguished Albertians' wall; and on the 20th wrote to Elizabeth Caffin:

> On the brink of departure [to Europe] I find myself inexplicably and inconveniently embarked on a sort of autobiography. I think of it like Yeats's *Reveries over Childhood and Youth* and will take it up to the beginning of 1956 when Kay and I left New Zealand for the first time. There's an idea in my head that anything and everything I have done or become are already in place as potential before I ever set foot offshore. I want the larger picture to be always visible – so it's not about me but about what I see and hear and learn – myself as eyes and ears. I began about ten days ago and it is just flowing so well – 12,000 words. Having resisted autobiography so long (despite publishers urging) I'm glad I waited because now I seem ready

to do it. The travel is inconvenient but I will take it with me and try to keep writing, especially during our month in France.

I have also been writing post-*Collected* poems and have one just out in the *New Yorker*, two in *Areté*, three coming in *PN Review*, two coming in the *Harvard Review*, plus the ones in the current *Landfall* and *Sport* – so there will be another new book before too long.

Family

The three elfin figures camping with their parents on the shores of Lake Como in Chapter 6 of *You Have a Lot to Lose* have largely vanished from my narrative. There have been only glimpses of them, and they will have their own stories to tell. But they were now adults, and parents, and we had seven grandchildren, five living in New Zealand, two in London; and already there was a great deal of visiting back and forth, and in some cases (depending on where the child was born) dual passports.

Like birds
on some

needless but
habitual migration
we've crossed skies

and crossed them
as our 'opposite isles'
chased each other

never to meet.
So what's belonging
unless it's to

one another
and to our own
history, the books which

made us what we are,
and those that will
tell our story?*

After a number of years as registrar at the Auckland Museum Oliver, whose PhD was in fine arts, had taken a senior post in the Australian National Library in Canberra; but far from wife Virginia and their two children he had become depressed and was now back in Auckland as deputy director of the James Wallace Trust. Charlotte, having qualified first in law, was now firmly established as a writer in New Zealand, with three novels and two collections of short stories published, and winning prizes (the Deutz Medal for example) which had eluded me. In London, Margaret, another qualified lawyer, had soon switched to publishing, and recently moved from Harvill to Atlantic Books as publishing director.

Around this time in a message to Margaret I told her my autobiography† was 'more or less finished' and said if she sent me Guy's e-address I would send it so he could print it out for her. She replied keen to see it and among other things reported:

> On Saturday George [her friend Georgina] took me to see *Gurrelieder* by Schoenberg at the Royal Festival Hall. I loved it – a huge orchestra and a choir of about 150 – very German and Wagnerian and rich, a series of lieder recounting a Norse myth, with a really weird spoken piece of poetry at the end. Have you ever seen it? I thought it terrific. I wondered whether

---

* 'Revisiting Bristol', *Collected Poems, 1951–2006*, p. 320.
† i.e. *South-West of Eden*.

> I'd find it too modern and complex but I was drawn in and excited. Then we had dinner looking out over the Thames which was bathed in golden light from the buildings opposite, and I thought that London is an addiction for me, from which I may never recover.

I was fascinated by this from the daughter who had always joked about her parents' addiction to classical music which she referred to collectively as 'Vivaldi'. Was there a potential Wagnerian here after all? My reply included:

> Yes I understand your addiction to London. I often worry that you might come back here and find it thin. Once you've been 'out' [i.e. of New Zealand] it's a way of life that has to be relearned. I see Charlotte yearning sometimes, as I did for many years, to get out of the cage. I will say, and only to you, what I have not said to ANYONE in private or public, that I really think I would have had a bigger, fuller life if I had not come back. (It almost hurts to say it, and should not be repeated.)

But now I have repeated it myself, and only because it's a half-truth, and the full truth would be a contradiction.

In addition to her successes with fiction Charlotte was winning prizes as a reviewer and literary journalist, a talent she exercised with a rare mix of sensitivity, penetrating intelligence and the necessary discretions. Her short stories brought international recognition too, with short-listings (twice) for the Frank O'Connor International Short Story Award. As fiction writer I thought her style could be seen to show we were father and daughter – there was a family likeness in the prose; but I always felt there was a magical quality about her novels which mine lacked.

In 2009 Oliver's book *Art Icons of New Zealand* with the subtitle *Lines in the Sand* had been short-listed for the Montana Book

Awards. The Montanas had become more than ever odd, adding strange new categories. Oliver's book was straight art history but there was no such category that year so he was short-listed in the 'Lifestyle and Contemporary Culture' section – and did not win. That section was won by a book called *Ladies a Plate* – a sort of cook book. I emailed him:

> I hope you're not too disappointed not to have won the prize. I was disappointed for you. I was sure you would win and was pissed off. But the Montanas are like that – homely and idiotic. Anyway I keep hearing more and more good (and deserved) comments about your book – last night Len Castle said how much he admired it; and last week Don Binney. You deserved to win which is why you didn't – it's almost a Montana rule.

He wrote back:

> I was disappointed – high as a kite on the fantasy of winning for a few days but made a conscious effort to sober up spiritually on Monday when I asked myself how I would cope if I didn't win.

My *Collected Poems, 1951–2006* had won (another absurd category) the Reference and Anthology section, and in accepting the prize I said I felt as if I was receiving it for editing the collected works of an obscure and long-dead poet, C. K. Stead. Oliver wrote:

> I'm thrilled for you that you won and you looked very snazzy on the podium in your cool new specs – like a Hollywood director. Your speech neatly captured the comic aspects of the prize distribution.

The Collected

Despite the absurdity of that Montana award AUP's publication of the 550-page *Collected Poems, 1951–2006* was of immense importance to me. The collection was so *there*, so big, so full of so much – not of me but of me-and-the-world, our interaction, our joint life. Poetry had always come first for me; everything else – fiction, literary criticism, memoirs, whatever – came second. So it was good that in the year following the Auckland publication Carcanet issued it in a beautiful big paperback. It was a UK confirmation of the NZ fact.

This meant that Kay and I were in that part of the world twice in 2009 – first in May–June when I took the Carcanet edition on a small reading tour – Grasmere (the Wordsworth Trust), Edinburgh (the Scottish Poetry Library), Manchester (the Public Library) and then London (BBC – the Radio 3 *Word* programme) and the launch at New Zealand House. After that we had our usual several weeks in Saint-Maximin and week in Menton – and home to Auckland. Then in August–September we were back again, for me to read at the Edinburgh Festival with Peter Porter and Hugo Williams, after which we had the month residency at Gaiole in Chianti followed by the fortieth-anniversary celebration of the Menton Mansfield fellowship where I and the old fantastical Duke were briefly reconciled with the joke that we'd eloped together.

I had always read Hugo Williams' columns in the *TLS*, and at the Edinburgh reading met him for the first time – charming, witty, handsome, posh (an Eton old-boy), actorly and son of a famous actor. Peter Porter, on the other hand, I knew well, a gritty intellectual Aussie, with whom I'd read in Sydney and at King's Lynn. I had dinner with him and his wife Christine that evening. He had come out of hospital for the reading and went back there – alas to die. Hugo in a subsequent column referred to Peter and me as 'heavyweights', by which I'm sure he didn't mean that he was a lightweight (he had won significant British poetry awards). It was just another glimpse of the charm of the posh Pom, confident enough to be absurdly self-deprecating. Rosemary Goring in the Glasgow *Herald* complained that we'd only been given an hour: 'I'd have cleared the schedule to allow this event double the time, so fine and rare was the company.'

I made one new friend in Edinburgh that year and left one trace behind. The friend was the Irish-born but Scots-by-adoption poet and James Joyce devotee (or fanatic) Hayden Murphy who writes and prints out with an illustration a new poem for Bloomsday each year, and in 2013 persuaded me to write one.* Hayden had worked for the publisher Martin Brian & O'Keefe when they were publishing Sargeson's late fiction, which he remembered fondly and felt it gave him a connection with New Zealand.

And the trace: for my visit that year the Scottish Poetry Library asked me to choose some favourite poems, which they would put on display (in original editions if they could find them) with my explanation of my choices to be published as a booklet. The poems I chose were ones more or less permanently lodged in my head, and what I wrote about them included:

> I have always been deeply interested in poetic form and in the case of Donne's 'A Nocturnal upon Saint Lucy's Day' and Hopkins' 'Thou art indeed just, Lord . . .' the rigour of the form set against the dramatic flow of the statement increases my sense of richness. Both are powerful, deeply felt poems, where the technical exactness does nothing to restrain the passion.
>
> 'Kubla Khan' is (to me) the *ur*-poem from which all poetry proceeds and to which all poetry aspires – a poem about poetry (about itself in fact), about the act of creation, and then about its own loss of itself – the ultimate illustration of the mystery. It's a poem which gives itself a geography rather than a history.

---

* 'That Stephen Dedalus will never be a poet', *That Derrida Whom I Derided Died*, Auckland University Press, 2018, pp. 96–97.

Allen Curnow was mentor, friend, colleague and neighbour over many years, and died in 2001. He has been widely acknowledged as New Zealand's finest poet of the 20th century, and 'You will know when you get there' is an example of his later style, capturing both the reality of place, and the unreality of time and death.

I am an ear person, and poetry is music – by which I mean literally it has a music that cannot be less (and may be more) important than its 'meanings'; but also that it is *like* music, in the sense that it has structure, tone, harmony, cadence.

Postscript:

One British reviewer of *My Name Was Judas* suggested (perhaps not entirely seriously) that its author should be awarded the Nobel Prize for literature.* In 2012 the UK English Association, which had made me an Honorary Fellow, and is 'one of the few learned societies in the UK invited to nominate individuals for the Nobel Prize for Literature', made the same proposal to the Nobel Committee in Stockholm. They accompanied this nomination with a detailed discussion of my career and concluded:

> There can be few men or women alive today who have contributed more to the international community of letters over so long a period than this New Zealander. The themes that have animated his work – the importance of language, the imperatives of global as well as local citizenship, and the responsibilities no less than the rights of the artist – resonate in our time. The English Association of Great Britain accordingly wishes to nominate Dr Christian Karlson Stead for the Nobel Prize for Literature for the year 2012.

---

* Roger Lewis, *Sunday Express*, 24 December 2006.

When informed of this by their chairman, Adrian Barlow, I thanked them sincerely but said it seemed to me extremely unlikely that a nomination which did not have support from the home country was ever likely to succeed, and I had not detected any such inclination in my favour in New Zealand.

16.
Nunc Dimittis

Moominpappa's Memoirs

You Have a Lot to Lose was to be Volume II of what is referred to in the family as 'Moominpappa's Memoirs', our children (and probably grandchildren) having read, or had read to them, Tove Jansson's Moomin stories. Volume I, *South-West of Eden*, published in 2010, was an account of my childhood and youth and went up to 1956 when Kay and I, already married, left New Zealand for the first time. I had enjoyed writing that book – it all flowed so easily and naturally, straight from memory, little need (except in the final two chapters) for reference to documents, of which there were few or none. In that sense Volume II was going to be very different; but there was something else quite unexpected had put me off the project and brought it to a halt for a considerable time. In *South-West of Eden* I had made the mistake of quoting a letter from Janet Frame without getting permission from the copyright holder, her niece Pamela Gordon. It was a letter to me and in my possession, so I was its legal owner; but I should have remembered that in law I owned the document, not the copyright. An understandable mistake you might think; and I have been assured by people experienced in publishing (daughter Margaret, Craig Raine) that these things happen from time to time and are usually amicably resolved. There was nothing amicable about the Frame faction's response. They wanted my book withdrawn, and when that was refused, they made it clear it was going to cost me and Auckland

University Press dearly. I am prevented by the legal agreement from spelling out the detail – but there was no profit in the book for me, and a significant loss for the Press and the university; and plans for a reissue in paperback and online have been scrapped. That is why there has been a ten-year gap between Volumes I and II. It also explains why nothing of Frame's is quoted in this book nor in *You Have a Lot to Lose*. If you own *South-West of Eden* you should perhaps treasure it and keep it in good condition. It would be a nice outcome from the author's point of view if this upsetting glitch, in which Gordon and her partner seemed to act against me with inexplicable and quite needless malice, should have made it a rare and sought-after book.

So when the Muse wasn't about I went back to fiction and literary criticism, and worked on my London money-meltdown novel, *Risk*, published in 2012, and *Shelf Life: Reviews, Replies and Reminiscences* in 2016. Between those came the poems, *The Yellow Buoy*, in 2013, with their registers of Bogliasco, Colombia and Venezuela – but of Auckland too, and swimming.

Harvill Secker, now part of the Random House empire and lacking Christopher MacLehose, offered to arrange publication of *Risk* as a Random House book in New Zealand, of which they would take copies for release in London. I knew well how unsatisfactory this kind of arrangement was and how it meant the book would be largely ignored in London where it very much belonged; so I offered it to Christopher for his new press, MacLehose. He welcomed it, and what was (once again) intended to be my last novel appeared in that imprint.

But Christopher was never for long entirely out of the reach, or the clutches, of the larger publishing predators, and his new publishing house soon had to function under the aegis of a larger firm, Quercus. His success with Stieg Larsson must have given him some protection and independence there, but not complete freedom; and when it came to what was in fact (and at last) my last novel, *The Necessary Angel*, he was not able to publish. So it was taken by daughter Margaret's London firm, Atlantic Books, now controlled by Australian-owned Allen & Unwin – though by the time it emerged as a book Margaret had moved on. Its London launch was desultory and in my absence (no New Zealand House celebration for this one), though it did get a stunning review and big-page welcome from the (UK) *Sunday Times* which greeted it with the headlines 'LITERARY SPARKLER' and 'NEW ZEALAND'S FINEST NOVELIST HAS WRITTEN A REAL GEM OF A BOOK'.

At home it was warmly welcomed, and my Auckland editor Jenny Hellen said I 'would just have to accept' that I'd written a best-seller. It was as if she thought I was the kind of author who would think best-sellerdom beneath me, something that only a vulgar populariser would want. This was another whiff of what had come with the popularity of *Smith's Dream*, and reminded me of that entry in Charles Brasch's journal when, on his last legs, he had asked himself, 'How can I be interested in Stead after this?' Even Frank Sargeson had been slightly unsure about *Smith's Dream*, telling Phil Wilson, 'If Karl's not careful he'll find himself our Graham Greene.'

The Necessary Angel came about by a sort of accident. In June 2014 I was in Paris for the Katherine Mansfield Society's conference at which I was to give one of several plenary papers. The conference dinner was held at a famous restaurant, Le Procope, on Midsummer's Night which in Paris is an occasion of extraordinary and noisy celebration. I had said publicly at the London launch of *Risk* that it would be my last novel; and to myself that if there *were* to be another it would never move from Auckland.

But contrary to this quite serious resolve, an idea for a novel began to creep up on me and take hold. It was partly a result of trying to imagine myself in the situation of my old friend Rob Dyer, Kiwi expatriate living in Paris with a French wife who was a distinguished academic and expert on the novels of Proust. There was no attempt to imagine my way into the mind and experience of Rob himself, who as I saw him was much too alien to figure at the centre of any fiction of mine. He was also retired and (like me) an old man, and my character had to be a viable middle age (mid-forties). Rob's wife was almost unknown to me; I had met and admired her and that was all. But my old obsession with France as the great unknowable, both close and remote, mysterious and irritating, meant the imagination wrestled with an idea which was really a question: how would it have been if I had ever taken an academic post (teaching English literature) in France, and could one do that as fiction? I began with that 2014 dinner at Le Procope, and the fiction soon established itself firmly in my imagination. But among the small set of characters there was one based on a strange and fascinating young woman, a New Zealander, who had called on me once in Auckland and had told us, Kay and me, about her manic-depressive problems, that she had sometimes had to use the medication lithium, and how it affected her.

She popped up, inexplicably, but welcome, quite early in the writing and established herself as the English student Helen – the most interesting character, I think, obsessed with language and fixated on certain poems and poets. Kay and I were back in Auckland at the end of June, and the writing of the novel ran on until, with 101 pages written towards the end of October 2014, I felt I had to get back to Paris, had to make a flying visit and capture it precisely in the autumn of that year.

The novel was shaping up to be unusually integrated – almost entirely in one city and for the space of just one year – the year in which it was being written. Insofar as it was destined to be any kind of success, I think this was the reason. I had so often irritated my readers by shifting times and locations, challenging them to remember where and when this or that happened and how it came about. Here was cruise mode, not quite the 'conventional fiction' I had been always determined to avoid, but nearer: a comfort zone for book groups perhaps. In a way this dash back to Paris for the sake of a work in hand was one of my simplest and most daring literary adventures. I booked cheap flights (one of which went briefly wrong, landing me in Amsterdam instead of Paris) and a two-star (but lovely) hotel in the quarter made famous by Hemingway; and I engaged my friend Claire Davison, with whom I had already discussed the idea during the Mansfield conference, to be available at least some of the time I was there, to help me with information and locations. I would be alone away from home and writing, with one project and nothing else – the situation I had always found most challenging, most arduous, most fulfilling and exciting.

Claire was English-born but (so to speak) embedded French – married to (and separated from) a Parisian police officer* with whom she'd had two sons, and now a full professor at the Sorbonne. We got on well together and her academic field was the one which had been mine – literary Modernism. But she taught to French and in French, and at that great and ancient institution. In that sense Claire would play the role my son-in-law Guy Clayton had played in the writing of *Risk*. She would provide information, show me important sites, introduce me to significant figures there (including the acting president of the university†) and correct any mistakes that crept into my narrative. It was a lot to ask of a very busy woman but she seemed to enjoy it, as if it was adding something exciting to the routines of her life. Claire's legs seemed almost as long as mine, and her walking pace even faster. When she led me about to see important locations I was made aware of my age, but didn't complain or restrain: this was what I was there for.

I was now engaged in research and yet still managing to do some of the writing, and my appointments diary of those Paris days keeps track of progress. In transit Auckland to Paris I read and annotated the 101 pages already written; and while there, I increased the page score to 123.

---

* By what would prove to be a lucky chance he was an officer in a branch of the Paris police, the 'Brigade against Traffic in Cultural Goods', which exactly suited the plot line when I returned to the novel after my lapse of confidence in it.

† I've forgotten his name but he was also expert in poetic Modernism and told me his doctoral subject had been something like 'Yeats and Inheritance'.

At home again the scoring continued, becoming mixed on the pages, as we moved towards summer, with my count of swims to the yellow buoy at Kohimarama. By early January the score was 175 pages – but now there was more mention of revisions, which sometimes sent the count into reverse. Soon the count of words and pages had been replaced entirely by the score of single and double visits to the yellow buoy, which petered out with the chill of the early autumn of 2015, and with my inauguration as Poet Laureate. Now my best energies were to be absorbed into the writing of my laureate blogs.

Somewhere during this period I had lost confidence in the novel. This was my habit – the inner critic in me who could always find fault and suffer embarrassments, often before there had been anything external to occasion them. I worried especially about the novel's bookishness: would publishers and booksellers (would *readers*) be interested? But more important was that it didn't have a sufficient 'story'; that it needed in fact an *end*, something decisive instead of a mysterious death and a rather French-arty *fade*.

So in the midst of my laureate duties I reduced what was good in it to a long short story centring on the character of the young English student Helen and her interaction with Max Jackson, the Kiwi teaching at the Sorbonne. I then put this together with a collection of stories new and old, including the story of 2010 'Last Season's Man' that had won the big prize, popular favourites like 'A Fitting Tribute', and others I thought in one way or another good or successful. Margaret, on a visit home, put me in touch with Jenny Hellen, the local rep of her London firm, Atlantic/Allen & Unwin. Jenny liked the collection and accepted it for the NZ/Australia market.

But now (of course) having put Helen White and Max Jackson into a short story, I returned to the novel and recognised where I had gone wrong. Helen, the most interesting character, had died in mysterious circumstances – a mystery I had not been able to think how to explain or resolve. Now I recognised that she had to survive;

and more than survive, she had to be the focal point of a climax that would rescue the novel as a narrative. Among many other events and travels here and there, and activities as laureate, this complete revision was achieved and the novel was offered to Christopher and to Atlantic/Allen & Unwin. Negotiations were complex and not of general interest; but it went to Margaret's firm who could do it both in the UK as Atlantic and here at home as Allen & Unwin.

A year later when Margaret sent me the *Sunday Times* review I sent it on to Christopher:

> I guess you will have seen this, Christopher. I so much wanted this one to be yours, and can't quite think why it didn't happen. I guess the short story collection which A & U published put a barrier in the way. Wishing you well as always from the South Seas.

Christopher replied:

> I am delighted for you and for the book. It's a wonderful review and I hope it gives the wise people at Allen & Unwin a terrific shot in the arm. It must be a happy feather in your cap. You are generous to write as you do and I thank you for sharing it.

I didn't see much evidence of Christopher's 'terrific shot in the arm' at the London end of Allen & Unwin, from which Margaret had by now gone; but the book flew in New Zealand, reprinting a number of times – hence the exchange when Jenny Hellen told me I would just have to accept I'd written a popular book. I did accept it, with pleasure – and even liked and was entertained by the story myself when I re-read it. I thought there was possibly a bit of a sag in the middle, but hoped the explosive end Helen had devised for her obsession with Max more than made up for it. One local review I especially liked was a measured affirmation from Jane Westaway in the blog-site magazine *The Spinoff* which concluded:

> My favourites of Karl Stead's novels are *All Visitors Ashore*, laden with nostalgia, and *Mansfield*, in which I got to know a real person rather than merely bowing to the religious icon. Reading these changed me. *The Necessary Angel* did not. It's an entertainment but in the best sense of the word – clever, rich and playful.

There had been however one further episode which very nearly spelled the death of this novel before it was born. In July 2017 Kay and I came back, flying straight through from Europe, in time for me to attend the Marlborough Book Festival where I stayed at a winery called Dog Point. There I suffered the worst jet-lag reaction I've ever experienced – so bad that reading final proofs of *The Necessary Angel* I became convinced that it was a disaster, a failure, so bad it must under no circumstance be published. I should have remembered *All Visitors Ashore* – my inability even to look at it, and its subsequent success. But this was depression, my most acute experience of it, so irrational that even knowing that that was what it was made no difference; and only Kay's strength of mind when I got back to Auckland saved me from withdrawing it.

But something else came of that episode. It was in the midst of one of those black 3 a.m. moments that I wandered out into the frosty Marlborough night and looked up at the southern sky and began working in my head – to keep my thoughts away from the awful thing I was about to publish – on a poem that keeps its essentially iambic measure through the sequence of two long sentences, and which I'm still deeply attached to because of the moment of despair and half-recovery it represents. I called it 'At Dog Point':

> After a day of frost and sunshine
> in the valley of winter vineyards and winding streams
> that teach the far brown hills by definition
> and the farther mountains by peaks and caps of snow

Dog Point at 4 a.m.
showed me the night of another world
created by gods and peopled by their children
each one distinct, a point of brilliant light
each family a constellation
and needing all together
a name to match and affirm their magnitude –
'the Heavens' for example or 'the canopy of the stars'.

There is a dream of love
so far from the avidities of lust
and dramas of fidelity and possession
it is like that southern sky at night
burned across by a single shooting star.

''Tis syntax, syntax, that hath ravished me!' – Allen's echo of Marlowe's Dr Faustus was entirely relevant to my writing of that poem; and perhaps it rescued my last novel by diverting my attention elsewhere.

In 2017 *The Necessary Angel* duly appeared in hardback in the UK and in Australia/New Zealand in paperback, and a year later in UK paperback. Kay re-read it recently and said it was '*le vrai C. K.* – with Sylvie the dream, Louise the reality (and wife) and Helen the writer's ur-self'.

Poet laureate

The idea of an official poet appointed to celebrate public occasions was one more thing we imported from Britain, but only recently. In Britain the laureate was appointed for life – until Masefield outlived his meagre talent and became an embarrassment. I have a dim memory of the verse he hacked out on the death of George VI, finishing with a line about 'the three Queens who mourn' – presumably the dead King's widow Elizabeth, now to be known as 'the Queen Mother', his daughter the still-with-us-Elizabeth II, and his mother, 'the old Queen Mary' as she had been known in my childhood. Masefield's verse had made the whole thing suggest a moderately good poker hand.

More recently the British laureate has been appointed for ten years. The New Zealand laureateship was established by the Te Mata Estate winery in 1997, in association with the local Matahiwi marae, whose carver, Jacob Scott, made a tokotoko for the first recipient of the award, Bill Manhire, and has continued with that tradition. In addition to the much-prized tokotoko, the New Zealand laureate receives a stipend of $80,000 (less tax) over two years, and regular supplies of Te Mata wines – this perhaps in modern imitation of the butt of sack the English laureate traditionally received from the sovereign. Each new laureate is inducted on the marae and receives their tokotoko, and the appointment is for two years.

After ten years, proprietorship of the organisation and appointment passed to the National Library in Wellington. One is appointed for only two years so we have had a number of New Zealand laureates and it can't be said to be a hugely significant honour except symbolically; but precisely for the symbolism I would rather have had it than not. I was laureate for 2015–17. Jacob Scott was in South East Asia when the call came to make my tokotoko so he used local materials – black ebony for the stick and buffalo horn for the handle. The ferrule and a metal band were steel. Ebony is a very hard wood so carving the name and office, and the small Māori motif, must have been challenging.

Most of the Stead whānau were there for the weekend of my inauguration – our three children and six of seven grandchildren (the one missing, Madsie Grimshaw, was overseas). Margaret had brought her two from London, leaving husband Guy in charge at home. I was able to nominate three poets to accompany me, and they were my two former students, Chris Price and Greg O'Brien, and fellow-Aucklander Paula Green. I spoke about my whenua, of growing up in Mt Eden in sight of the three maunga – Maungawhau, Maungakiekie and Ōwairaka – and extracts were read from my poem 'Scoria'. Charlotte wrote about the whole event for *The Spinoff*. She described me as a 'control freak', but the tone was fond and affectionate.

The New Zealand laureate is not required to do anything in particular, but there is a laureate blog and I wrote for that substantially and regularly without looking to see what kinds of thing my predecessors used it for. For me it was just a place to write about poetry, its importance to me, its history, my own experience writing it and teaching it. I included six of those blogs at the end of my most recent collection of literary essays and reviews.*

It has been up to each of us to decide which (if any) public events we commemorate or respond to; but I did get one semi-formal request early on. The New Zealand Navy was to celebrate its seventy-fifth birthday since independence from the Royal Navy of which it had been part until World War II. There was to be a commemorative publication, and a page they thought might be kept for a poem from New Zealand's official laureate. Could I do this? I thought I could – try at least – but how much time could they give me? They were going to press tomorrow. I said it was impossible; and then, when they said the print date couldn't be changed, that I would try; but I told them to have something else ready for that space because a publishable outcome was extremely unlikely. I cursed and complained a great deal that day and on into the night, making many drafts and redrafts, telling Kay and anyone else in earshot that it was impossible, ridiculous, something only one of the armed services could be stupid enough to think could be done. But I 'went over the top' as commanded and came up with a poem I called 'A Birthday' which duly appeared in the commemorative publication.† I reprinted it in my next collection exactly as it had

---

* *Shelf Life*, pp. 389–436.

† *Courage, Commitment, Comradeship*, 2015.

emerged, on time, meeting its deadline, and without revision or improvement. Anything else would have felt like cheating, and would have been at odds with the Navy's commemorative publication.

I did get a few gentle suggestions from the Ministry. My two-year term ran slap in the middle of centenary commemorations of the 1914–18 'war to end all wars'; and a kindly hint was that I might find a way to register the importance of our women in World War I. I was free to ignore this; but it had an effect of triggering the Catullus in me. In other words it gave me the feeling that there was something to kick against; something, not so much to ignore, as to acknowledge and *not* do. The inoffensive and tentative Ministry became my Caesar. I thought first of the two famous Latin tags – Catullus's mellifluous farewell to his dead brother – 'Frater ave atque vale', and Horace's deplorably sinuous 'Dulce et decorum est pro patria mori' – and wrote a few introductory lines to say I could do one but not the other. So indeed I did commemorate some aspects of New Zealand's military role in World War I, but in forms of almost excessive sparseness: no heightened tone, no rolling Churchillian cadences or ringing rhymes, and if there were hero tales, they were only of a conscientious objector (Archibald Baxter – father of James K.), of a deserter shot at dawn (Jack Braithwaite), and of the ones with no names:

> My brother is a number
> and so is my cousin
>   and my cousin's cousin
> and so now am I
> one of a number.

The great Gallipoli disaster received only this:

> Paddy was the doctor's dog
> and died of shrapnel wounds
> in the same good cause

and for the same good reason
the soldiers died.

What was it again?

As for the suggestion about the role of women, that produced:

The Ministry wants one on . . .

the contribution of women
so Catullus records
that Clodia gave white feathers
to cowards
and lived to shed
                    tears for them.

'Feathers and tears'
says Catullus.

'Feathers and tears'.

The contribution of women also crept into one about the Battle of the Somme, in which I allowed myself a nod to my great-uncle Owen and the bronze plaque his death earned my grandmother. That rather beautiful object in a round wooden frame hung on our dining-room wall in my childhood, and Grandmother Karlson wept over it often, blaming herself for not discouraging her little brother from volunteering for the great adventure a war had seemed to represent.

The Somme

Mud – to drown in
but don't forget

the boozing and singing
the brotherhood-in-blood
and those easeful epiphanies
in the brothels of Bruges.

Tell the Ministry
it was a man's war –
to men most of the pride,
to men all of the shame,
and to Owen Vincent Freeman
a grave in Armentières
and a bronze plaque saying
'He died for Freedom and Honour.'

So my laureateship had no notable outcome; but I was there along with my fellow-laureates for various public occasions. There were my blogs – and there was the symbolism.

The laureate's last

His last
was not least
nor yet his best
but shaped for a shoe
his size
and like his sighs
not to last.

I, Karlson

In 2016 I had three publications: the collection of poems *That Derrida Whom I Derided Died*, another collection of critical essays and literary reviews, *Shelf Life: Reviews, Replies and Reminiscences*, and my 1994 novel *The Singing Whakapapa* reissued as one of six

Penguin Award Winning Classics. Though the print run appeared to be quite small, I was especially pleased about the last because it was a handsome hardcover and the original Penguin paperback had seemed such a scrappy poorly designed book with an amateurish cover. I thought it was a novel that deserved serious notice, and it had a better chance of survival in this new edition.

Shelf Life followed three earlier collections of literary criticism each of which had sold surprisingly well. It seemed there were still numbers of serious readers who enjoyed my thoughts and commentaries and critical analysis, which I had tried to keep detailed enough to convince but well short of inducing impatience or boredom. In fact I had always suspected, even as far back as my PhD (a necessarily boring style of writing), that there was a hidden factor in my critical writing which kept the reader alert and interested; and it had not been entirely a joke when I referred to *The New Poetic* as my first novel. It seemed I had profited by my faith in Virginia Woolf's 'Common Reader' (an entity rejected by literary theorists) and my preference for intelligibility; but perhaps above all by trusting (while I could sustain confidence) my own 'voice', in the sense Nabokov means when he says we read Dickens not for the story or the message, but for the *voice*.

That Derrida Whom I Derided Died contained my laureate poems, including the one suggesting that Tāmaki-makau-rau should be reinstated as the name of what we now call Auckland. There was a poem, 'Syllabics for young rooster', tracing the story of how I tracked down (too late, alas – they were both dead) Les Parker and Jean Lamont, friends of my youth who figure in *South-West of Eden*. There was a quiet goodbye to the writing of fiction, 'By the back door', written after *Risk* but before I had embarked, as a sort of late afterthought, on *The Necessary Angel*. There was a distant farewell wave to Diane ('The moon'), and a poem for Kay ('Beauty') remembering a party in Takapuna in 1955, which ended:

Much wine was drunk,

and so, soon, were the drinkers.
There was a moon on the sea
right out to Rangitoto.

You were beautiful, and I
sang, as I could in those days
all the way home – like a bird.

My late mother was there with me as I swam on my back at Kohimarama reading the clouds, and there were subtleties the aesthete in her would have liked – 'the laureate's last' for example; or the three lines written after seeing a signer for the deaf bizarrely posted stage left at the performance of an opera at Covent Garden:

Not singing but signing
with subtle hands and mobile features she makes
something of nothing and a song of silence;

or even (with a mild wince at the 'swearword') the sun rising seen as

that ball of bullshit fire
in all its gold glory.

There were poems for Paula Green at sixty and Fleur Adcock at eighty; and elegies for Peter Porter ('In the June rain'), Nick Tarling ('Unusual obsequies') and Jeny Curnow ('The widow will not be returning'). 'The year was '69' was a sort of commemoration of that year of action and how Maurice Shadbolt, Colin McCahon, Pat Hanly, and 'the usual suspects', figured in it along with Richard Nixon and the moon landing and the war in Vietnam – and with lines I liked so well I had stolen them from my own novel, *Risk*:

when songs had words you could remember
        and tunes you couldn't forget.

That poem, dedicated to the younger poet Sam Sampson, was a favourite (if the author may have favourites). So was 'Rain':

Now iron roofs and gutters
                    come into their own
                as drummers, timpanists
calling on Noah & Sons
and praying that the god of
rainbows
remember his promise.

The big drain chokes on its swallow
                        and throws up,
the tide-out bay
has the sheen and reflect of fullness,
        and everywhere, even in a lull
there's the rustle still,
the whisper and whistle of water.

                Green is never so green
as the colour of after-rain
                    when birds set in,
                and Tamaki-makau-rau
wahine with a thousand lovers
shakes east and westward
over two harbours
                and an isthmus of cones
                        her cloak
                    of feathered cloud.

It's a poem, like so much else in the collection, which seems to echo back – for example to Chapter 16, the Auckland rainstorm, in *The Death of the Body*, to Scoria's 'lay language' and chook speak, back to *South-West of Eden*'s colonial conjunctions of Dominion Road, Balmoral Road and Kensington Avenue with Maungawhau School, Maungakiekie Avenue and Ōwairaka – its family of five ('three and two halves to town'), four of them now dead and I, Karlson, about to be, having, as usual, the last word (the last laugh?) – completing a long loop back to these, my beginnings.

Appendix: Absent Friends

I am aware of many gaps in this account – too many 'absent friends', who might have expected to find a word or two, or many, in the foregoing narrative. For example . . .

. . . **Ann and Anthony Thwaite**, she the biographer, first of Edmund Gosse (1985), then A. A. Milne (1990), Frances Hodgson Burnett (1991), Emily Tennyson (1997), and Philip Henry Gosse (2002); he the poet, literary editor at various periods of the *Listener* (BBC), the *New Statesman, Encounter* (co-editor), for many years editor of Secker & Warburg's poetry list, and probably best known in later years as editor of Philip Larkin's work. It might be hard to decide which of this couple (both Fellows of the Royal Society of Literature) is the more distinguished, but she is at least his equal in literary eminence. As one of the Movement poets Anthony has been an adroit formalist, though never matching the sad mordancy of Larkin, and destined to make his way partly in Larkin's shadow which is, however, itself a mark of distinction.

Ann, my exact contemporary, was British-born but of New Zealand parents, and was sent to New Zealand with her brother for safety during World War II. She went to school in Wellington, but was often in Auckland with relatives during school holidays and swam, as I did, at the Mt Eden baths. I like to think (a fantasy) that we encountered one another as children and can imagine a bossy little English Ann dismissing me briskly as a silly Kiwi kid. She returned to her parents in England after the war, and she and Anthony met as students at Oxford. They have four daughters.

Anthony and I have read together once in Wellington and at least twice in King's Lynn. The Kiwi expat banker, Sam Nola, in my money-meltdown novel *Risk*, reports on what is happening in the small ground-floor business across the street, watching from the front first-floor window of what was in fact the Thwaites' *pied à terre* apartment in Paddington; and my English student Helen White in *The Necessary Angel* goes home to her parents' house (modelled on the Thwaites' Mill House at Low Tharston, Norfolk), where she reads a Martin Amis novel in a punt on the stream among the green and gold reeds and hovering turquoise damselflies.

I helped Ann find a publisher (Otago University Press) for her last biographical work, *Passageways*, about her forebears in New Zealand. I have played outdoor table tennis with her in the woods at Low Tharston, and Kay once fell out of their punt into the stream – the classic punting accident, hands and forearms supporting her weight on the landing, and knees on the floor of the boat as it drifted out into the stream. Ann's scream brought me running, Anthony just behind, and it was Kay's response – laughter – that especially impressed Ann. Our encounters with the Thwaites, here or there or wherever, have always been the same – warm 'round-the-fire' or 'out-in-the-garden' literary talk-and-gossip fests.

And then there's . . .

. . . **Roger and Joselyn Morton** our theatre friends who came back to New Zealand after their OE had stretched into two or three decades, mainly in London. For a few years in Auckland they did wonderfully vivid productions of plays by Steven Berkoff who had become their friend during the ten years Roger acted as photographer for his productions, and travelled with Berkoff's theatre group when it toured Europe. Joselyn had been a magazine editor in London and a casting agent for movies, and Roger was stage manager, first of the Roundhouse in Chalk Farm and later at the ICA (Institute of Contemporary Arts) Theatre. After their return to New Zealand Joselyn tried to interest movie people in my *Sister Hollywood* – and it was her interest in that novel that brought us together.

For his production of Berkoff's *Kvetch* at BATS Theatre in Wellington Roger won Director of the Year in 1994. They had a lovely house and a swimming pool at Murrays Bay on Auckland's North Shore, and a yacht which slept four for summer sailing.

Once, invited to dinner at Tohunga Crescent, they asked if they could bring a visitor from Britain, an actress, Cheryl. Finding myself across the corner of the table from her, where she swung her rather lovely auburn hair this way and that as she talked, I asked about her current work. She told me that when she went back she was to act in 'the Scottish play' at the Royal Shakespeare. Impressed, I asked what was her role?

Oh, she said, I'm Missus.

This took me so much by surprise I said, thinking of Lady Macbeth's fearsome grandeur, the first thing that came into my head. 'But you're quite small.'

I was in England soon afterwards and Cheryl, whom I now knew as the famous Cheryl Campbell, sent me a ticket for the performance. We met afterwards for a drink in the theatre bar and I told her how impressed I had been by her performance. Derek Jacobi had been the Macbeth to whom she'd had to say 'Infirm of purpose – give me the daggers.'

Not too small? she asked.

The Mortons' Auckland productions were successful sell-outs, but they were made to feel they were still 'outsiders' in the New Zealand theatre world and had difficulty extracting assistance from the Arts Council, so had to raise money privately to support each new show. And then their undoubtedly rising profile was all at once scuppered by an experimental musical, *Meatworks*, which failed dismally, I think simply for want of real (tuneful, memorable, uplifting, captivating) *music*! What it needed and had absolutely lacked was (to use lines from my poem '1969') 'words you could remember / and tunes you couldn't forget'.

After that disappointment they returned to Europe and have been living in rural France – Verteillac – where their unmatched talent for friendship has gained them access to a rural community, a new social network in a lovely part of the world. And Roger's photographs of people in the theatre world of the 1980s and '90s have given him a continued professional identity online.*

And then . . .

. . . Bill Gavin

We met Bill at a party at the Mortons' Murrays Bay house. He was like the Mortons in having a genius for friendship. He was also like them in having returned home to New Zealand after more than twenty highly successful years abroad. In that time he had married and divorced twice (the first wife a Mary Quant model), fathered three children, and made his name first as a motor-racing journalist, covering the international Grand Prix circuit, and then as an impresario and movie producer. He had become a friend of famous drivers (including New Zealander Bruce McLaren) more than a few of whom were killed in action. He wrote the biography of one of them, Jim Clark, who was world champion in 1963 and '65, and died at the wheel in 1968. I suspect this was the part of Bill's professional life he enjoyed most. What he loved about it was its intellectual edge and intensity. According to Bill every one of those top drivers was exceptionally intelligent – their minds moved, had to move, so fast; and for that reason they were wonderful – and daring – company. Back in Auckland (but I'm sure this was not new) there was always a girlfriend in Bill's life, sometimes two who had to be kept discreetly apart, Darling One never referred to in the company of Darling Two. It was from Bill I borrowed Bertie Winterstoke's bad-taste joke/boast in *Talking about O'Dwyer*, that there wasn't anything he missed about marriage except the adultery.

Bill lived when we first knew him in a very tasty duplex apartment in Endeans Building in Lower Queen Street with views

---

* See www.rogermortonphotographer.com. He has had shows of his photographs on both sides of the Channel.

out over the harbour; and later in a house in Ponsonby. He loved to entertain, either at home or in restaurants – generously, and I remember a dinner in Parnell when he had sold a waterfront property and the waiter was instructed to replace the bottles of ('top-end' of course) wine as they emptied. Bill's anecdotes about his dealing with famous racing drivers, movie stars and rock groups in his years away were always vivid and full of intelligence (both senses). His narrative style was peculiar, with many hesitations, ums and ahs and especially 'and so on', which I thought should be the title of the autobiography I harried him to write. But they always had shape, a beginning, a middle and an end (usually a very loud laugh). He always promised he would write the book I demanded of him, and sometimes gave me progress reports, and even once a sample chapter. He did write a book he was commissioned to do about his early career in motor racing, but I'm not aware it was published. And with help from John Barnett and Cliff Curtis he was said to be dictating the rest of his life story; but if anything came of that it is yet to appear. Really the account needed Bill himself; he was a keen and intelligent reader, and (despite, or even because of, the hesitancy) a great talker. Perhaps not a writer – though he had been a successful journalist, and there had been that biography of Jim Clark.

While he was back in New Zealand he acted as producer for *What Becomes of the Broken Hearted* (the sequel to *Once Were Warriors*); and I think when the movie of *Whale Rider* was threatened with collapse for want of money he made a quick trip to Europe and secured what was needed to keep it afloat.

And then after perhaps a decade back in Auckland, Bill departed again for London and a senior position in a new movie production company. He was soon living the high life again. I remember a party at his flat in Turnham Green where most of the cast of *Whale Rider* appeared, and we went up on the roof for a long view of London at night. Next he moved to a beautiful flat in Carnaby Street, the heart of London fashion.

And then it all collapsed and Bill came home to Auckland, broke.

Probably none of his friends knew – Kay and I certainly didn't – that he had put all his money into the new film enterprise. My guess is that he had always lived like that – dangerously; but this time there was to be no financial recovery. He was to live in a council flat in an apartment block in Greys Avenue, probably with no more income than an old-age pension. What was extraordinary about this was that he didn't ever comment on his changed circumstances, or complain; he just carried on, inviting friends and cooking for us, or coming when invited, and still entertaining us all with those stories about what had been his great days. His walls were adorned with posters of famous people he had worked with. The leather furniture was too big for the flat, but he kept it, and his friends crowded into the space and carried on as if nothing had changed. Bill was still Bill and we were still his friends. It was his courage and resilience in this that were so remarkable – and optimism. I don't think he ever gave up hope that something new would turn up to call on his talents and he would be once again 'in the money'. Meanwhile he stayed afloat and in good spirits.

And then just a few months ago he was taken into hospital with what proved to be a malignant brain tumour. It was during the Covid 19 Level 4 lockdown and he couldn't be visited; but we did get through to him once by phone and though he was having great difficulty talking at all, he did manage to say 'You and Kay have been such wonderful friends' – a sentiment that was reciprocated twice over. In his final days, which came mercifully quickly, some of his family, and his good friend John Barnett, managed to get him back home into his council flat and he died there with friends in attendance.

Acknowledgements

My debts to the University of Auckland, first for educating me, then employing me, and finally publishing me, have been duly acknowledged in the second volume of these memoirs, and my sincere thanks are repeated here. That I have not approved of some of the directions the institution has taken was recorded in passing in *You Have a Lot to Lose*, but with a recognition that if universities are compromising what Newman called 'the idea of a university' with practices from business schools and management studies programmes, and making a financial enterprise of what should be the pure pursuit of knowledge, they are doing this 'worldwide' and in unison. This volume records my escapes from 'all that' but it was never a complete severance, and I am proud still of my connection and my title of emeritus professor. My gratitude to Sam Elworthy and his team at Auckland University Press is ongoing: their combination of expertise with human warmth has been constantly an encouragement and a lesson.

My thanks are due to the following: to Tim Curnow and Auckland University Press for permission to quote from letters, emails and poems of Allen Curnow; to Amanda Taylor-Ace for permission to quote from her book *My French Affair*; to Keith Ovenden for permission to quote from *A Fighting Withdrawal*, his biography of Dan Davin; to Janet Wilson for permission to quote statements by Nuala O'Faolain from her book *Intimate Stranger: Reminiscences of Dan Davin*; to Kay Stead, Anthony Axelrad, Christopher MacLehose, Kevin Ireland, Eva Reid, Helen Vendler, Craig Raine, Michael Schmidt, Witi Ihimaera and Jadranka Pintarić for permission to quote from letters and email exchanges; to Gerrard Friedlander for permission to quote from Marti's letters and emails; to Alan Roddick for permission to quote from the *Journals* of Charles Brasch; to Charlotte Grimshaw for permission to quote from her short story 'The Olive Grove'; to Rachel Scott for permission to quote from letters and emails of her mother Margaret Scott; to Rachael King for permission to quote from her father Michael King's emails and a dedication; to Sean Shadbolt for permission to quote from his father Maurice Shadbolt's fiction and letters; to Professor Natalie Mauriac-Dyer for permission to quote from her husband Robert Dyer's letters, emails and poems; and to Hinewairangi Tocker-Fenton for permission to quote emails and a poem by her mother Mahinarangi Tocker.

C. K. Stead

Index

Page references in **bold** refer to photographs in the image sections.